VIDEO GIRL AI ™

Volume 2: Mix Down

Story & Art by **Masakazu Katsura**

VIDEO GIRL AI™
Volume 2
Mix Down
Action Edition

STORY & ART BY MASAKAZU KATSURA

This volume contains the VIDEO GIRL AI installments from ANIMERICA EXTRA
Vol. 2, No. 8, through Vol. 3, No. 4, in their entirety.

Translation/Yuji Oniki
Touch-up Art & Lettering/Freeman Wong
Design/Hidemi Sahara
Editor, 1st Edition/William Flanagan
Editor, Action Edition/Elizabeth Kawasaki

Managing Editor/Annette Roman
Editorial Director/Alvin Lu
Director of Production/Noboru Watanabe
Sr. Director of Licensing & Acquisitions/Rika Inouye
V.P. of Sales & Marketing/Liza Coppola
Executive Vice President/Hyoe Narita
Publisher/Seiji Horibuchi

Printed in the U.S.A.

Published by VIZ, LLC
P.O. Box 77010
San Francisco, CA 94107

Action Edition
10 9 8 7 6 5 4 3 2
First printing, June 2004
Second printing, September 2004
First English edition, July 2000

www.viz.com

STORY THUS FAR

High school student Yota Moteuchi is so unpopular with girls that his classmates have nicknamed him "Dateless." But that doesn't stop him from falling for sweet co-ed Moemi. Before Yota can tell Moemi how he feels, she tells him that she's in love with his best friend, the handsome and popular Takashi. Instead of feeling sorry for himself, Yota sympathizes with Moemi and her hopeless crush on his friend.

That night, Yota enters a mysterious video shop, Gokuraku, which only rents tapes to the "pure of heart," and picks up a video starring the cute, young idol Ai Amano. When he pops the film into his broken VCR, Ai promises to cheer Yota up, then she emerges from the TV and lands in Yota's bed. But the real Ai is different from her video persona – she swears, makes dirty jokes, and cooks very badly, but she has a kind heart and truly wants to see Yota happily dating Moemi.

Yota eventually grows closer to Moemi, but as her friend/confidante, not her boyfriend. When Moemi and Takashi start dating, Yota gives up on his love. Meanwhile, Yota begins to rely on Ai emotionally more and more. Ai is also discovering emotions that a Video Girl should not have, emotions forbidden by the creator of Video Girls: jealousy, longing and love. Further complicating things, Yota's broken VCR has been causing Ai physical problems – some are comical, but others are deadly serious. While running an errand for Yota, Ai collapses in a deserted alley...

CONTENTS

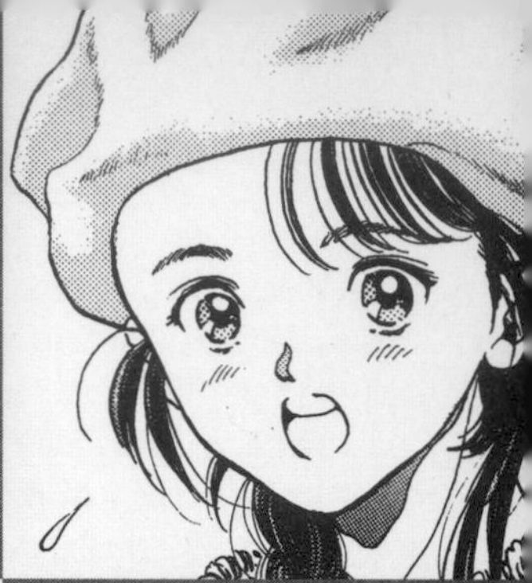

Yota Moteuchi

Yota is not very popular with girls and has been nicknamed "Dateless" by his classmates. He's in love with kindhearted Moemi.

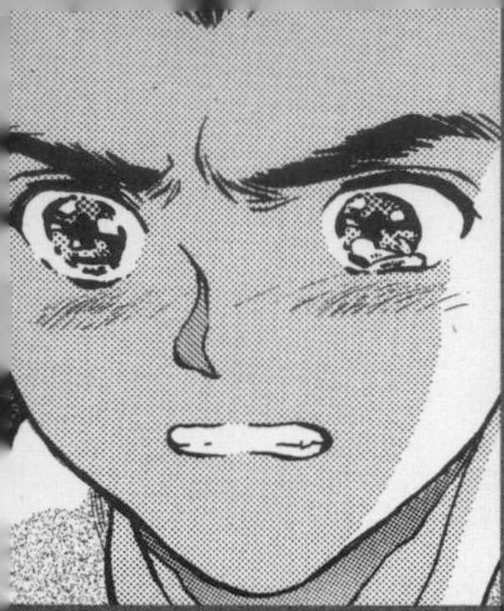

Moemi Hayakawa

Moemi is a quiet high school student who has fallen for Yota's popular friend, Takashi Niimai. She doesn't know Yota has a crush on her.

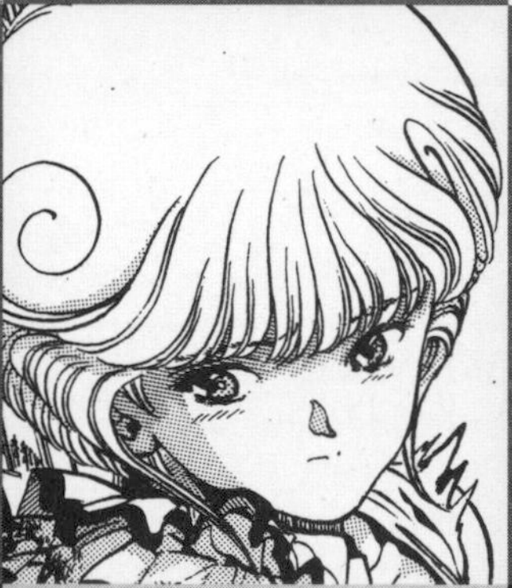

Ai Amano

Ai is a Video Girl who has popped out of Yota's broken VCR to cheer him up and help him win Moemi's heart.

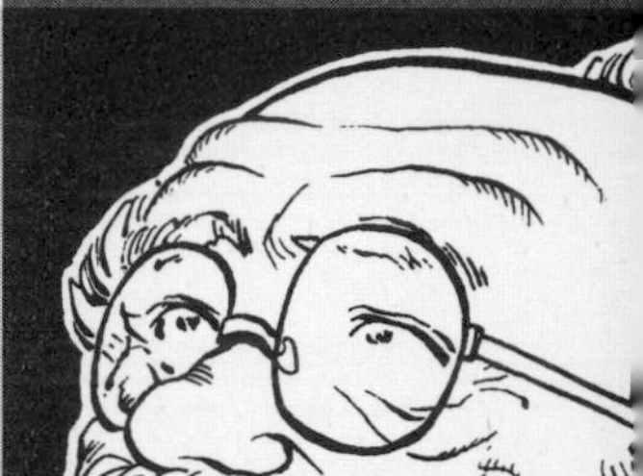

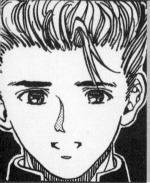

Takashi Niimai

Takashi is the most popular guy in school and is Yota's best friend. He's not particularly interested in romance.

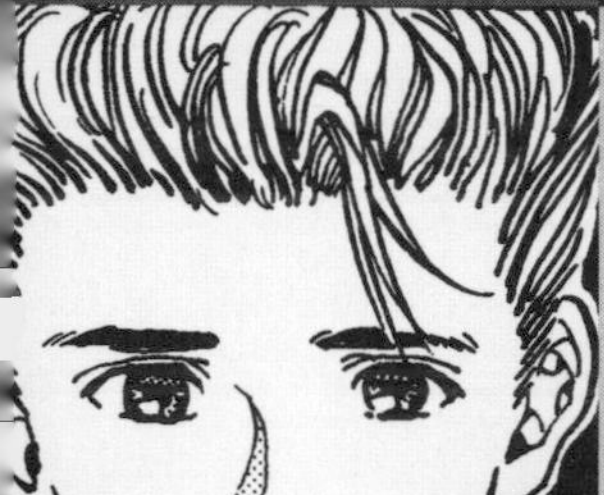

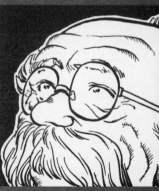

Gokuraku Clerk

This kindhearted old man works at the Gokuraku video shop and allows Yota to rent Ai's tape.

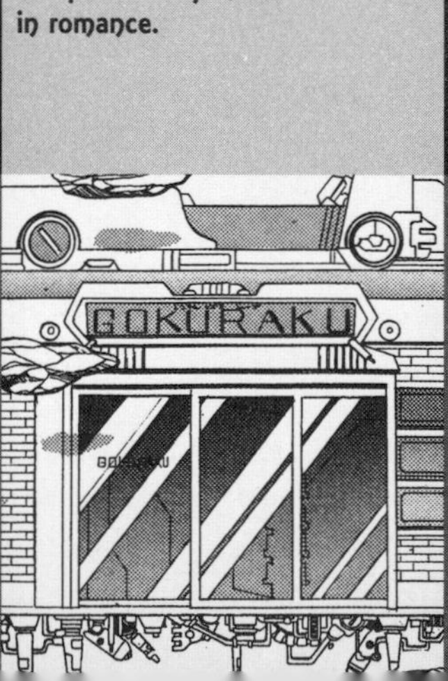
GOKURAKU

Gokuraku

The mysterious video shop has free rentals, but only for the pure of heart.

■ ❚❚ ►► ► *CHAPTER NINE*
Where Ai Has Gone

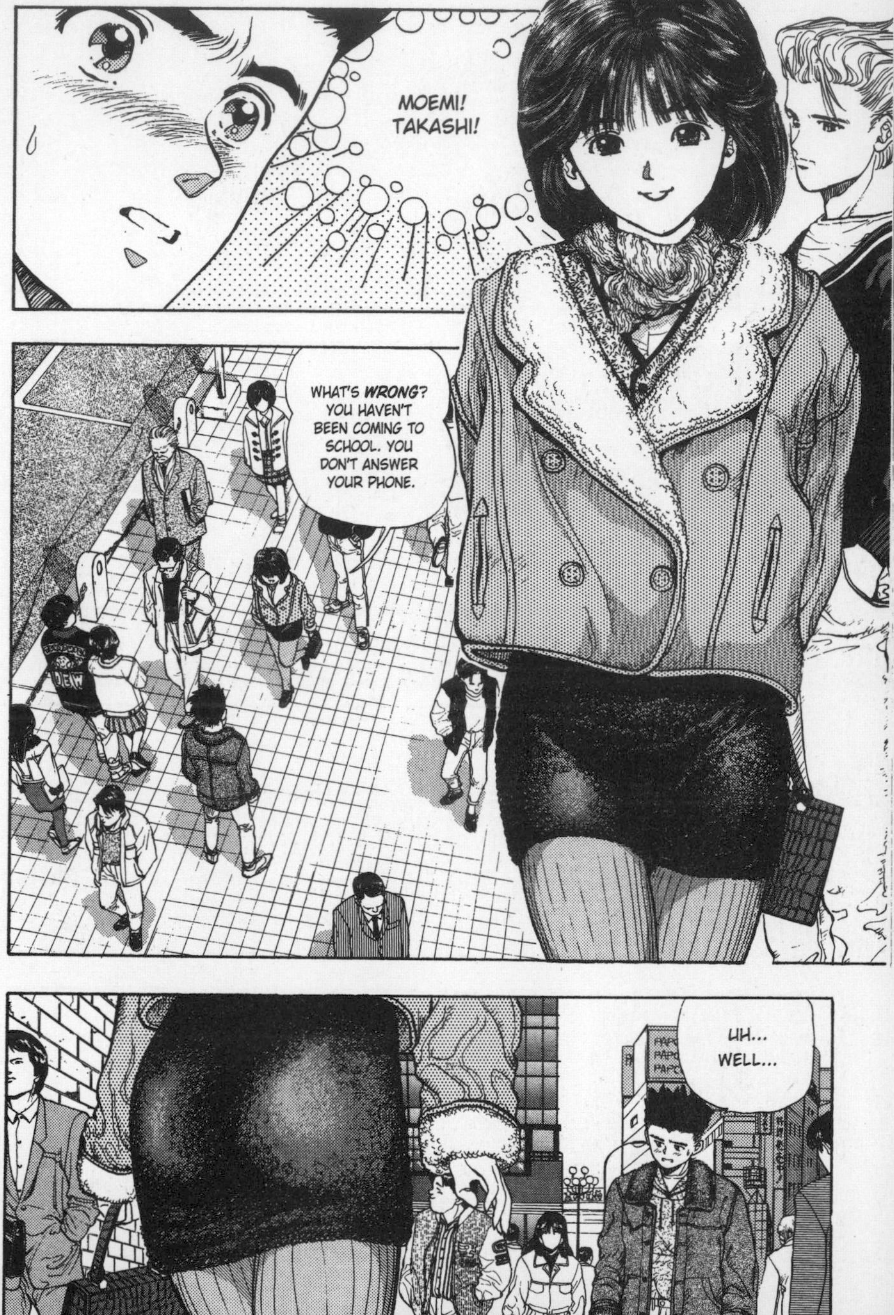
MOEMI! TAKASHI!
WHAT'S ***WRONG***? YOU HAVEN'T BEEN COMING TO SCHOOL. YOU DON'T ANSWER YOUR PHONE.
UH... WELL...

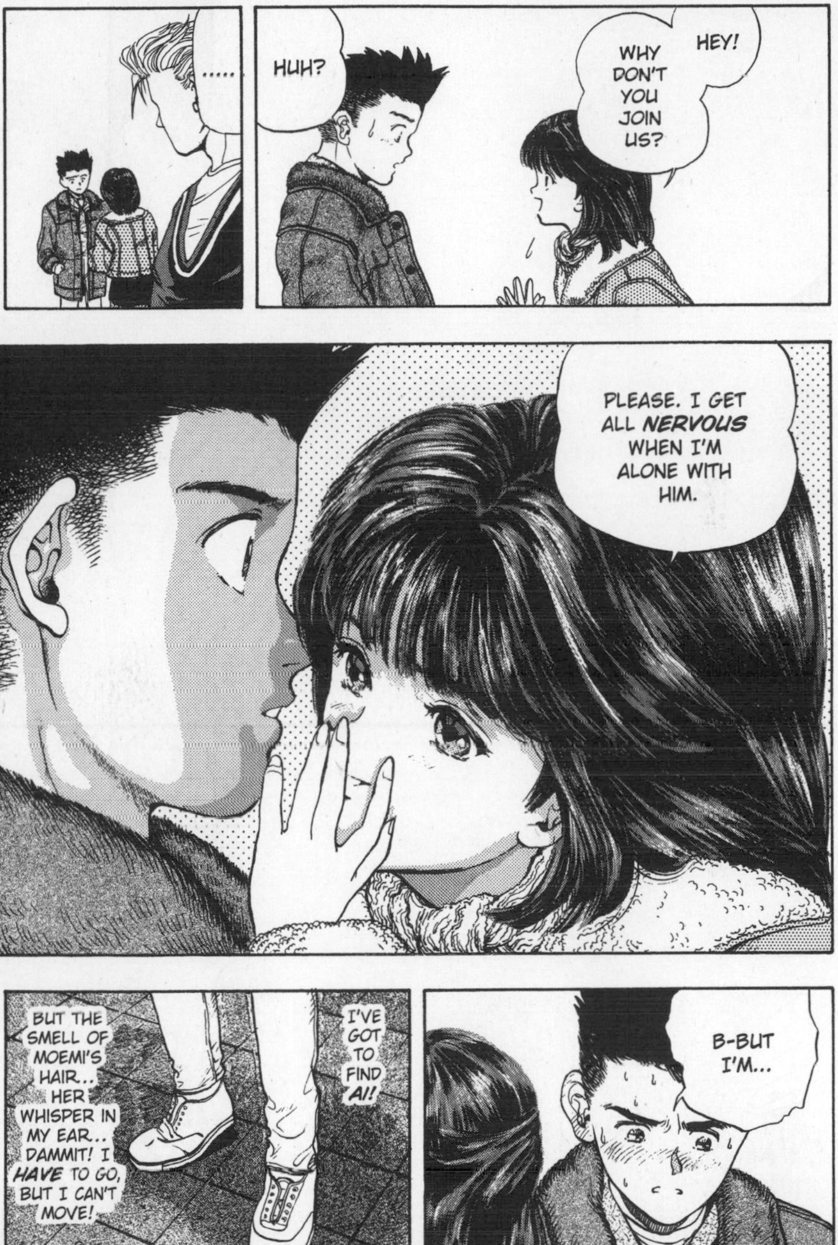
HEY!
WHY DON'T YOU JOIN US?
HUH?
......
PLEASE. I GET ALL ***NERVOUS*** WHEN I'M ALONE WITH HIM.
B-BUT I'M...
I'VE GOT TO FIND ***AI!***
BUT THE SMELL OF MOEMI'S HAIR.. HER WHISPER IN MY EAR.. DAMMIT! I ***HAVE*** TO GO, BUT I CAN'T MOVE!

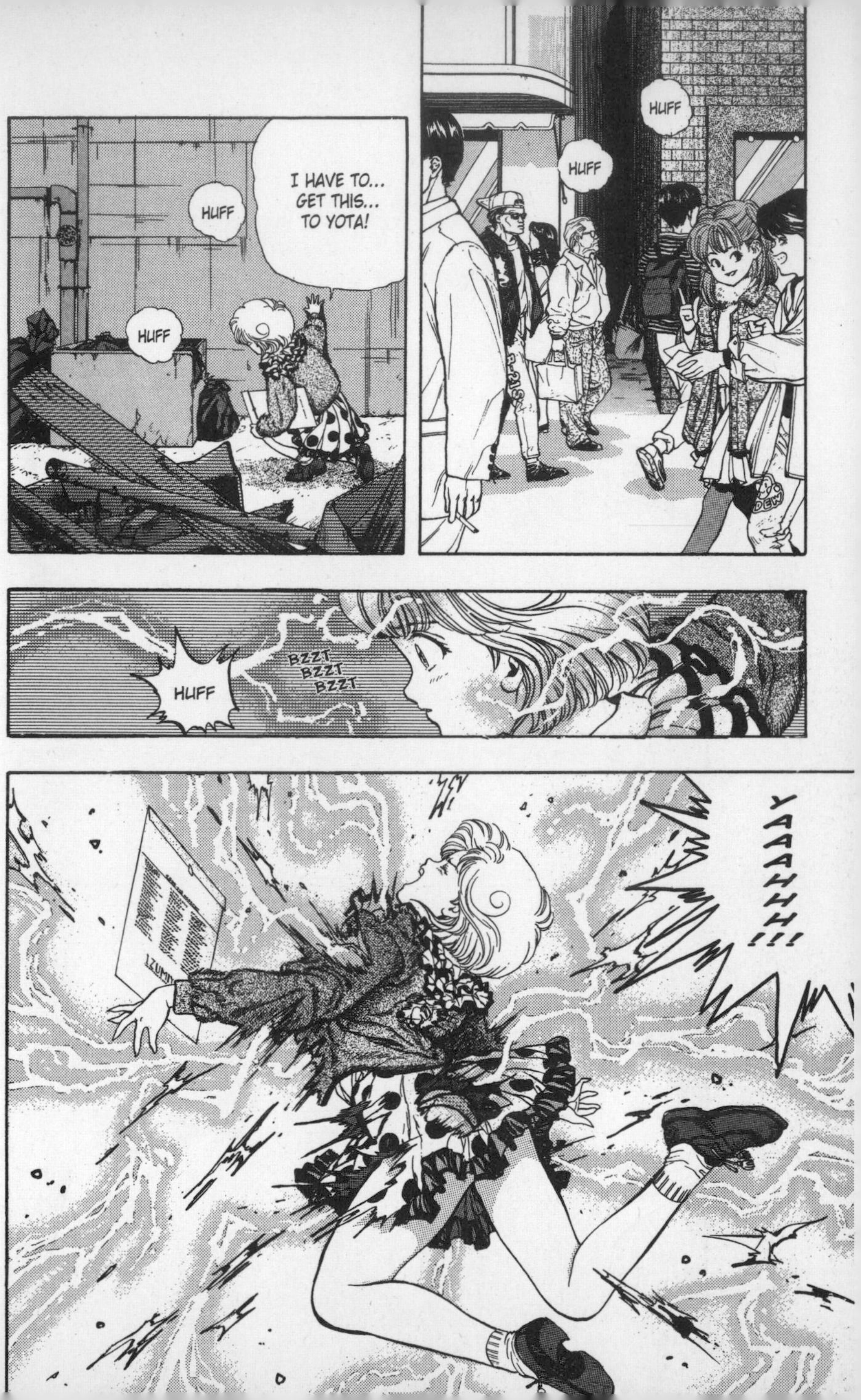
HUFF
HUFF
I HAVE TO... GET THIS... TO YOTA!
HUFF
HUFF
BZZT BZZT BZZT
HUFF
YAAAHHH!!!

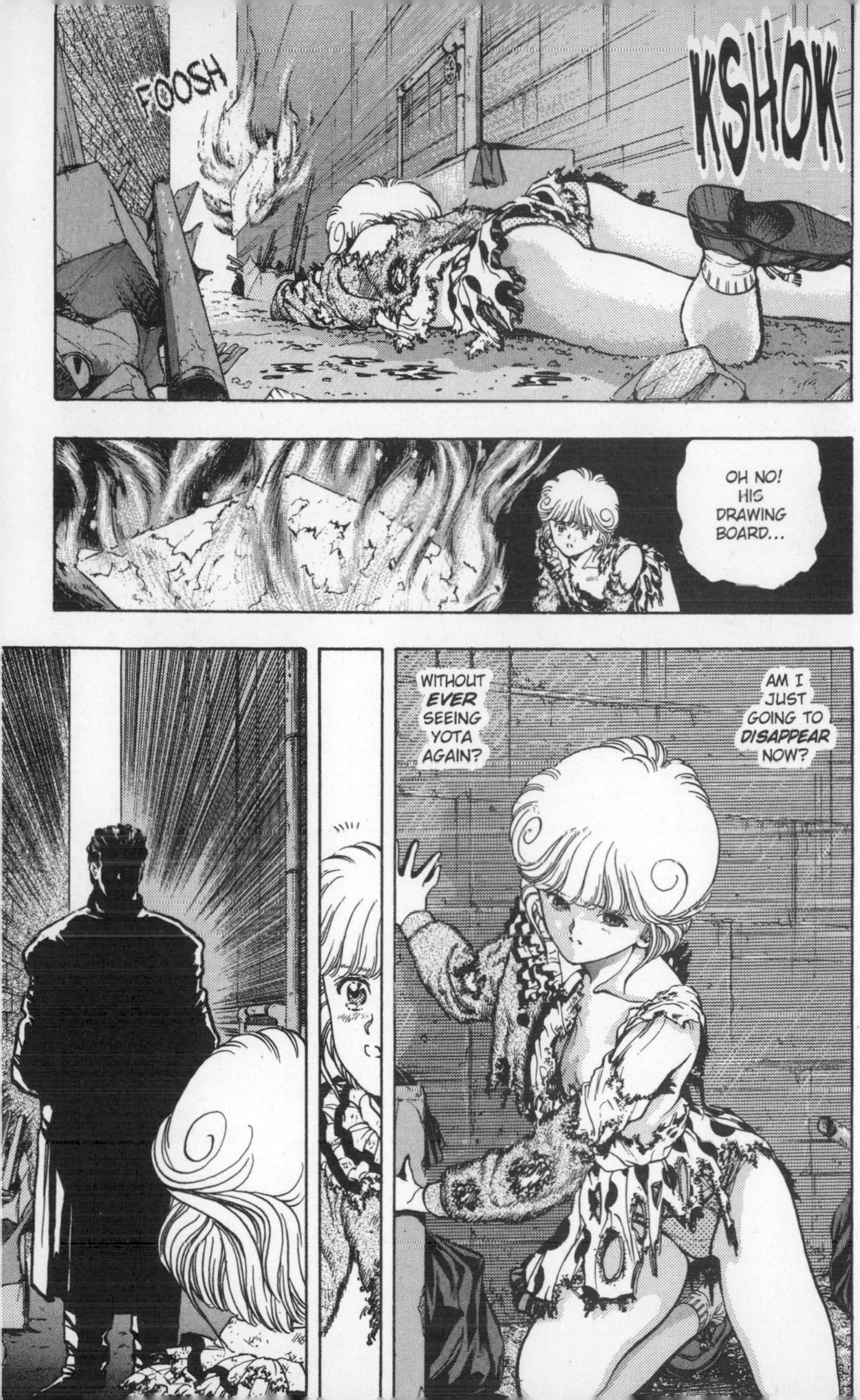
KSHOK
FOOSH
OH NO! HIS DRAWING BOARD...
AM I JUST GOING TO DISAPPEAR NOW?
WITHOUT EVER SEEING YOTA AGAIN?

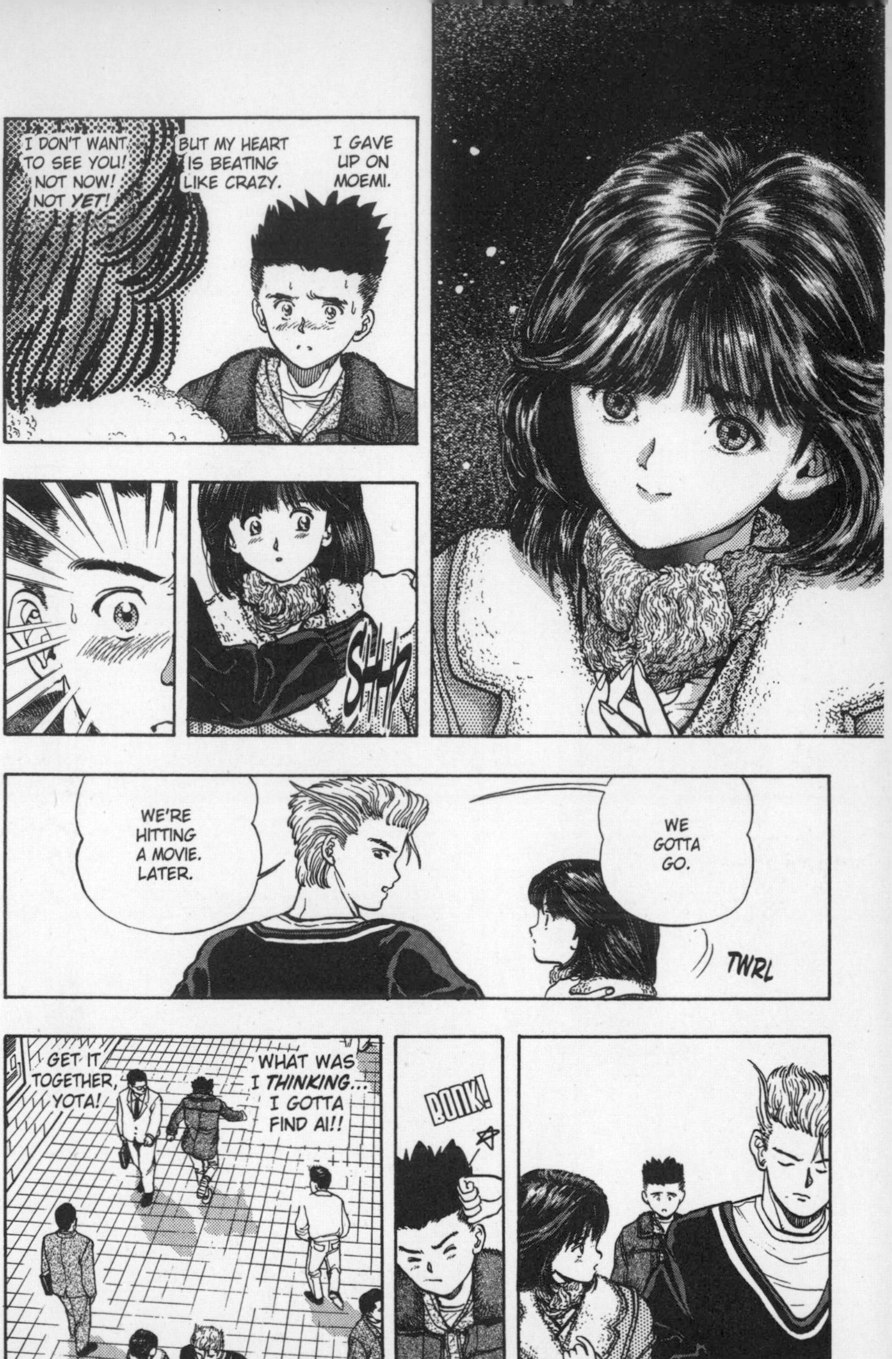
I GAVE UP ON MOEMI.
BUT MY HEART IS BEATING LIKE CRAZY.
I DON'T WANT TO SEE YOU! NOT NOW! NOT YET!
WE GOTTA GO.
TWRL
WE'RE HITTING A MOVIE. LATER.
BONK!
WHAT WAS I THINKING... I GOTTA FIND AI!!
GET IT TOGETHER, YOTA!

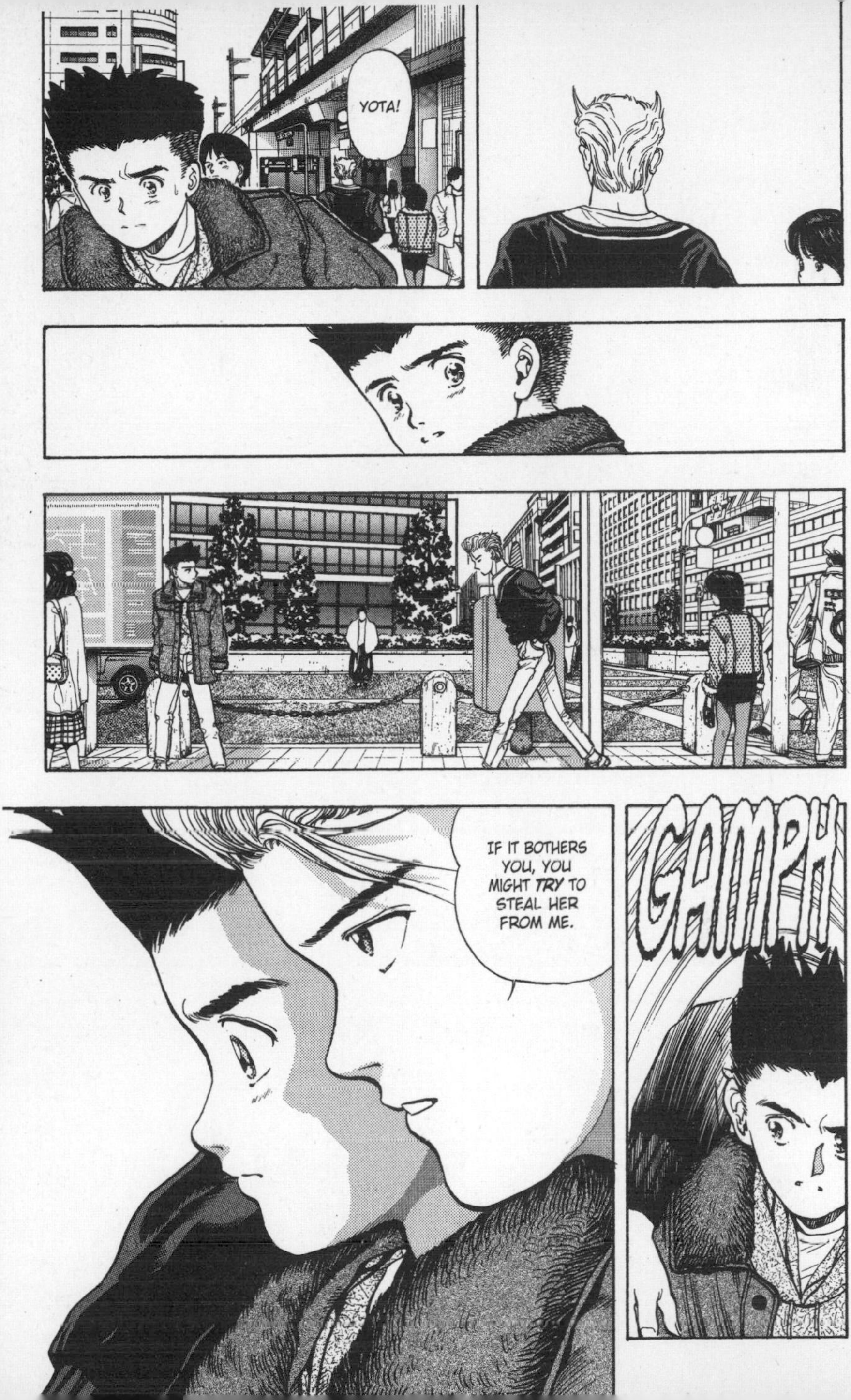
YOTA!
GAMPH
IF IT BOTHERS YOU, YOU MIGHT *TRY* TO STEAL HER FROM ME.

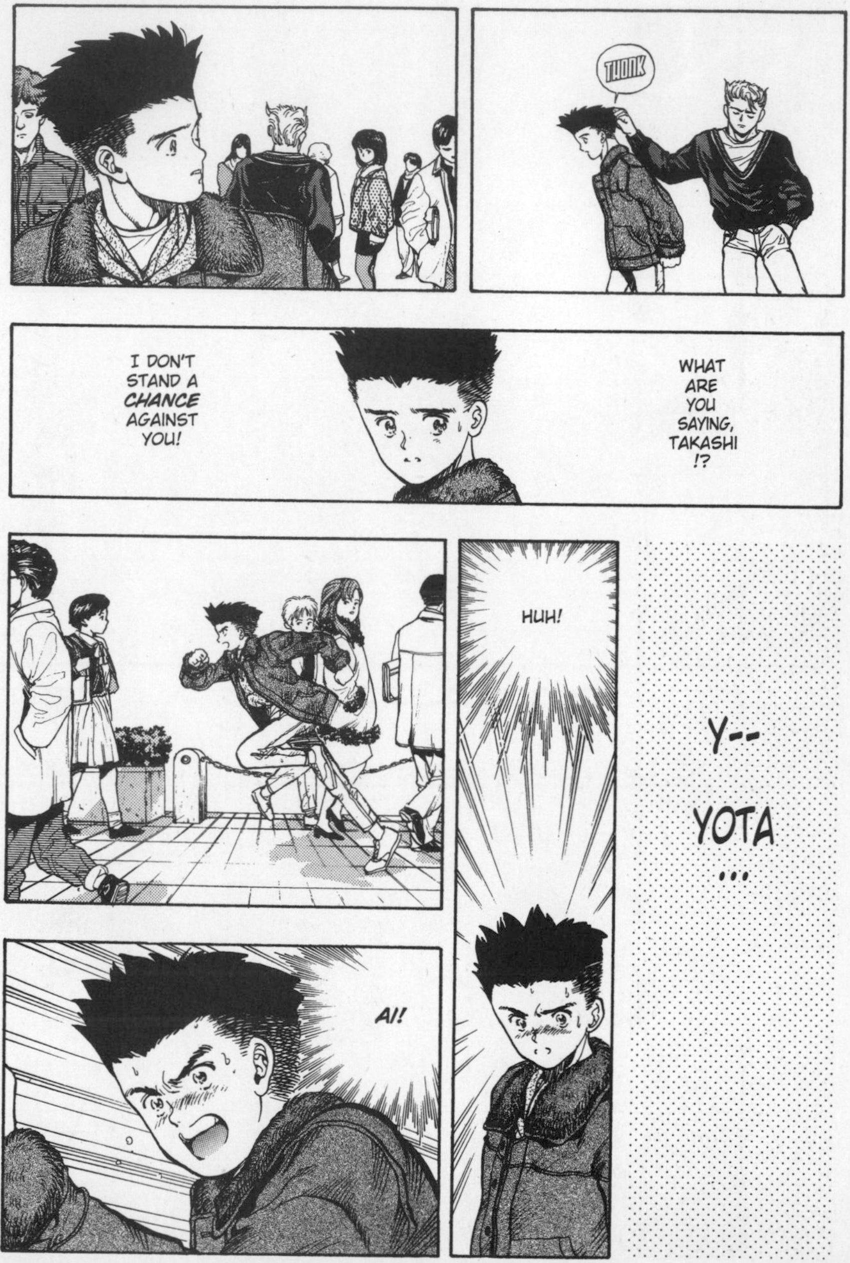
THONK
WHAT ARE YOU SAYING, TAKASHI!?
I DON'T STAND A *CHANCE* AGAINST YOU!
Y-- YOTA ...
HUH!
AI!

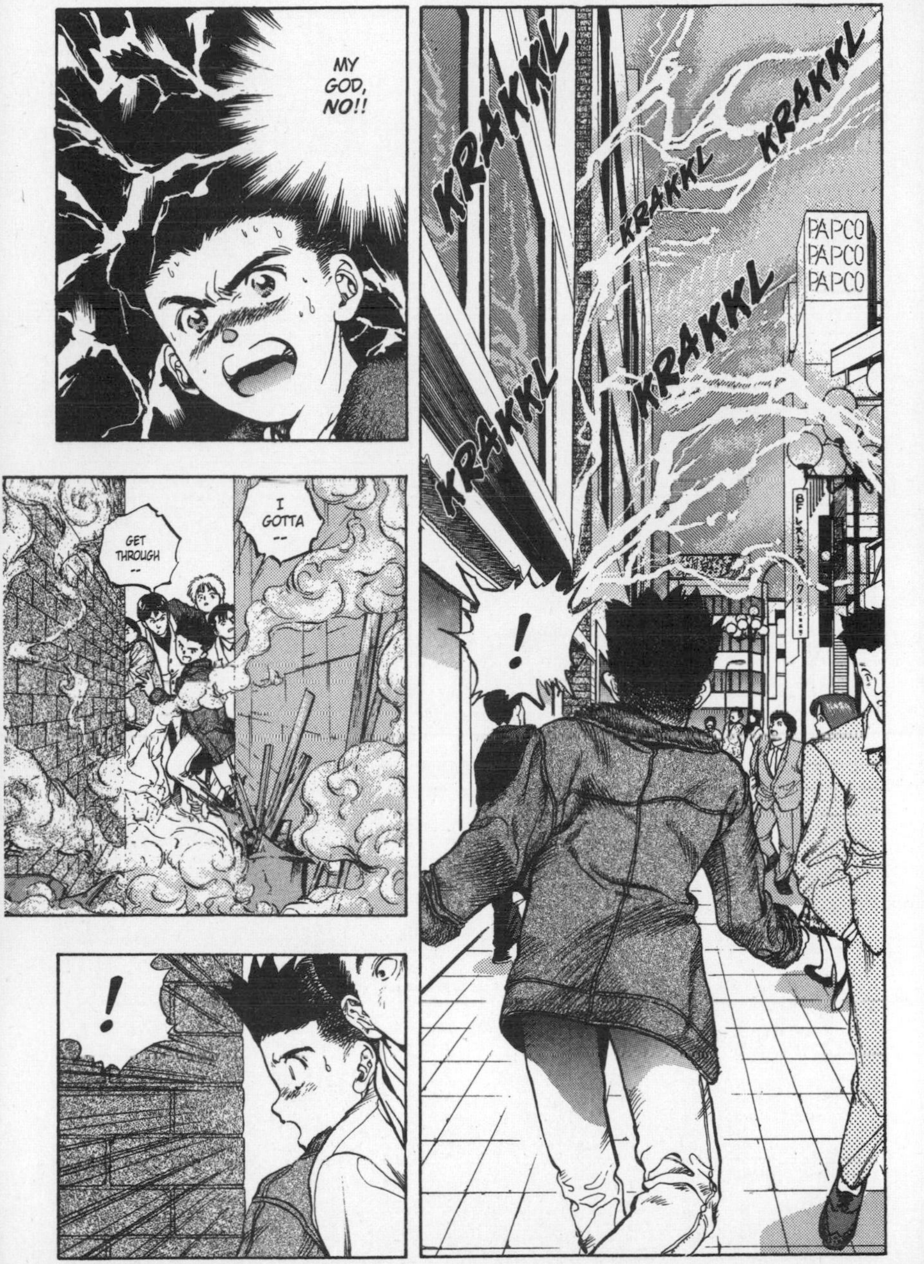
KRAKKL
KRAKKL
KRAKKL
KRAKKL
KRAKKL
PAPCO
PAPCO
PAPCO
!
MY GOD, NO!!
I GOTTA --
GET THROUGH --
!

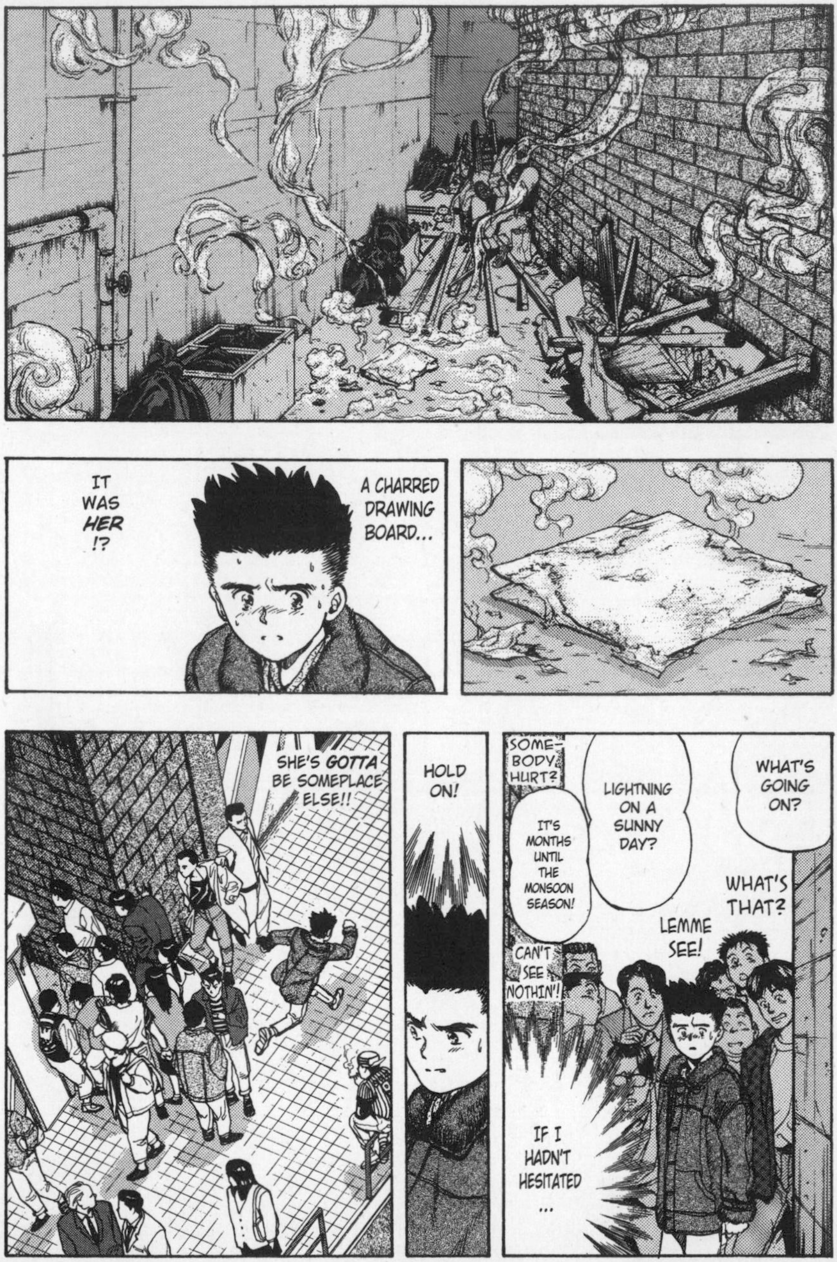
A CHARRED DRAWING BOARD...
IT WAS *HER* !?
WHAT'S GOING ON?
LIGHTNING ON A SUNNY DAY?
SOME-BODY HURT?
IT'S MONTHS UNTIL THE MONSOON SEASON!
WHAT'S THAT?
LEMME SEE!
CAN'T SEE NOTHIN'!
IF I HADN'T HESITATED ...
HOLD ON!
SHE'S *GOTTA* BE SOMEPLACE ELSE!!

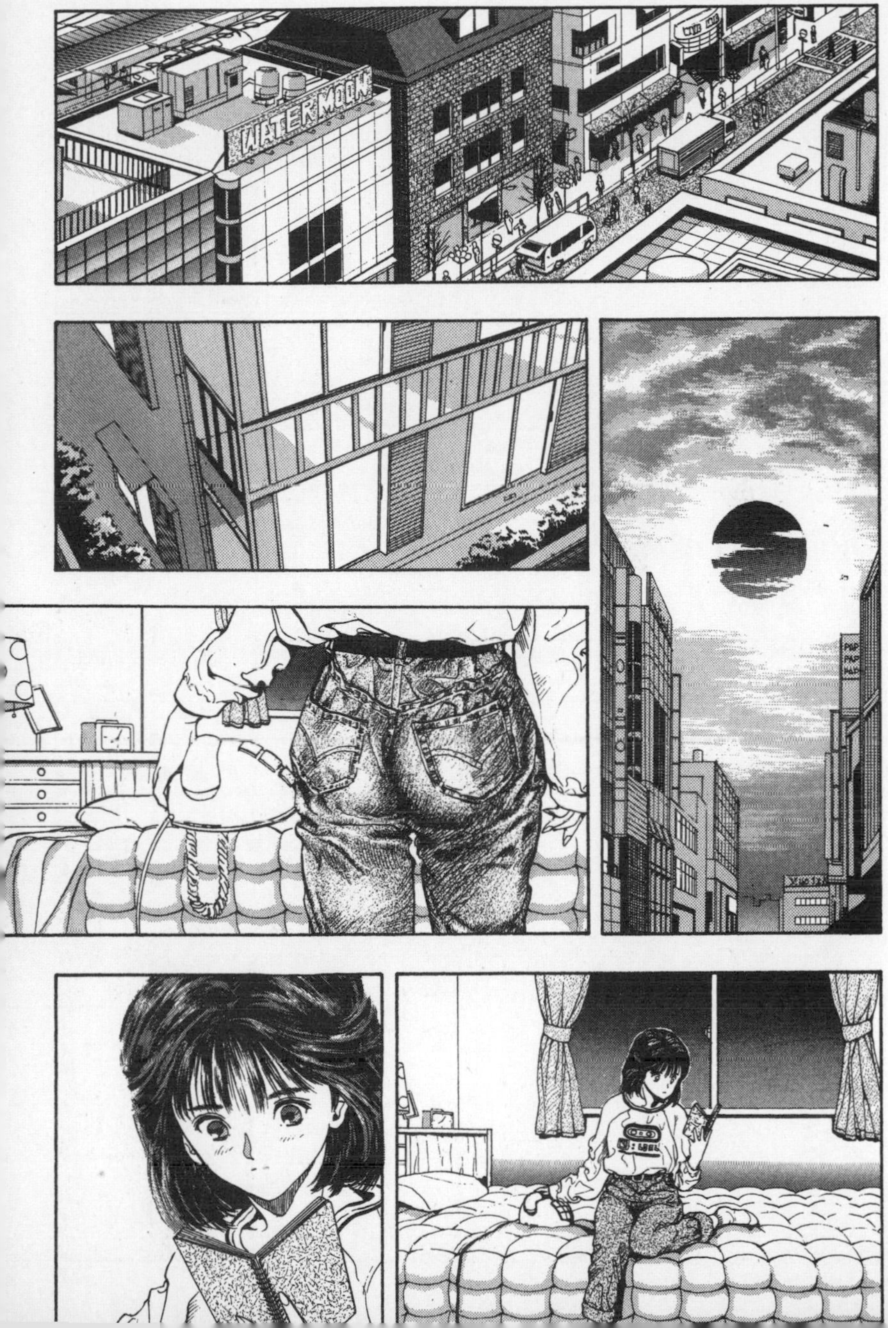
WATER MOON

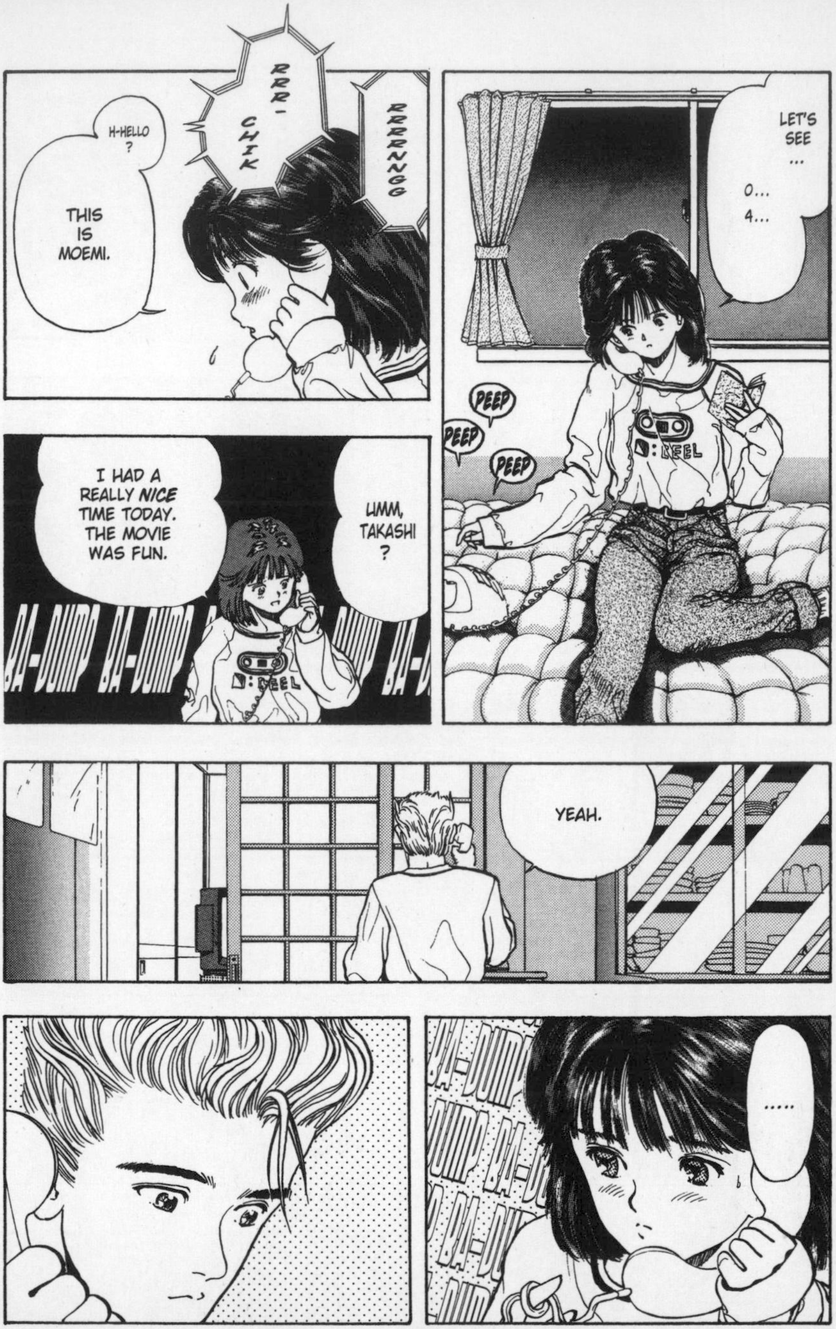

LET'S SEE ... 0... 4...
PEEP
PEEP
PEEP
RRRRNNGG
RRR- CHIK
H-HELLO ?
THIS IS MOEMI.
UMM, TAKASHI ?
I HAD A REALLY *NICE* TIME TODAY. THE MOVIE WAS FUN.
BA-DUMP BA-DUMP BA-DUMP BA-DUMP
YEAH.
.....
BA-DUMP BA-DUMP BA-DUMP

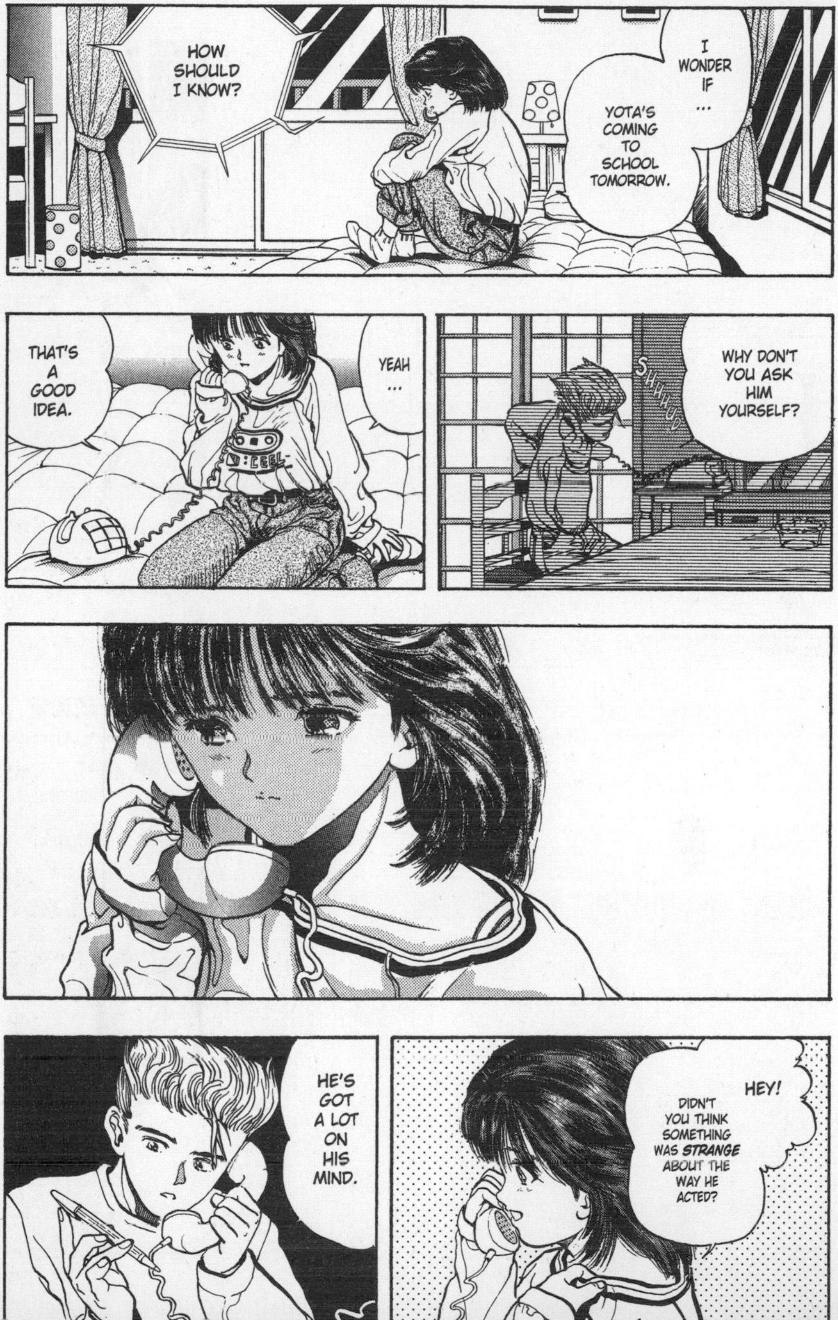

I WONDER IF ... YOTA'S COMING TO SCHOOL TOMORROW.
HOW SHOULD I KNOW?
WHY DON'T YOU ASK HIM YOURSELF?
YEAH ...
THAT'S A GOOD IDEA.
HEY!
DIDN'T YOU THINK SOMETHING WAS *STRANGE* ABOUT THE WAY HE ACTED?
HE'S GOT A LOT ON HIS MIND.

LISTEN ...

I WAS WONDERING IF YOTA ...

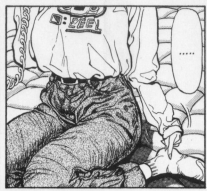
.....

DO YOU ALWAYS TALK ABOUT *HIM* !?

CHAK

U-- UH-HUH.

I'LL SEE YOU TOMORROW AT SCHOOL.

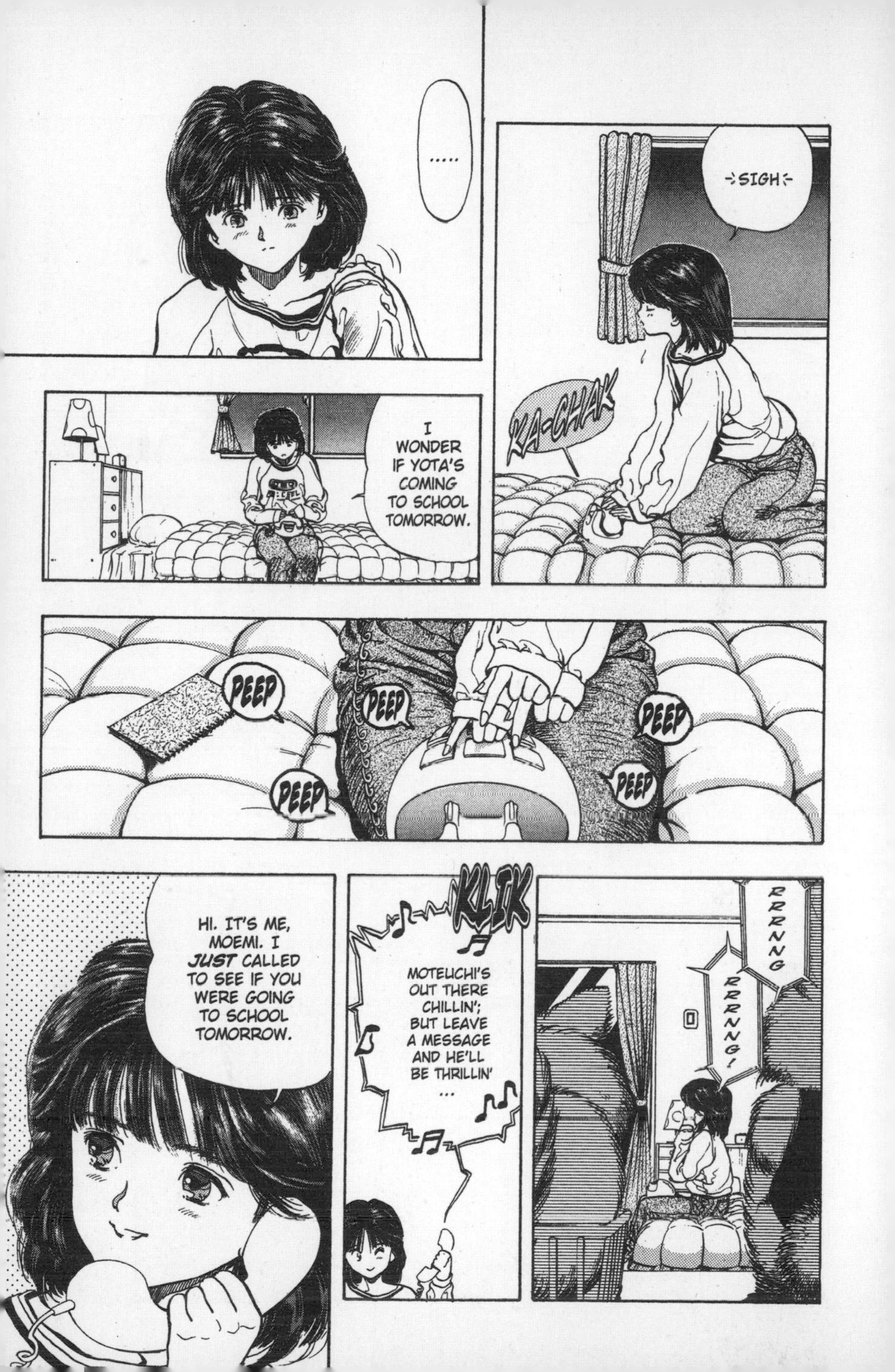
SIGH
KA-CHAK
......
I WONDER IF YOTA'S COMING TO SCHOOL TOMORROW.
PEEP
PEEP
PEEP
PEEP
PEEP
RRRNNG
RRRNNG!
KLIK
MOTEUCHI'S OUT THERE CHILLIN'; BUT LEAVE A MESSAGE AND HE'LL BE THRILLIN' ...
HI. IT'S ME, MOEMI. I *JUST* CALLED TO SEE IF YOU WERE GOING TO SCHOOL TOMORROW.

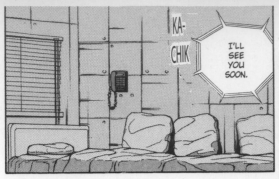

PLEASE CALL BACK.
KA-CHIK
I'LL SEE YOU SOON.
CHA-KAK
I CAN'T FIND HER. SHE'S GONE... GONE...

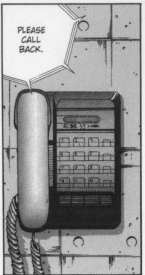

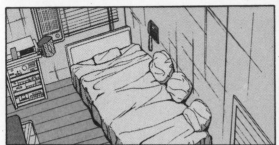

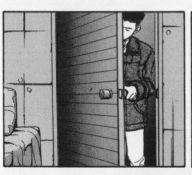

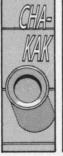

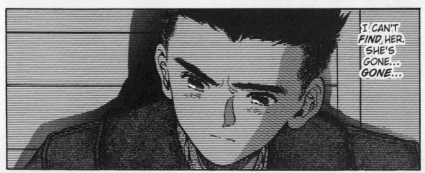

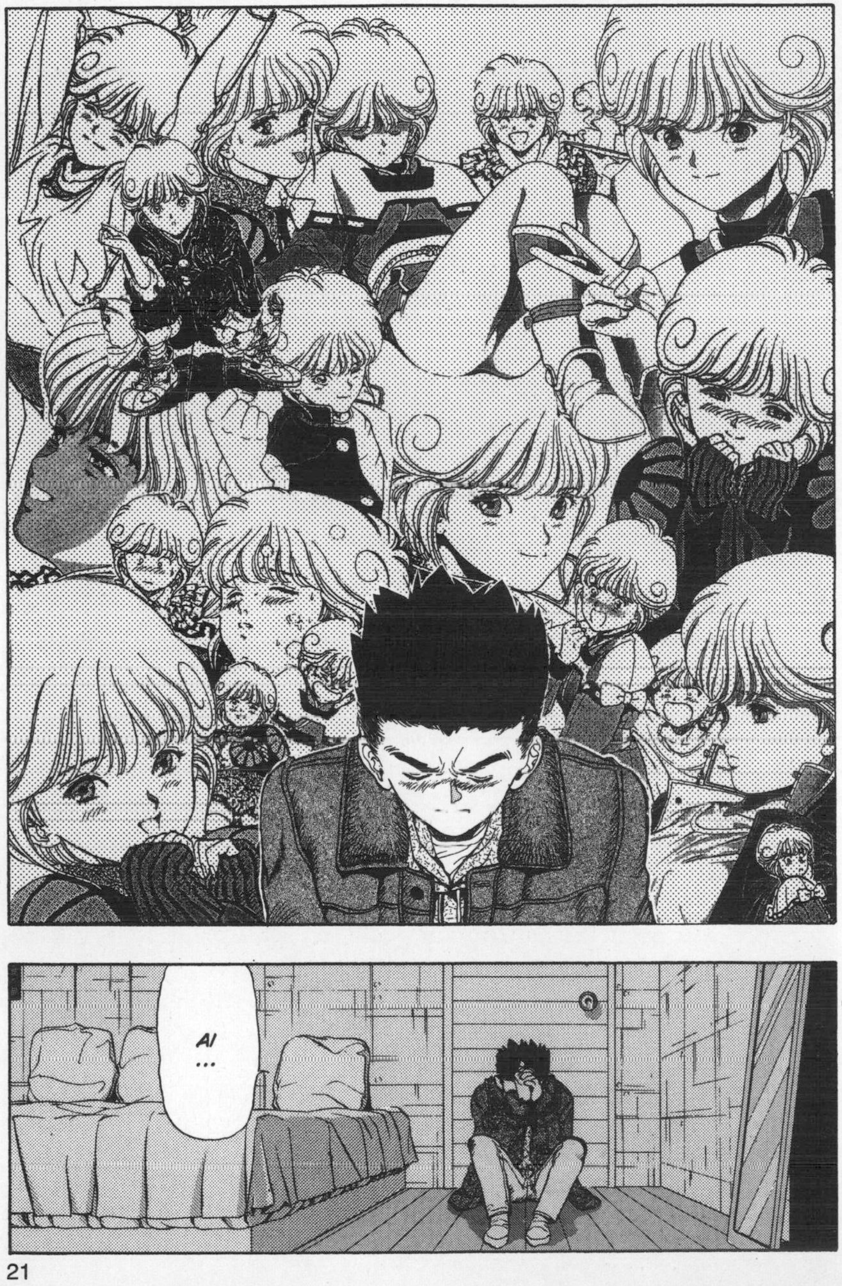
AI ...

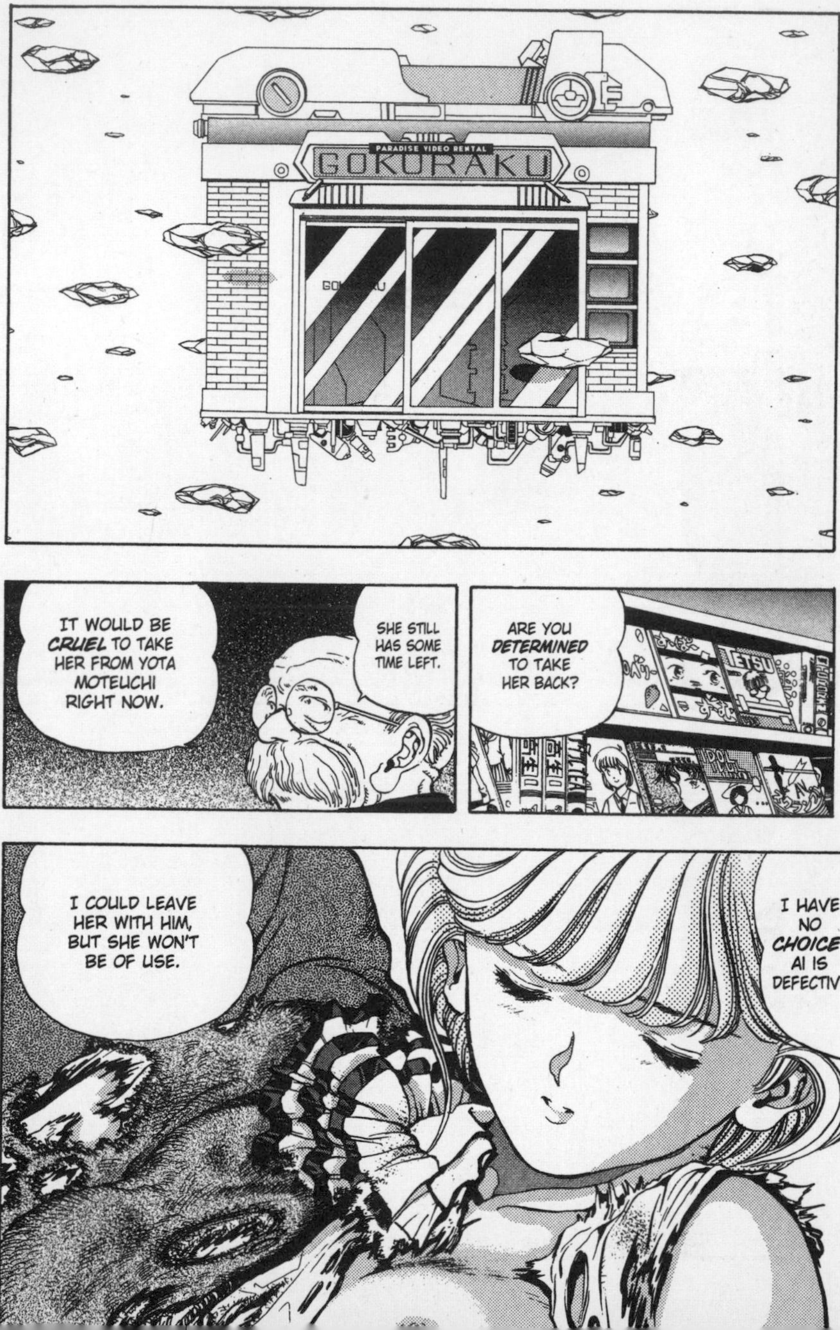
PARADISE VIDEO RENTAL
GOKURAKU
ARE YOU *DETERMINED* TO TAKE HER BACK?
SHE STILL HAS SOME TIME LEFT.
IT WOULD BE *CRUEL* TO TAKE HER FROM YOTA MOTEUCHI RIGHT NOW.
I HAVE NO *CHOICE*. AI IS DEFECTIVE.
I COULD LEAVE HER WITH HIM, BUT SHE WON'T BE OF USE.

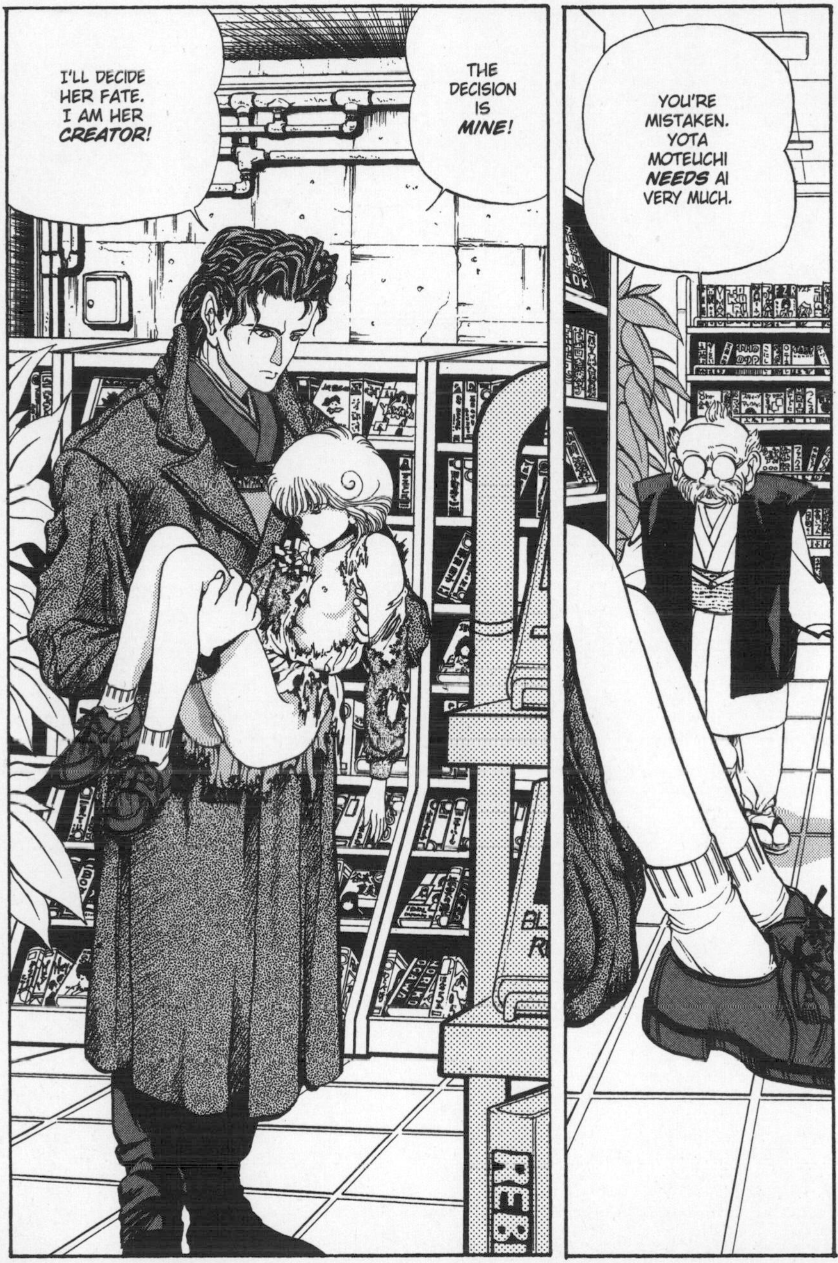
YOU'RE MISTAKEN. YOTA MOTEUCHI *NEEDS* AI VERY MUCH.
THE DECISION IS *MINE!*
I'LL DECIDE HER FATE. I AM HER *CREATOR!*

■ ▲ ■ II ■ ►► ■ ► ■ *CHAPTER TEN*
Gone!

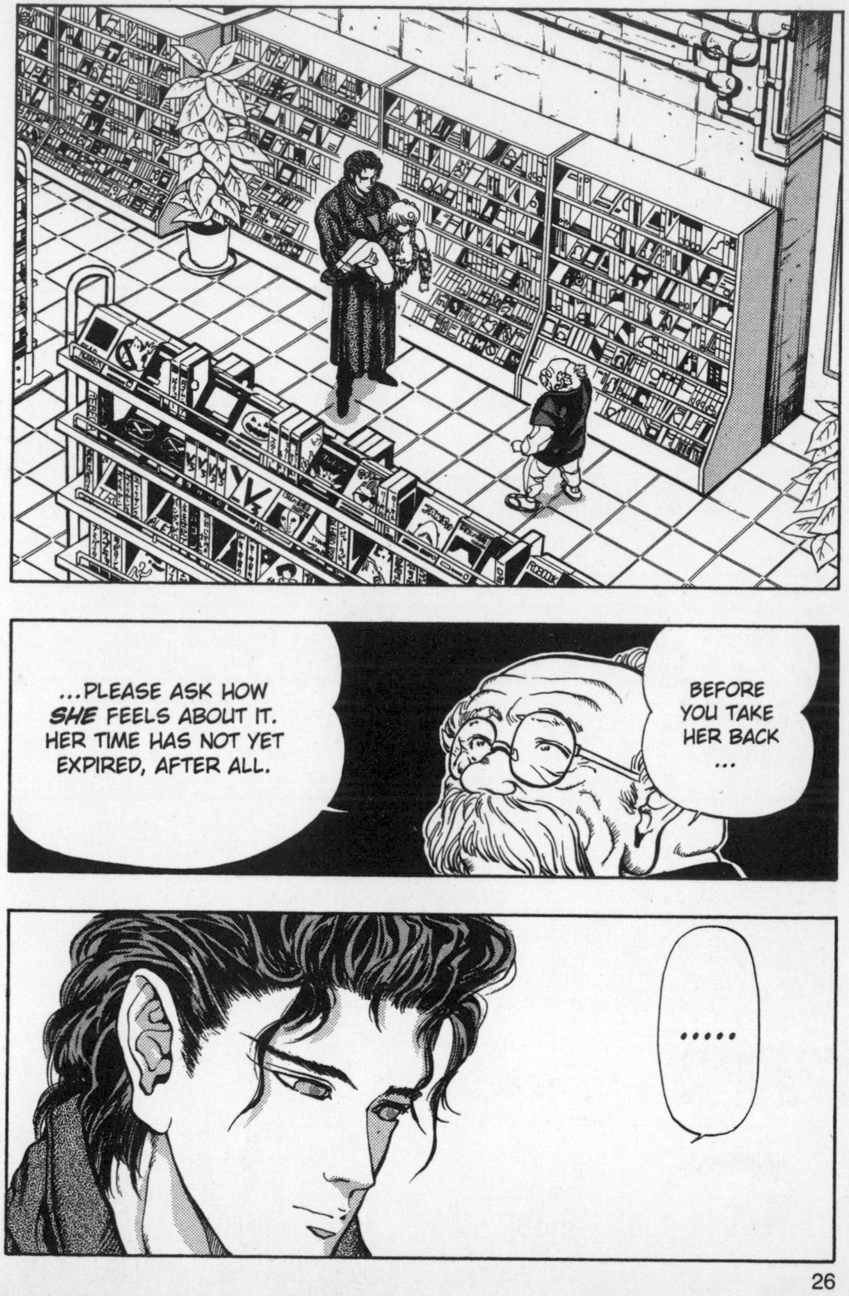
BEFORE YOU TAKE HER BACK ...
...PLEASE ASK HOW *SHE* FEELS ABOUT IT. HER TIME HAS NOT YET EXPIRED, AFTER ALL.
.....

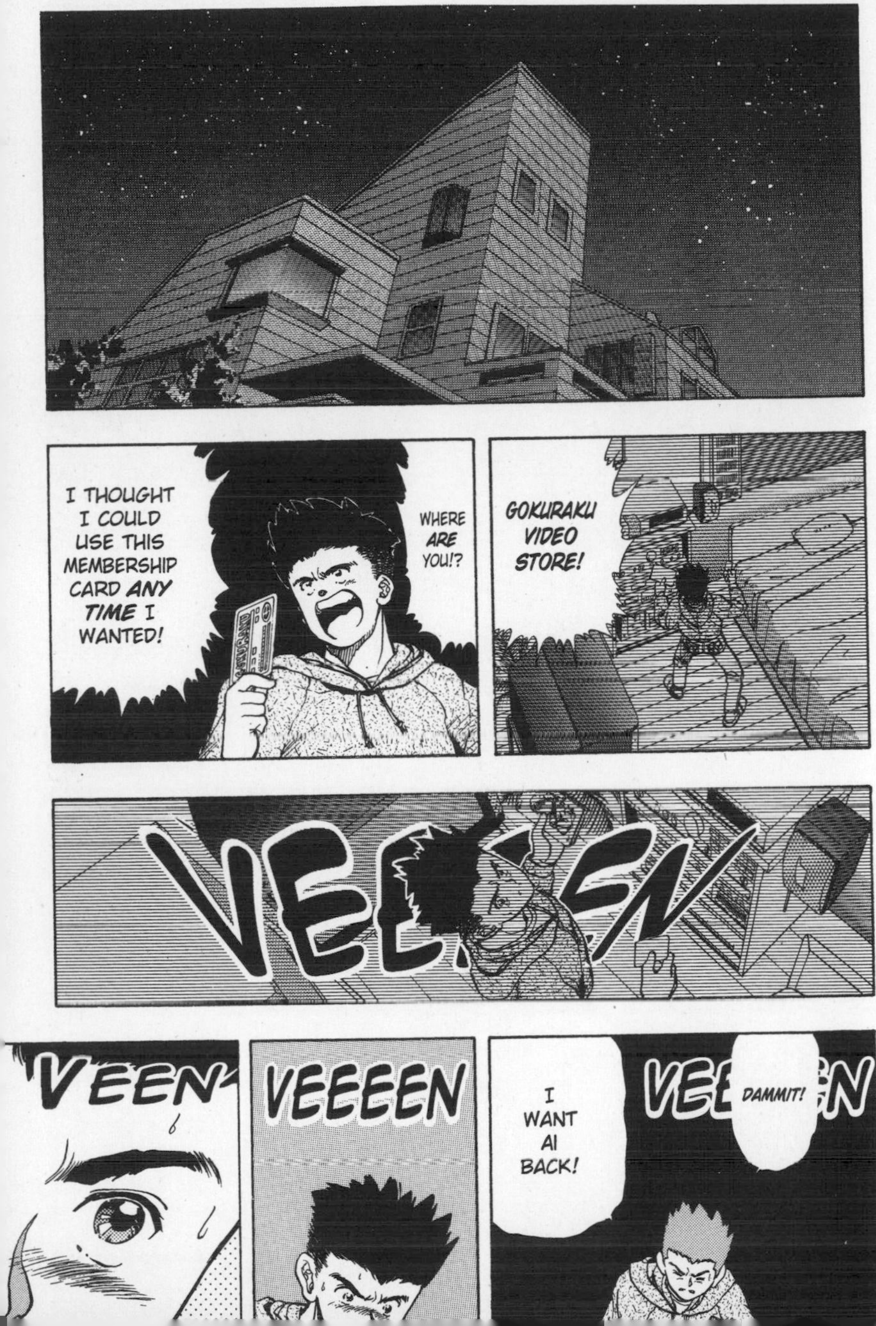
GOKURAKU VIDEO STORE!
WHERE ARE YOU!?
I THOUGHT I COULD USE THIS MEMBERSHIP CARD ANY TIME I WANTED!
DAMMIT!
I WANT AI BACK!
VEEEEN
VEEN

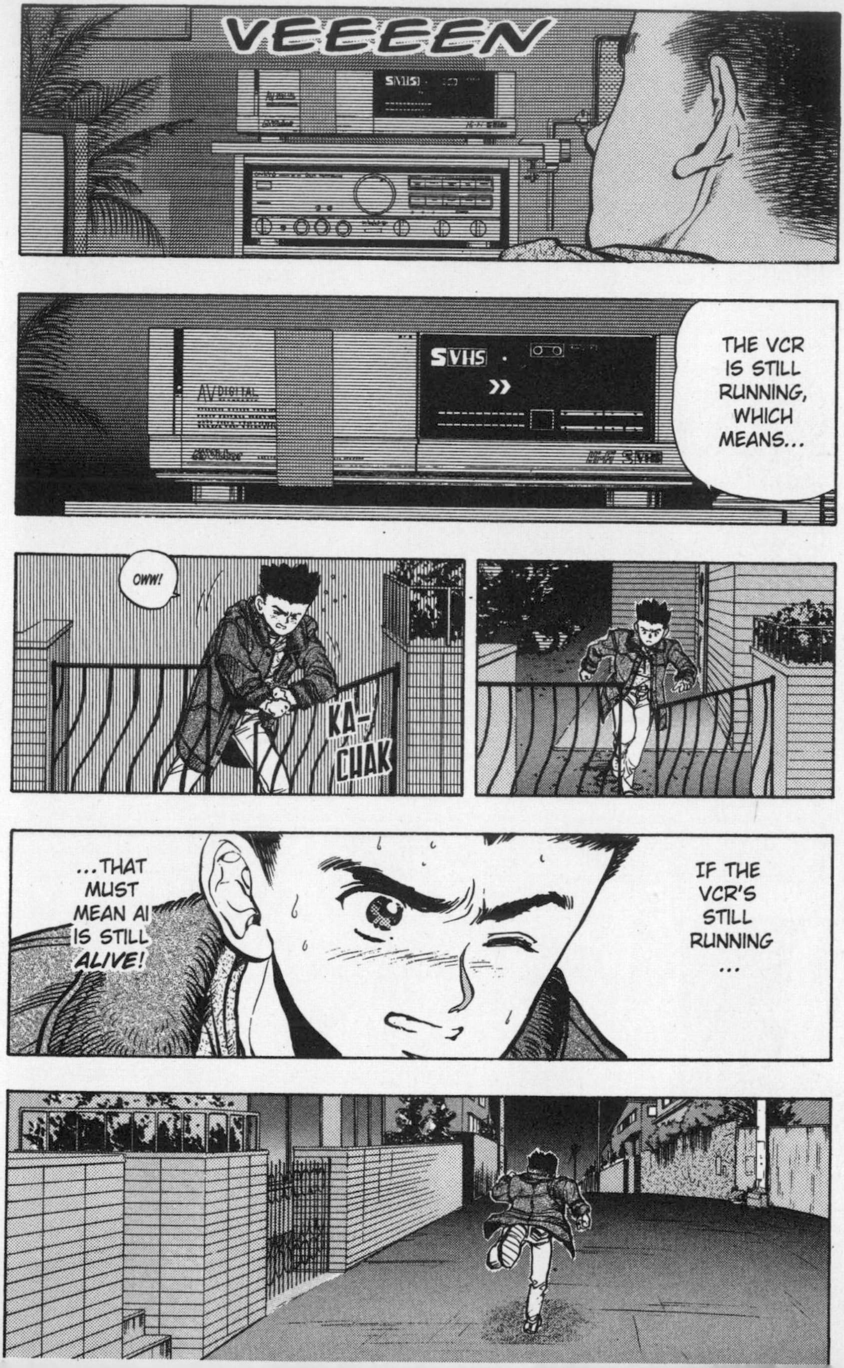
VEEEEN
THE VCR IS STILL RUNNING, WHICH MEANS...
OWW!
KA-CHAK
IF THE VCR'S STILL RUNNING ...
...THAT MUST MEAN AI IS STILL ALIVE!

...I CONTINUED TO LOOK FOR AI...

THE NEXT DAY...

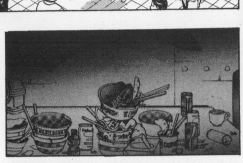

ARE YOU, AI?

ARE YOU REALLY GONE?

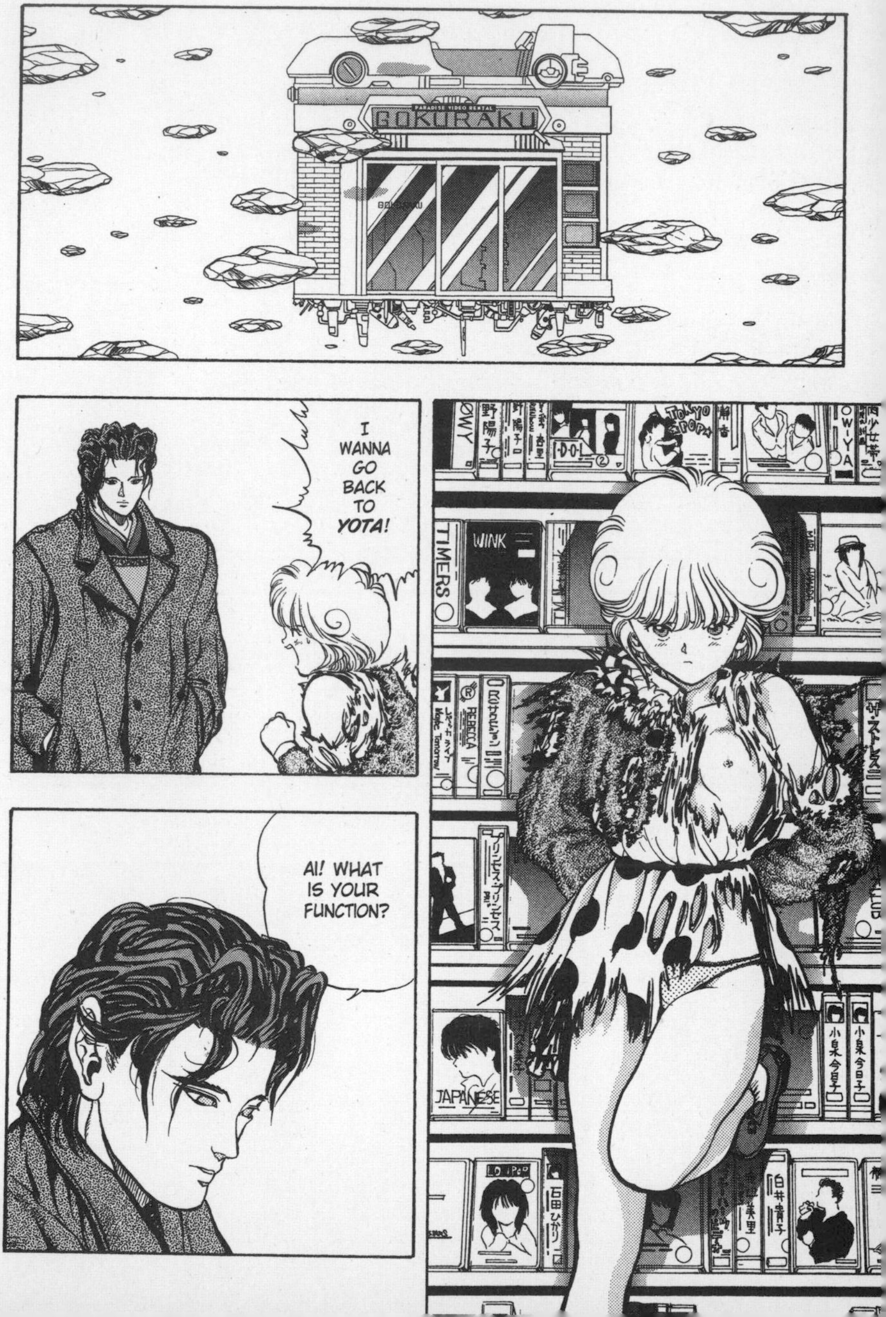
PARADISE VIDEO RENTAL
GOKURAKU
TOKYO POP
WINK
TIMERS
REBECCA
JAPANESE
I WANNA GO BACK TO *YOTA!*
AI! WHAT IS YOUR FUNCTION?

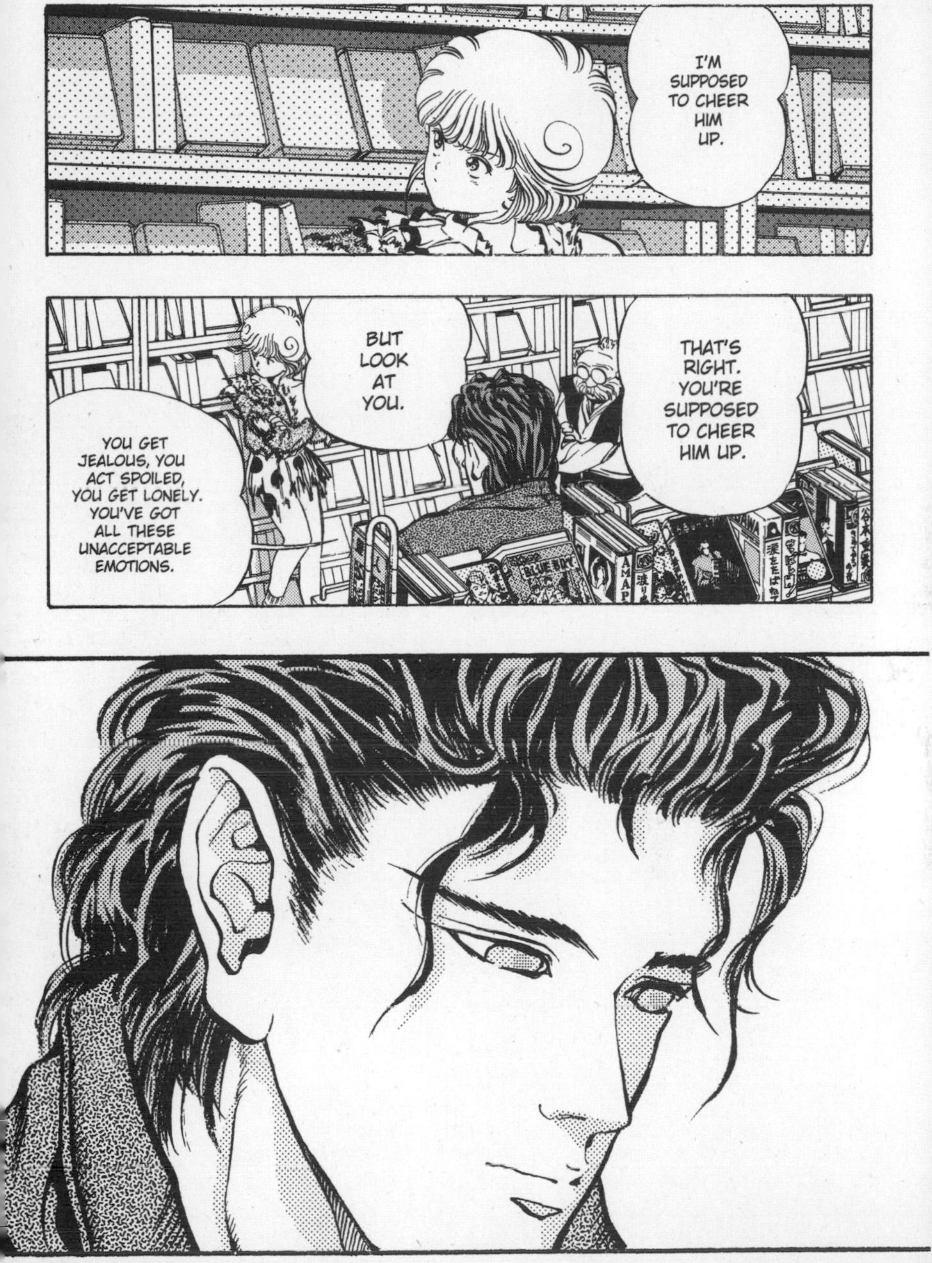
I'M SUPPOSED TO CHEER HIM UP.
THAT'S RIGHT. YOU'RE SUPPOSED TO CHEER HIM UP.
BUT LOOK AT YOU.
YOU GET JEALOUS, YOU ACT SPOILED, YOU GET LONELY. YOU'VE GOT ALL THESE UNACCEPTABLE EMOTIONS.

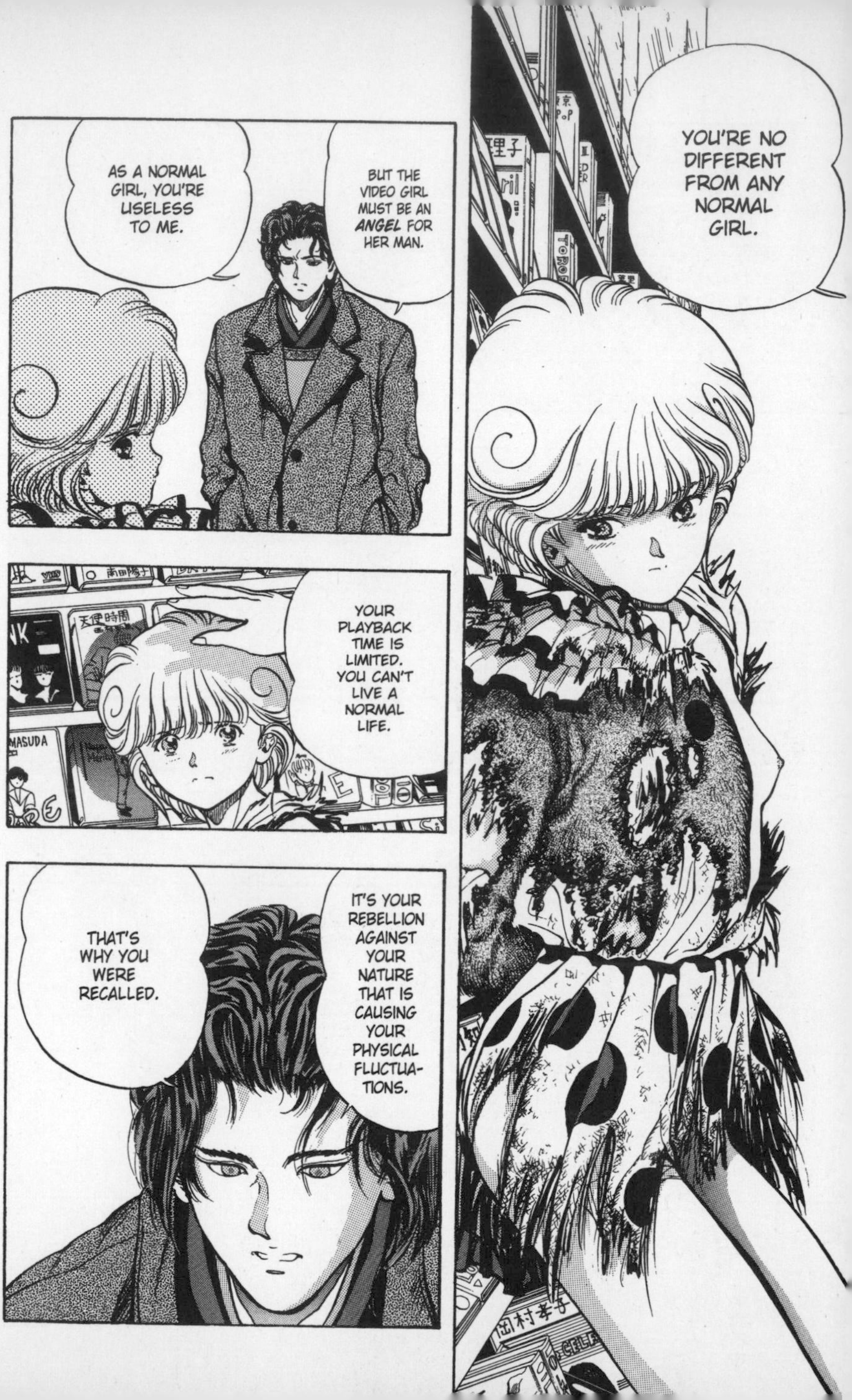
YOU'RE NO DIFFERENT FROM ANY NORMAL GIRL.
BUT THE VIDEO GIRL MUST BE AN ANGEL FOR HER MAN.
AS A NORMAL GIRL, YOU'RE USELESS TO ME.
YOUR PLAYBACK TIME IS LIMITED. YOU CAN'T LIVE A NORMAL LIFE.
IT'S YOUR REBELLION AGAINST YOUR NATURE THAT IS CAUSING YOUR PHYSICAL FLUCTUATIONS.
THAT'S WHY YOU WERE RECALLED.

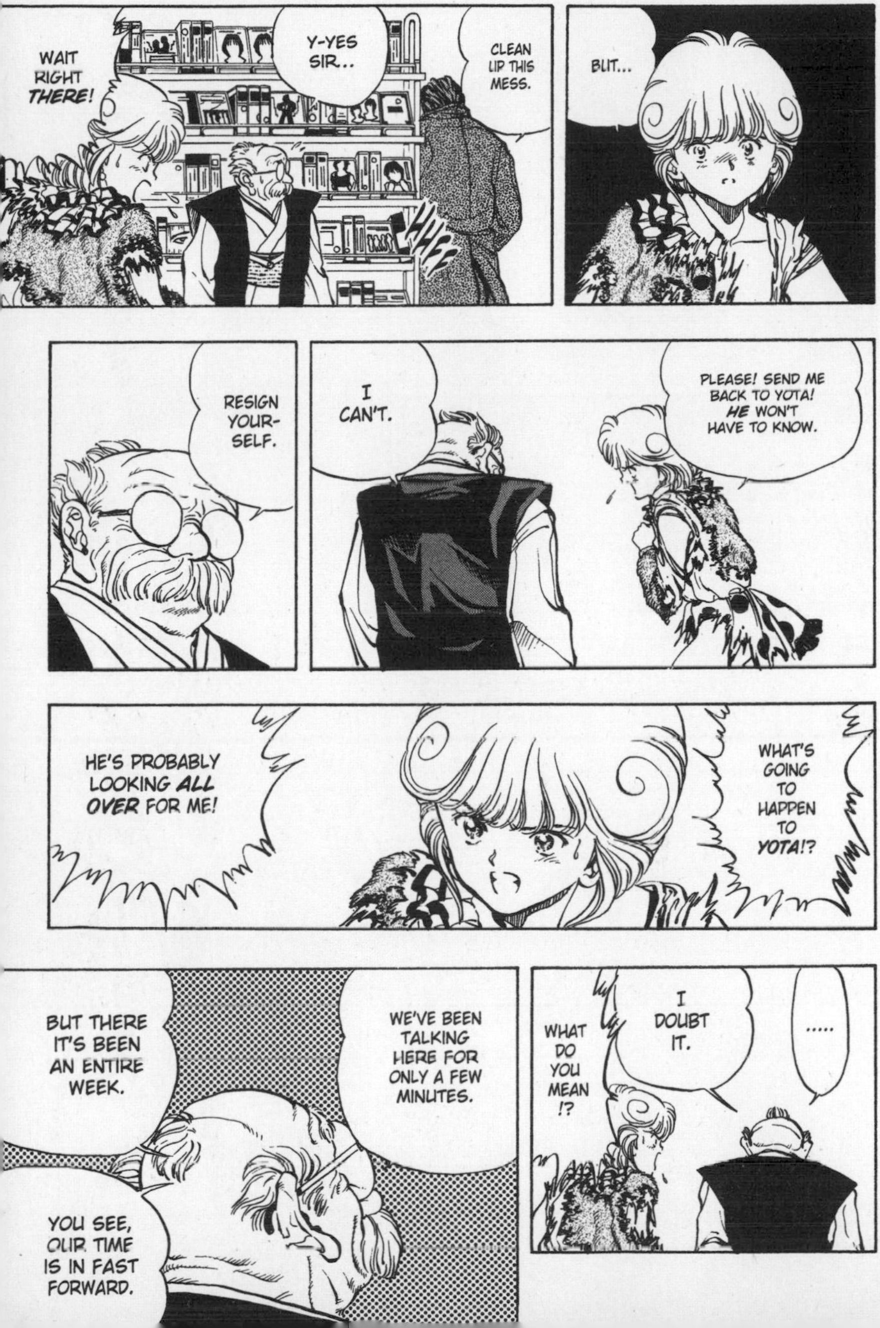
BUT...
CLEAN UP THIS MESS.
Y-YES SIR...
WAIT RIGHT *THERE*!
PLEASE! SEND ME BACK TO YOTA! *HE* WON'T HAVE TO KNOW.
I CAN'T.
RESIGN YOURSELF.
WHAT'S GOING TO HAPPEN TO *YOTA*!?
HE'S PROBABLY LOOKING ***ALL OVER*** FOR ME!
.....
I DOUBT IT.
WHAT DO YOU MEAN!?
WE'VE BEEN TALKING HERE FOR ONLY A FEW MINUTES.
BUT THERE IT'S BEEN AN ENTIRE WEEK.
YOU SEE, OUR TIME IS IN FAST FORWARD.

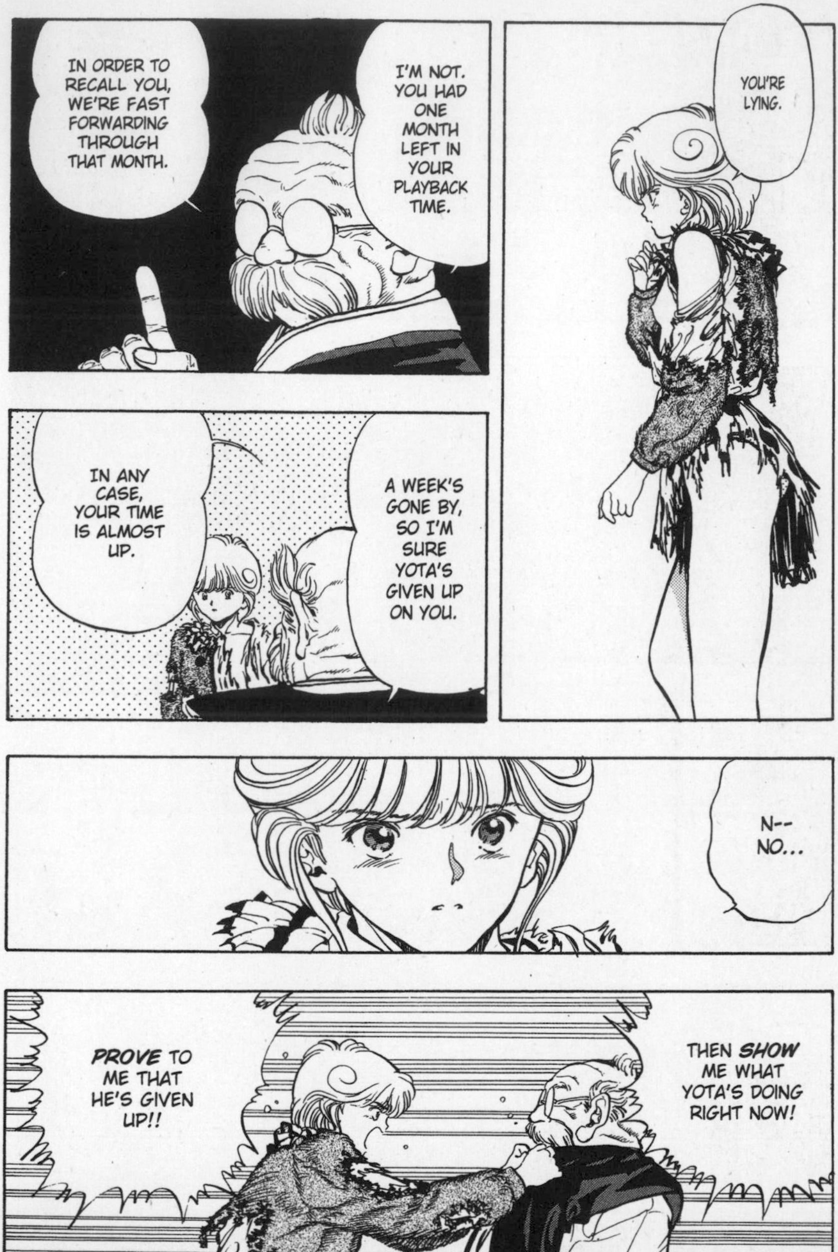
YOU'RE LYING.
I'M NOT. YOU HAD ONE MONTH LEFT IN YOUR PLAYBACK TIME.
IN ORDER TO RECALL YOU, WE'RE FAST FORWARDING THROUGH THAT MONTH.
A WEEK'S GONE BY, SO I'M SURE YOTA'S GIVEN UP ON YOU.
IN ANY CASE, YOUR TIME IS ALMOST UP.
N-- NO...
THEN *SHOW* ME WHAT YOTA'S DOING RIGHT NOW!
PROVE TO ME THAT HE'S GIVEN UP!!

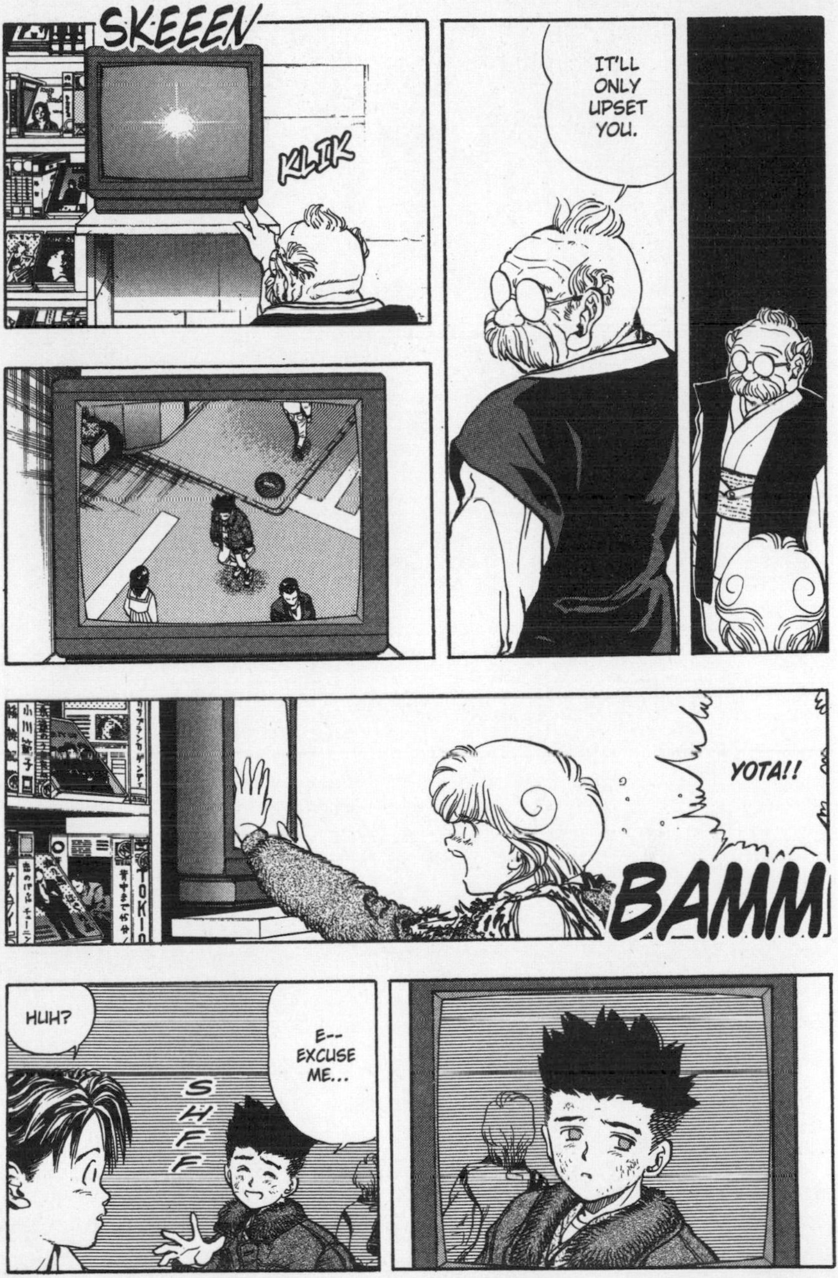
IT'LL ONLY UPSET YOU.
SKEEEN
KLIK
YOTA!!
BAMM
E-- EXCUSE ME...
SHFF
HUH?

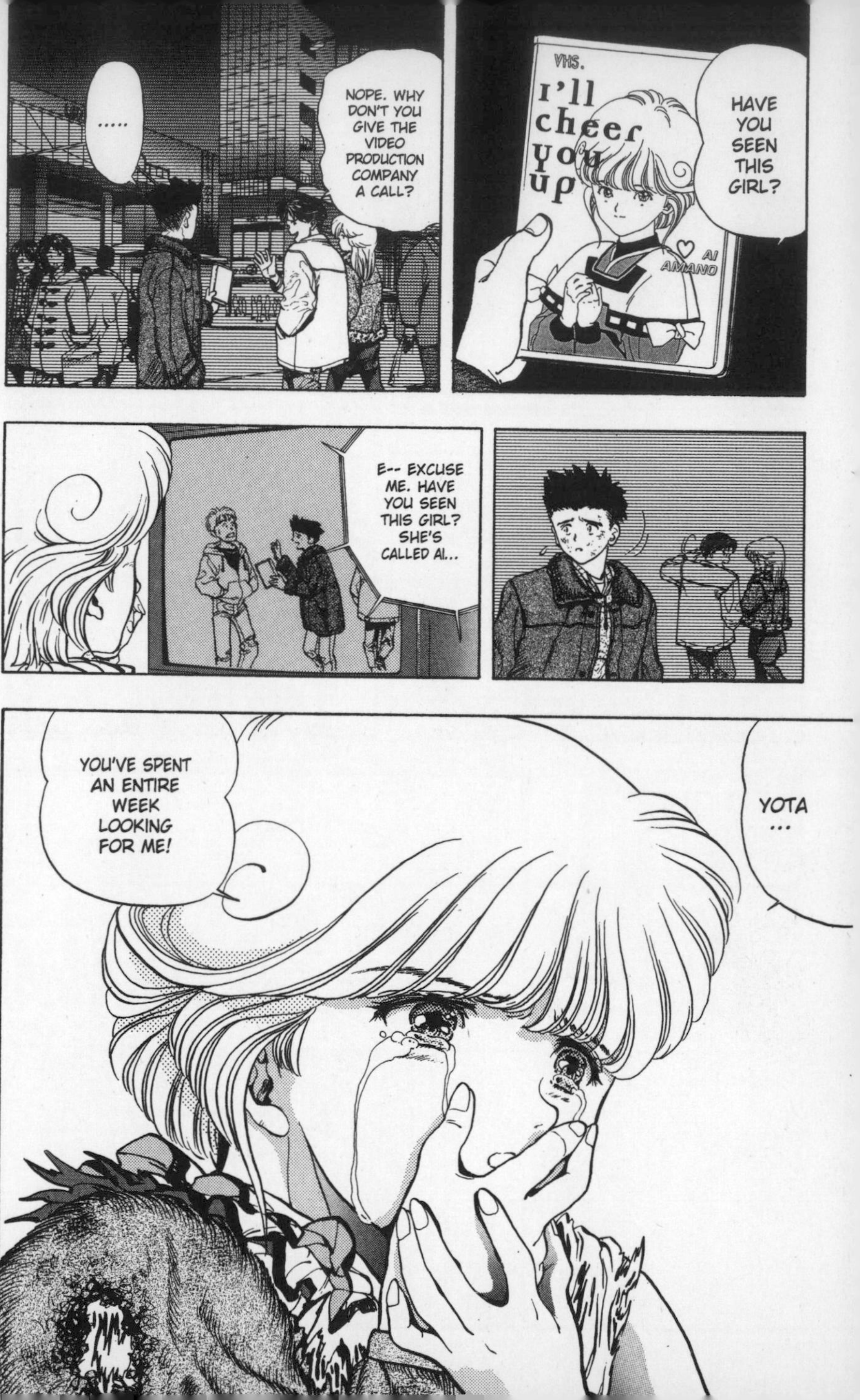
HAVE YOU SEEN THIS GIRL?
VHS.
I'll cheer you up
AI AMANO
NOPE. WHY DON'T YOU GIVE THE VIDEO PRODUCTION COMPANY A CALL?
......
E-- EXCUSE ME. HAVE YOU SEEN THIS GIRL? SHE'S CALLED AI...
YOTA ...
YOU'VE SPENT AN ENTIRE WEEK LOOKING FOR ME!

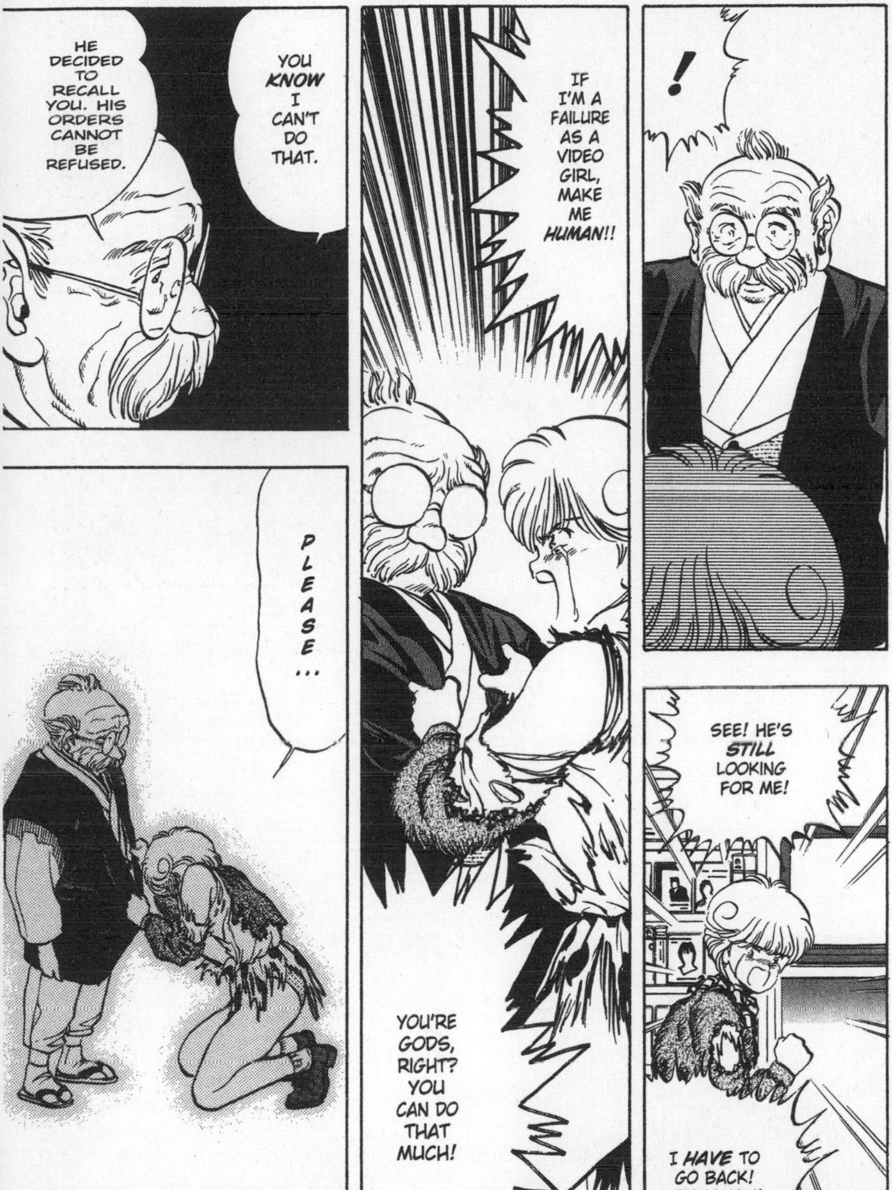
HE DECIDED TO RECALL YOU. HIS ORDERS CANNOT BE REFUSED.
YOU *KNOW* I CAN'T DO THAT.
PLEASE...
IF I'M A FAILURE AS A VIDEO GIRL, MAKE ME *HUMAN*!!
YOU'RE GODS, RIGHT? YOU CAN DO THAT MUCH!
!
SEE! HE'S *STILL* LOOKING FOR ME!
I *HAVE* TO GO BACK! RIGHT NOW!

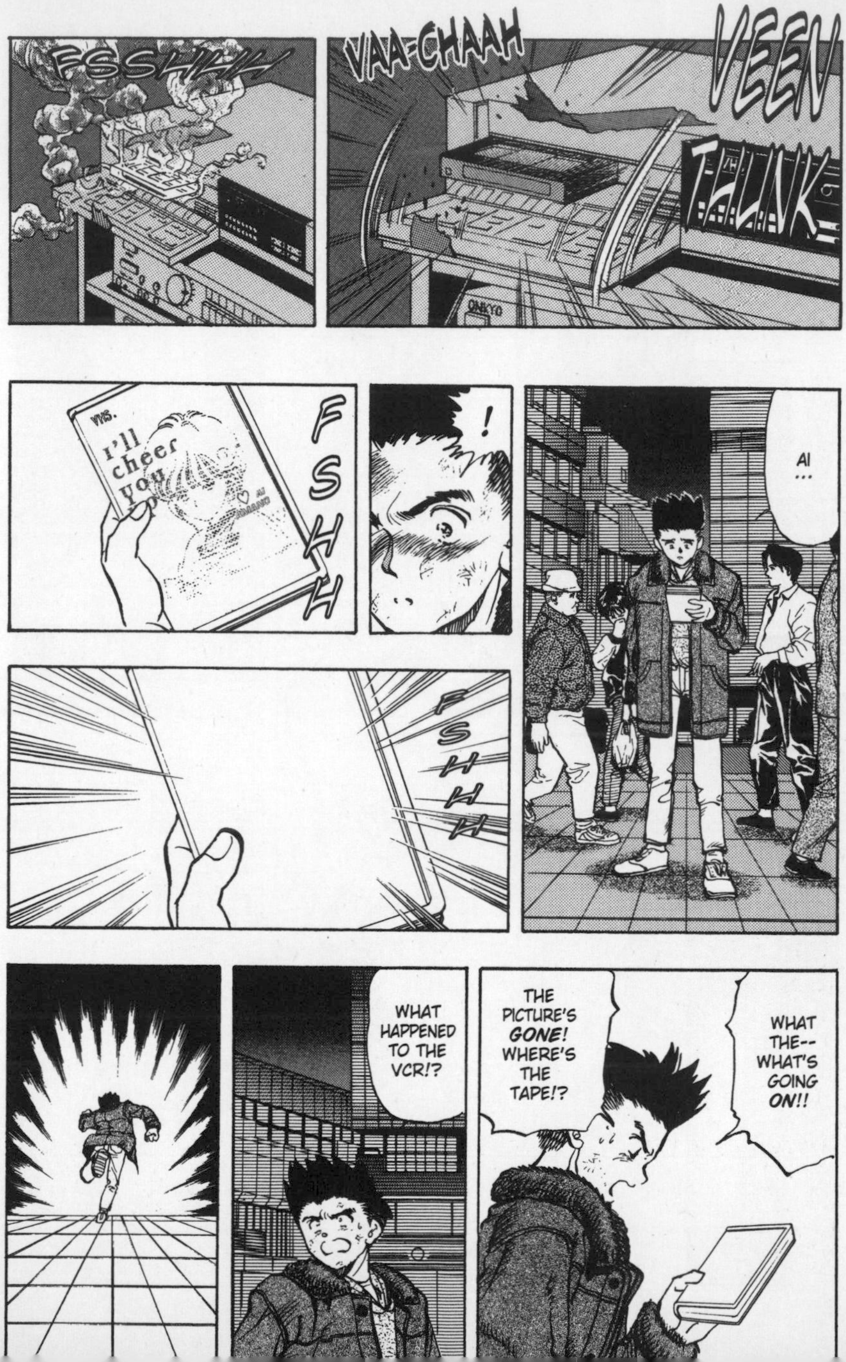
VAA-CHAAH
VEEN
THUNK
ONKYO
FSSHHH
AI...
!
VHS.
i'll cheer you
AI AMANO
FSHHH
FSHHH
WHAT THE-- WHAT'S GOING ON!!
THE PICTURE'S GONE! WHERE'S THE TAPE!?
WHAT HAPPENED TO THE VCR!?

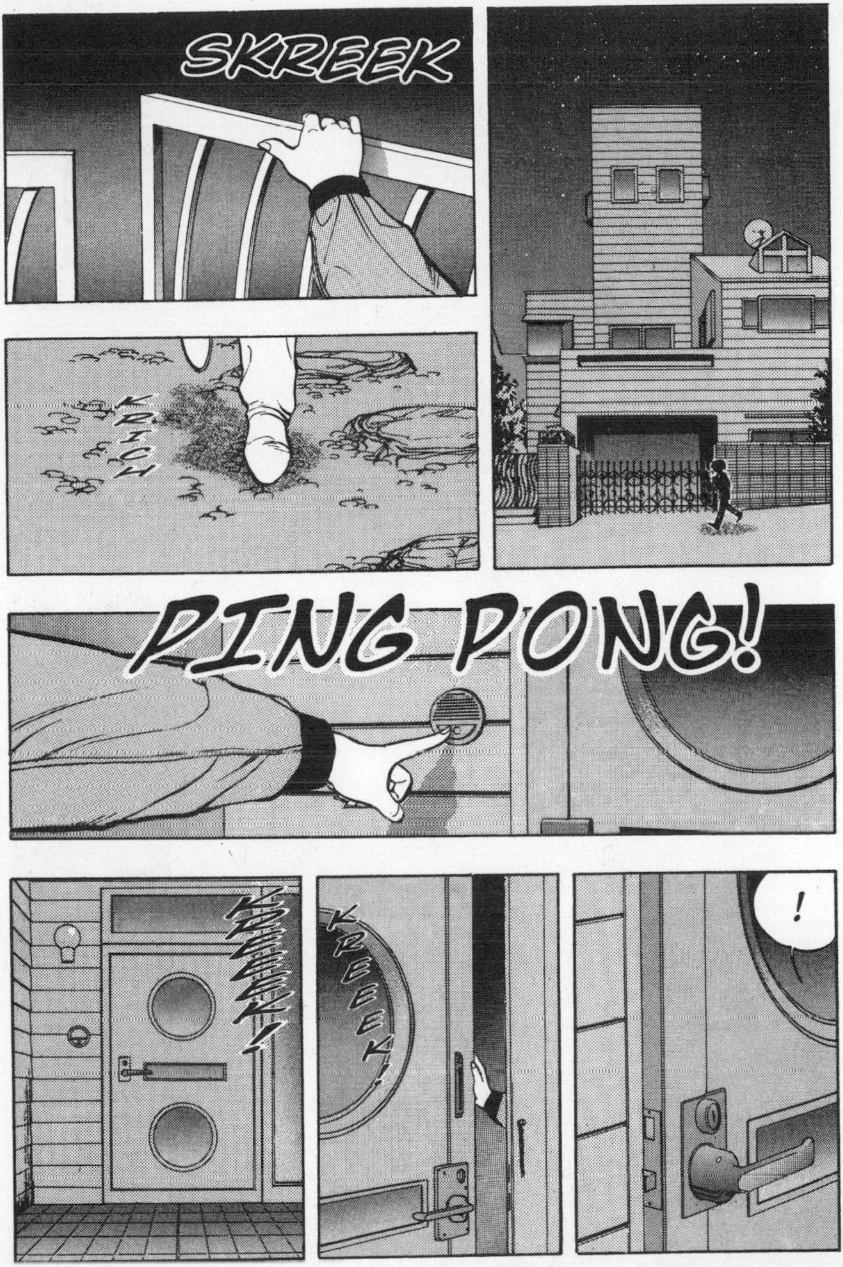
SKREEK
KRICH
PING PONG!
!
KREEEK!
KREEEEK!

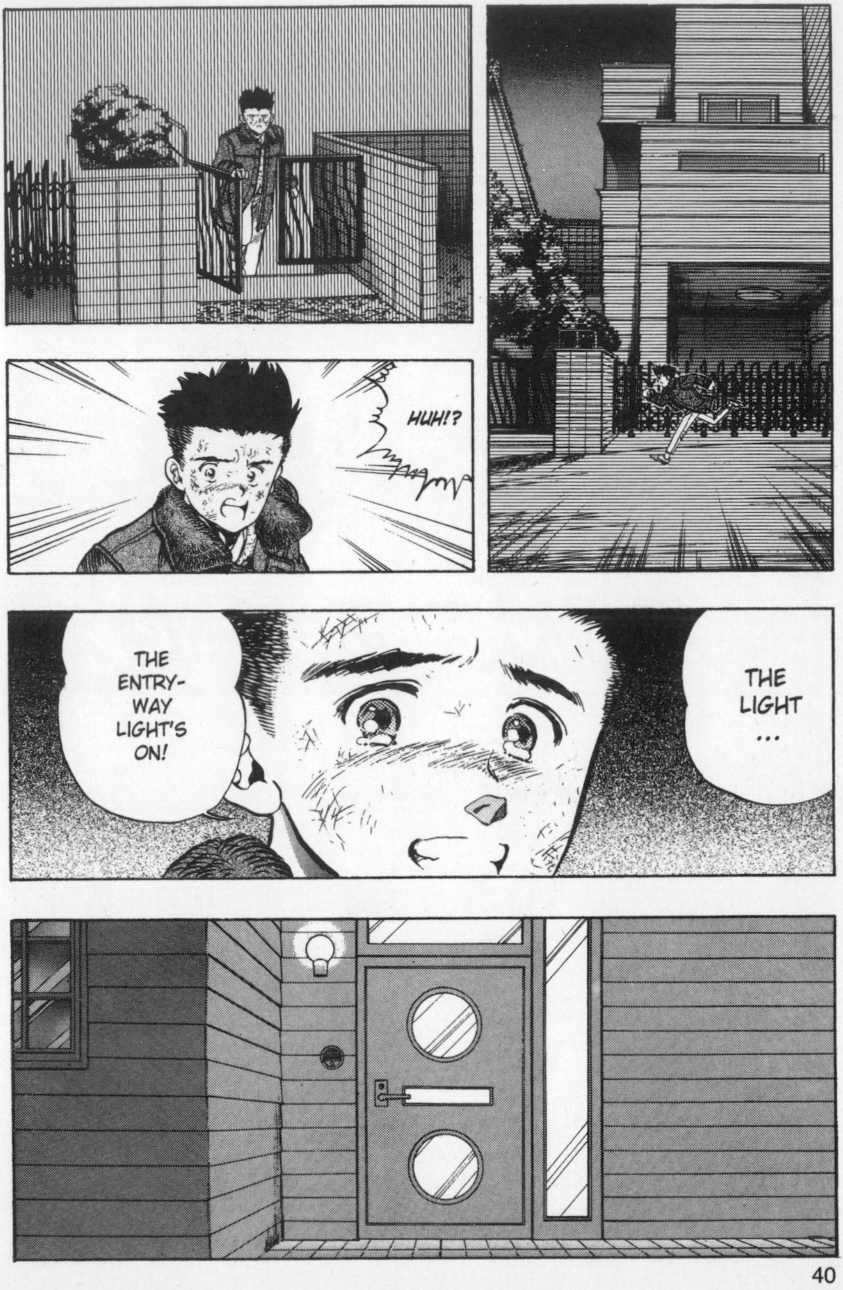
HUH!?
THE LIGHT ...
THE ENTRY-WAY LIGHT'S ON!

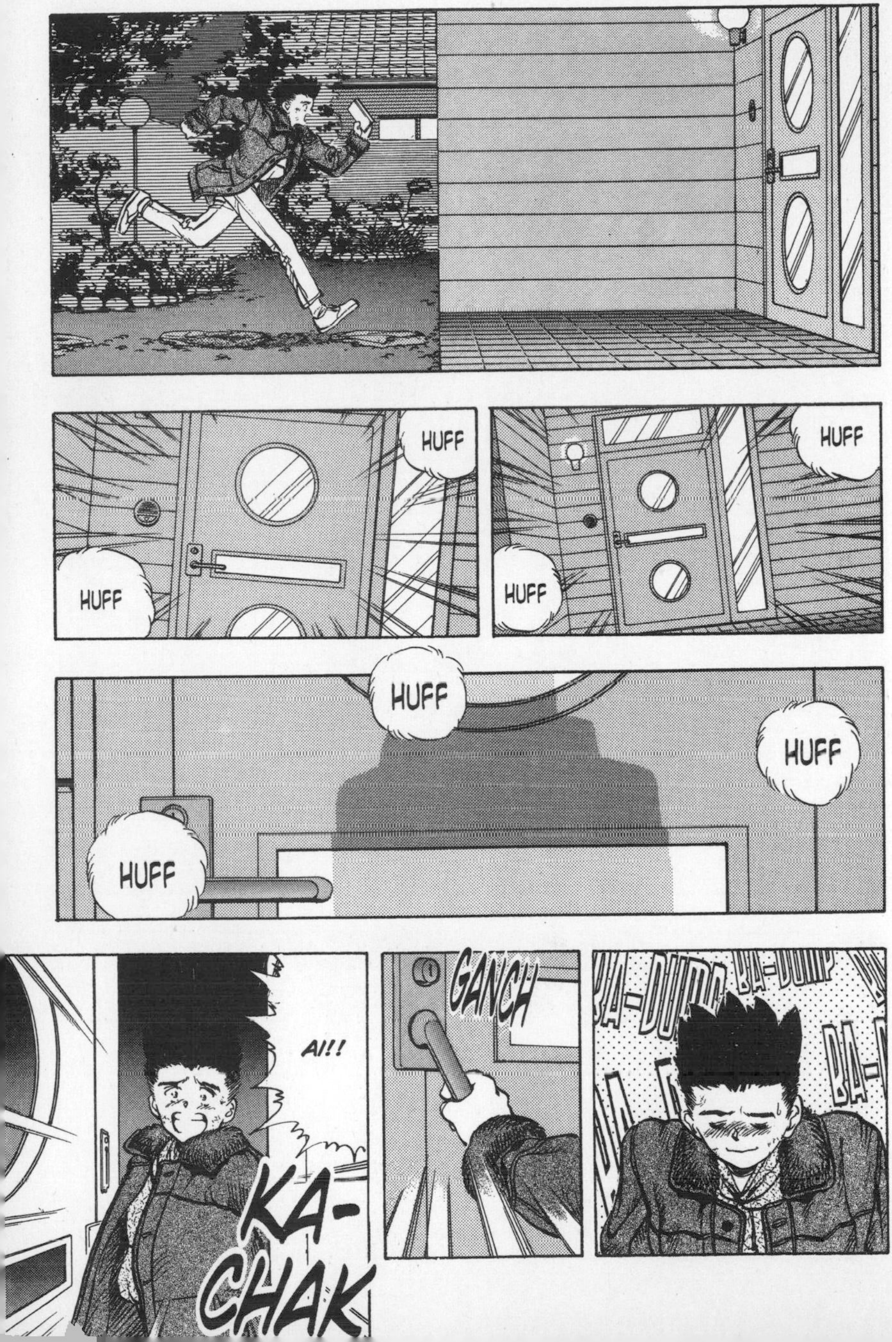

HUFF
HUFF
HUFF
HUFF
HUFF
HUFF
HUFF
BA-DUMP
BA-DUMP
GANCH
AI!!
KA-CHAK

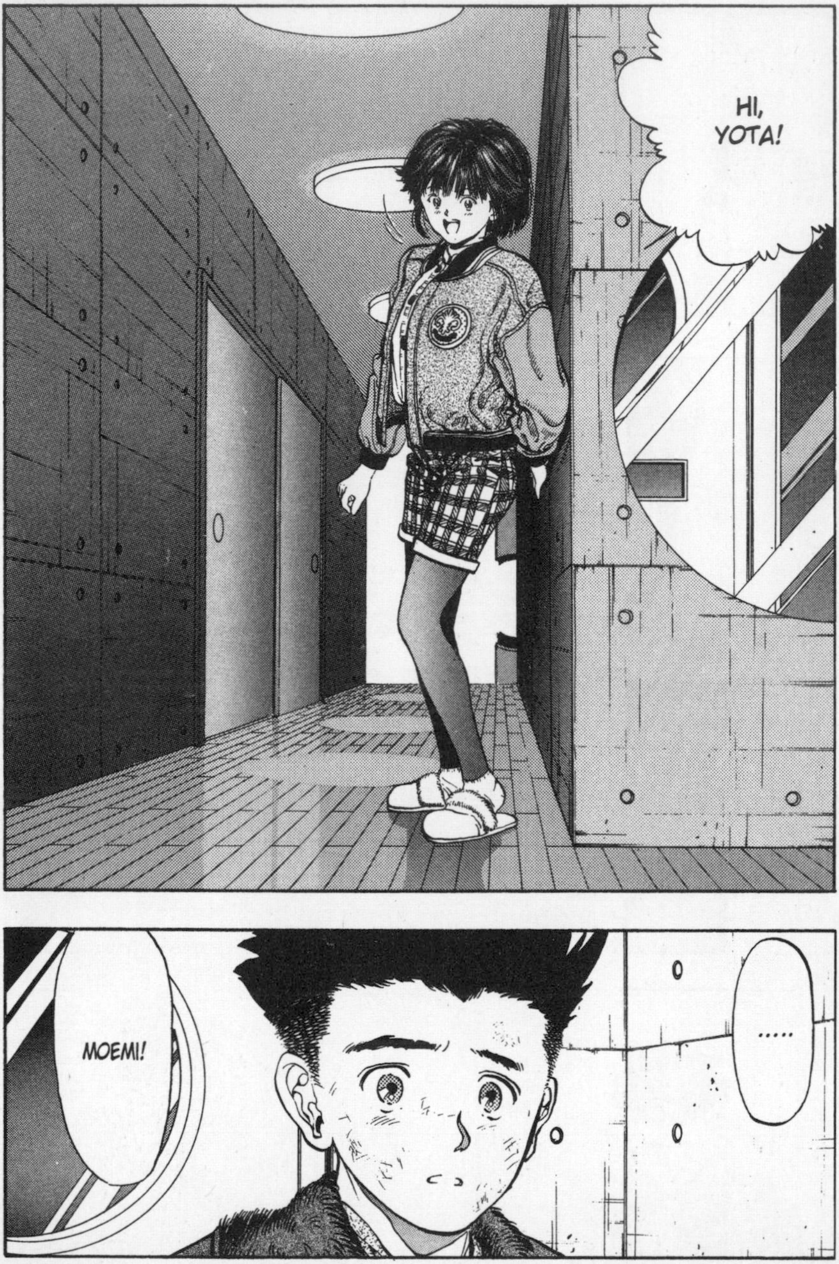
HI, YOTA!
.....
MOEMI!

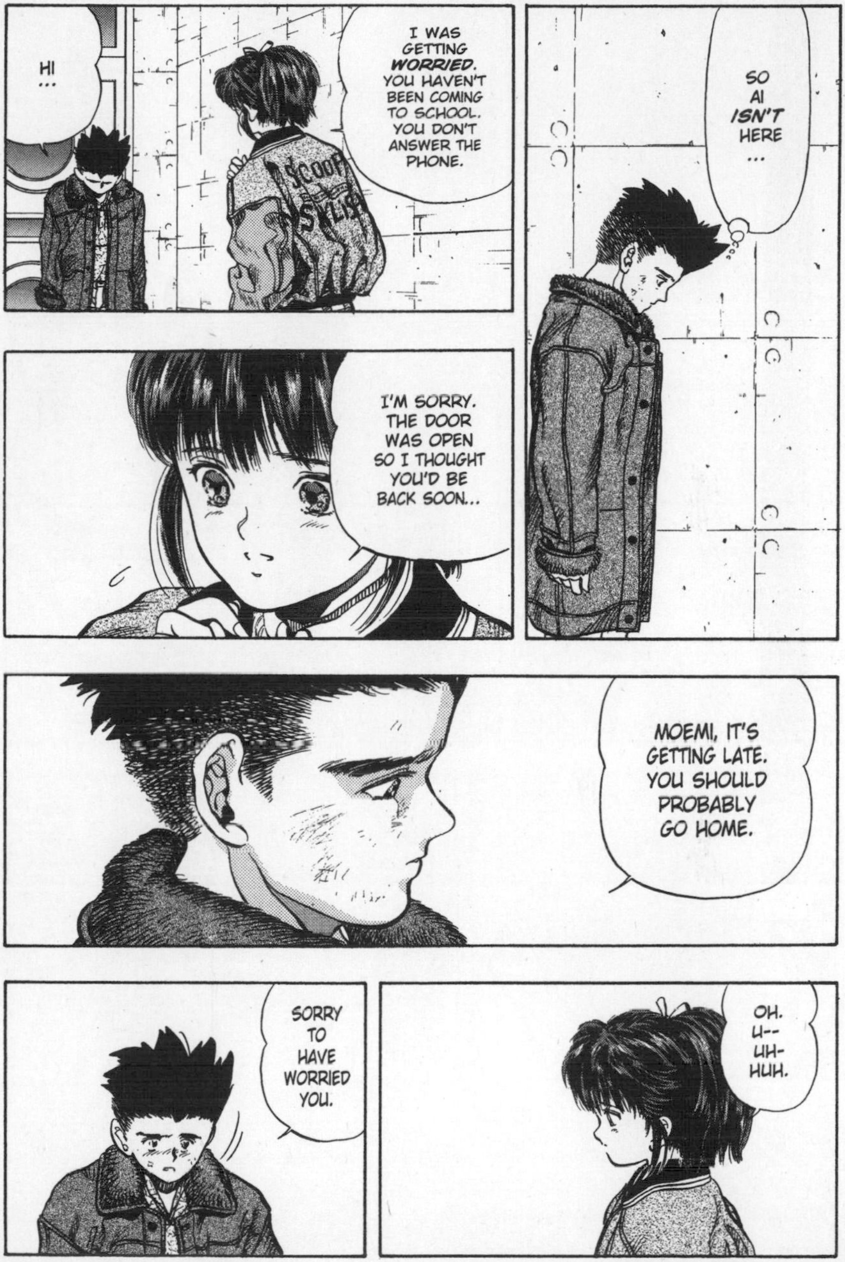
SO AI *ISN'T* HERE ...
I WAS GETTING ***WORRIED***. YOU HAVEN'T BEEN COMING TO SCHOOL. YOU DON'T ANSWER THE PHONE.
HI ...
I'M SORRY. THE DOOR WAS OPEN SO I THOUGHT YOU'D BE BACK SOON...
MOEMI, IT'S GETTING LATE. YOU SHOULD PROBABLY GO HOME.
OH. U-- UH-HUH.
SORRY TO HAVE WORRIED YOU.

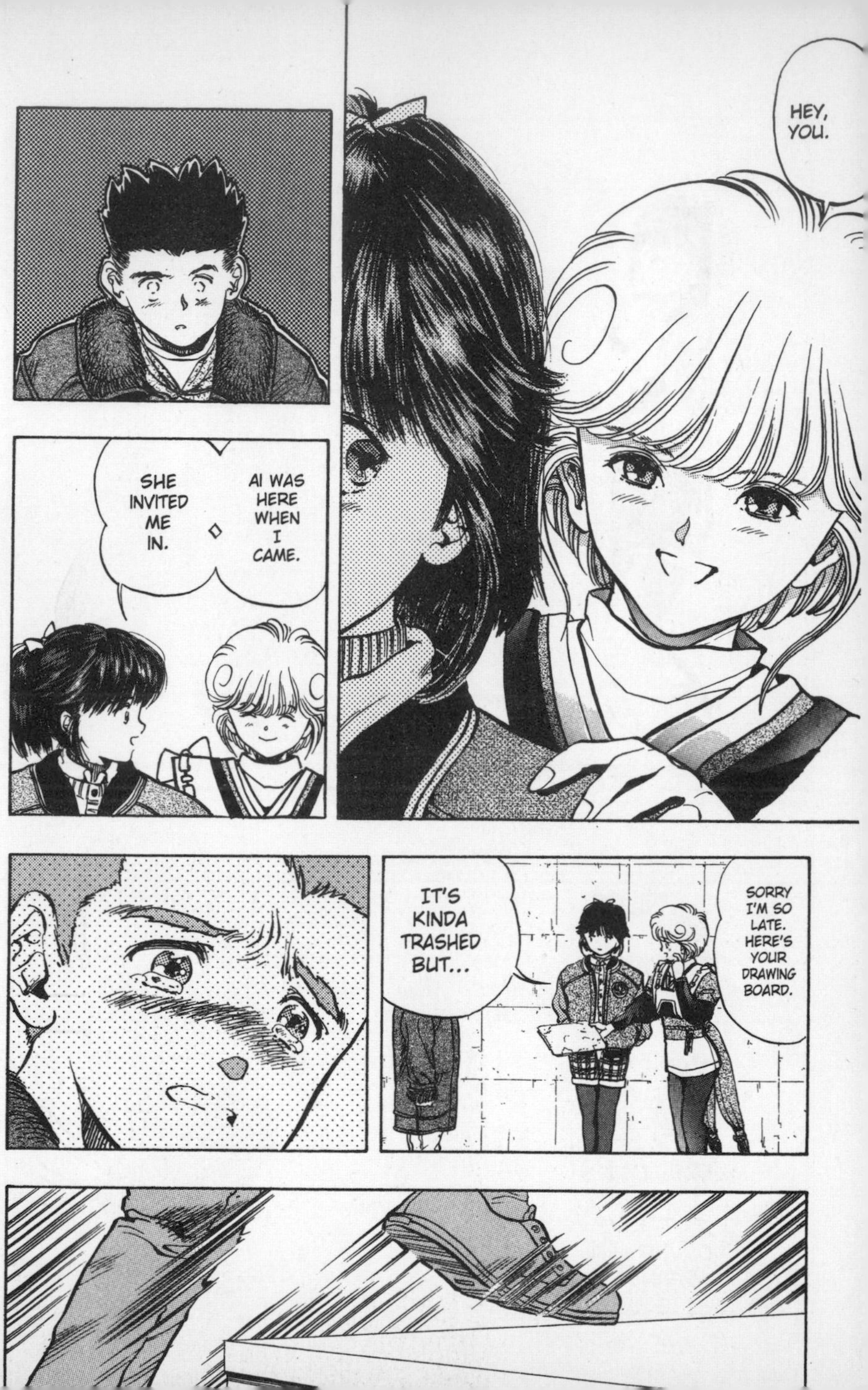
HEY, YOU.
AI WAS HERE WHEN I CAME.
SHE INVITED ME IN.
SORRY I'M SO LATE. HERE'S YOUR DRAWING BOARD.
IT'S KINDA TRASHED BUT...

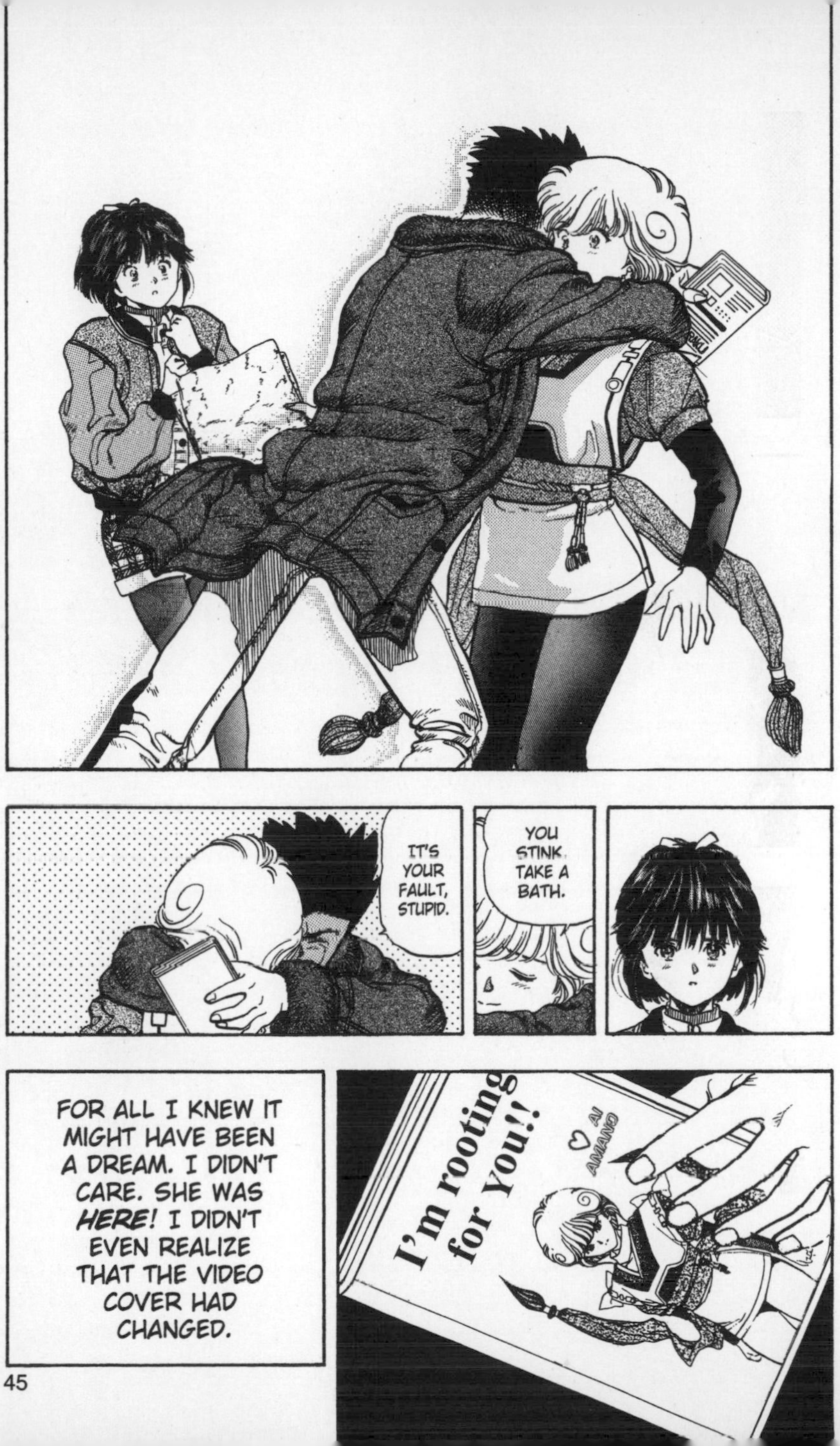
YOU STINK. TAKE A BATH.
IT'S YOUR FAULT, STUPID.
I'm rooting for You!!
♥ AI AMANO
FOR ALL I KNEW IT MIGHT HAVE BEEN A DREAM. I DIDN'T CARE. SHE WAS *HERE*! I DIDN'T EVEN REALIZE THAT THE VIDEO COVER HAD CHANGED.

◢ ❙❙ ►► ► *CHAPTER ELEVEN*
Distance From Yota

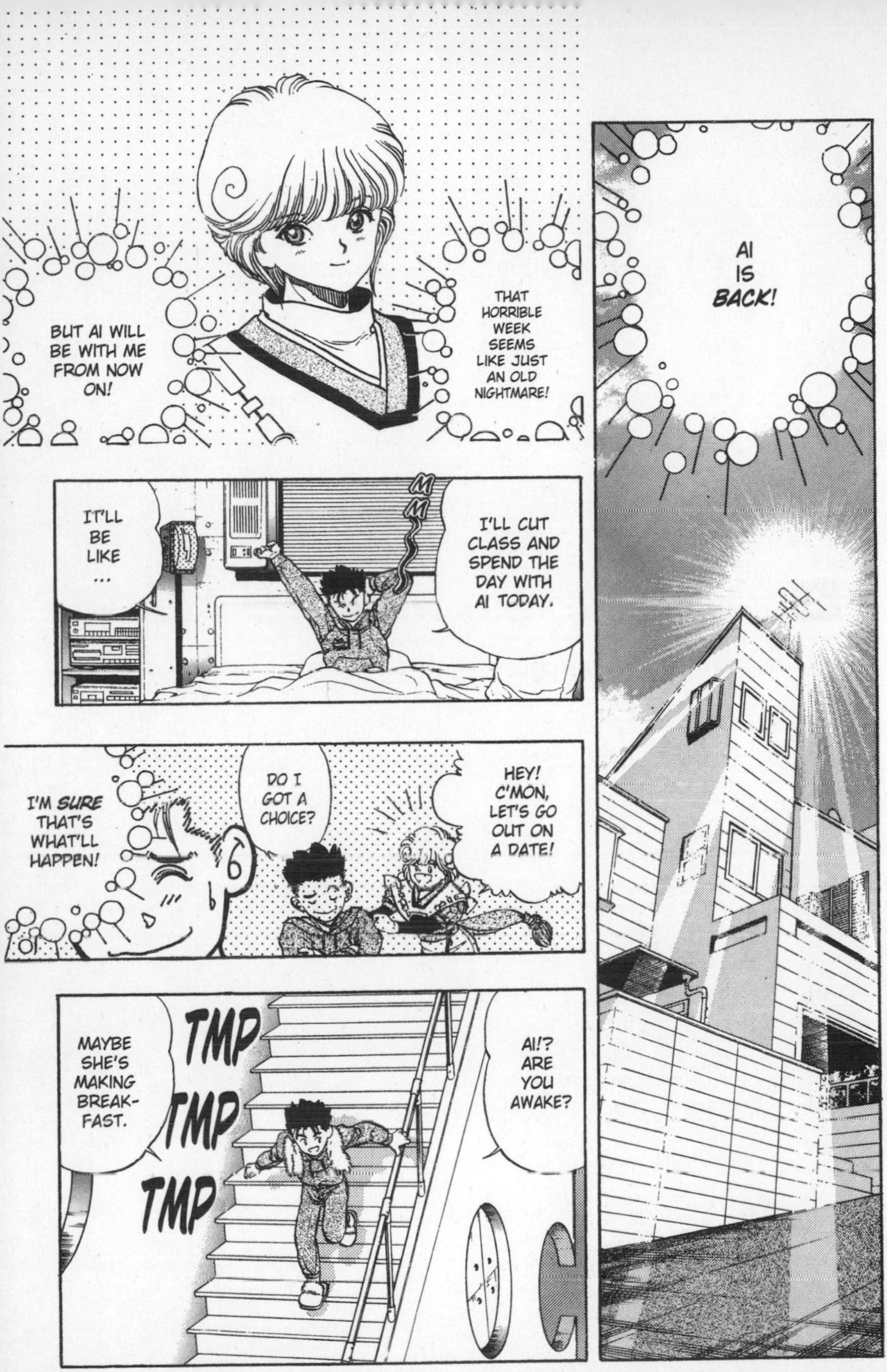
AI IS *BACK!*
THAT HORRIBLE WEEK SEEMS LIKE JUST AN OLD NIGHTMARE!
BUT AI WILL BE WITH ME FROM NOW ON!
MM
I'LL CUT CLASS AND SPEND THE DAY WITH AI TODAY.
IT'LL BE LIKE ...
HEY! C'MON, LET'S GO OUT ON A DATE!
DO I GOT A CHOICE?
I'M *SURE* THAT'S WHAT'LL HAPPEN!
AI!? ARE YOU AWAKE?
TMP
TMP
TMP
MAYBE SHE'S MAKING BREAK-FAST.

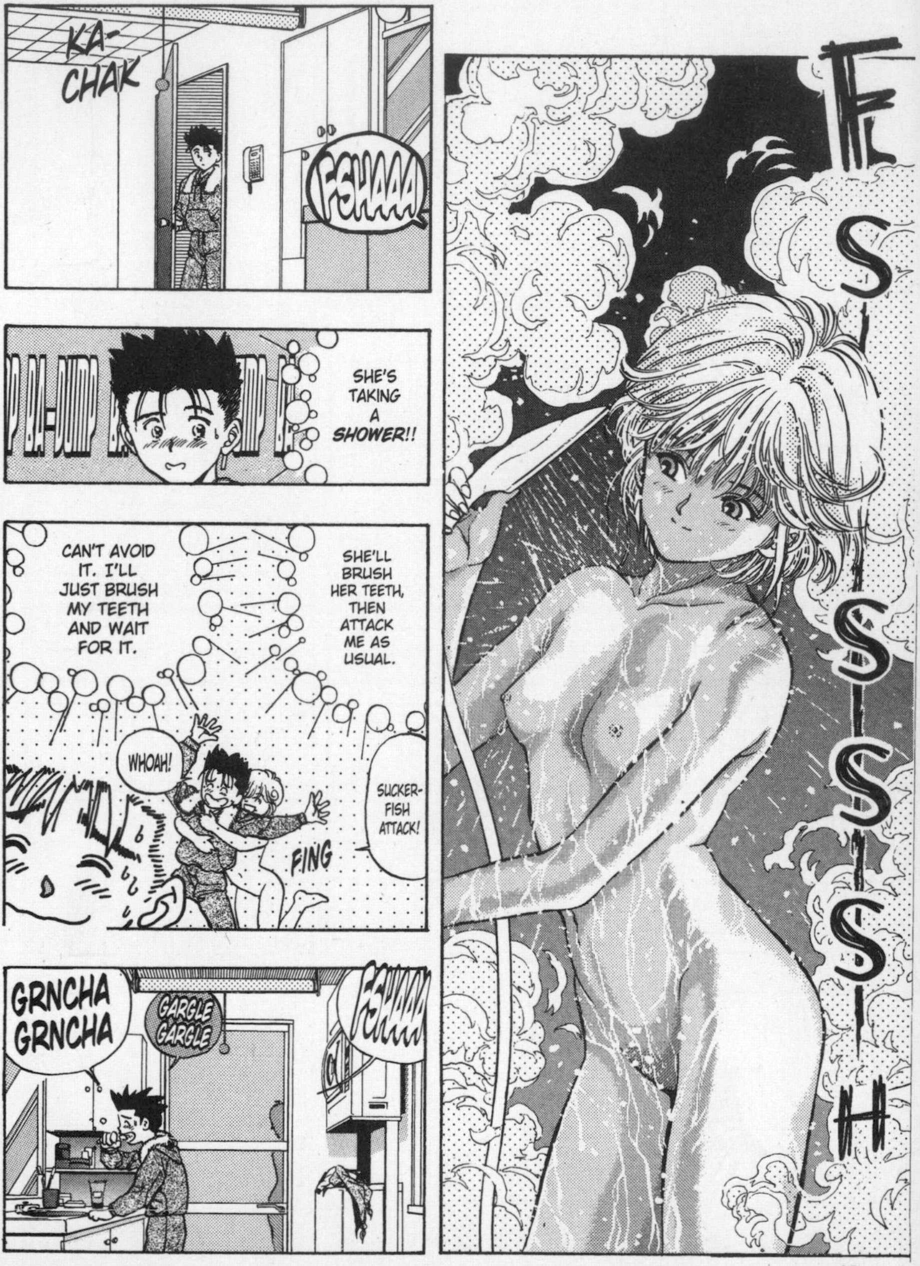
FSSSSH
KA-CHAK
FSHAAA
BA-DUMP
SHE'S TAKING A SHOWER!!
SHE'LL BRUSH HER TEETH, THEN ATTACK ME AS USUAL.
CAN'T AVOID IT. I'LL JUST BRUSH MY TEETH AND WAIT FOR IT.
SUCKER-FISH ATTACK!
WHOAH!
FING
FSHAAA
GARGLE GARGLE
GRNCHA GRNCHA

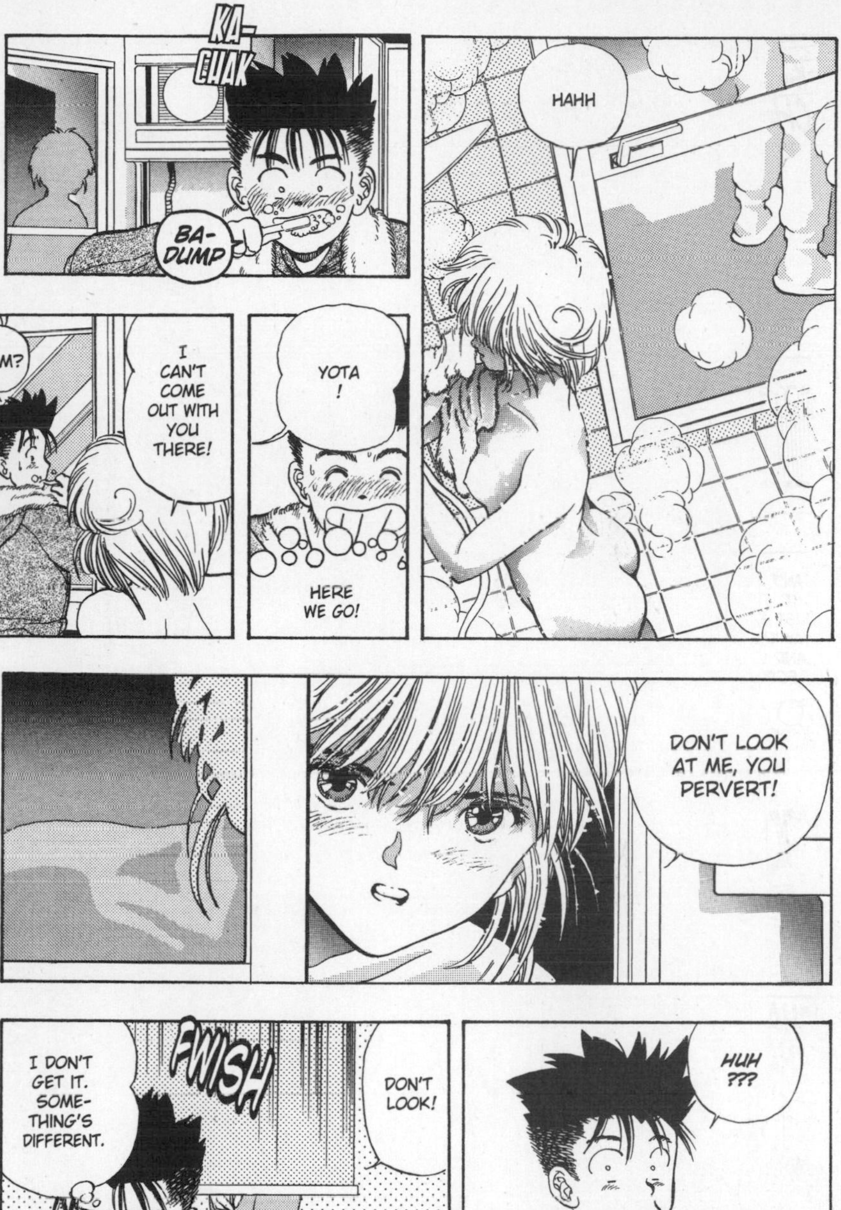
HAHH
KA-CHAK
BA-DUMP
YOTA!
HERE WE GO!
I CAN'T COME OUT WITH YOU THERE!
HM?
DON'T LOOK AT ME, YOU PERVERT!
HUH ???
DON'T LOOK!
FWISH
I DON'T GET IT. SOME-THING'S DIFFERENT.

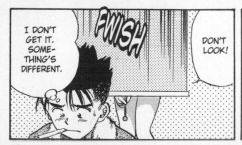

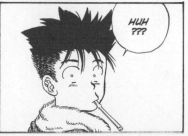

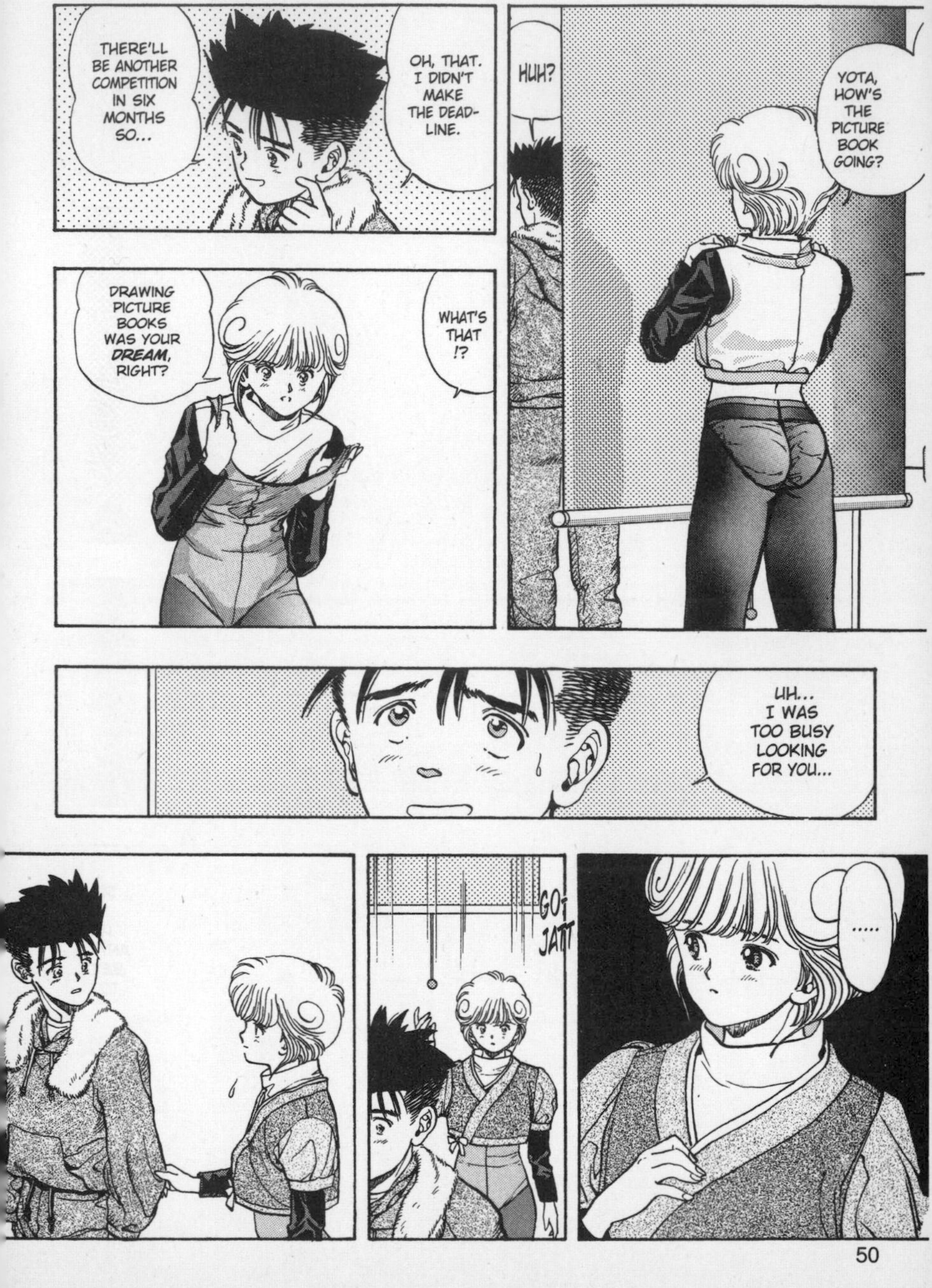
YOTA, HOW'S THE PICTURE BOOK GOING?
HUH?
OH, THAT. I DIDN'T MAKE THE DEAD-LINE.
THERE'LL BE ANOTHER COMPETITION IN SIX MONTHS SO...
WHAT'S THAT !?
DRAWING PICTURE BOOKS WAS YOUR *DREAM*, RIGHT?
UH... I WAS TOO BUSY LOOKING FOR YOU...
.....
GO-JATT

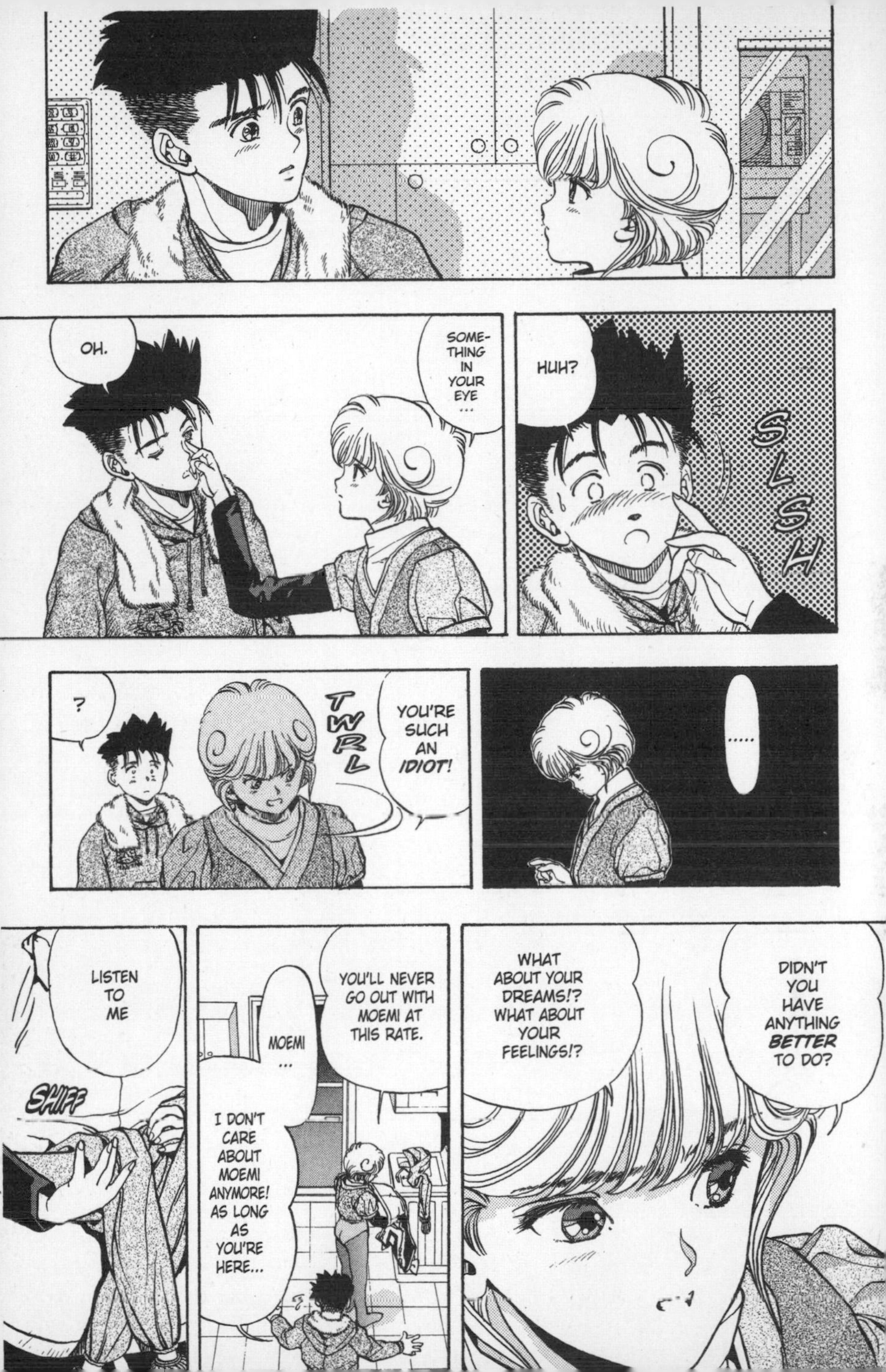
HUH?
SLSH
SOMETHING IN YOUR EYE ...
OH.
.....
YOU'RE SUCH AN *IDIOT*!
TWRL
?
DIDN'T YOU HAVE ANYTHING *BETTER* TO DO?
WHAT ABOUT YOUR DREAMS!? WHAT ABOUT YOUR FEELINGS!?
YOU'LL NEVER GO OUT WITH MOEMI AT THIS RATE.
MOEMI ...
I DON'T CARE ABOUT MOEMI ANYMORE! AS LONG AS YOU'RE HERE...
LISTEN TO ME
SHIFF

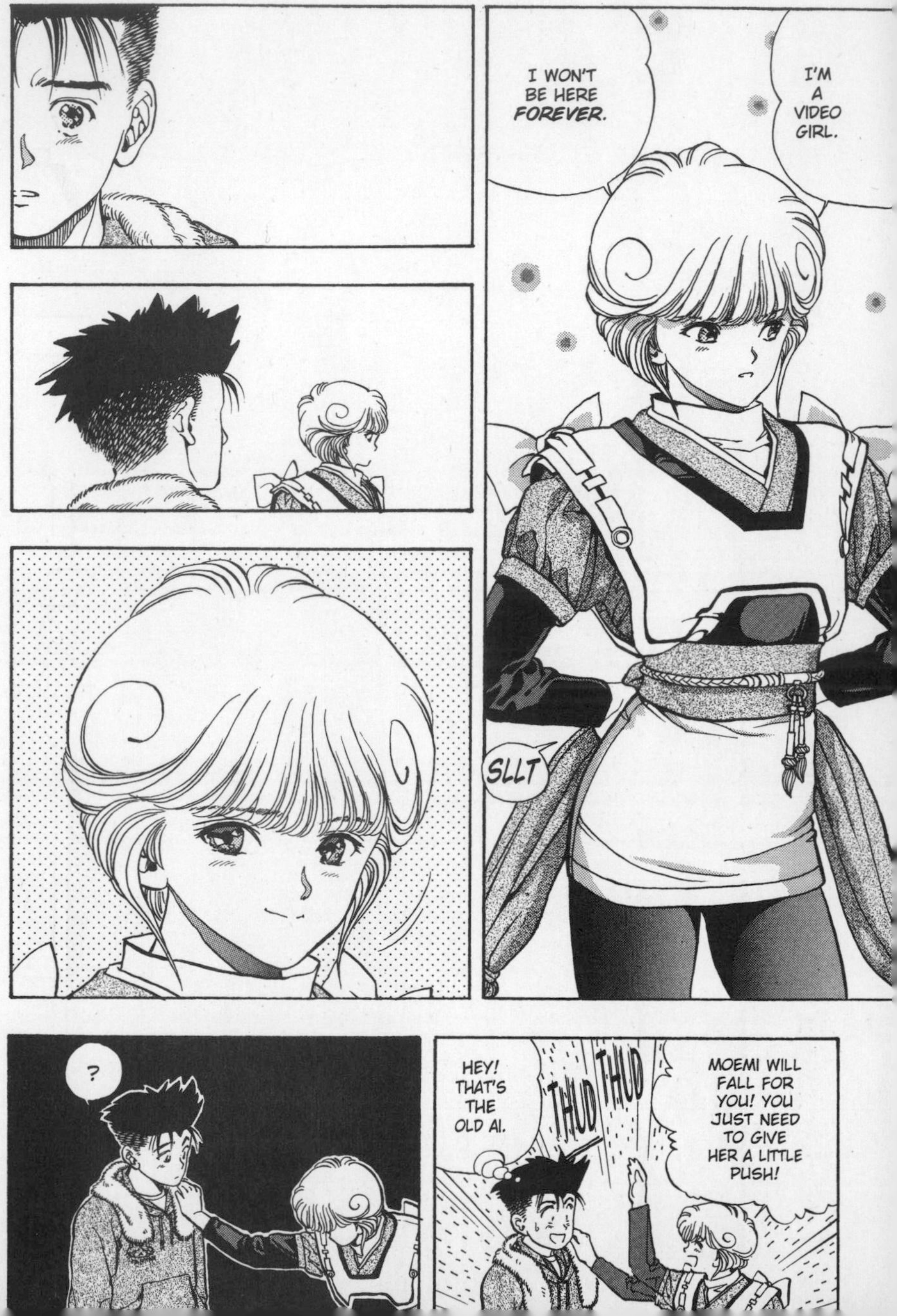
I'M A VIDEO GIRL.
I WON'T BE HERE FOREVER.
SLLT
MOEMI WILL FALL FOR YOU! YOU JUST NEED TO GIVE HER A LITTLE PUSH!
THUD THUD
HEY! THAT'S THE OLD AI.
?

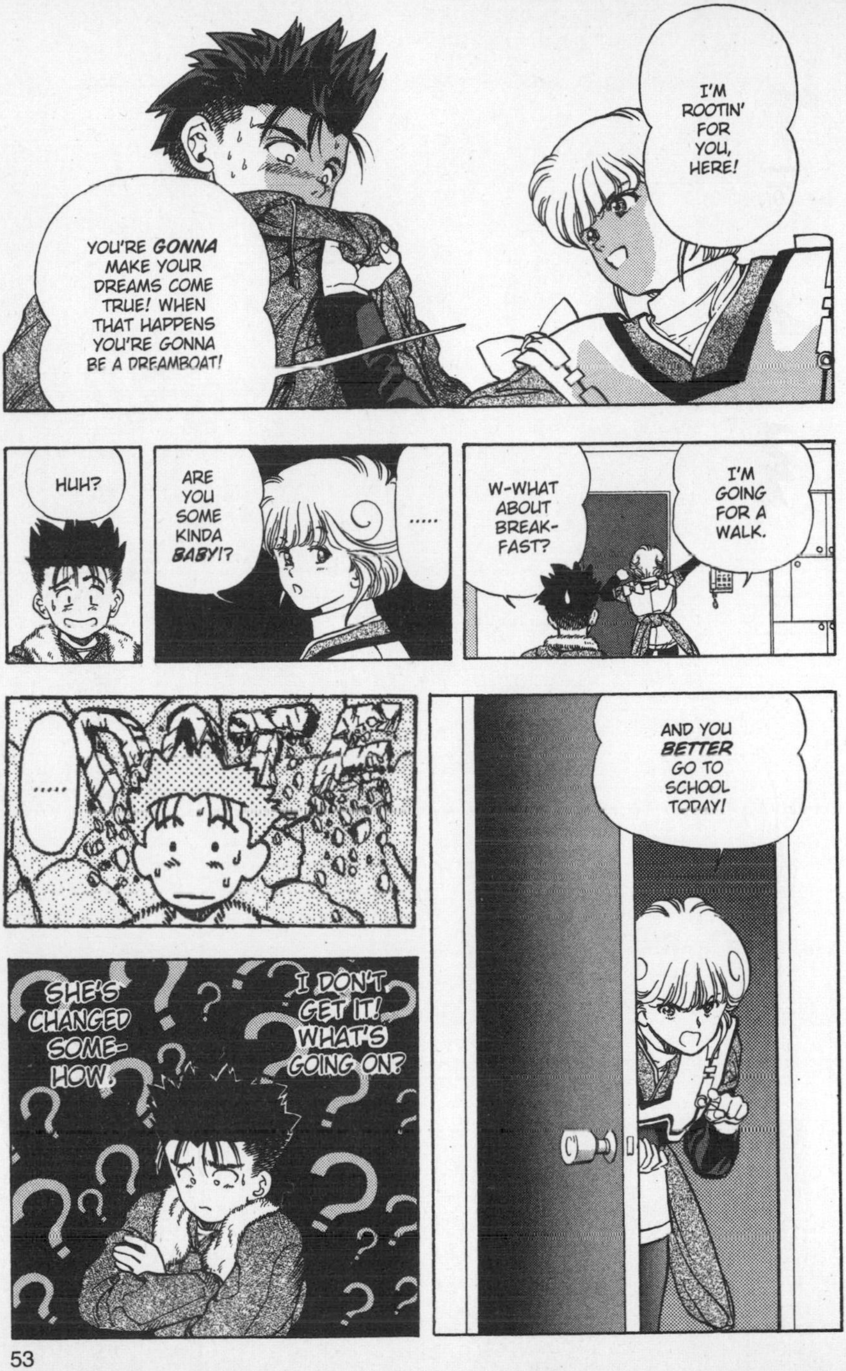
I'M ROOTIN' FOR YOU, HERE!
YOU'RE GONNA MAKE YOUR DREAMS COME TRUE! WHEN THAT HAPPENS YOU'RE GONNA BE A DREAMBOAT!
I'M GOING FOR A WALK.
W-WHAT ABOUT BREAK-FAST?
.....
ARE YOU SOME KINDA BABY!?
HUH?
AND YOU BETTER GO TO SCHOOL TODAY!
.....
I DON'T GET IT! WHAT'S GOING ON?
SHE'S CHANGED SOME-HOW.

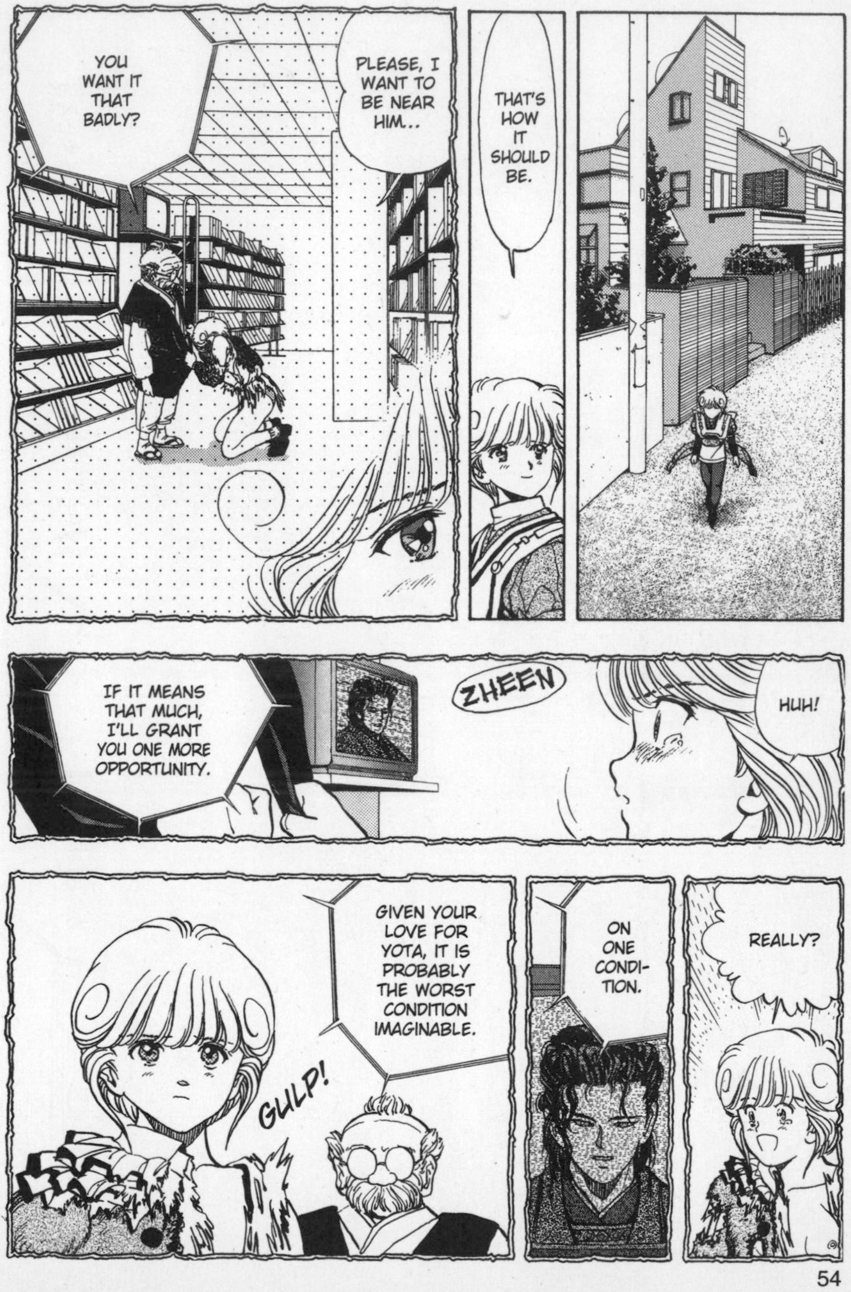
THAT'S HOW IT SHOULD BE.
PLEASE, I WANT TO BE NEAR HIM..
YOU WANT IT THAT BADLY?
HUH!
ZHEEN
IF IT MEANS THAT MUCH, I'LL GRANT YOU ONE MORE OPPORTUNITY.
REALLY?
ON ONE CONDITION.
GIVEN YOUR LOVE FOR YOTA, IT IS PROBABLY THE WORST CONDITION IMAGINABLE.
GULP!

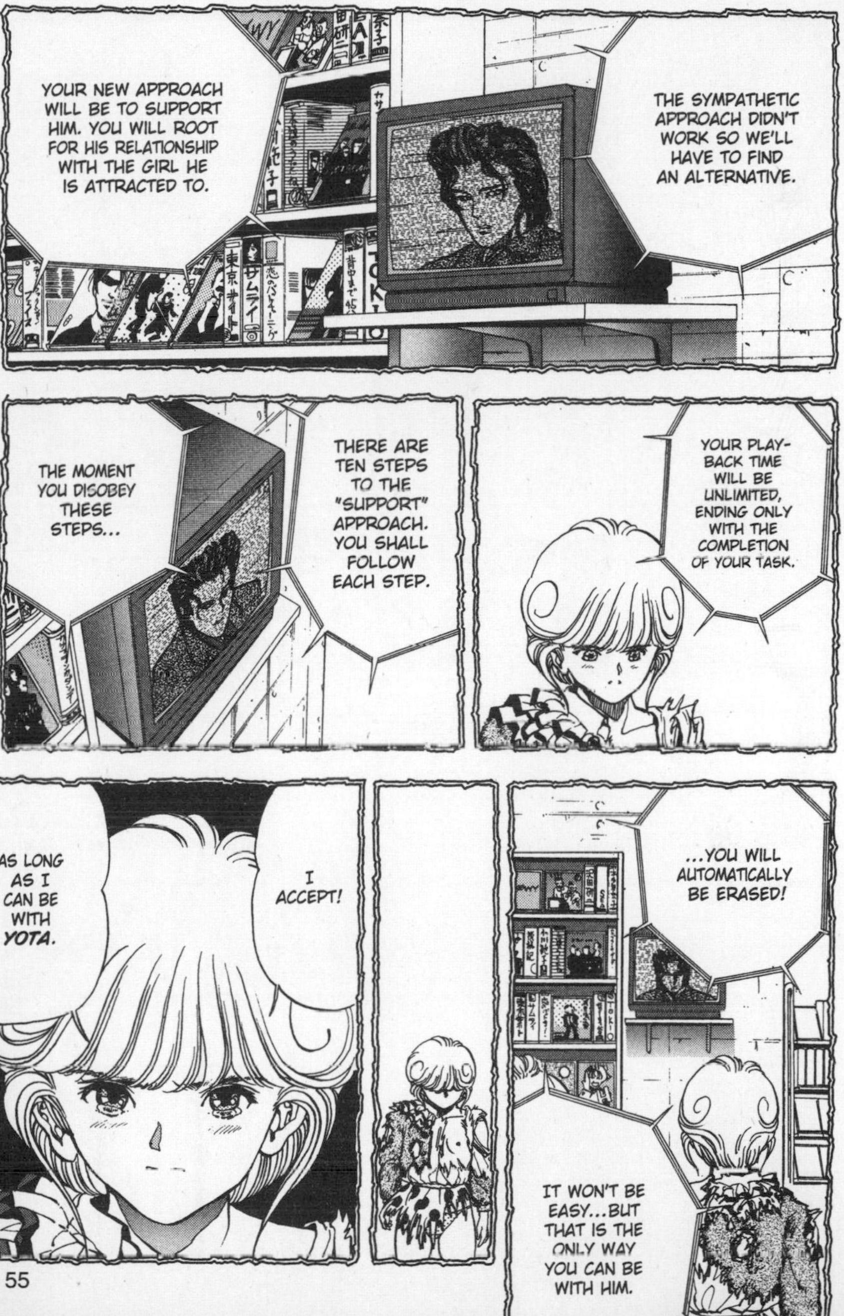
THE SYMPATHETIC APPROACH DIDN'T WORK SO WE'LL HAVE TO FIND AN ALTERNATIVE.
YOUR NEW APPROACH WILL BE TO SUPPORT HIM. YOU WILL ROOT FOR HIS RELATIONSHIP WITH THE GIRL HE IS ATTRACTED TO.
YOUR PLAY-BACK TIME WILL BE UNLIMITED, ENDING ONLY WITH THE COMPLETION OF YOUR TASK.
THERE ARE TEN STEPS TO THE "SUPPORT" APPROACH. YOU SHALL FOLLOW EACH STEP.
THE MOMENT YOU DISOBEY THESE STEPS...
...YOU WILL AUTOMATICALLY BE ERASED!
IT WON'T BE EASY...BUT THAT IS THE ONLY WAY YOU CAN BE WITH HIM.
I ACCEPT!
AS LONG AS I CAN BE WITH *YOTA*.

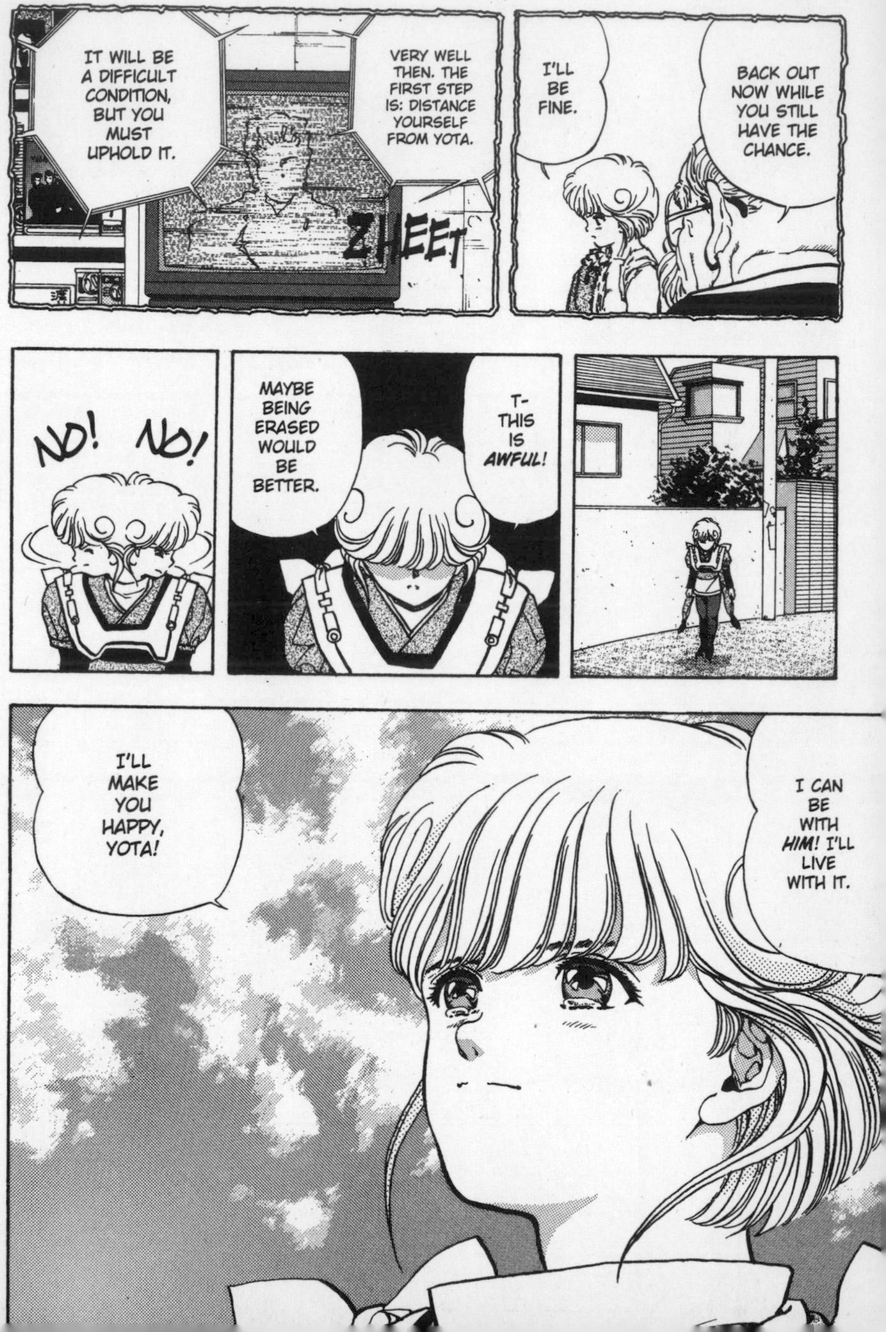
BACK OUT NOW WHILE YOU STILL HAVE THE CHANCE.
I'LL BE FINE.
VERY WELL THEN. THE FIRST STEP IS: DISTANCE YOURSELF FROM YOTA.
IT WILL BE A DIFFICULT CONDITION, BUT YOU MUST UPHOLD IT.
ZHEET
T-THIS IS *AWFUL!*
MAYBE BEING ERASED WOULD BE BETTER.
NO! NO!
I CAN BE WITH *HIM!* I'LL LIVE WITH IT.
I'LL MAKE YOU HAPPY, YOTA!

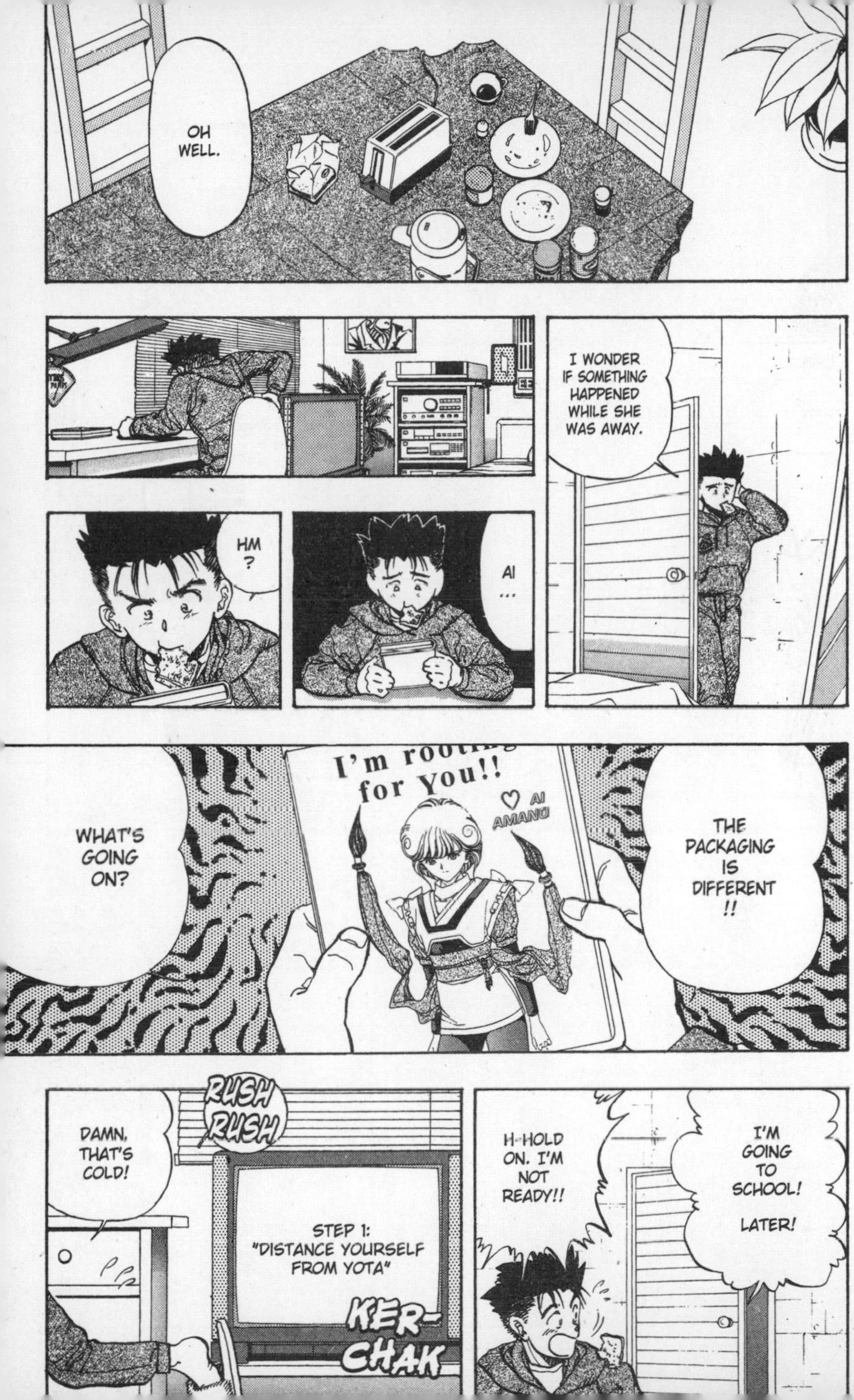

OH WELL.
I WONDER IF SOMETHING HAPPENED WHILE SHE WAS AWAY.
AI ...
HM ?
THE PACKAGING IS DIFFERENT !!
I'm rooti
for You!!
♡ AI AMANO
WHAT'S GOING ON?
I'M GOING TO SCHOOL!
LATER!
H-HOLD ON. I'M NOT READY!!
RUSH RUSH
DAMN, THAT'S COLD!
STEP 1: "DISTANCE YOURSELF FROM YOTA"
KER-CHAK

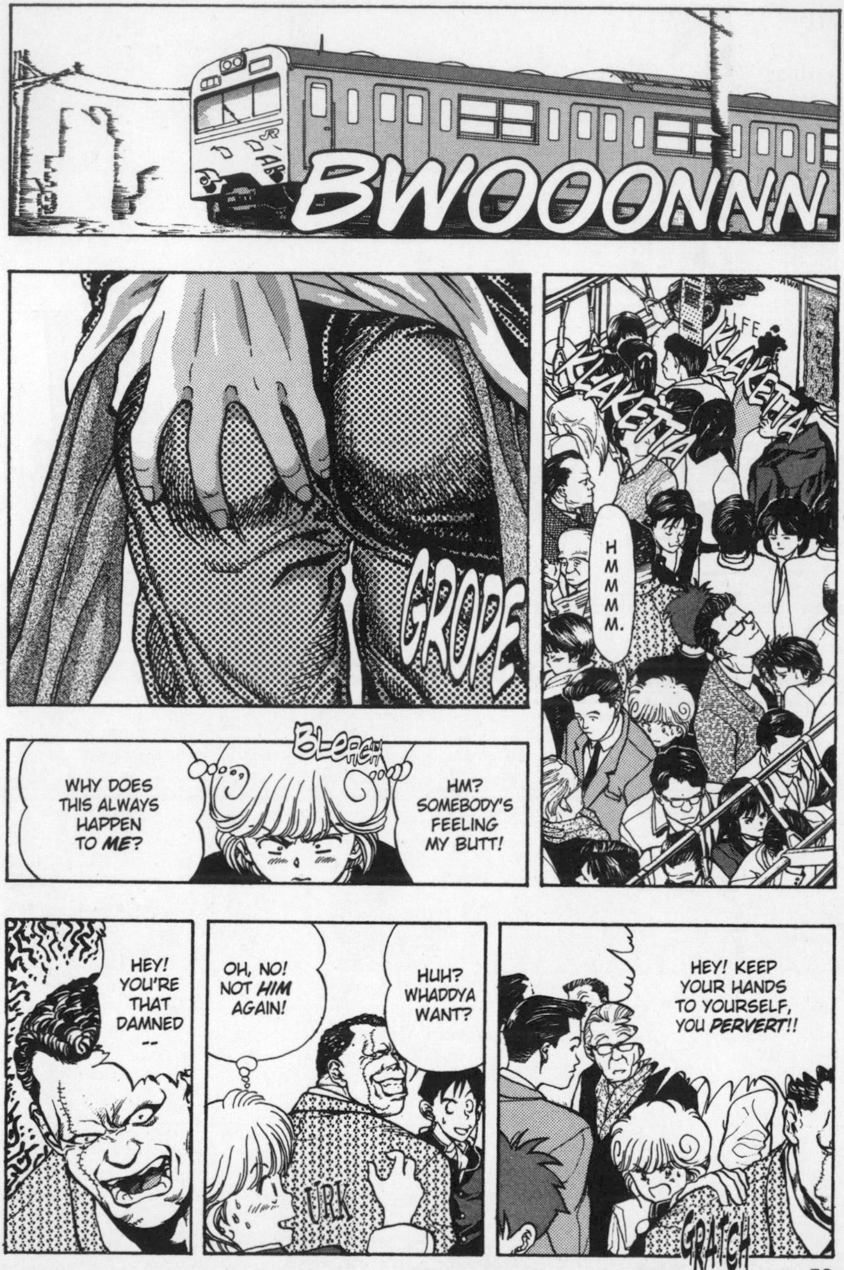
BWOOONNN
KLAKETTA
KLAKETTA
HMMMM.
GROPE
BLEACH
HM? SOMEBODY'S FEELING MY BUTT!
WHY DOES THIS ALWAYS HAPPEN TO ME?
HEY! KEEP YOUR HANDS TO YOURSELF, YOU PERVERT!!
GRATCH
HUH? WHADDYA WANT?
OH, NO! NOT HIM AGAIN!
URK
HEY! YOU'RE THAT DAMNED --

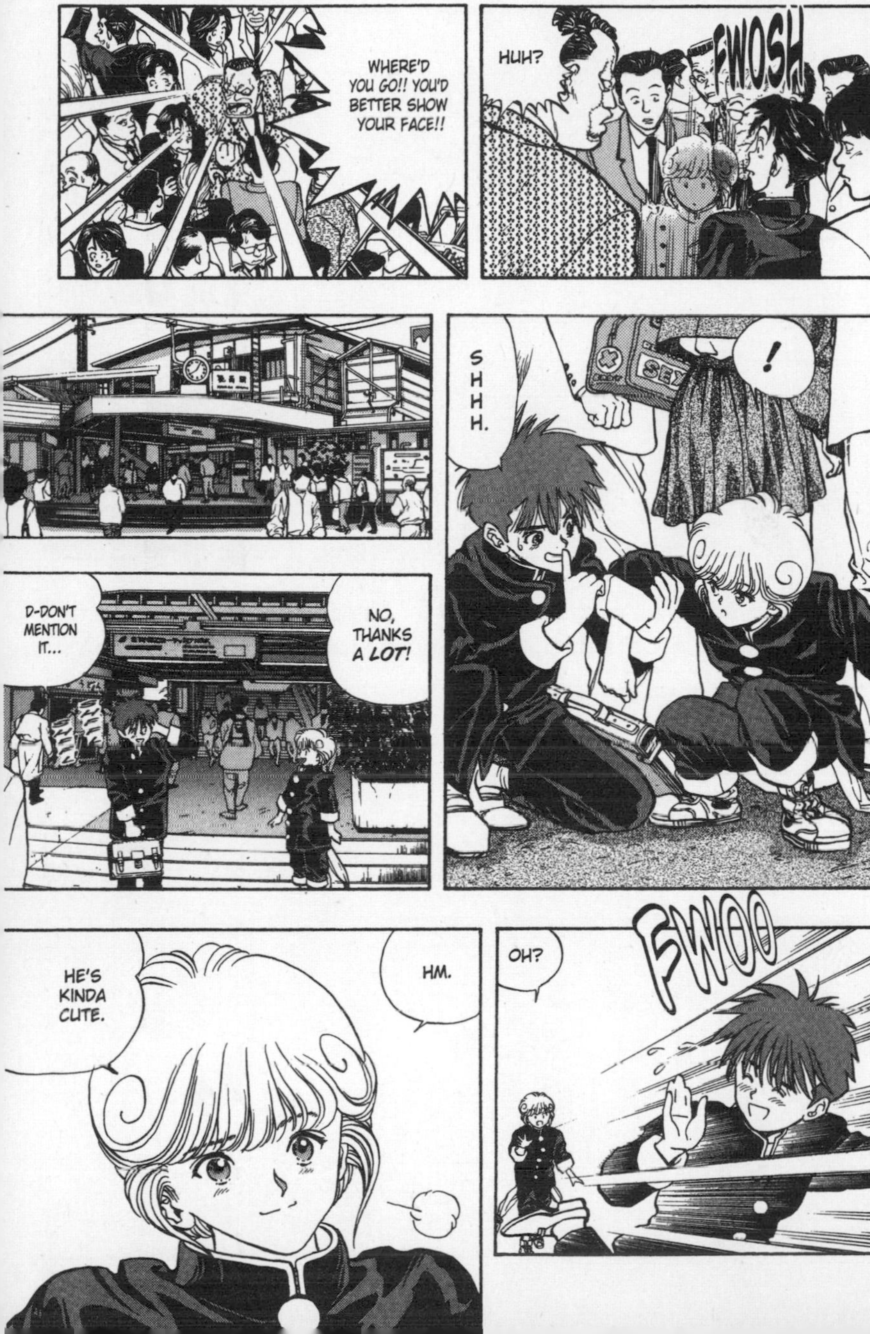
HUH?
FWOSH
WHERE'D YOU GO!! YOU'D BETTER SHOW YOUR FACE!!
!
SHHH.
NO, THANKS A LOT!
D-DON'T MENTION IT...
FWOO
OH?
HM.
HE'S KINDA CUTE.

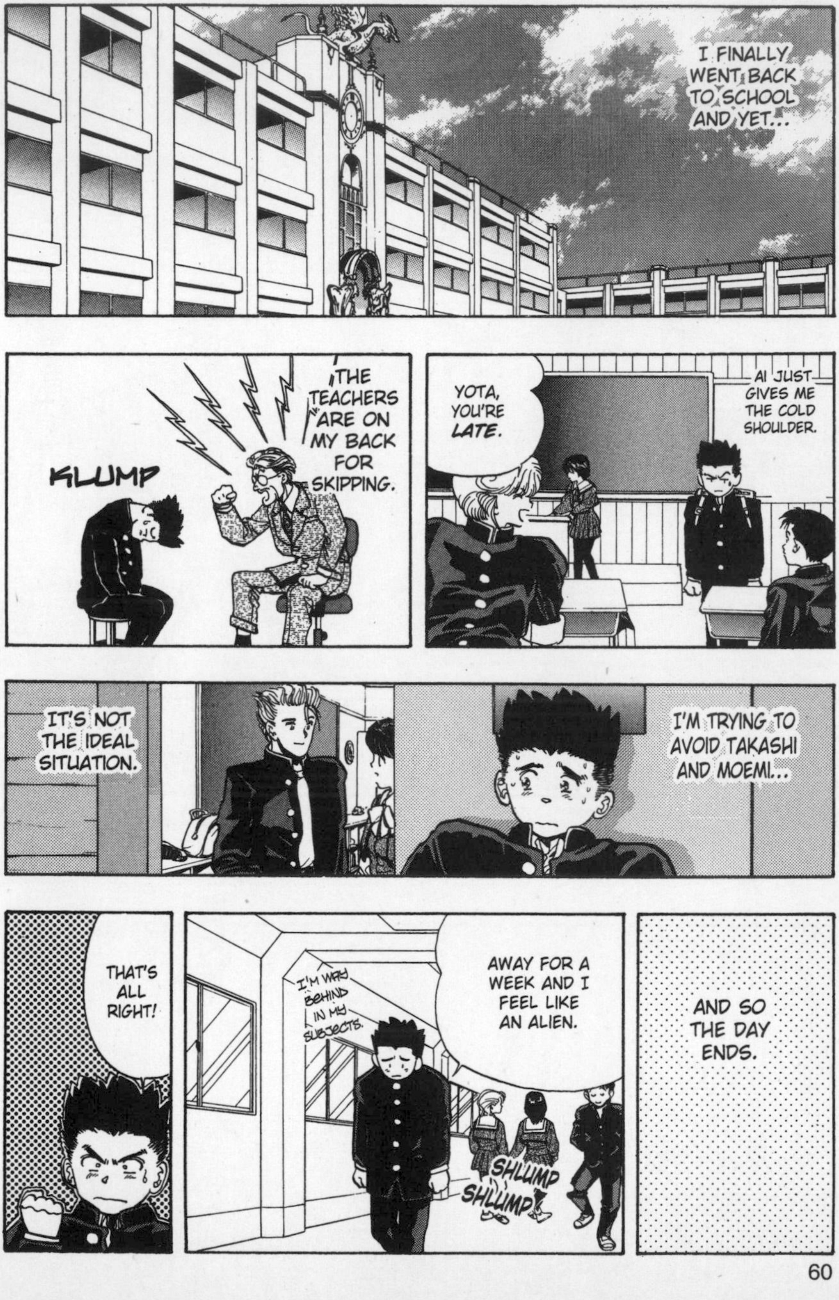
I FINALLY WENT BACK TO SCHOOL AND YET...
AI JUST GIVES ME THE COLD SHOULDER.
YOTA, YOU'RE *LATE*.
THE TEACHERS ARE ON MY BACK FOR SKIPPING.
KLUMP
I'M TRYING TO AVOID TAKASHI AND MOEMI...
IT'S NOT THE IDEAL SITUATION.
AND SO THE DAY ENDS.
AWAY FOR A WEEK AND I FEEL LIKE AN ALIEN.
I'M WAY BEHIND IN MY SUBJECTS.
SHLUMP
SHLUMP
THAT'S ALL RIGHT!

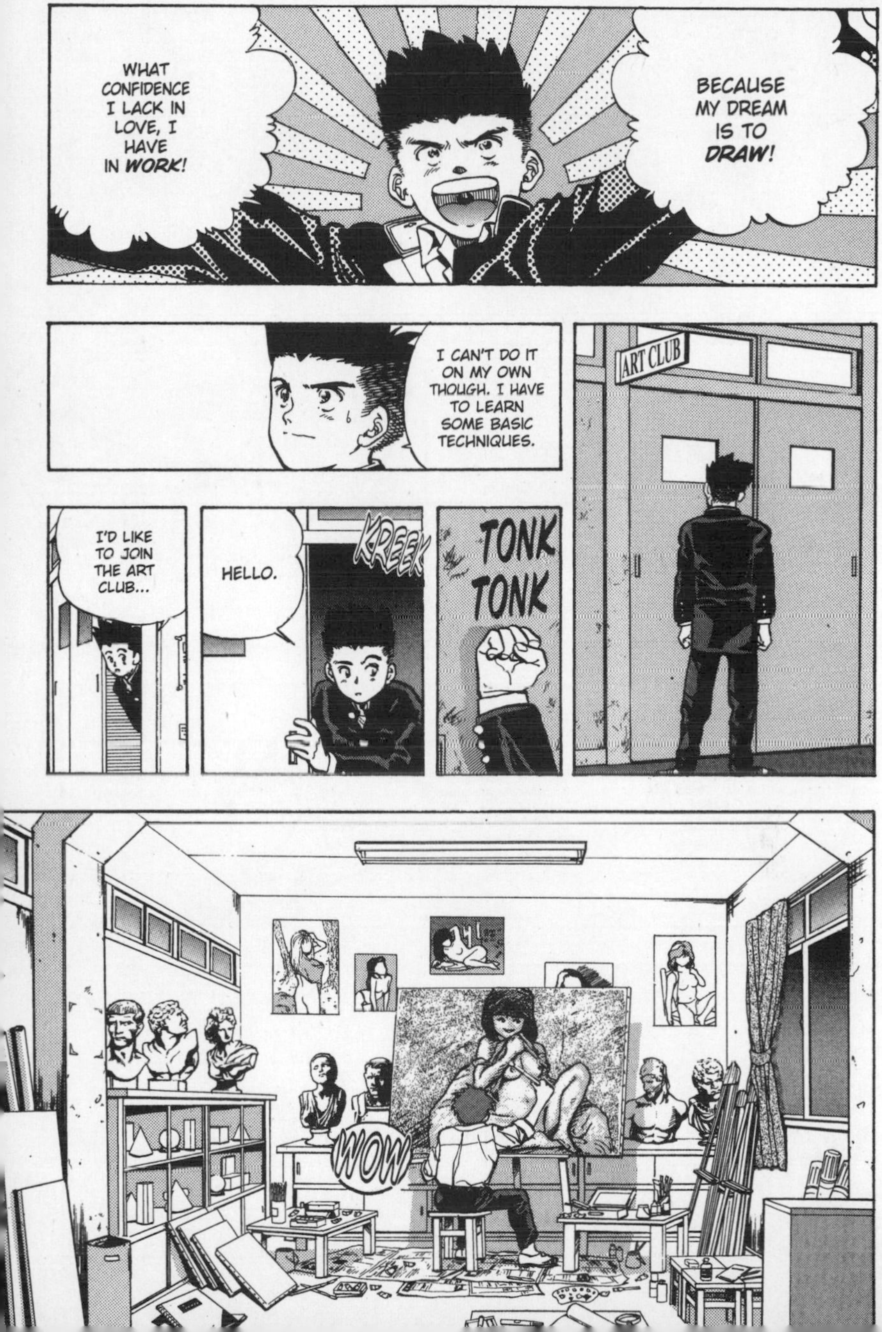
WHAT CONFIDENCE I LACK IN LOVE, I HAVE IN **WORK**!
BECAUSE MY DREAM IS TO **DRAW**!
ART CLUB
I CAN'T DO IT ON MY OWN THOUGH. I HAVE TO LEARN SOME BASIC TECHNIQUES.
TONK TONK
KREEK
HELLO.
I'D LIKE TO JOIN THE ART CLUB...
WOW

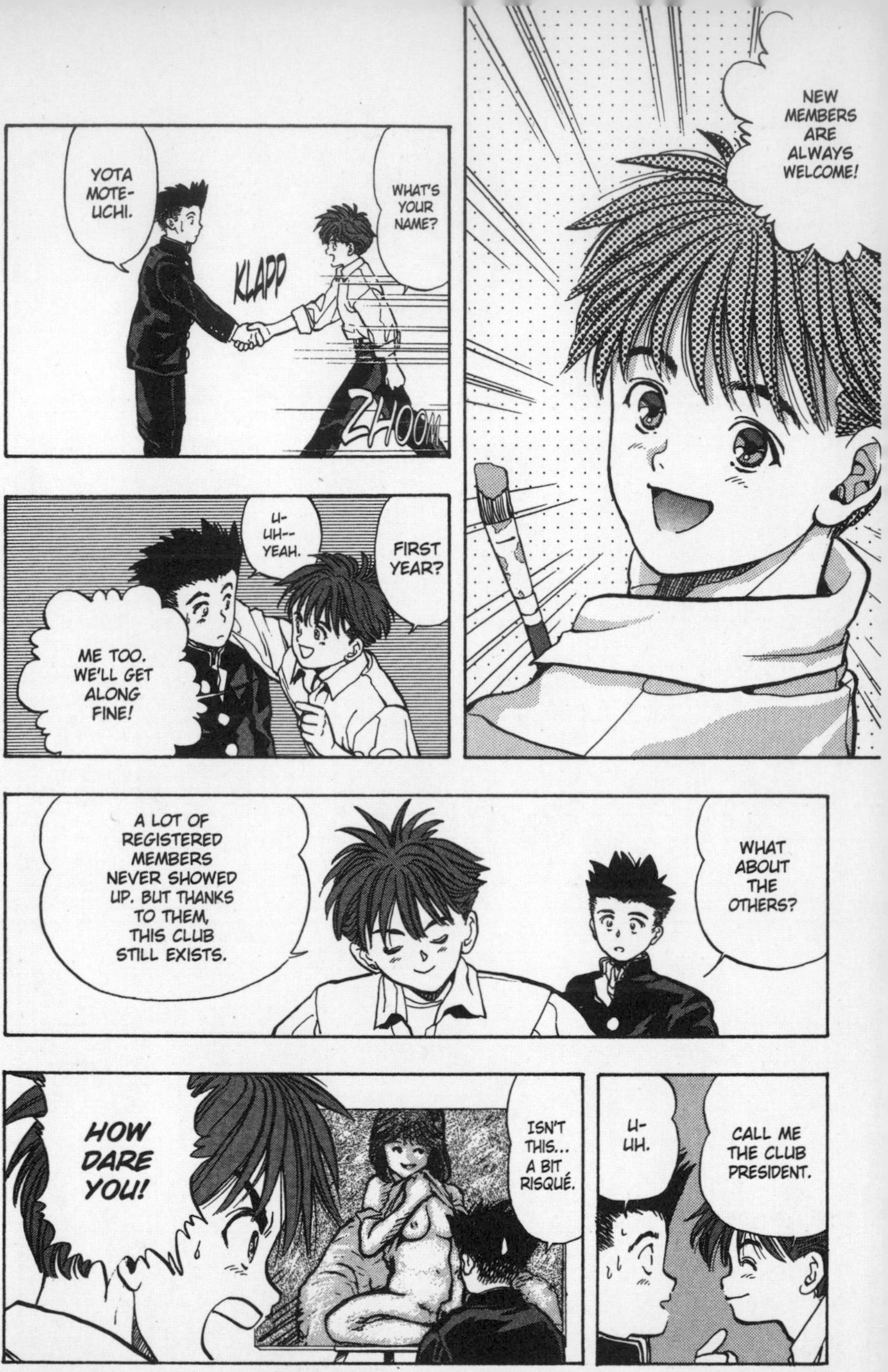
NEW MEMBERS ARE ALWAYS WELCOME!
WHAT'S YOUR NAME?
YOTA MOTE-UCHI.
KLAPP
ZHOOM
FIRST YEAR?
U-UH--YEAH.
ME TOO. WE'LL GET ALONG FINE!
WHAT ABOUT THE OTHERS?
A LOT OF REGISTERED MEMBERS NEVER SHOWED UP. BUT THANKS TO THEM, THIS CLUB STILL EXISTS.
CALL ME THE CLUB PRESIDENT.
U-UH.
ISN'T THIS... A BIT RISQUÉ.
HOW DARE YOU!

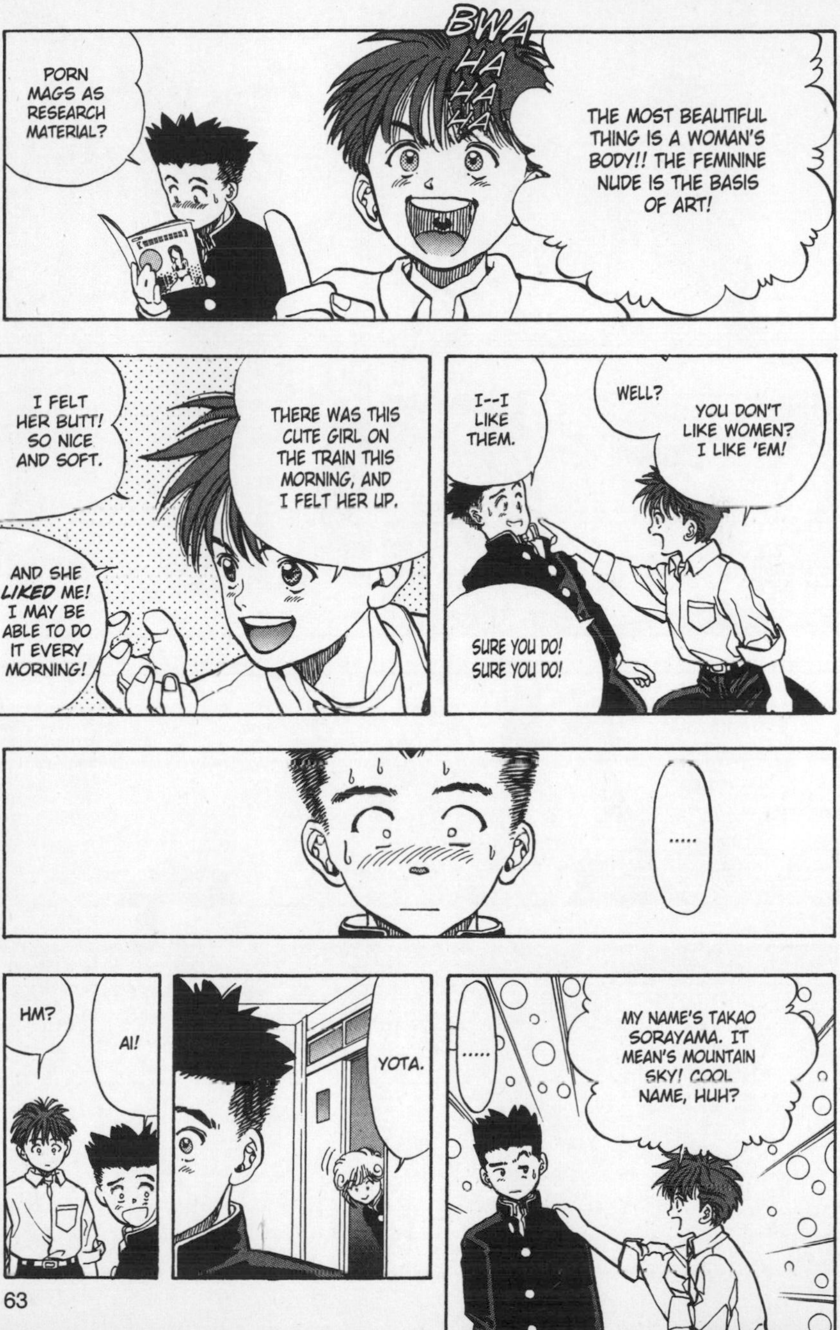
BWA HA HA HA HA
THE MOST BEAUTIFUL THING IS A WOMAN'S BODY!! THE FEMININE NUDE IS THE BASIS OF ART!
PORN MAGS AS RESEARCH MATERIAL?
WELL?
YOU DON'T LIKE WOMEN? I LIKE 'EM!
I--I LIKE THEM.
SURE YOU DO! SURE YOU DO!
THERE WAS THIS CUTE GIRL ON THE TRAIN THIS MORNING, AND I FELT HER UP.
I FELT HER BUTT! SO NICE AND SOFT.
AND SHE *LIKED* ME! I MAY BE ABLE TO DO IT EVERY MORNING!
.....
MY NAME'S TAKAO SORAYAMA. IT MEAN'S MOUNTAIN SKY! COOL NAME, HUH?
.....
YOTA.
AI!
HM?

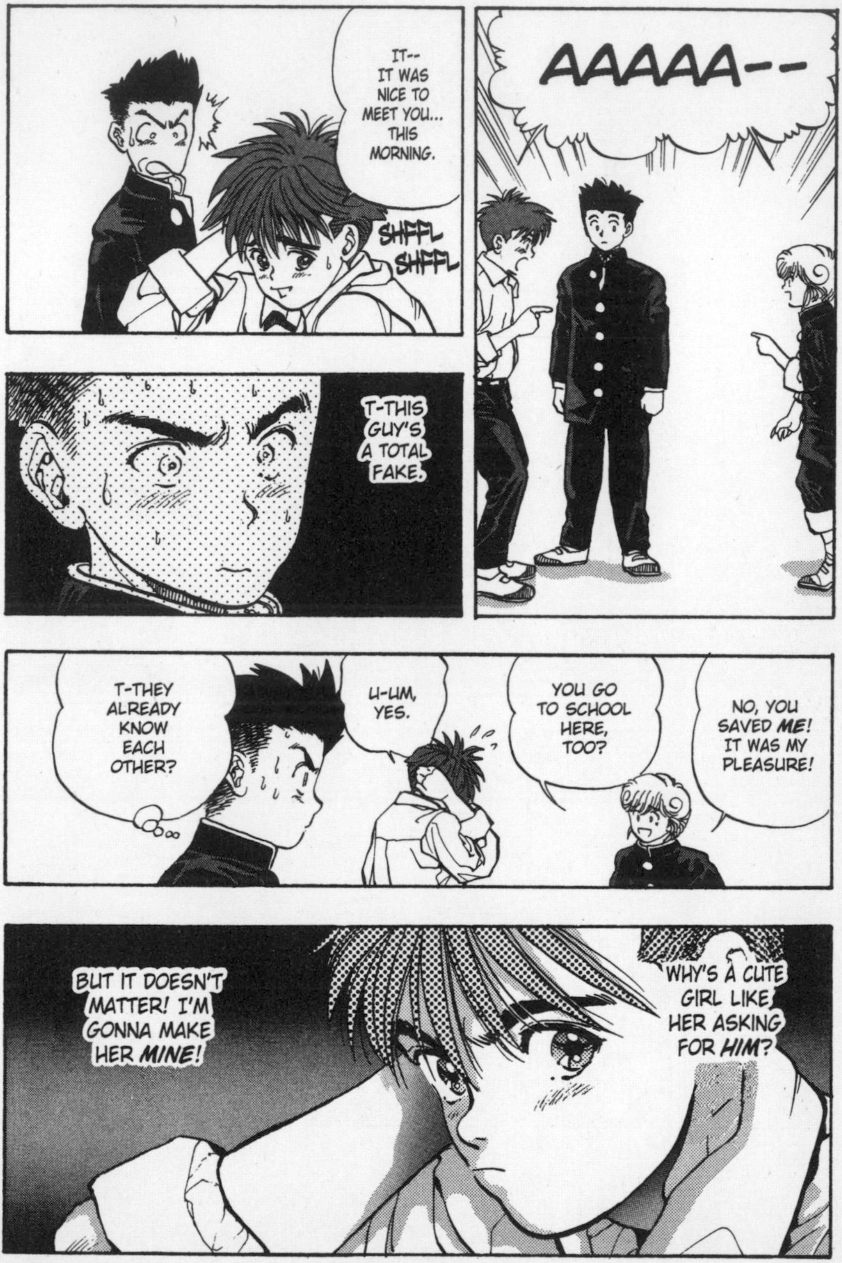
AAAAA--
IT-- IT WAS NICE TO MEET YOU... THIS MORNING.
SHFFL SHFFL
T-THIS GUY'S A TOTAL FAKE.
NO, YOU SAVED ME! IT WAS MY PLEASURE!
YOU GO TO SCHOOL HERE, TOO?
U-UM, YES.
T-THEY ALREADY KNOW EACH OTHER?
WHY'S A CUTE GIRL LIKE HER ASKING FOR HIM?
BUT IT DOESN'T MATTER! I'M GONNA MAKE HER MINE!

■ ▲ ❚❚ ►► ► *CHAPTER TWELVE*
Don't You Like Me?

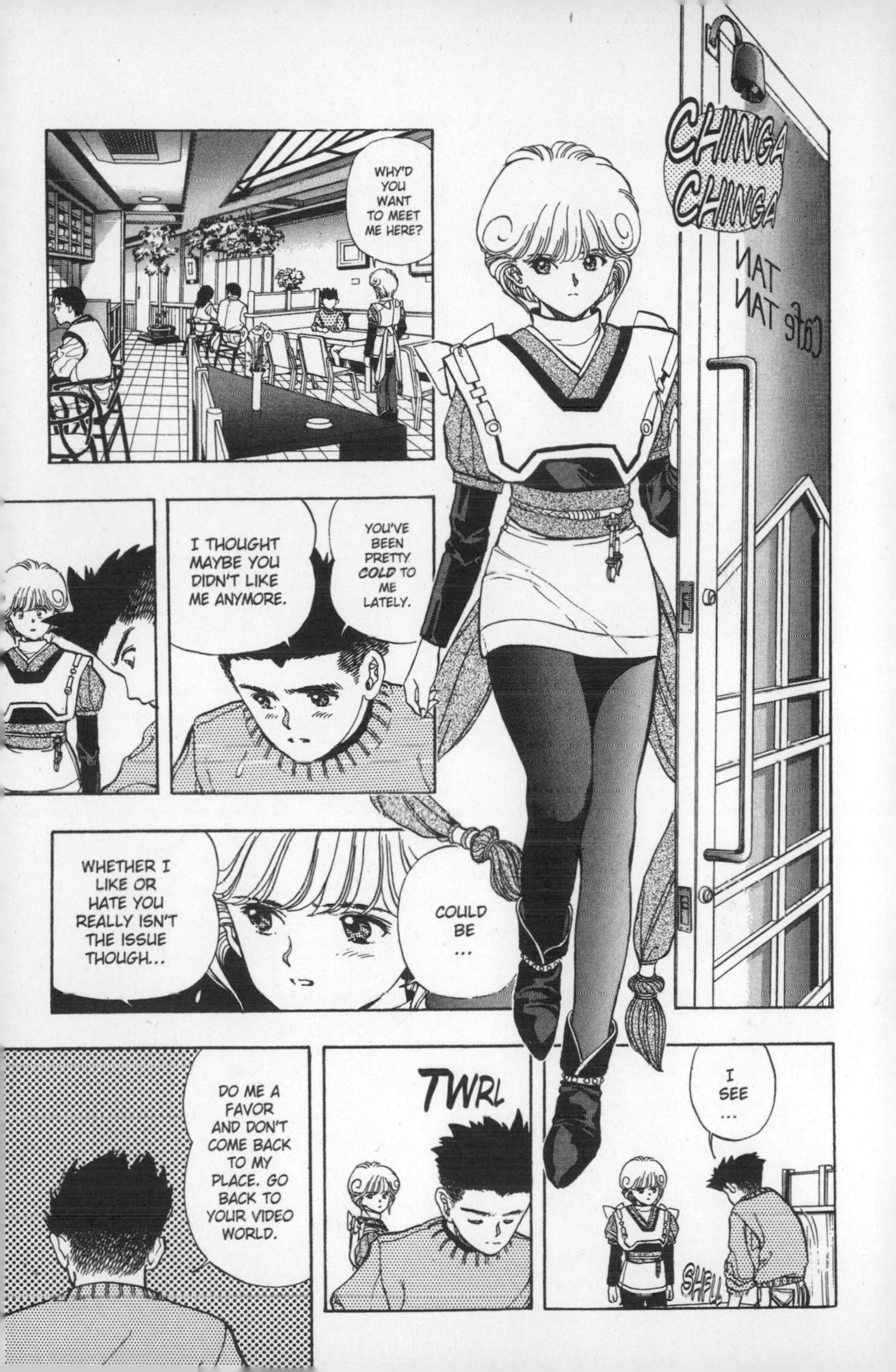
CHINGA CHINGA
Cafe TAN TAN
WHY'D YOU WANT TO MEET ME HERE?
YOU'VE BEEN PRETTY *COLD* TO ME LATELY.
I THOUGHT MAYBE YOU DIDN'T LIKE ME ANYMORE.
COULD BE ...
WHETHER I LIKE OR HATE YOU REALLY ISN'T THE ISSUE THOUGH...
I SEE ...
SHFFL
TWRL
DO ME A FAVOR AND DON'T COME BACK TO MY PLACE. GO BACK TO YOUR VIDEO WORLD.

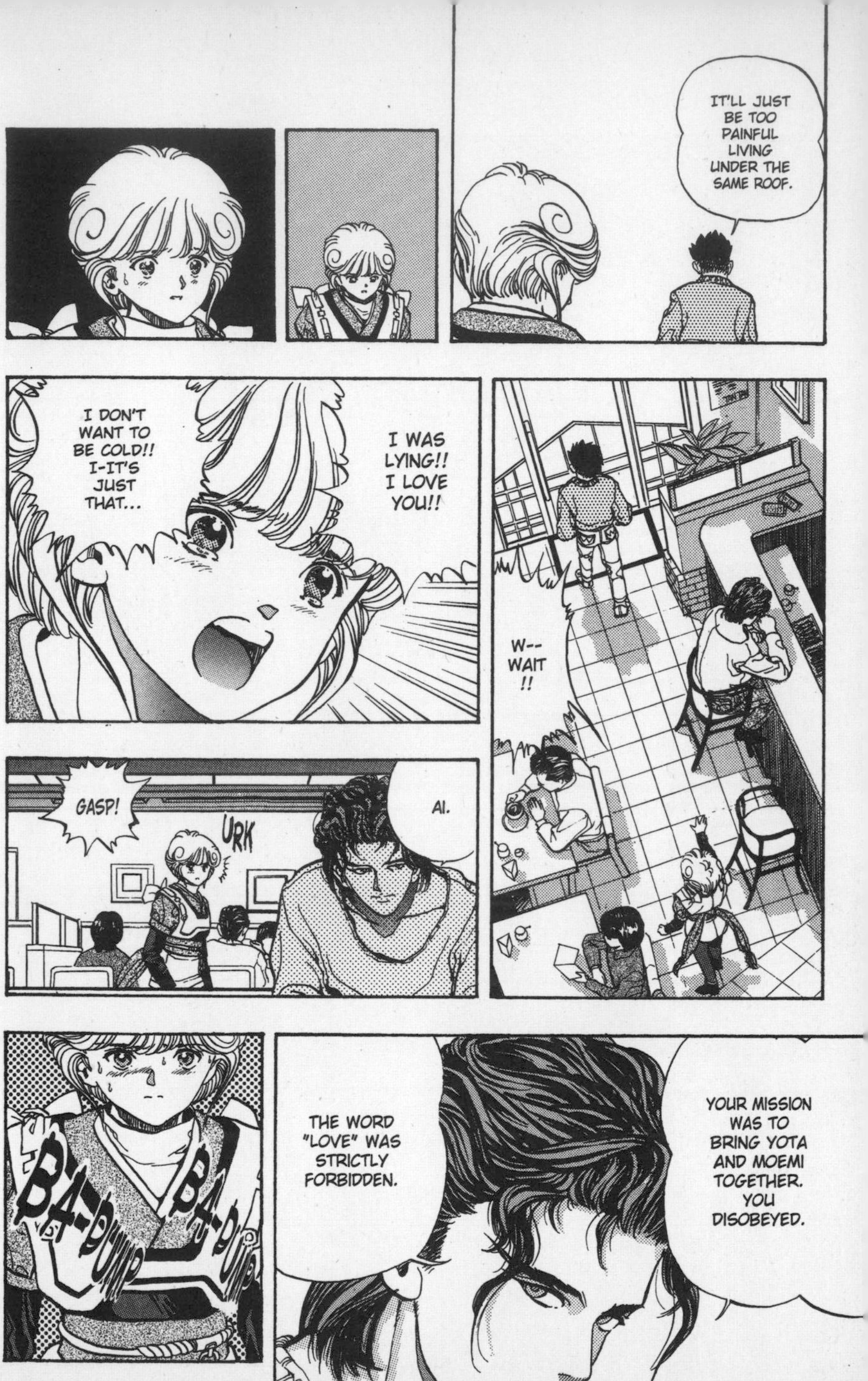
IT'LL JUST BE TOO PAINFUL LIVING UNDER THE SAME ROOF.
W-- WAIT !!
I WAS LYING!! I LOVE YOU!!
I DON'T WANT TO BE COLD!! I-IT'S JUST THAT...
AI.
URK
GASP!
YOUR MISSION WAS TO BRING YOTA AND MOEMI TOGETHER. YOU DISOBEYED.
THE WORD "LOVE" WAS STRICTLY FORBIDDEN.
BA-DUMP
BA-DUMP

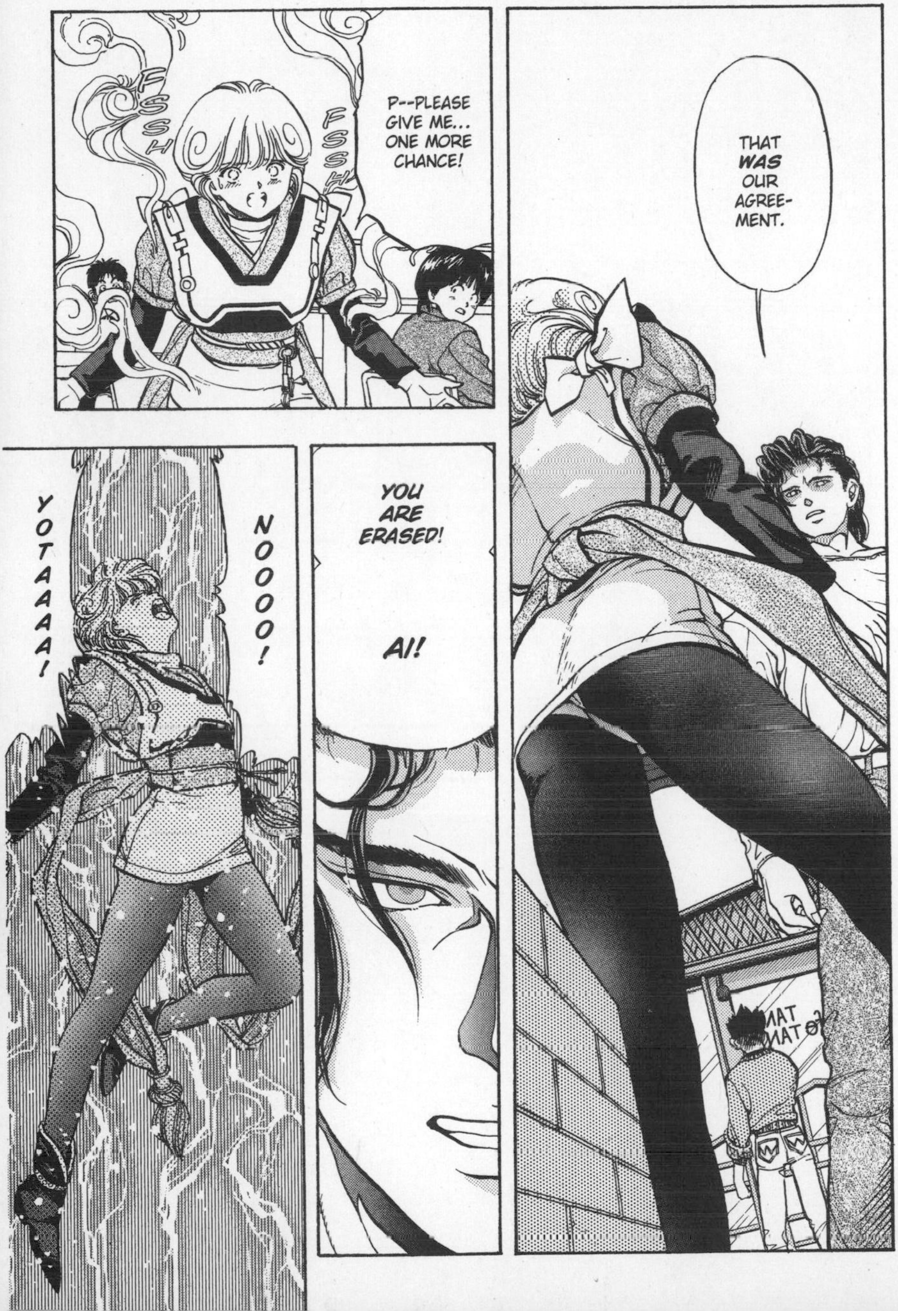
THAT **WAS** OUR AGREEMENT.
FSSH
FSSH
P--PLEASE GIVE ME... ONE MORE CHANCE!
YOU ARE ERASED!
AI!
NOOOOO!
YOTAAAAA!

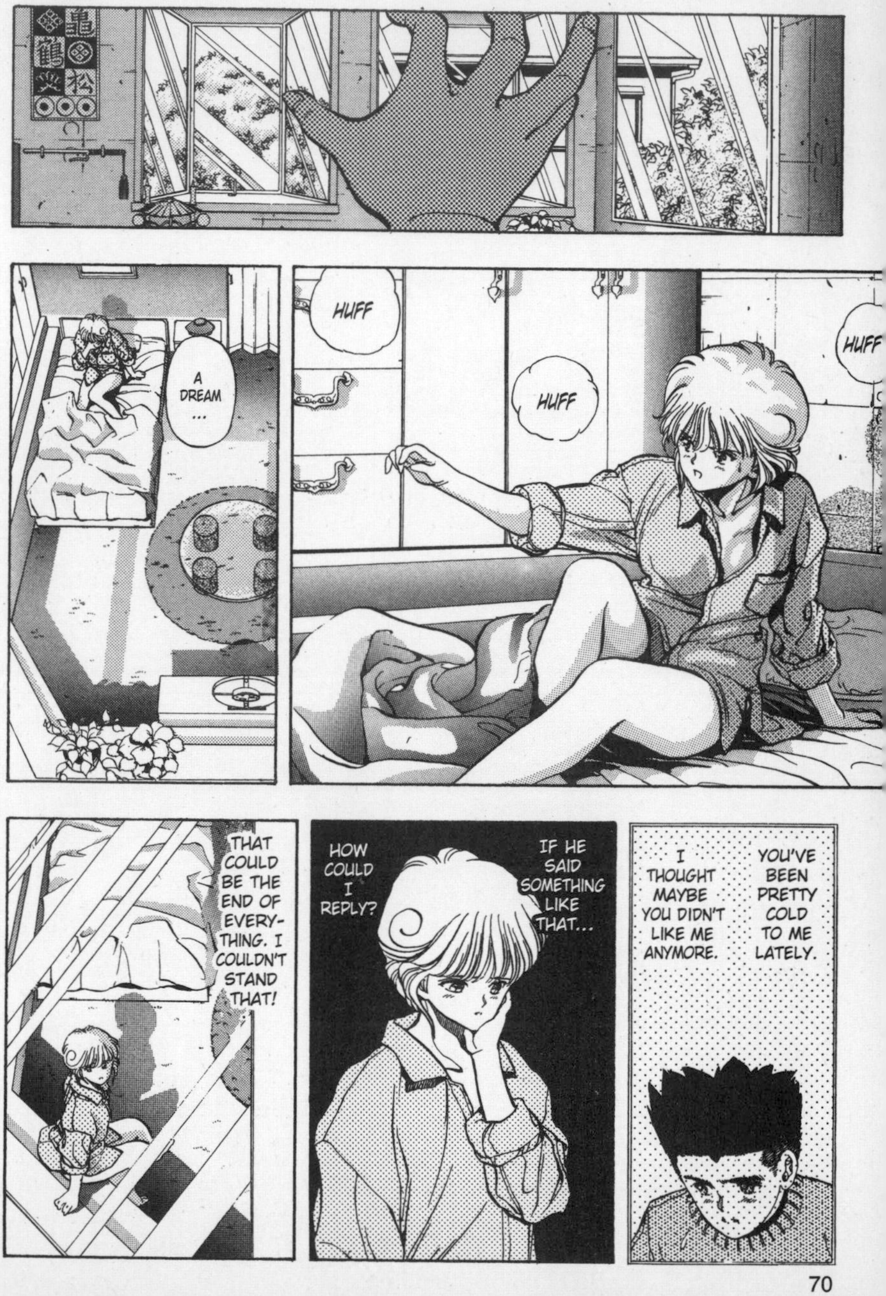
HUFF
HUFF
HUFF
A DREAM ...
YOU'VE BEEN PRETTY COLD TO ME LATELY.
I THOUGHT MAYBE YOU DIDN'T LIKE ME ANYMORE.
IF HE SAID SOMETHING LIKE THAT...
HOW COULD I REPLY?
THAT COULD BE THE END OF EVERY-THING. I COULDN'T STAND THAT!

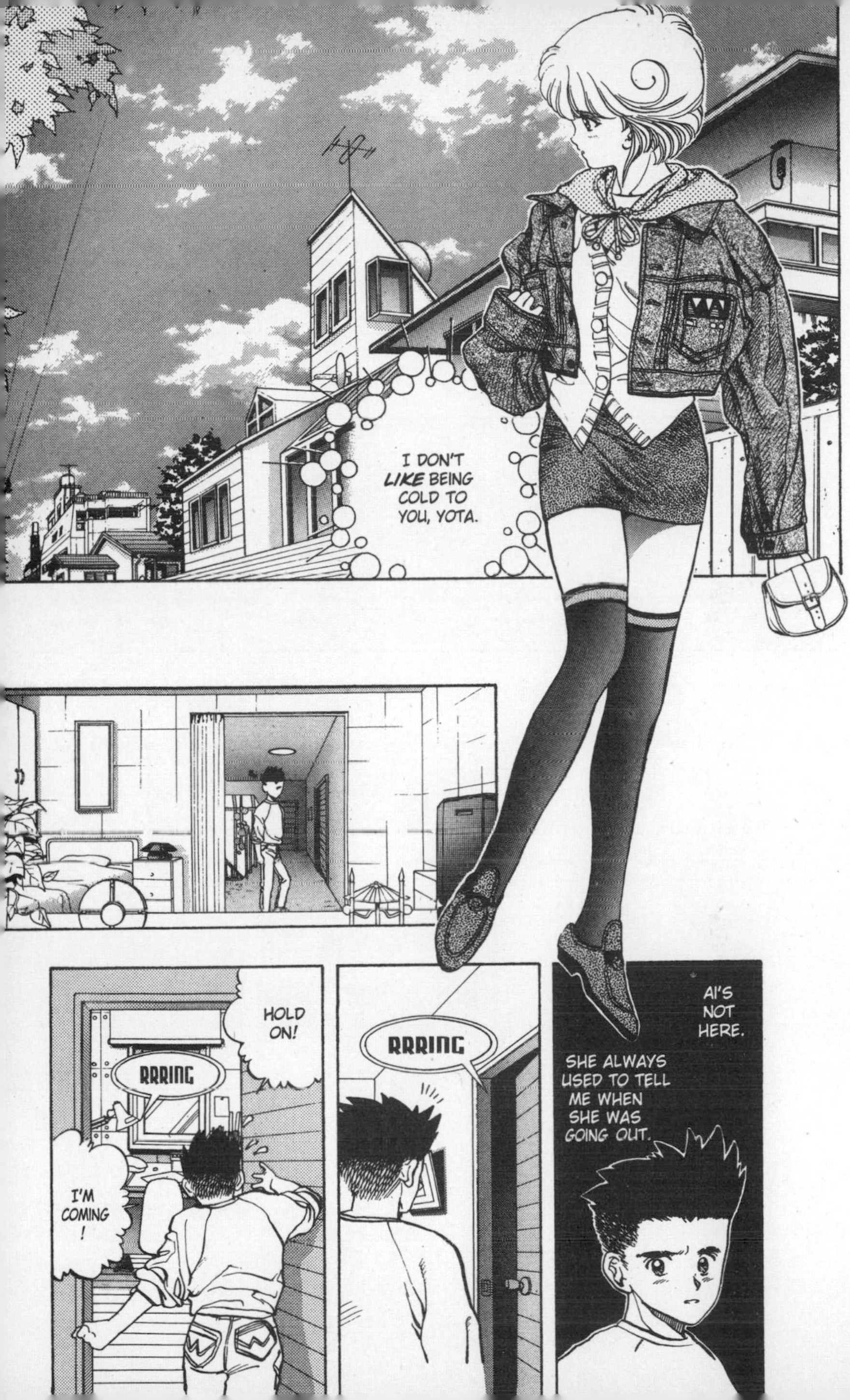
I DON'T LIKE BEING COLD TO YOU, YOTA.
AI'S NOT HERE.
SHE ALWAYS USED TO TELL ME WHEN SHE WAS GOING OUT.
RRRING
HOLD ON!
RRRING
I'M COMING!

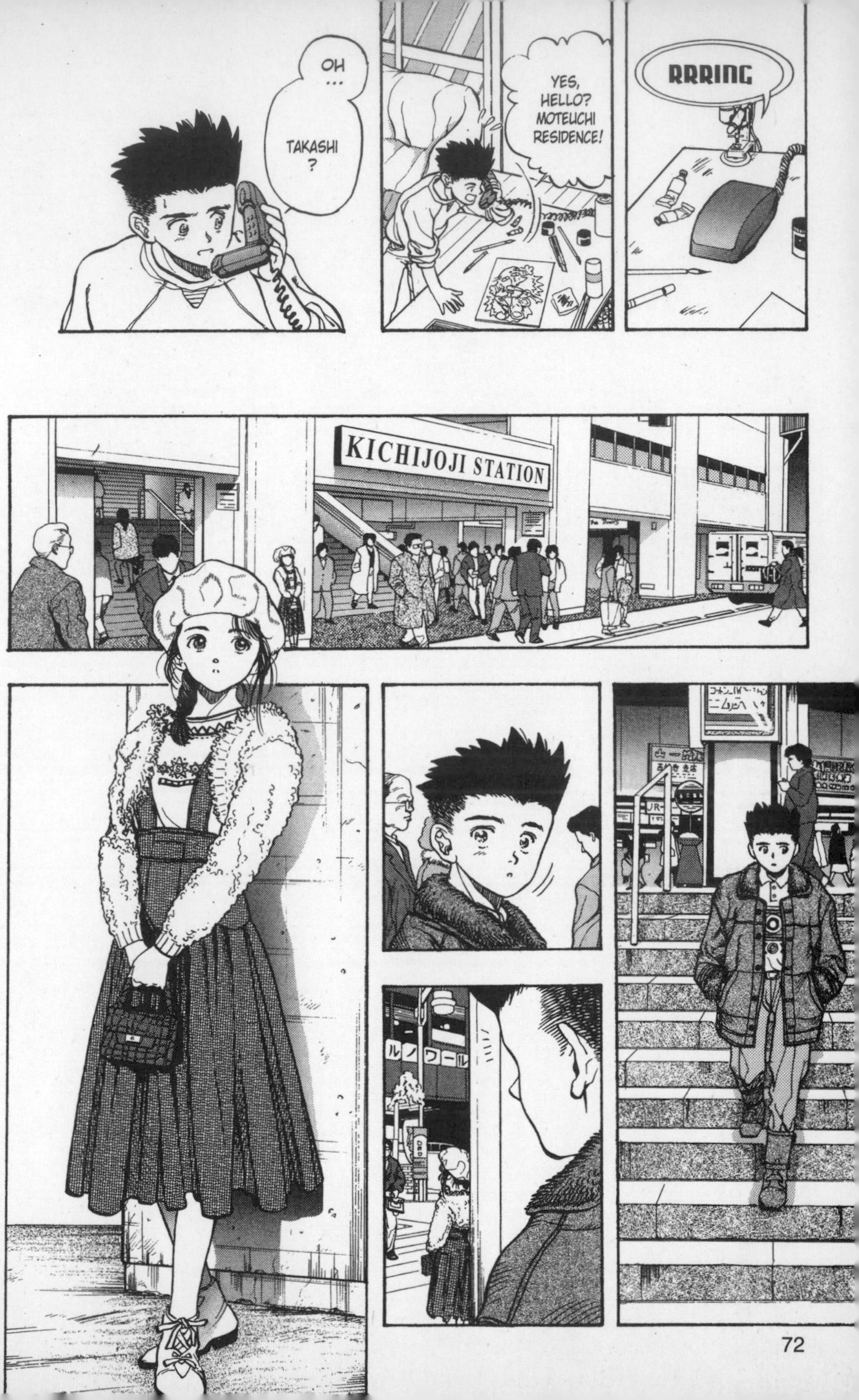
RRRING
YES, HELLO? MOTEUCHI RESIDENCE!
OH ... TAKASHI ?
KICHIJOJI STATION

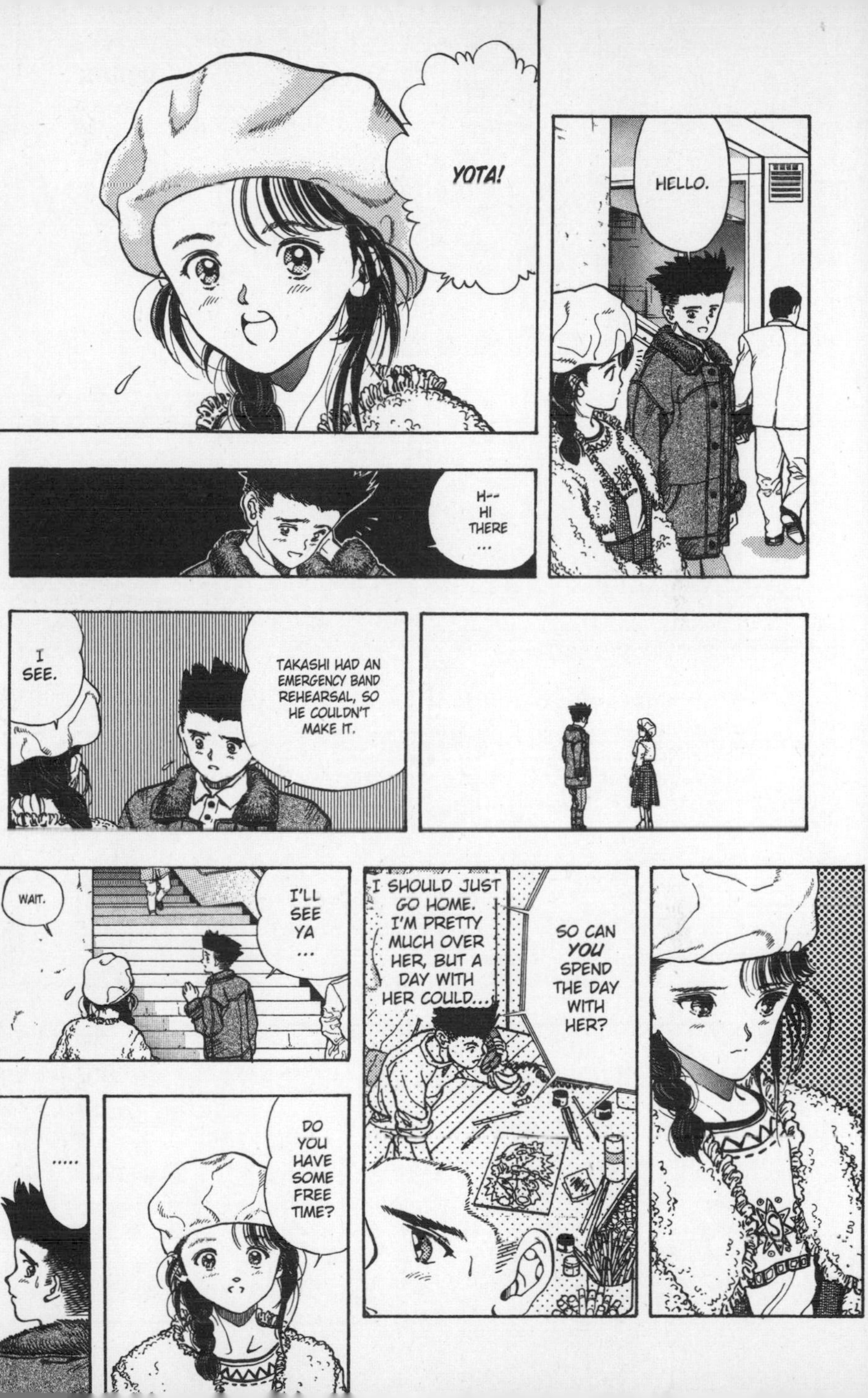
HELLO.
YOTA!
H-- HI THERE ...
TAKASHI HAD AN EMERGENCY BAND REHEARSAL, SO HE COULDN'T MAKE IT.
I SEE.
SO CAN YOU SPEND THE DAY WITH HER?
I SHOULD JUST GO HOME. I'M PRETTY MUCH OVER HER, BUT A DAY WITH HER COULD...
I'LL SEE YA ...
WAIT.
DO YOU HAVE SOME FREE TIME?
.....

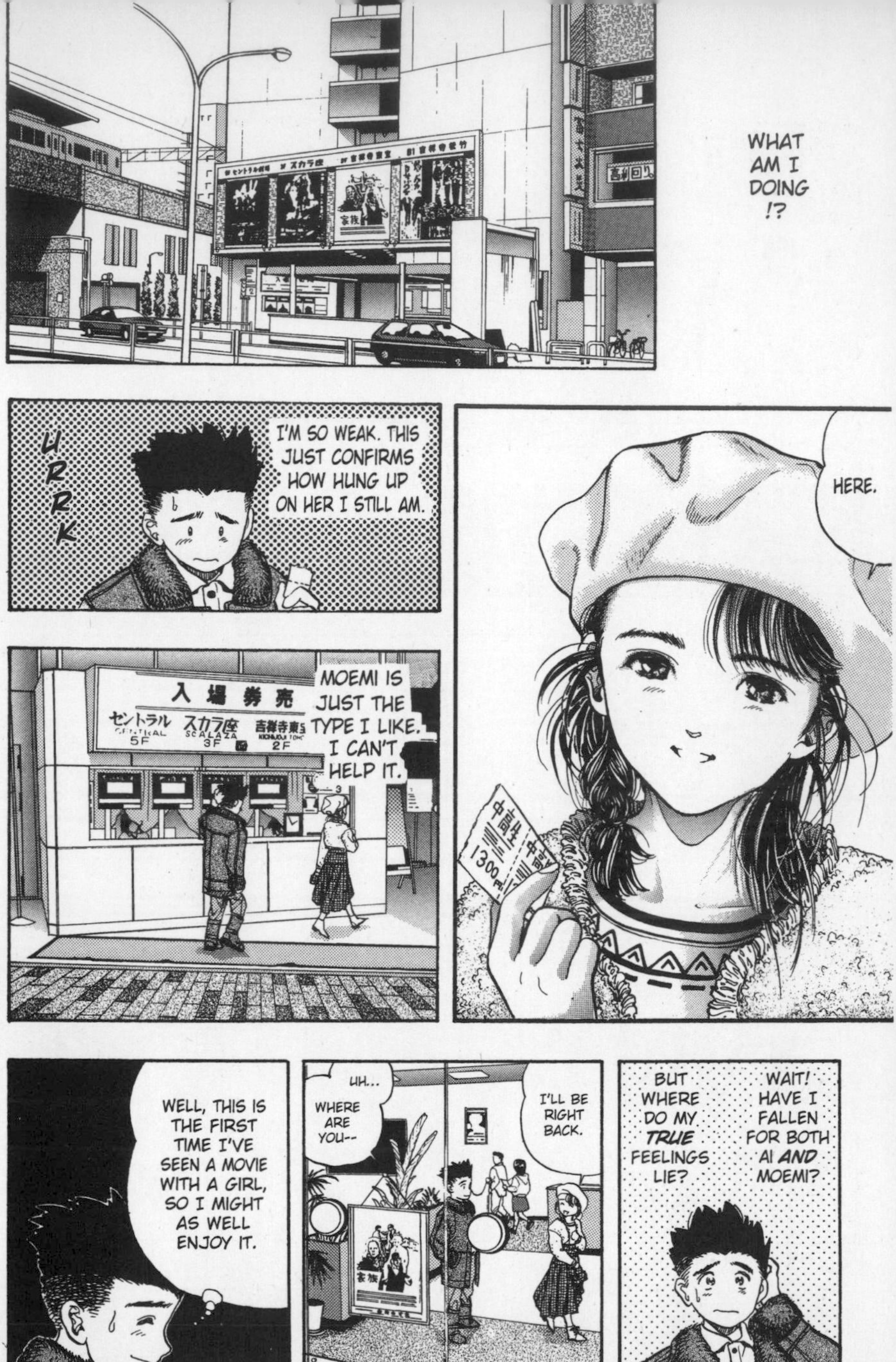

WHAT AM I DOING !?
HERE.
URRK
I'M SO WEAK. THIS JUST CONFIRMS HOW HUNG UP ON HER I STILL AM.
MOEMI IS JUST THE TYPE I LIKE. I CAN'T HELP IT.
WAIT! HAVE I FALLEN FOR BOTH AI *AND* MOEMI?
BUT WHERE DO MY *TRUE* FEELINGS LIE?
I'LL BE RIGHT BACK.
UH... WHERE ARE YOU--
WELL, THIS IS THE FIRST TIME I'VE SEEN A MOVIE WITH A GIRL, SO I MIGHT AS WELL ENJOY IT.

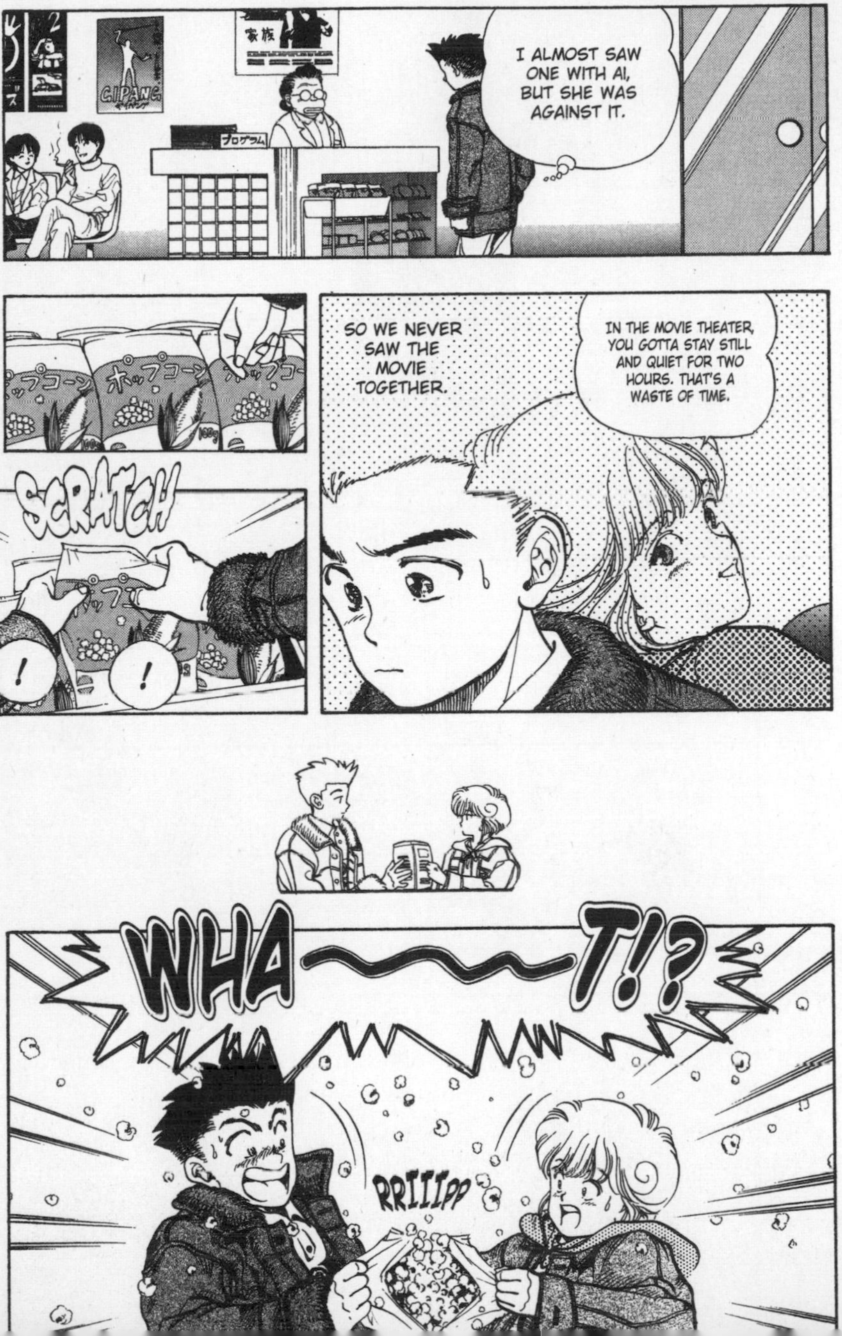

I ALMOST SAW ONE WITH AI, BUT SHE WAS AGAINST IT.
家族
GIPANG
プログラム
IN THE MOVIE THEATER, YOU GOTTA STAY STILL AND QUIET FOR TWO HOURS. THAT'S A WASTE OF TIME.
SO WE NEVER SAW THE MOVIE TOGETHER.
SCRATCH
!
!
WHA~~~T!?
RRIIIPP

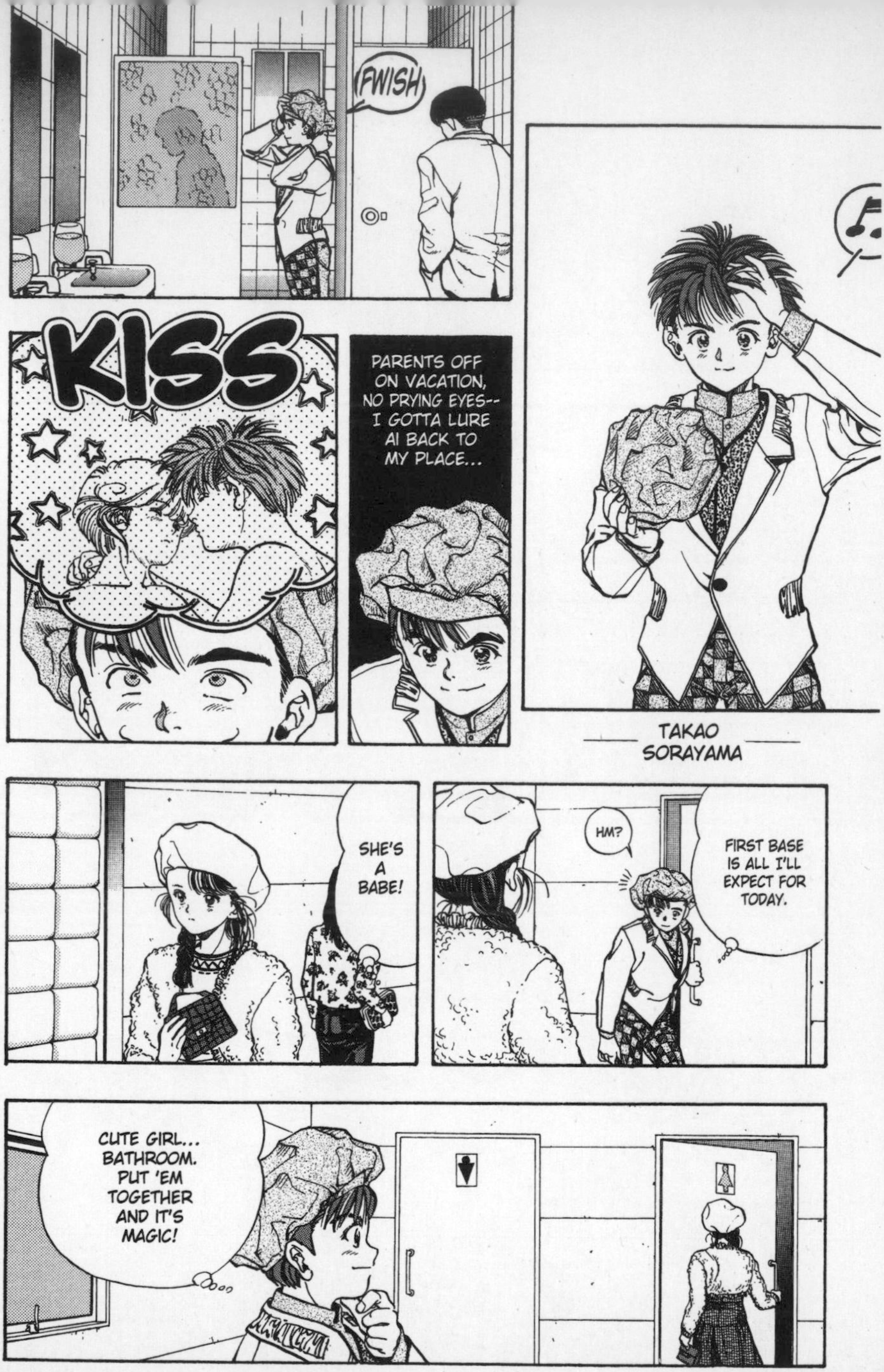
TAKAO SORAYAMA
FWISH
PARENTS OFF ON VACATION, NO PRYING EYES-- I GOTTA LURE AI BACK TO MY PLACE...
KISS
HM?
FIRST BASE IS ALL I'LL EXPECT FOR TODAY.
SHE'S A BABE!
CUTE GIRL... BATHROOM. PUT 'EM TOGETHER AND IT'S MAGIC!

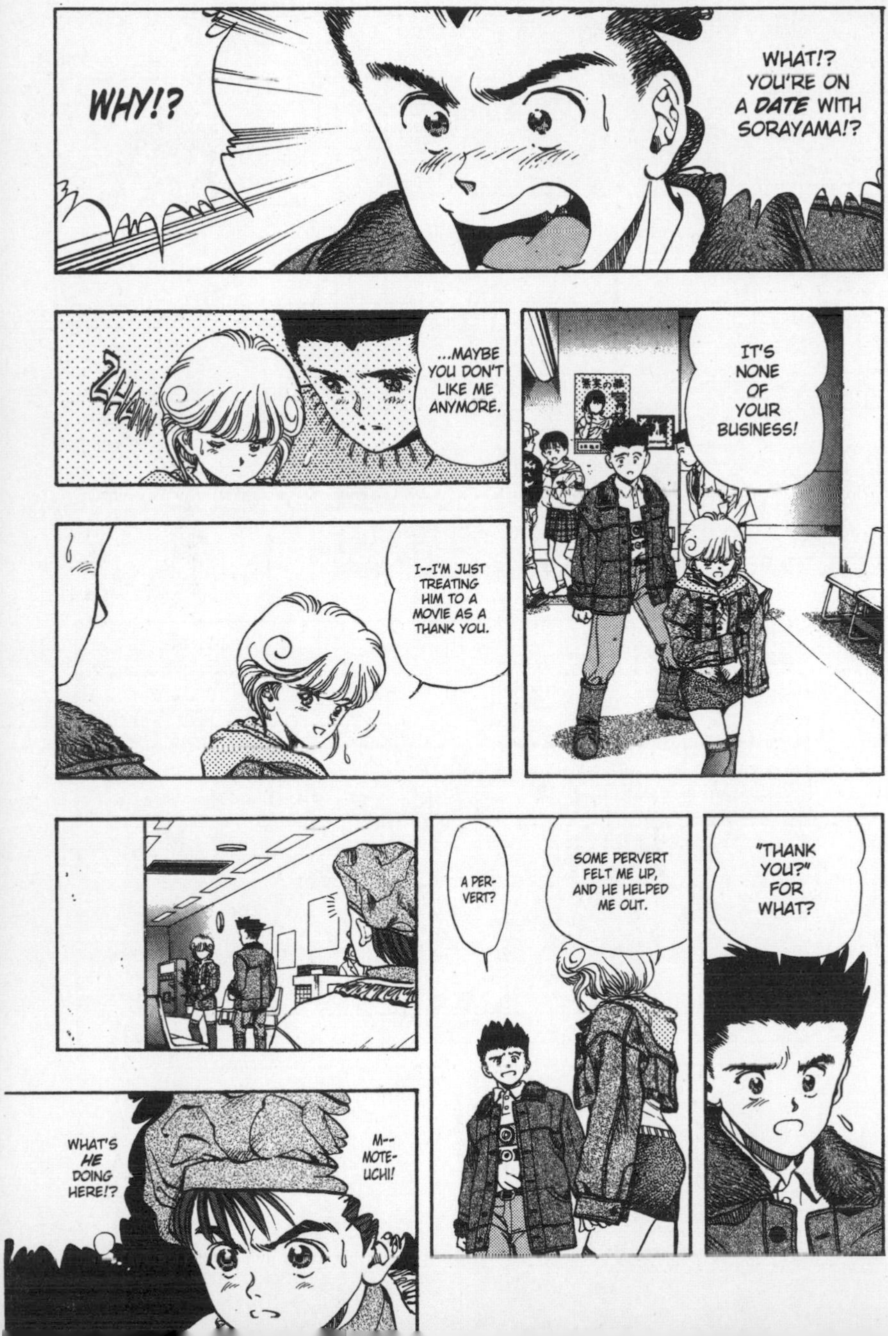
WHAT!? YOU'RE ON A DATE WITH SORAYAMA!?
WHY!?
IT'S NONE OF YOUR BUSINESS!
...MAYBE YOU DON'T LIKE ME ANYMORE.
ZHANN
I--I'M JUST TREATING HIM TO A MOVIE AS A THANK YOU.
"THANK YOU?" FOR WHAT?
SOME PERVERT FELT ME UP, AND HE HELPED ME OUT.
A PER-VERT?
M--MOTE-UCHI!
WHAT'S HE DOING HERE!?

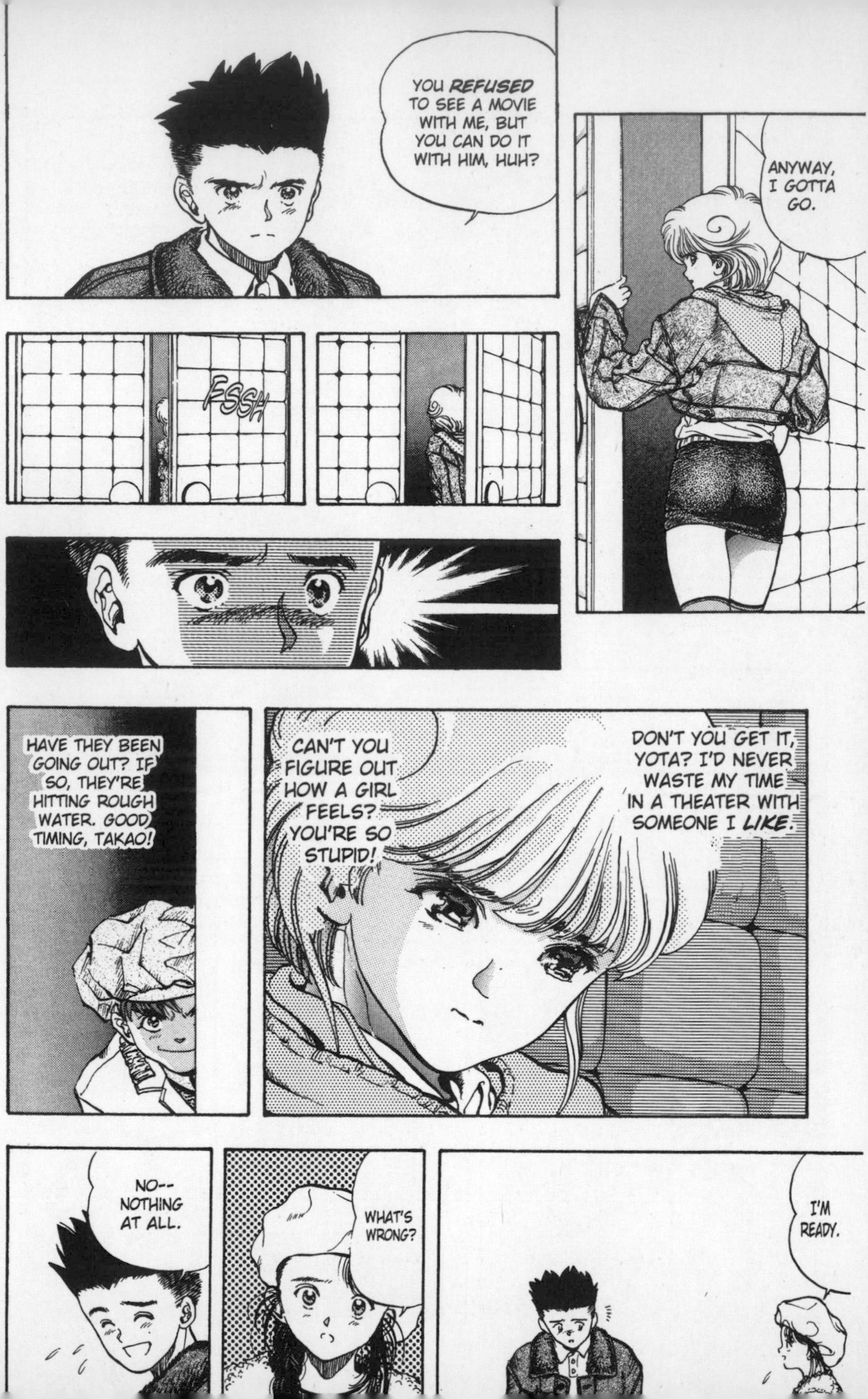

ANYWAY, I GOTTA GO.
YOU **REFUSED** TO SEE A MOVIE WITH ME, BUT YOU CAN DO IT WITH HIM, HUH?
FSSH
DON'T YOU GET IT, YOTA? I'D NEVER WASTE MY TIME IN A THEATER WITH SOMEONE I ***LIKE***.
CAN'T YOU FIGURE OUT HOW A GIRL FEELS? YOU'RE SO STUPID!
HAVE THEY BEEN GOING OUT? IF SO, THEY'RE HITTING ROUGH WATER. GOOD TIMING, TAKAO!
I'M READY.
WHAT'S WRONG?
NO-- NOTHING AT ALL.

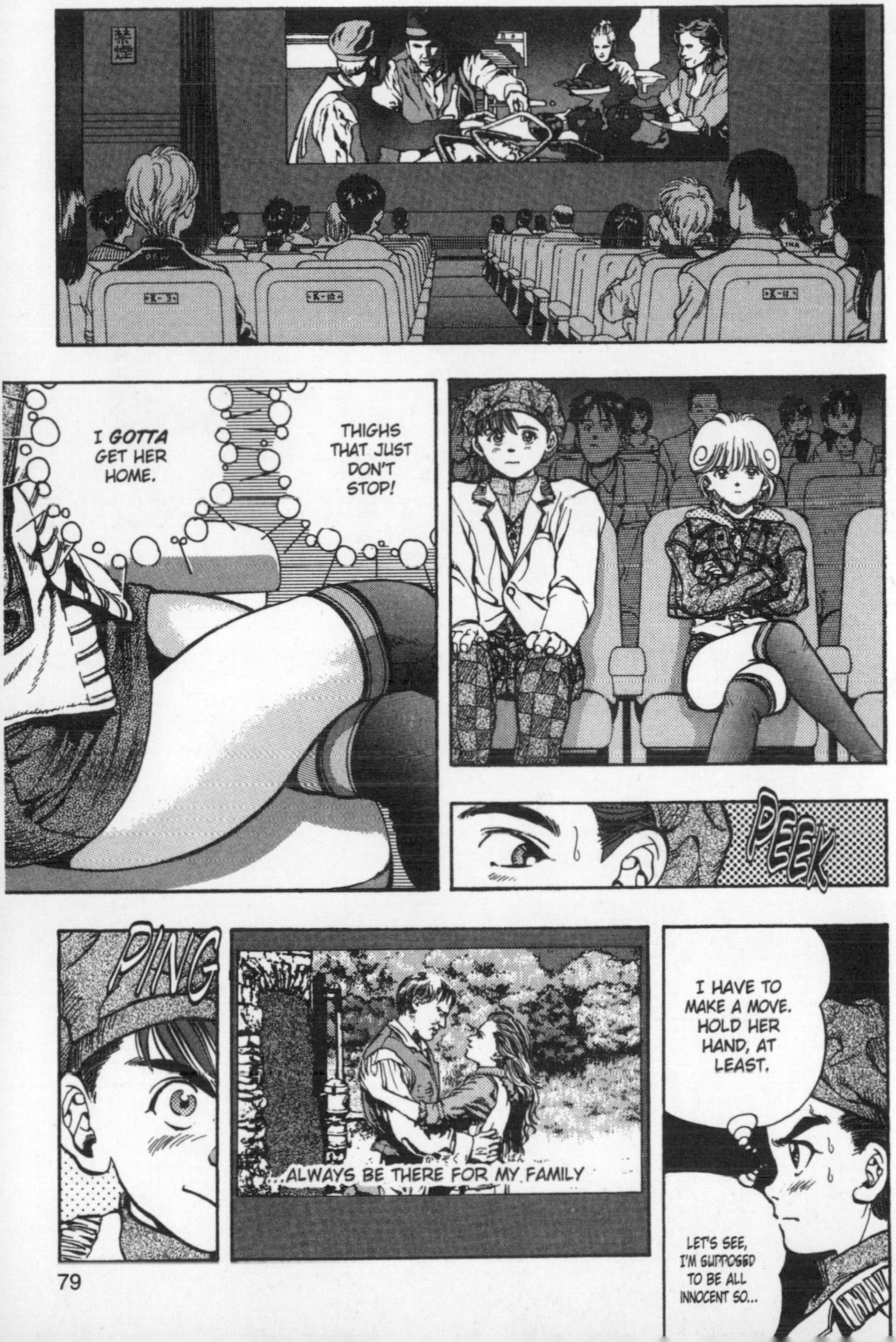
PEEK
THIGHS THAT JUST DON'T STOP!
I GOTTA GET HER HOME.
I HAVE TO MAKE A MOVE. HOLD HER HAND, AT LEAST.
LET'S SEE, I'M SUPPOSED TO BE ALL INNOCENT SO...
...ALWAYS BE THERE FOR MY FAMILY
PING

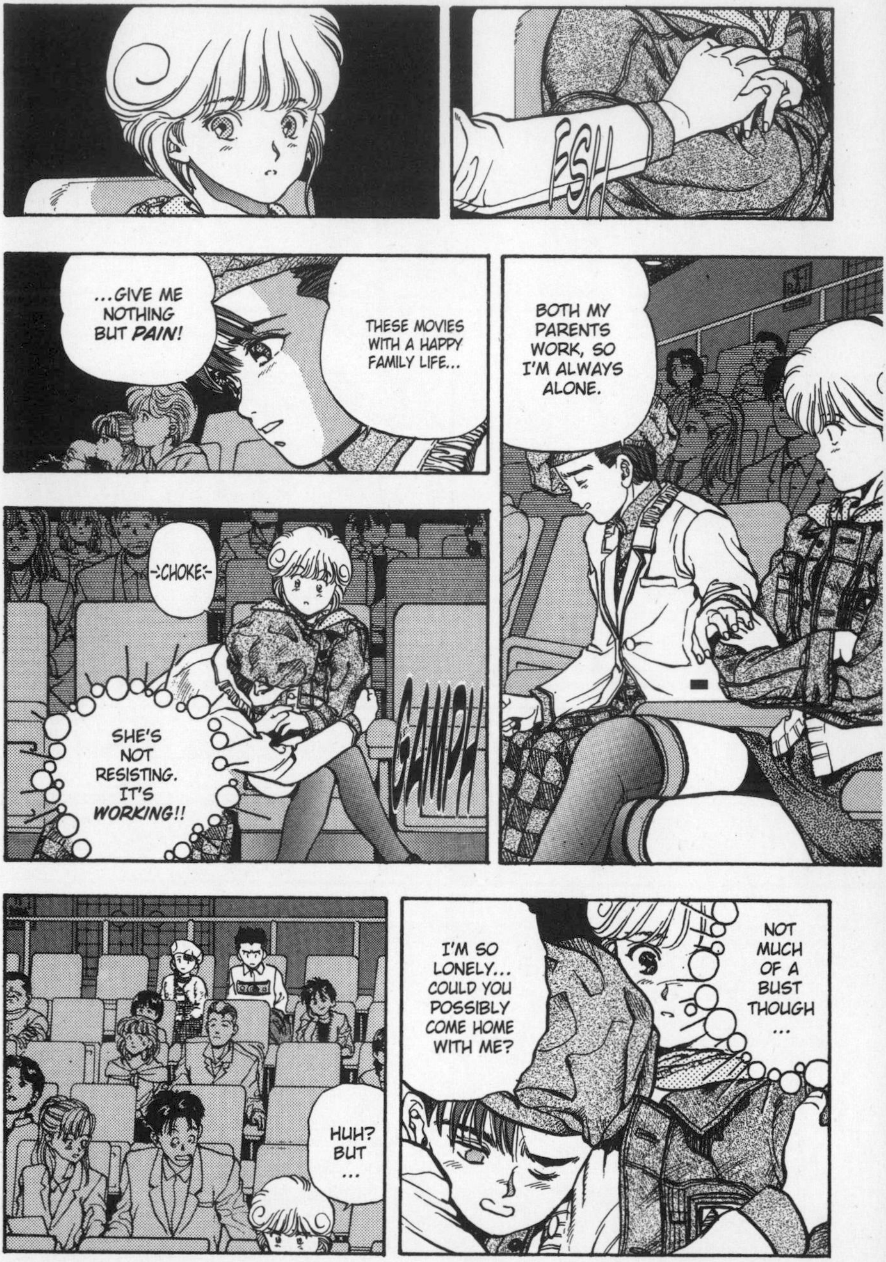
FSH
BOTH MY PARENTS WORK, SO I'M ALWAYS ALONE.
THESE MOVIES WITH A HAPPY FAMILY LIFE...
...GIVE ME NOTHING BUT PAIN!
-CHOKE-
GAMPH
SHE'S NOT RESISTING. IT'S WORKING!!
NOT MUCH OF A BUST THOUGH ...
I'M SO LONELY... COULD YOU POSSIBLY COME HOME WITH ME?
HUH? BUT ...

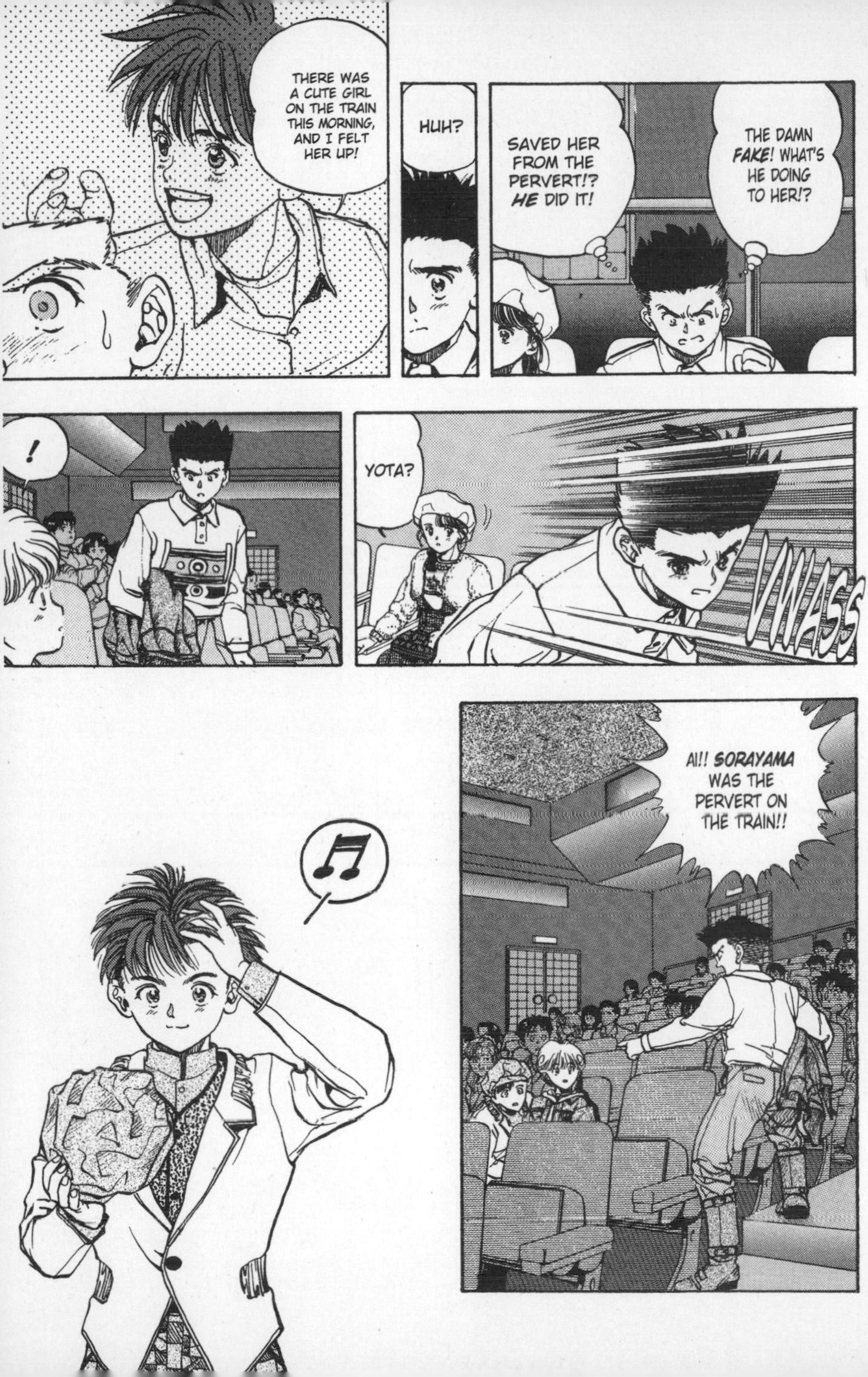
THE DAMN FAKE! WHAT'S HE DOING TO HER!?
SAVED HER FROM THE PERVERT!? HE DID IT!
HUH?
THERE WAS A CUTE GIRL ON THE TRAIN THIS MORNING, AND I FELT HER UP!
YOTA?
VWASS
!
AI!! SORAYAMA WAS THE PERVERT ON THE TRAIN!!

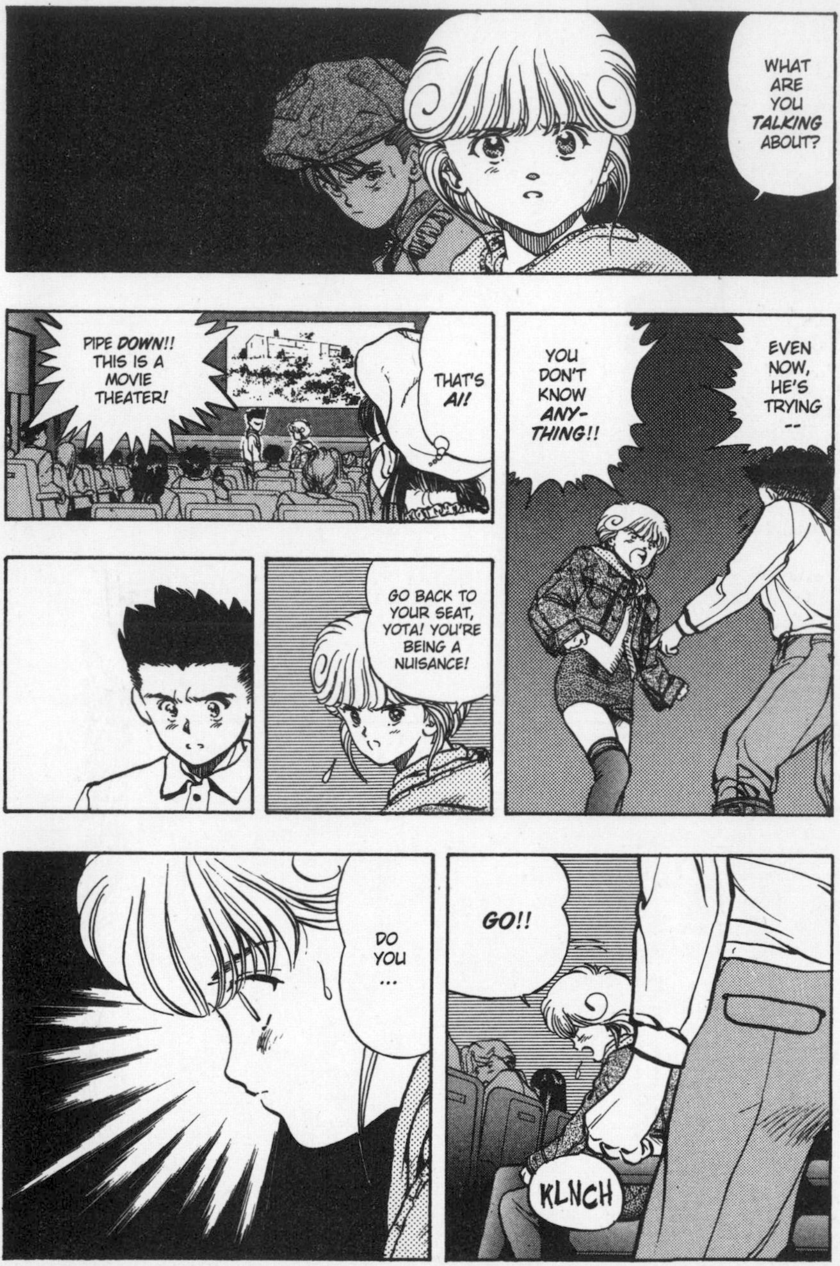
WHAT ARE YOU TALKING ABOUT?
EVEN NOW, HE'S TRYING --
YOU DON'T KNOW ANYTHING!!
THAT'S AI!
PIPE DOWN!! THIS IS A MOVIE THEATER!
GO BACK TO YOUR SEAT, YOTA! YOU'RE BEING A NUISANCE!
GO!!
KLNCH
DO YOU ...

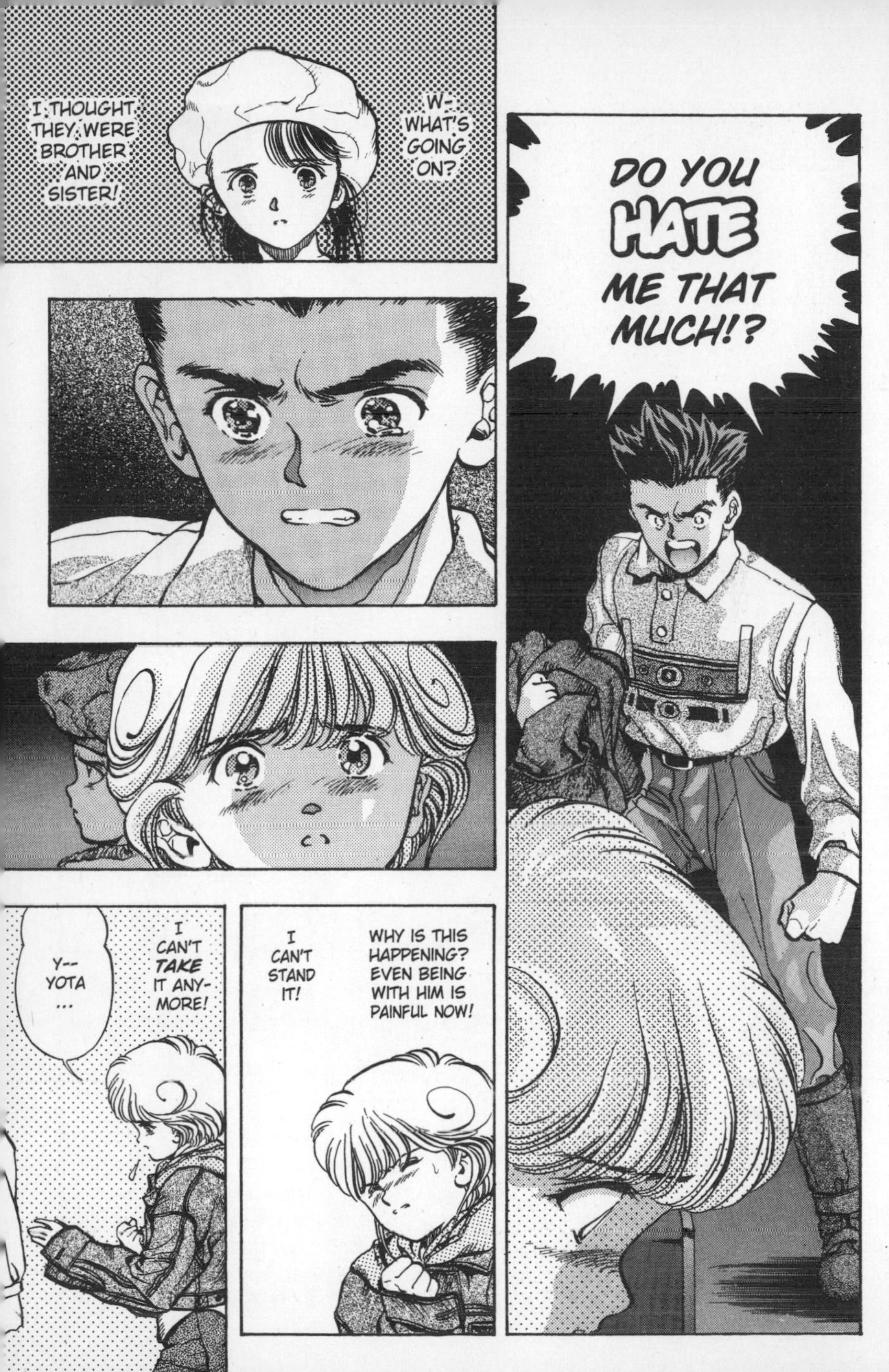
DO YOU HATE ME THAT MUCH!?
W-WHAT'S GOING ON?
I THOUGHT THEY WERE BROTHER AND SISTER!
WHY IS THIS HAPPENING? EVEN BEING WITH HIM IS PAINFUL NOW!
I CAN'T STAND IT!
I CAN'T TAKE IT ANY-MORE!
Y-- YOTA ...

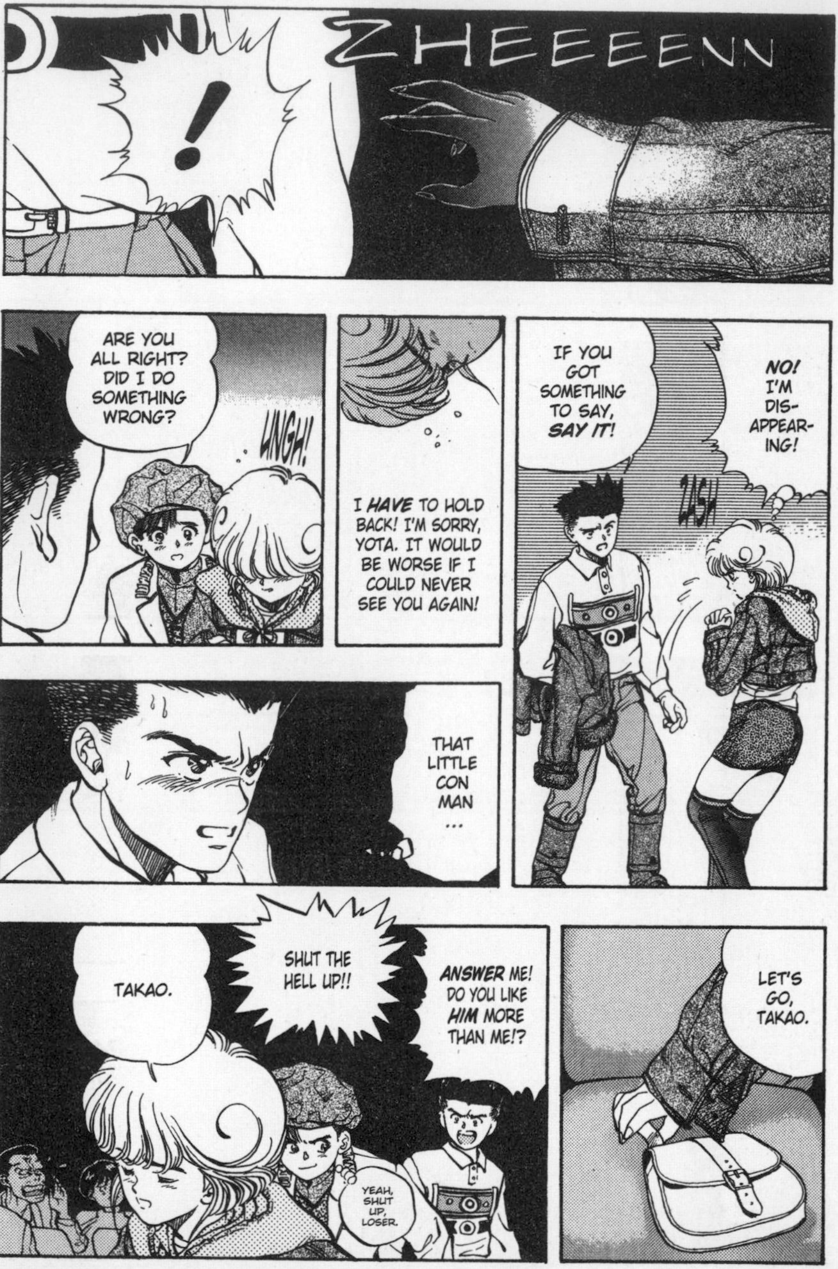
ZHEEEEENN
!
NO! I'M DIS-APPEARING!
IF YOU GOT SOMETHING TO SAY, SAY IT!
ZASH
I HAVE TO HOLD BACK! I'M SORRY, YOTA. IT WOULD BE WORSE IF I COULD NEVER SEE YOU AGAIN!
ARE YOU ALL RIGHT? DID I DO SOMETHING WRONG?
UNGH!
THAT LITTLE CON MAN ...
LET'S GO, TAKAO.
ANSWER ME! DO YOU LIKE HIM MORE THAN ME!?
SHUT THE HELL UP!!
TAKAO.
YEAH, SHUT UP, LOSER.

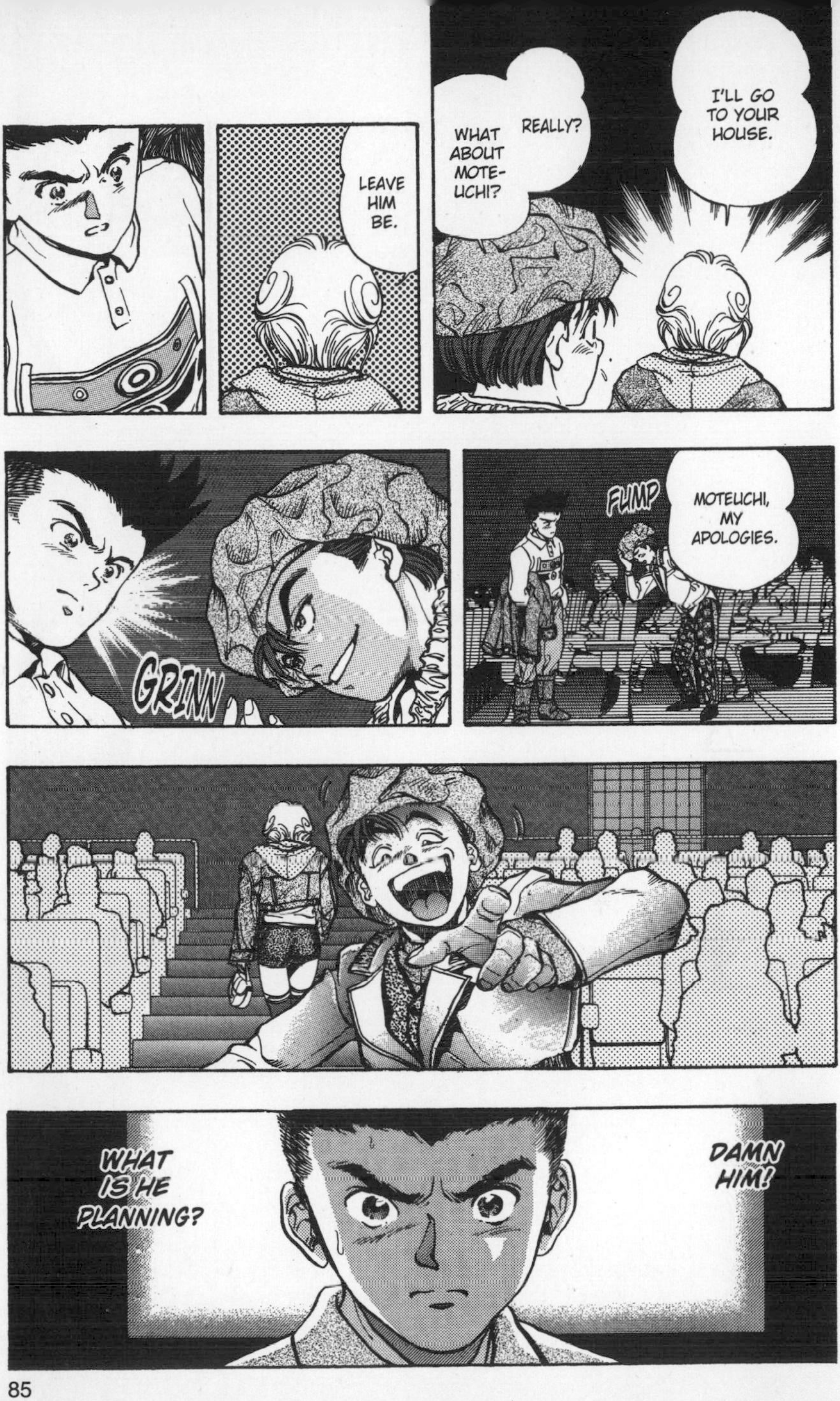
I'LL GO TO YOUR HOUSE.
REALLY?
WHAT ABOUT MOTE-UCHI?
LEAVE HIM BE.
MOTEUCHI, MY APOLOGIES.
FLUMP
GRINN
DAMN HIM!
WHAT IS HE PLANNING?

■ ▲ ■ II ■ ►► ■ ► *CHAPTER THIRTEEN*
His House

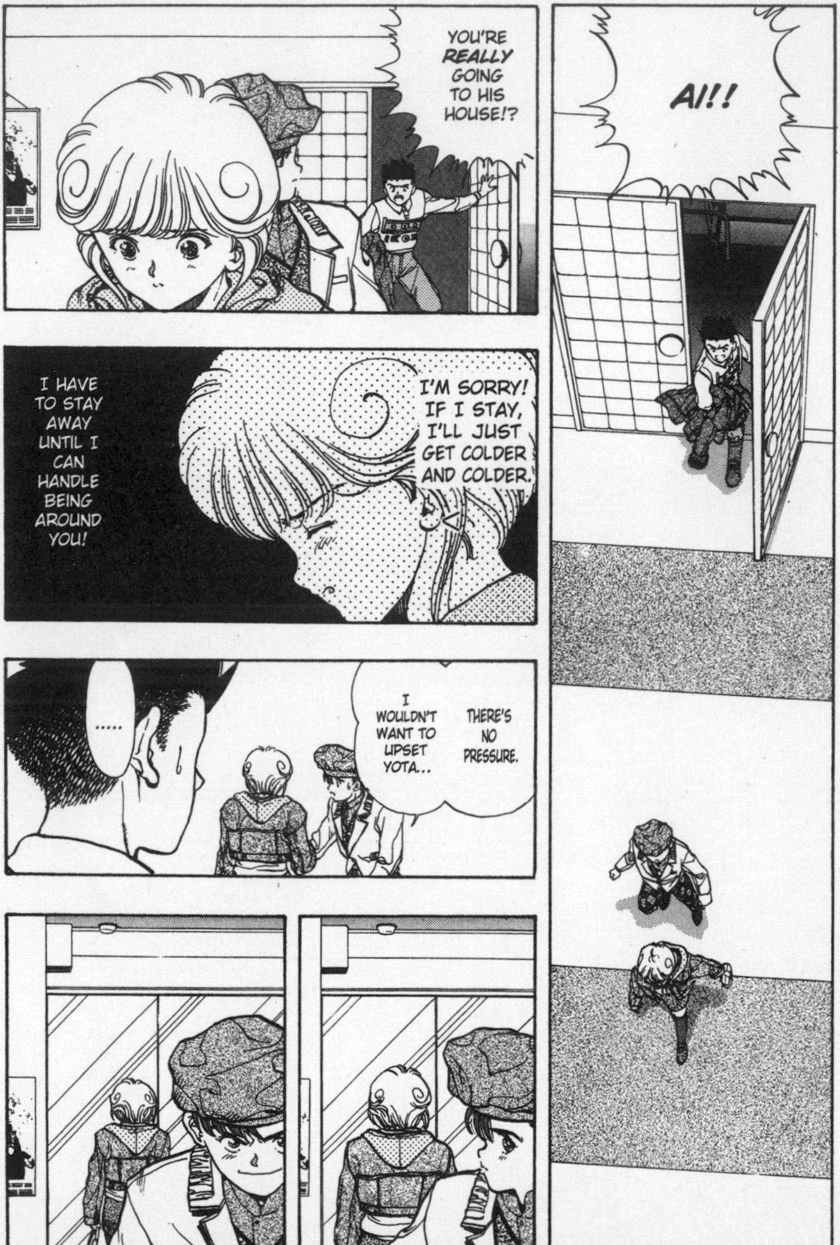
AI!!
YOU'RE *REALLY* GOING TO HIS HOUSE!?
I'M SORRY! IF I STAY, I'LL JUST GET COLDER AND COLDER.
I HAVE TO STAY AWAY UNTIL I CAN HANDLE BEING AROUND YOU!
THERE'S NO PRESSURE.
I WOULDN'T WANT TO UPSET YOTA...
......

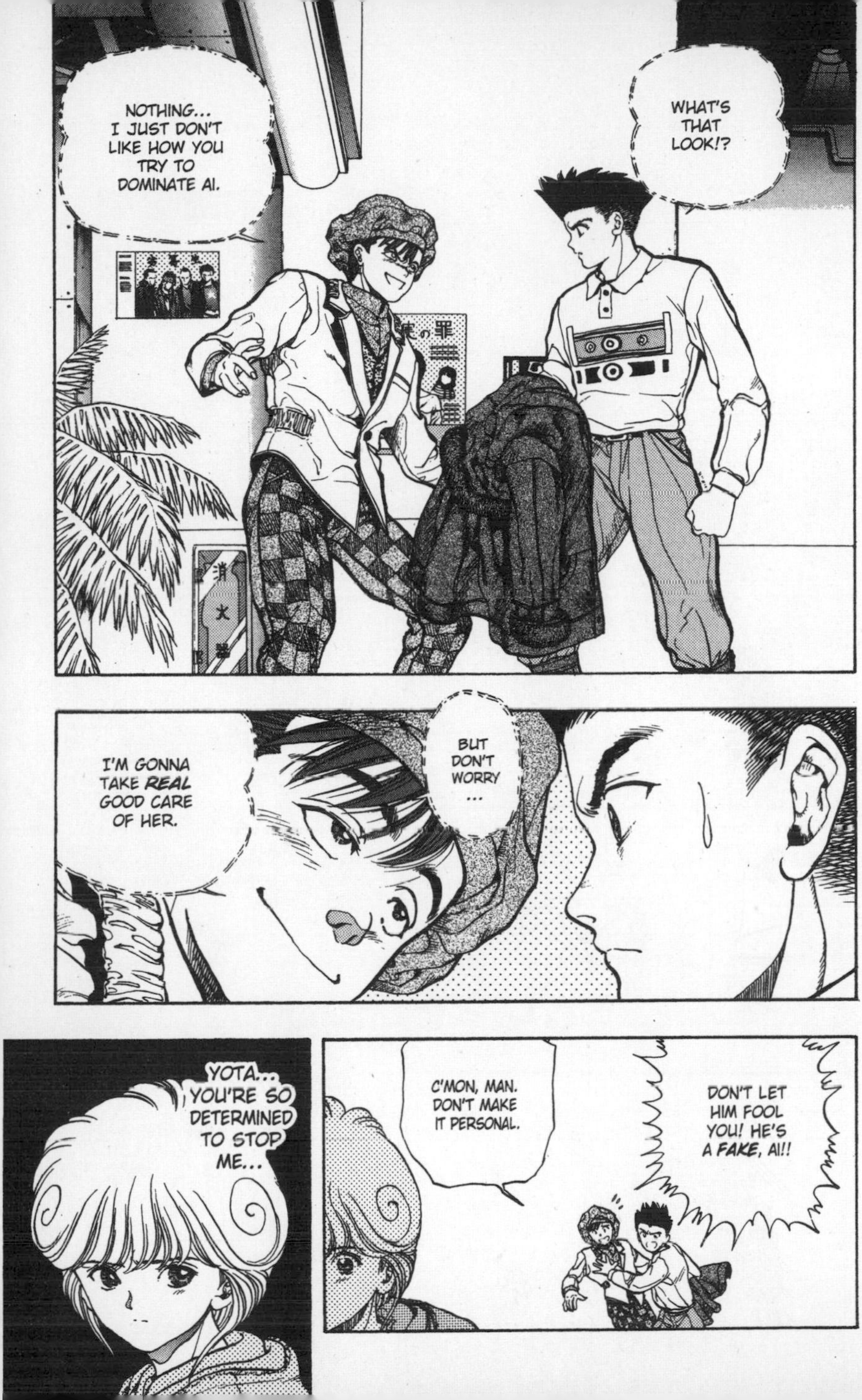
WHAT'S THAT LOOK!?
NOTHING... I JUST DON'T LIKE HOW YOU TRY TO DOMINATE AI.
BUT DON'T WORRY ...
I'M GONNA TAKE *REAL* GOOD CARE OF HER.
DON'T LET HIM FOOL YOU! HE'S A *FAKE*, AI!!
C'MON, MAN. DON'T MAKE IT PERSONAL.
YOTA... YOU'RE SO DETERMINED TO STOP ME...

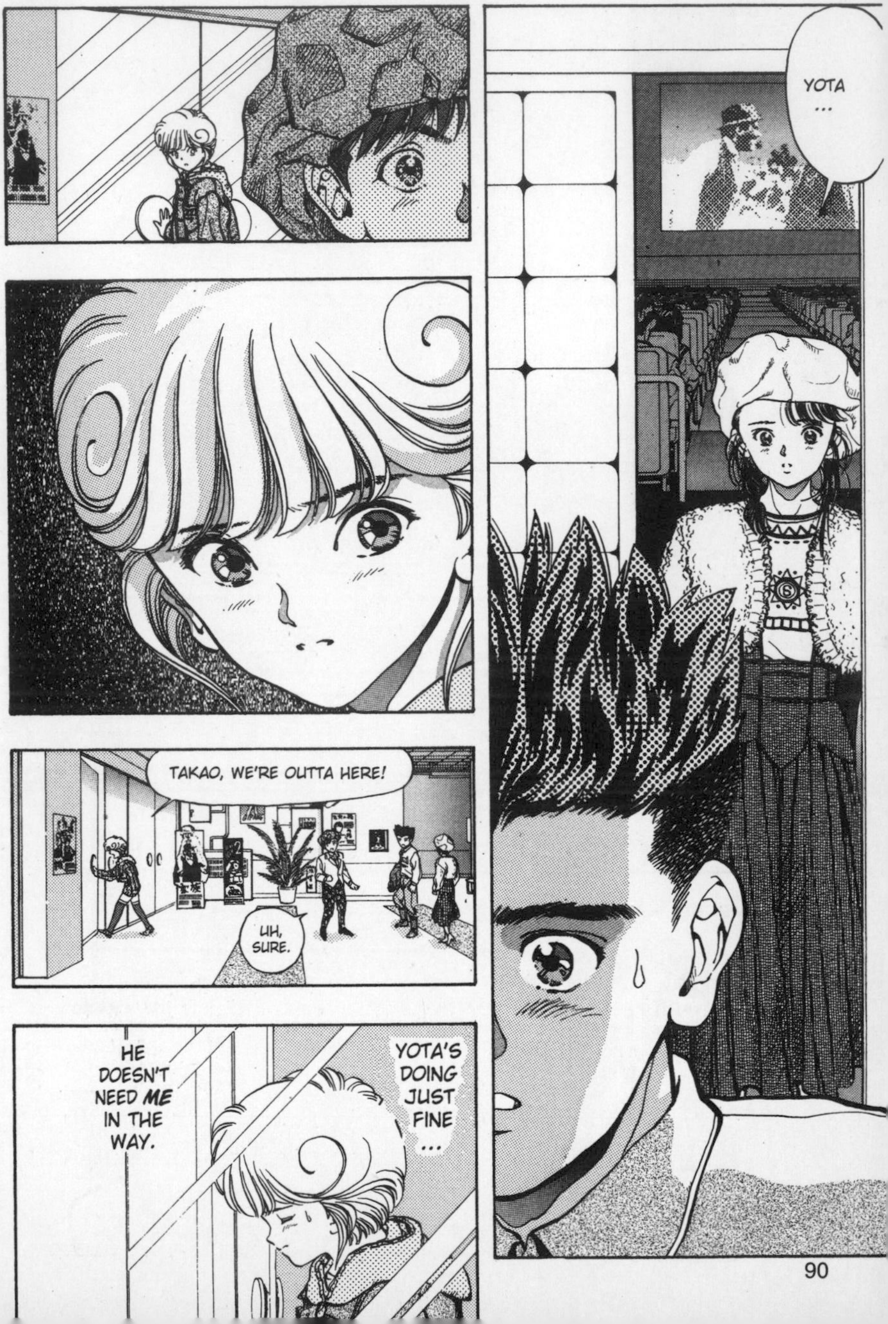
YOTA ...
TAKAO, WE'RE OUTTA HERE!
UH, SURE.
YOTA'S DOING JUST FINE ...
HE DOESN'T NEED *ME* IN THE WAY.

I--
I'M
NOT
...

CHASE TWO RABBITS, AND YOU END UP WITH NONE.

I'M REALLY BEGINNING TO *DESPISE* YOU.

Y'KNOW
...

WHAT'S WRONG?

LATER.

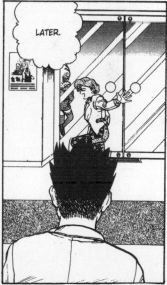

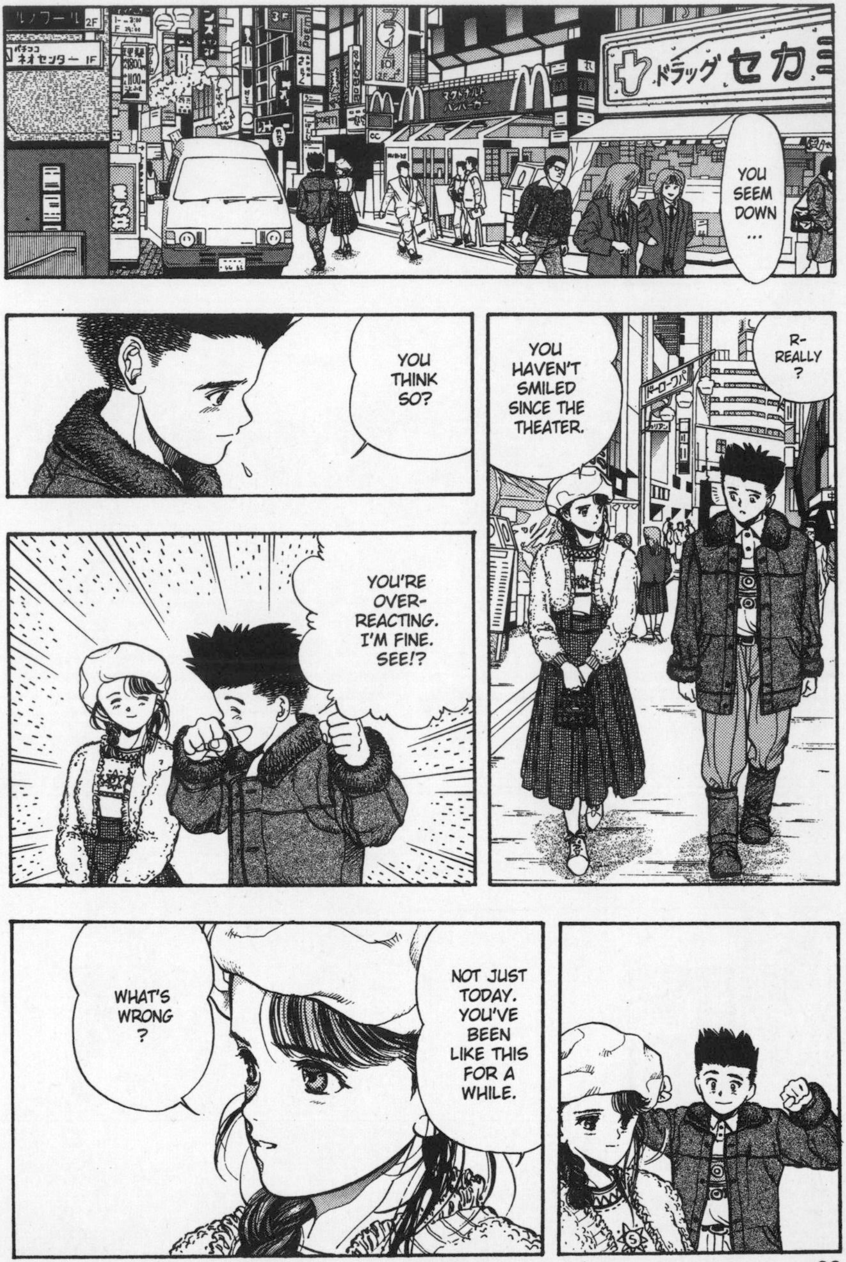
YOU SEEM DOWN ...
R-REALLY?
YOU HAVEN'T SMILED SINCE THE THEATER.
YOU THINK SO?
YOU'RE OVER-REACTING. I'M FINE. SEE!?
NOT JUST TODAY. YOU'VE BEEN LIKE THIS FOR A WHILE.
WHAT'S WRONG?

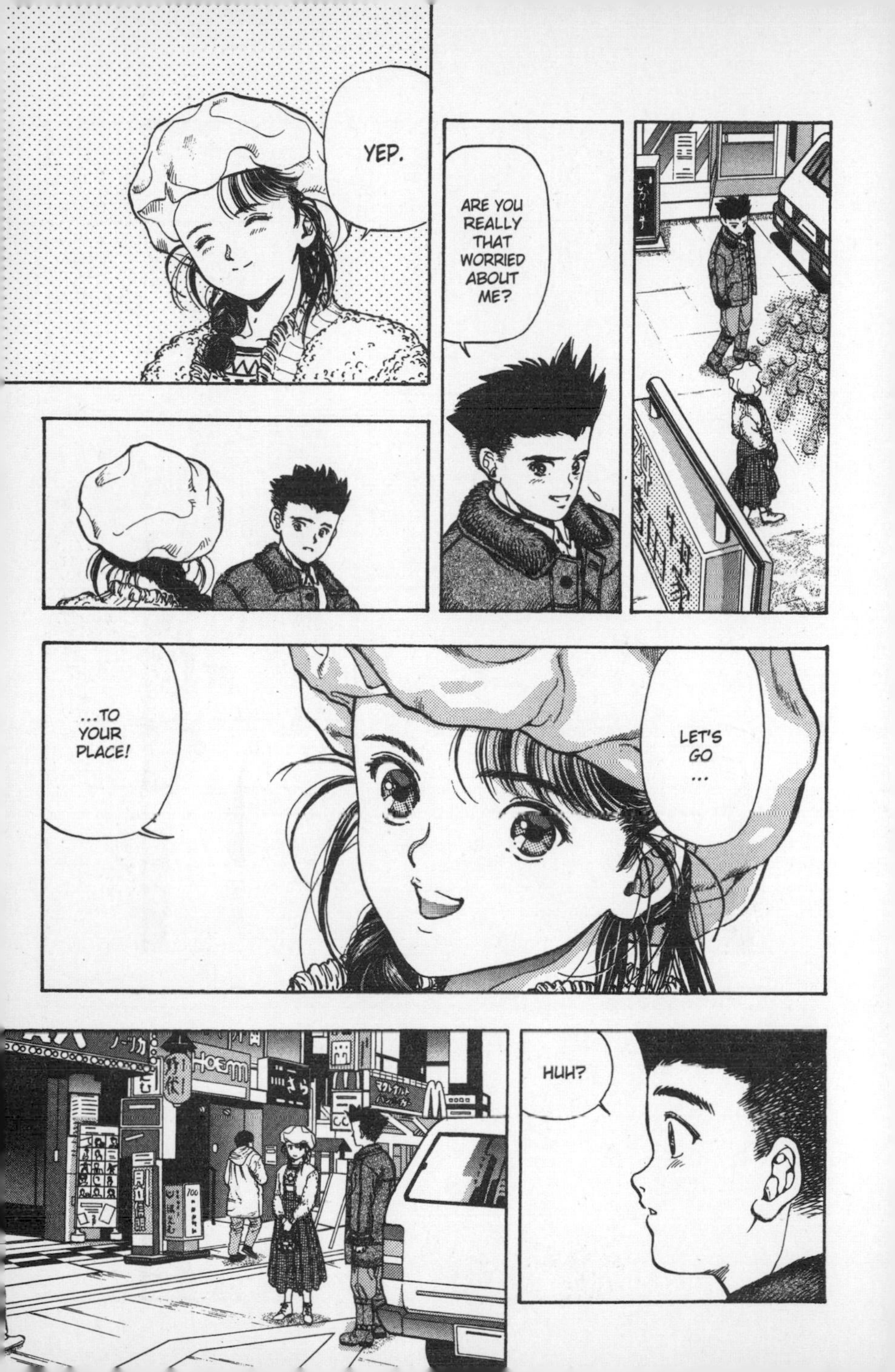
ARE YOU REALLY THAT WORRIED ABOUT ME?
YEP.
LET'S GO ...
...TO YOUR PLACE!
HUH?

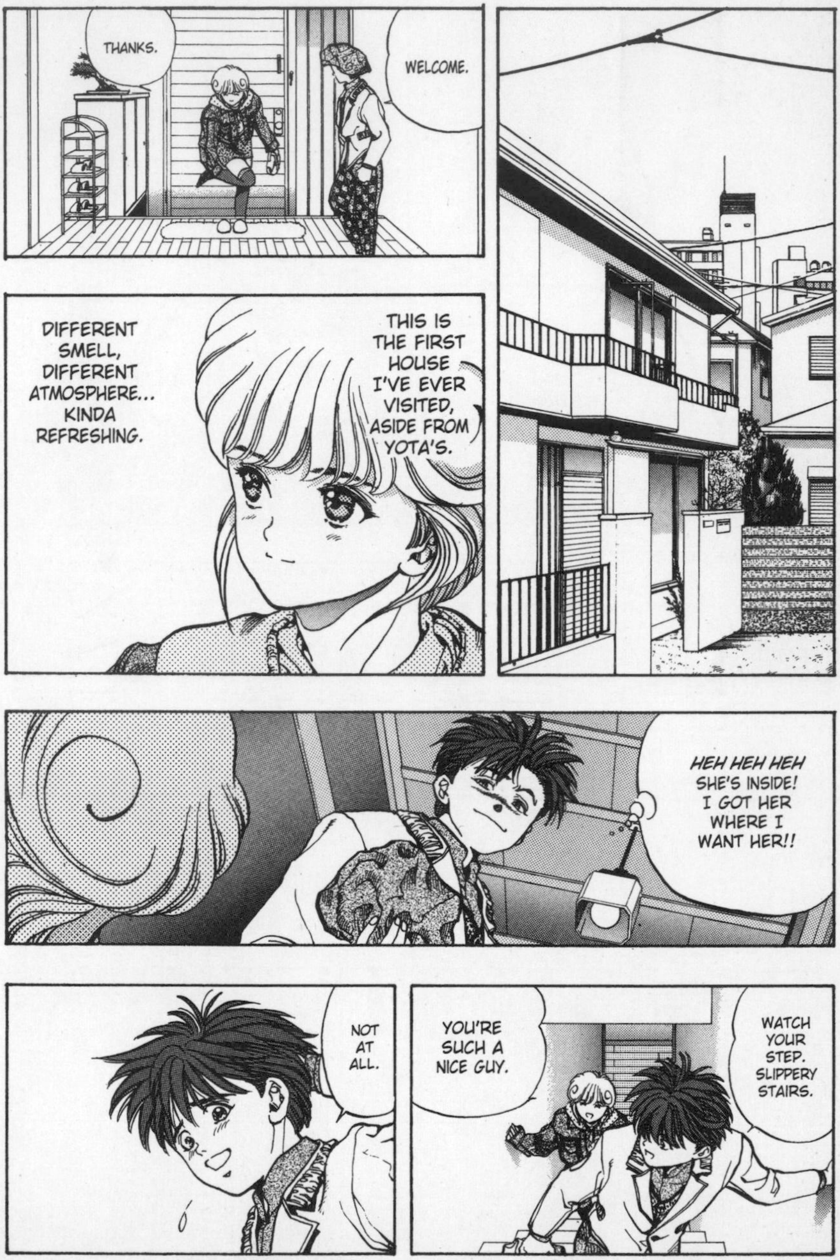
WELCOME.
THANKS.
THIS IS THE FIRST HOUSE I'VE EVER VISITED, ASIDE FROM YOTA'S.
DIFFERENT SMELL, DIFFERENT ATMOSPHERE... KINDA REFRESHING.
HEH HEH HEH SHE'S INSIDE! I GOT HER WHERE I WANT HER!!
WATCH YOUR STEP. SLIPPERY STAIRS.
YOU'RE SUCH A NICE GUY.
NOT AT ALL.

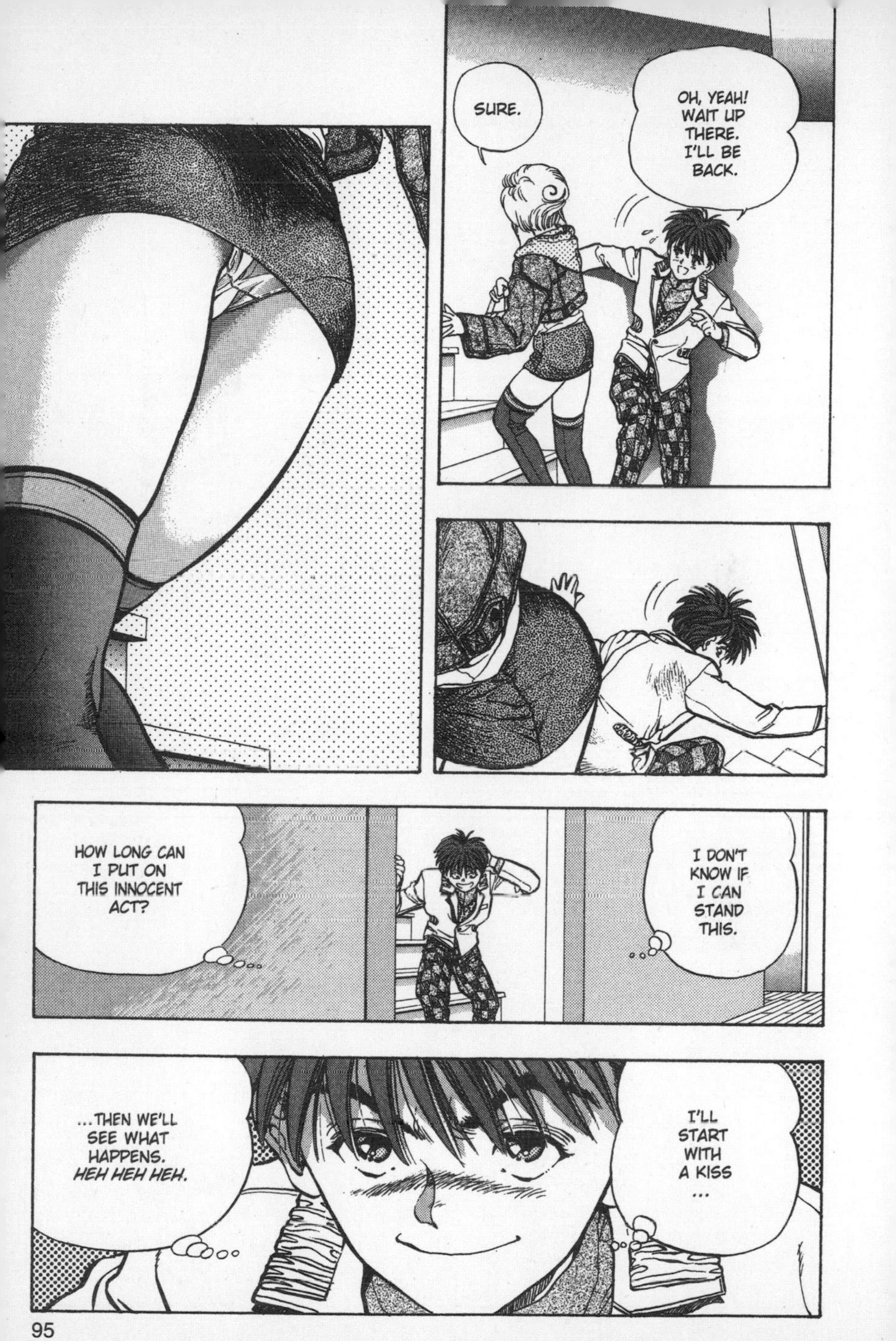
OH, YEAH! WAIT UP THERE. I'LL BE BACK.
SURE.
I DON'T KNOW IF I CAN STAND THIS.
HOW LONG CAN I PUT ON THIS INNOCENT ACT?
I'LL START WITH A KISS ...
...THEN WE'LL SEE WHAT HAPPENS. *HEH HEH HEH.*

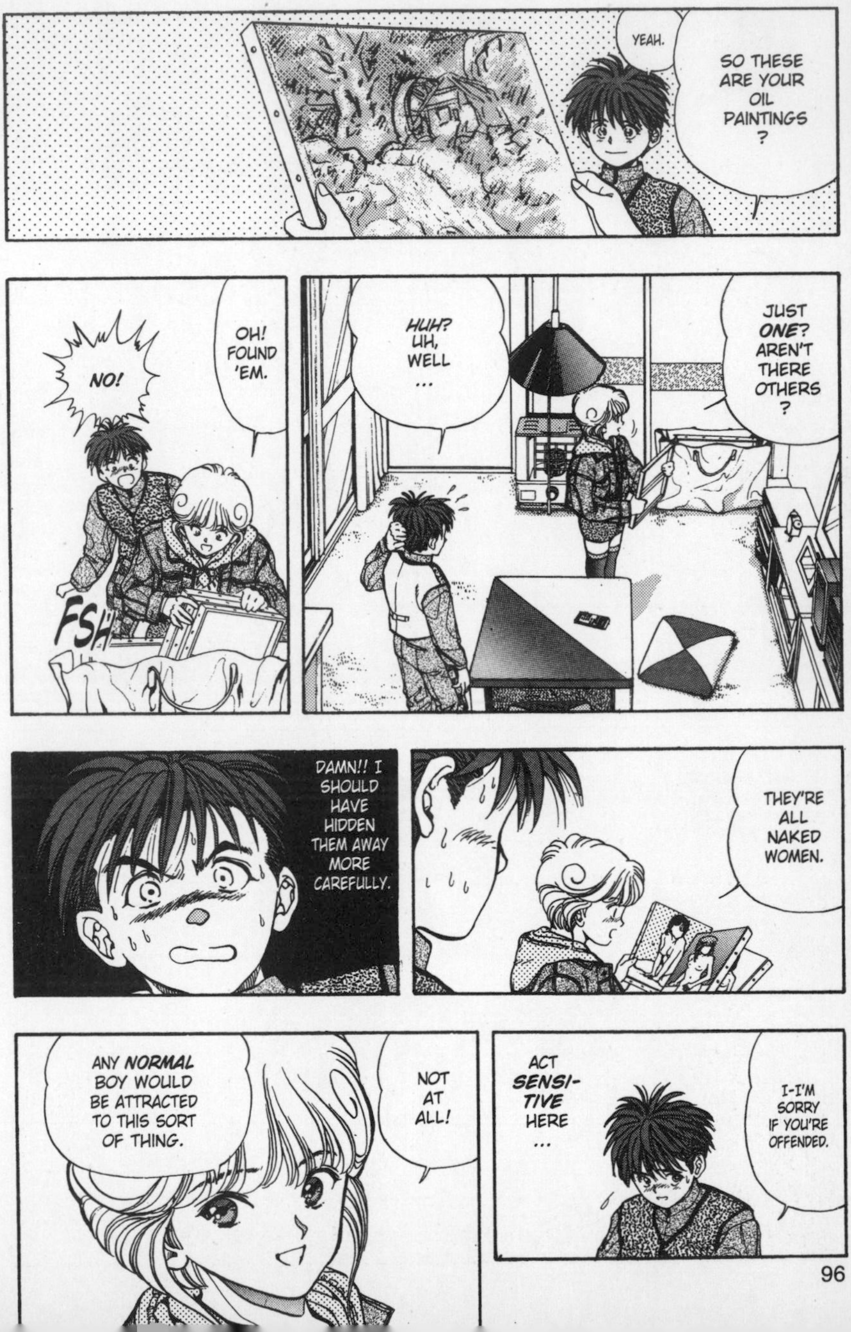
SO THESE ARE YOUR OIL PAINTINGS?
YEAH.
JUST **ONE**? AREN'T THERE OTHERS?
HUH? UH, WELL ...
OH! FOUND 'EM.
NO!
FSH
THEY'RE ALL NAKED WOMEN.
DAMN!! I SHOULD HAVE HIDDEN THEM AWAY MORE CAREFULLY.
I-I'M SORRY IF YOU'RE OFFENDED.
ACT ***SENSI-TIVE*** HERE ...
NOT AT ALL!
ANY ***NORMAL*** BOY WOULD BE ATTRACTED TO THIS SORT OF THING.

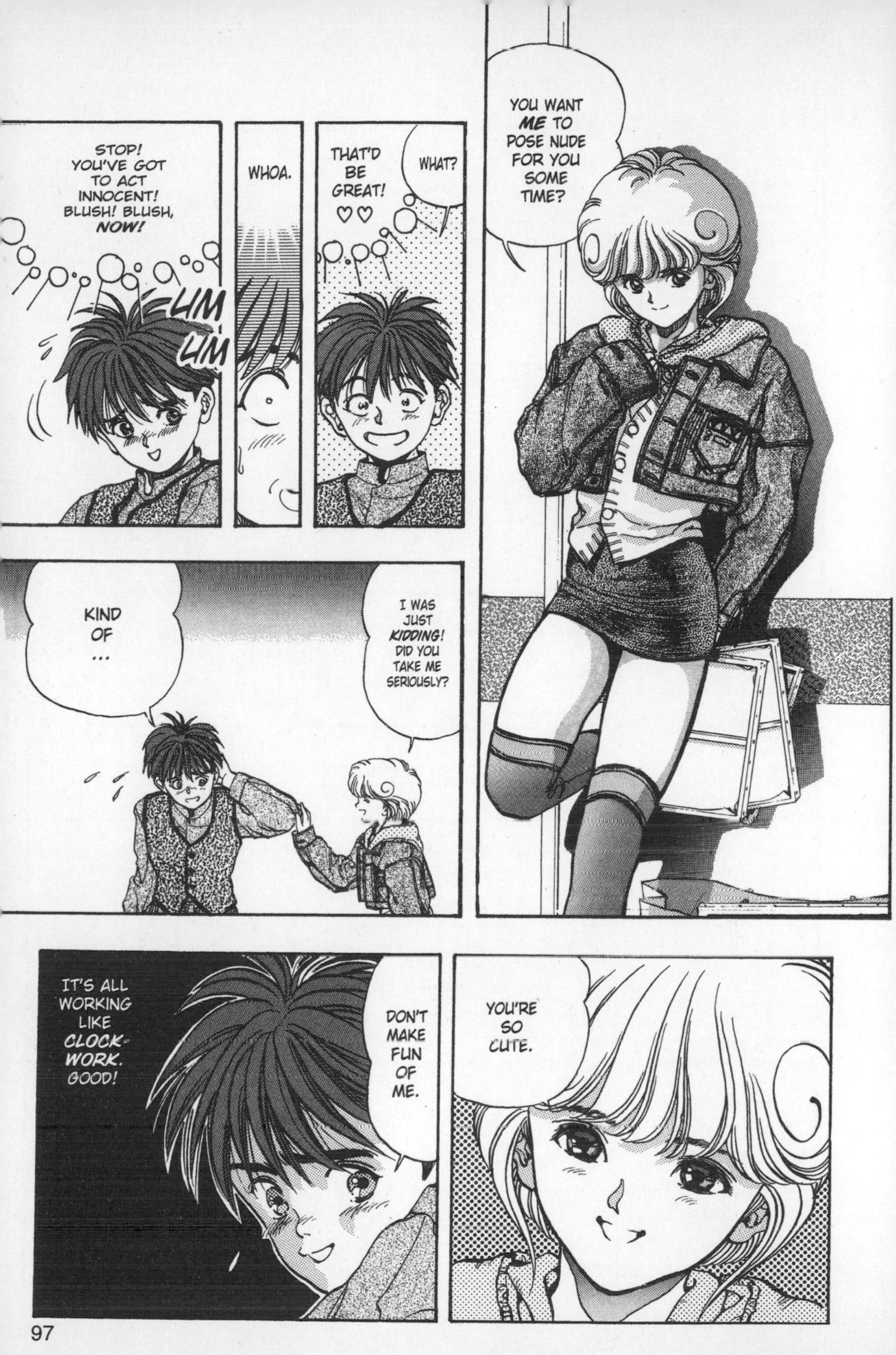
YOU WANT ME TO POSE NUDE FOR YOU SOME TIME?
WHAT?
THAT'D BE GREAT! ♡♡
WHOA.
STOP! YOU'VE GOT TO ACT INNOCENT! BLUSH! BLUSH, NOW!
UM UM
I WAS JUST KIDDING! DID YOU TAKE ME SERIOUSLY?
KIND OF ...
YOU'RE SO CUTE.
DON'T MAKE FUN OF ME.
IT'S ALL WORKING LIKE CLOCKWORK. GOOD!

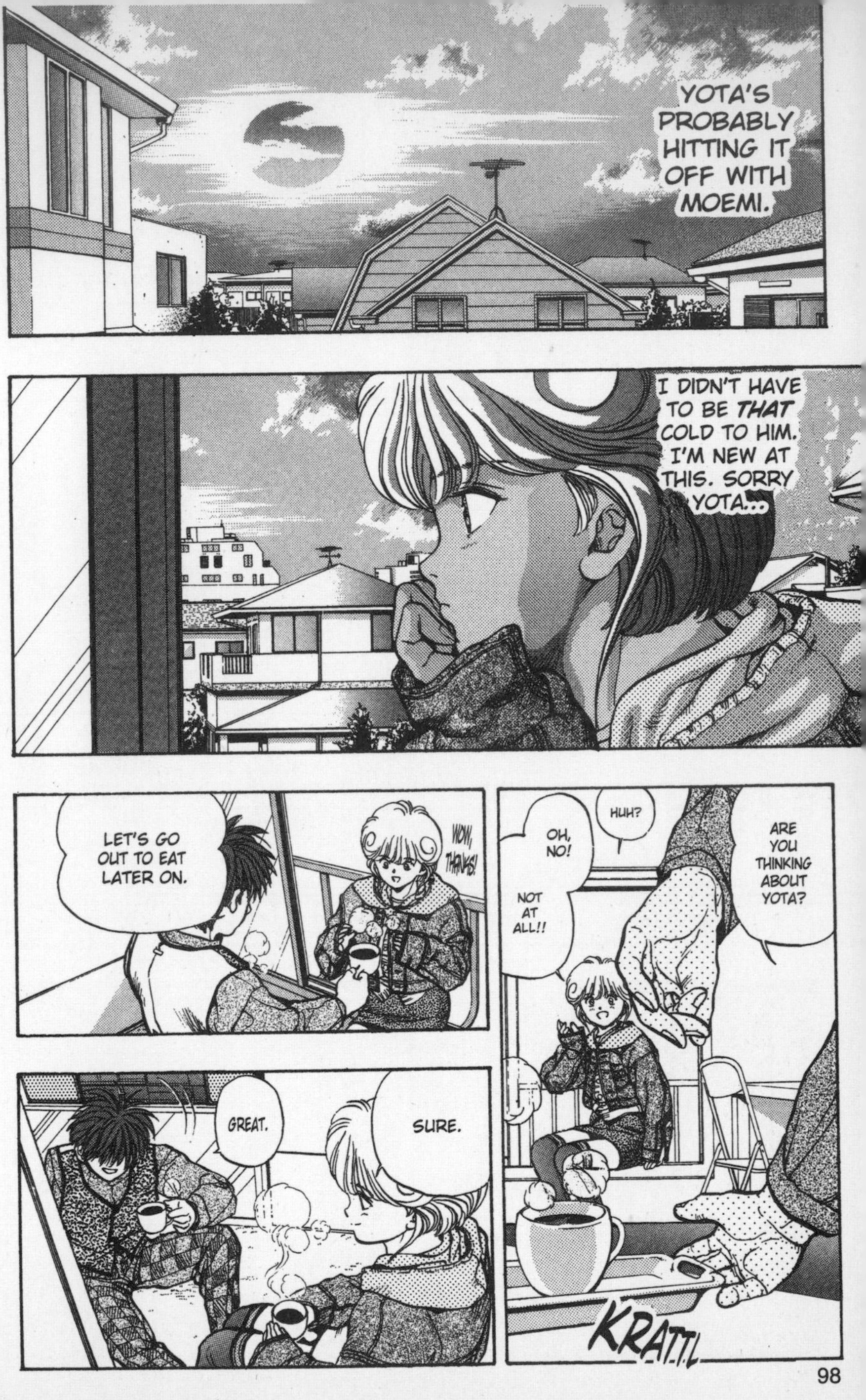
YOTA'S PROBABLY HITTING IT OFF WITH MOEMI.
I DIDN'T HAVE TO BE *THAT* COLD TO HIM. I'M NEW AT THIS. SORRY YOTA...
ARE YOU THINKING ABOUT YOTA?
HUH?
OH, NO!
NOT AT ALL!!
KRATTL
LET'S GO OUT TO EAT LATER ON.
WOW, THANKS!
SURE.
GREAT.

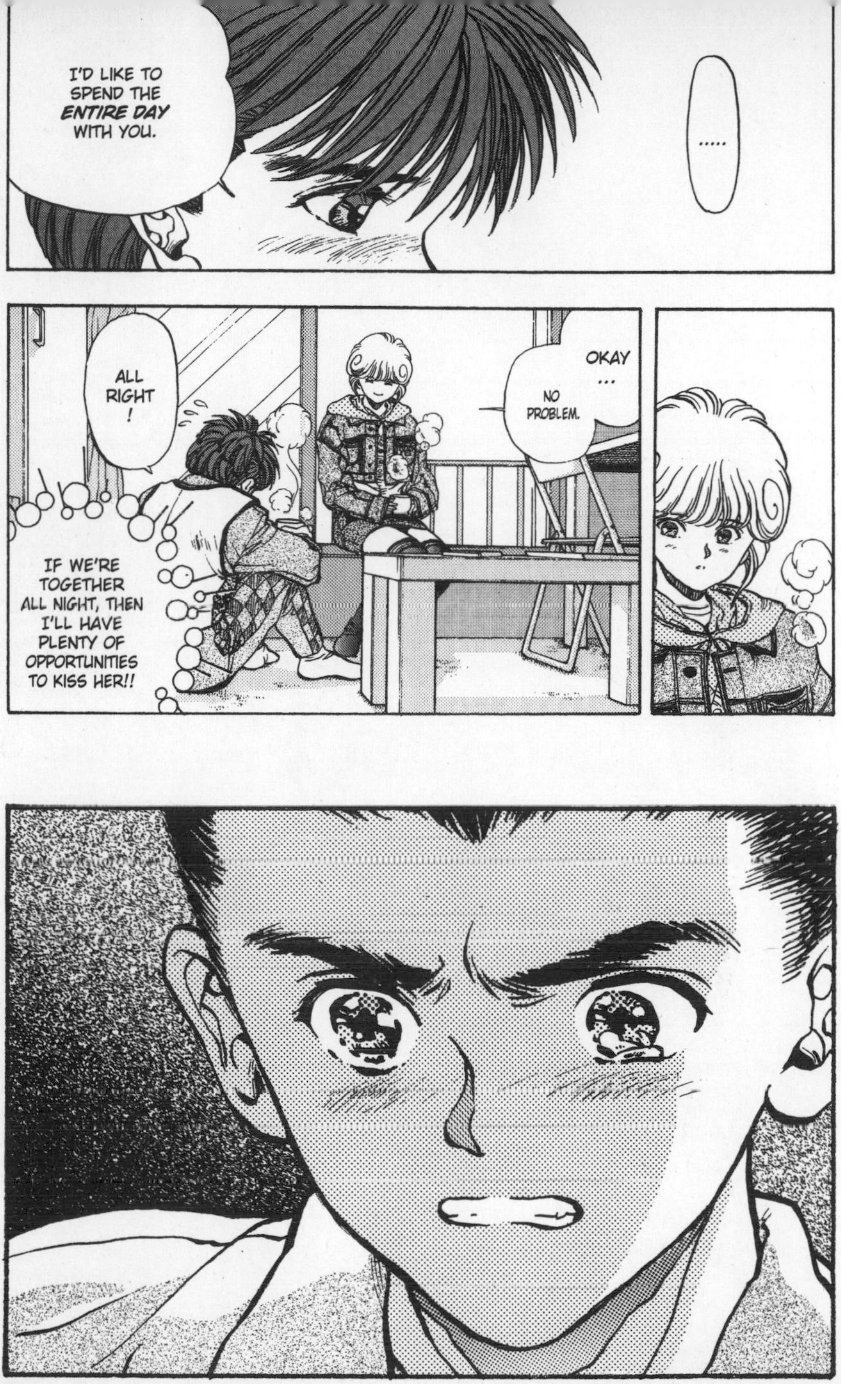
.....
I'D LIKE TO SPEND THE ENTIRE DAY WITH YOU.
OKAY ...
NO PROBLEM.
ALL RIGHT !
IF WE'RE TOGETHER ALL NIGHT, THEN I'LL HAVE PLENTY OF OPPORTUNITIES TO KISS HER!!

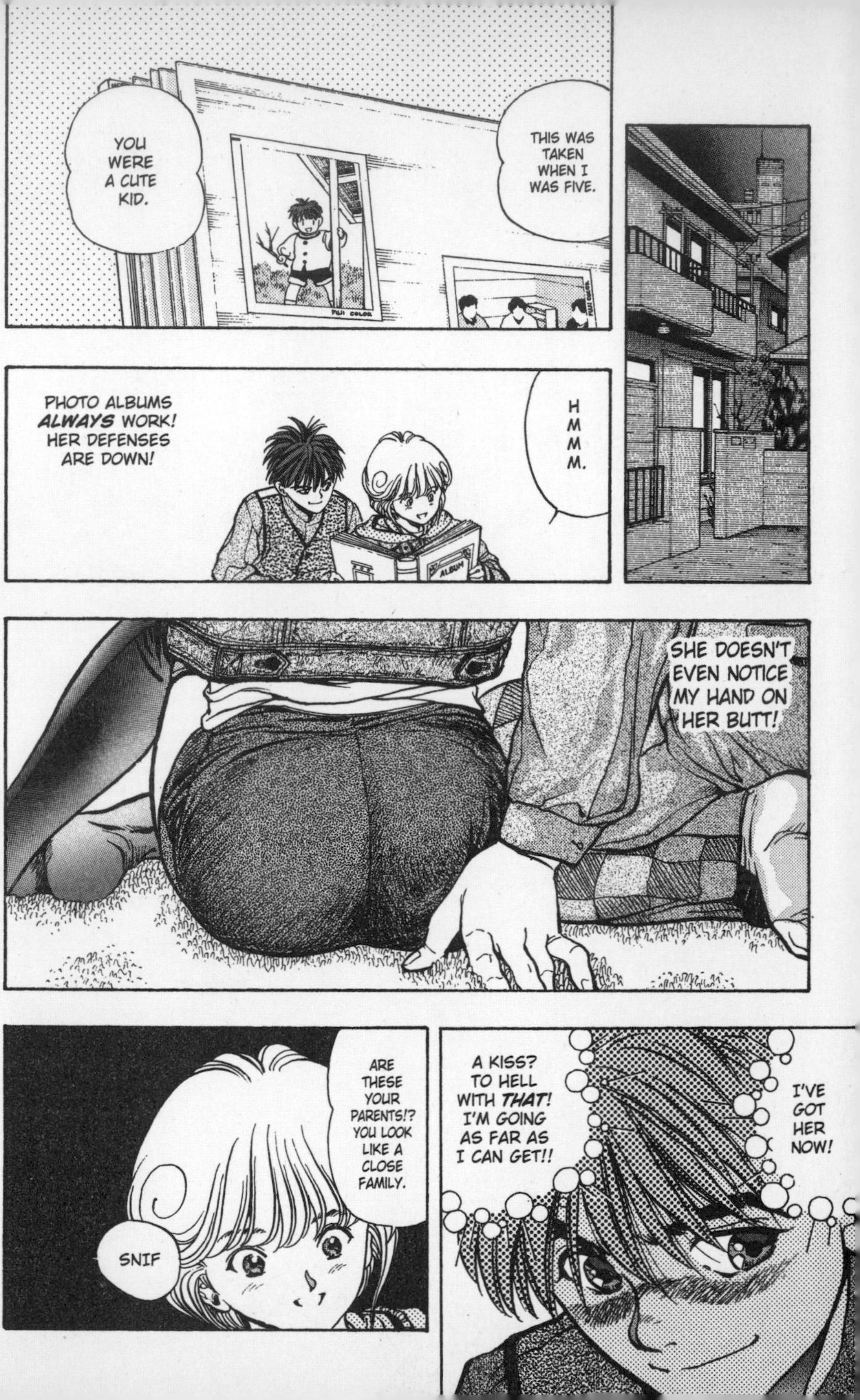
THIS WAS TAKEN WHEN I WAS FIVE.
YOU WERE A CUTE KID.
HMMM.
PHOTO ALBUMS *ALWAYS* WORK! HER DEFENSES ARE DOWN!
SHE DOESN'T EVEN NOTICE MY HAND ON HER BUTT!
I'VE GOT HER NOW!
A KISS? TO HELL WITH *THAT*! I'M GOING AS FAR AS I CAN GET!!
ARE THESE YOUR PARENTS!? YOU LOOK LIKE A CLOSE FAMILY.
SNIF

I FORGOT HE'S SENSITIVE ABOUT HIS FAMILY.

I'M SORRY...

WHEN MOM AND DAD GOT ALONG. AT LEAST IN FRONT OF ME.

THOSE WERE THE *GOOD* TIMES...

SNIFFL SNIFFL

NOW ...I'M ALONE...

BUT NOW YOTA'S... I THINK I UNDERSTAND WHERE HE'S COMING FROM.

I DON'T HAVE A FAMILY... THE CLOSEST THING I HAVE IS YOTA...

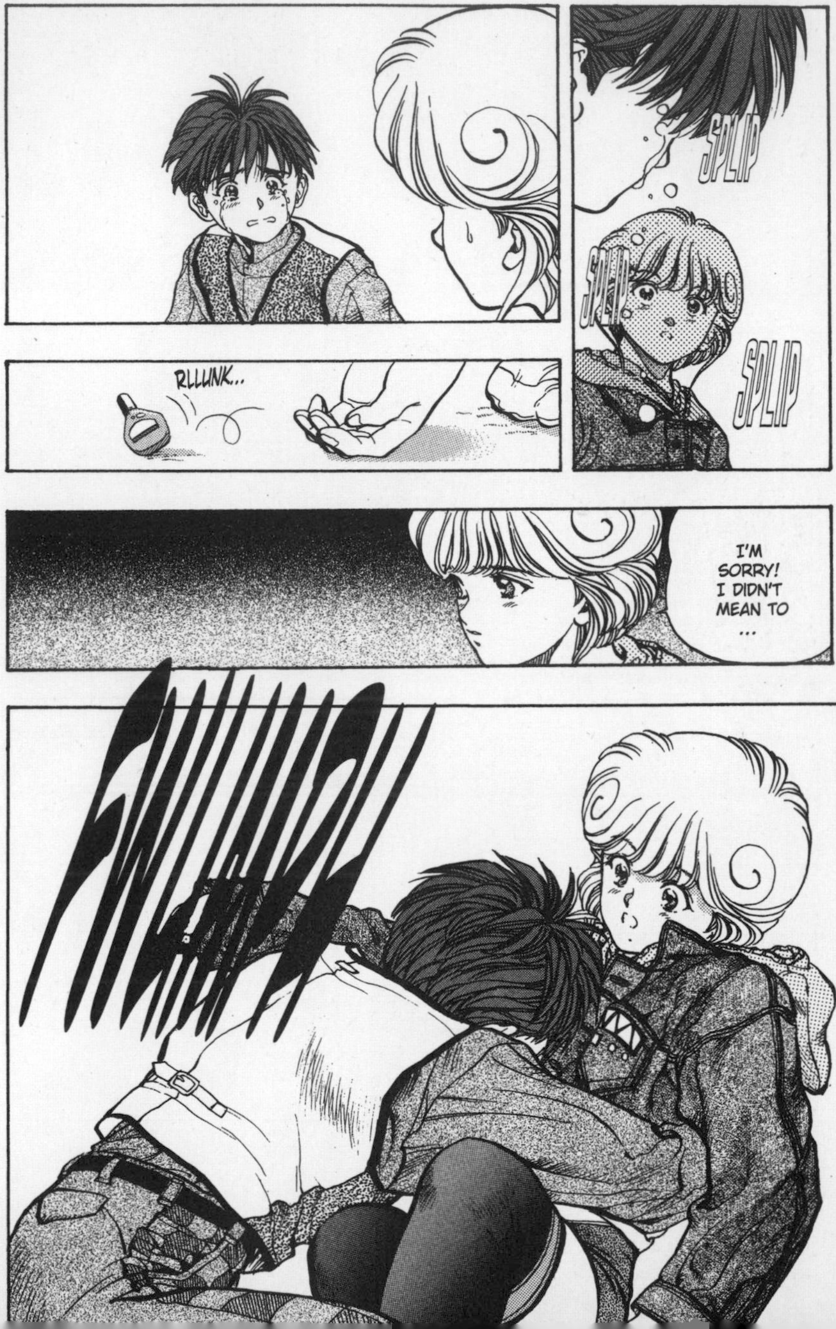
SPLIP
SPLIP
SPLIP
RLLUNK...
I'M SORRY! I DIDN'T MEAN TO ...

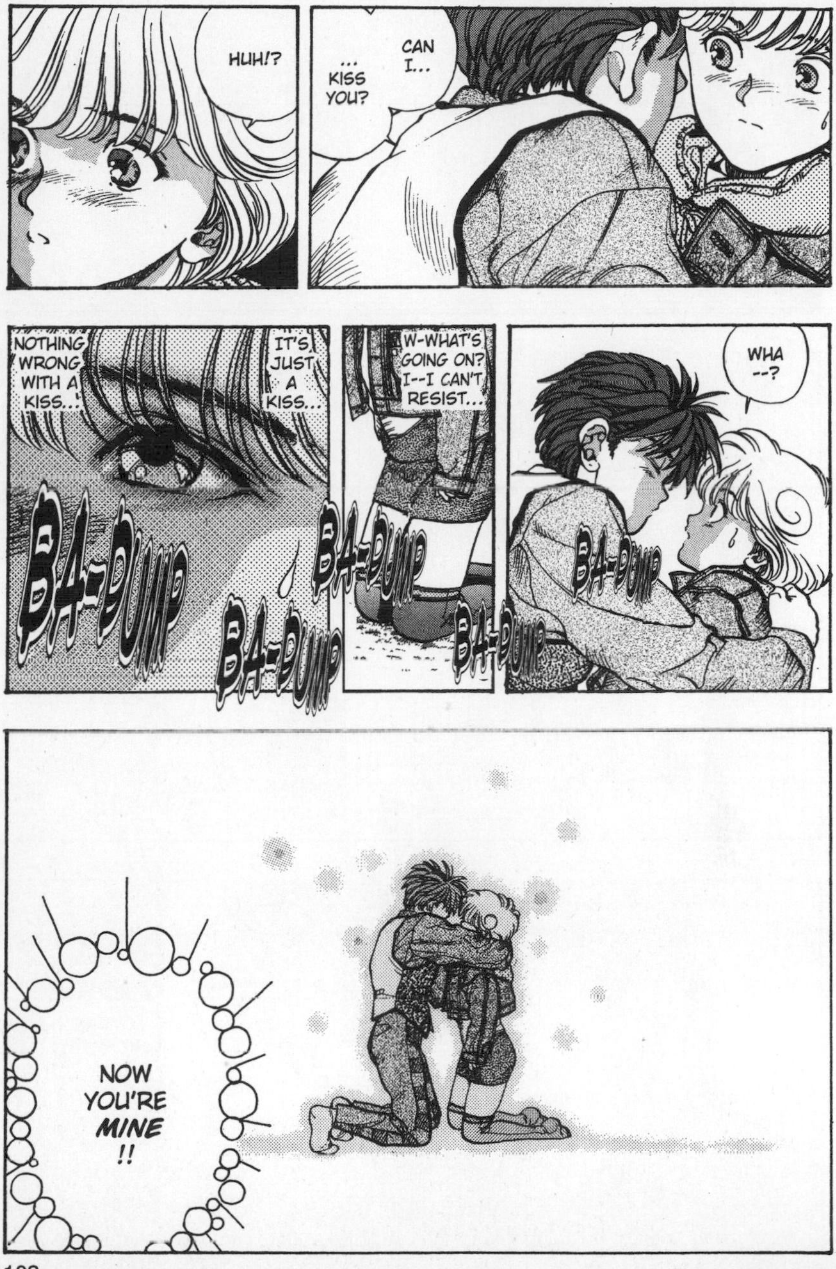
CAN I... ...KISS YOU?
HUH!?
WHA --?
BA-DUMP
BA-DUMP
W-WHAT'S GOING ON? I--I CAN'T RESIST...
BA-DUMP
BA-DUMP
IT'S JUST A KISS...
NOTHING WRONG WITH A KISS...
BA-DUMP
NOW YOU'RE MINE !!

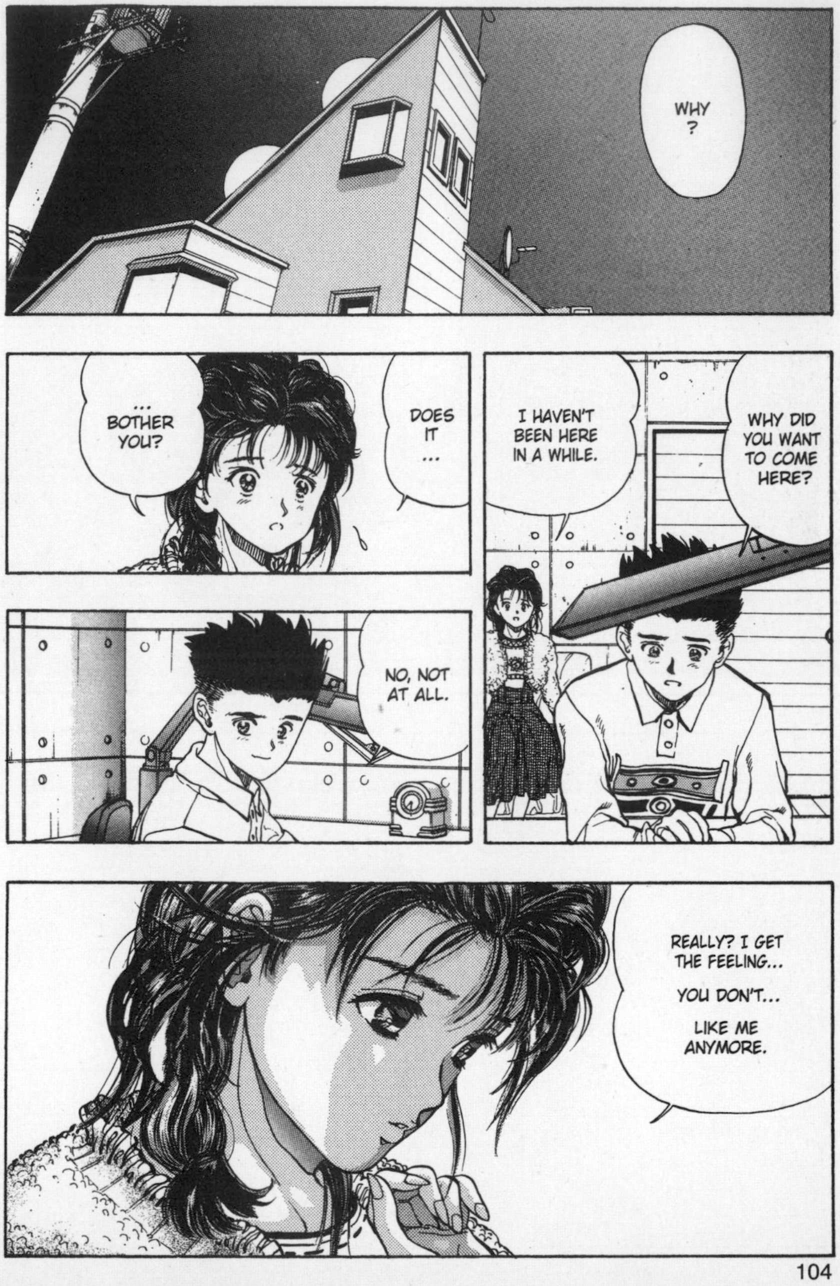
WHY ?
WHY DID YOU WANT TO COME HERE?
I HAVEN'T BEEN HERE IN A WHILE.
DOES IT ...
... BOTHER YOU?
NO, NOT AT ALL.
REALLY? I GET THE FEELING... YOU DON'T... LIKE ME ANYMORE.

HUH?

THINGS AREN'T WORKING OUT WITH TAKASHI?

JUST FINE!

EVERY- THING'S FINE!

.....

IF EVERY- THING'S FINE, THEN...

WHAT DOES ...

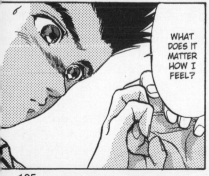

WHAT DOES IT MATTER HOW I FEEL?

105

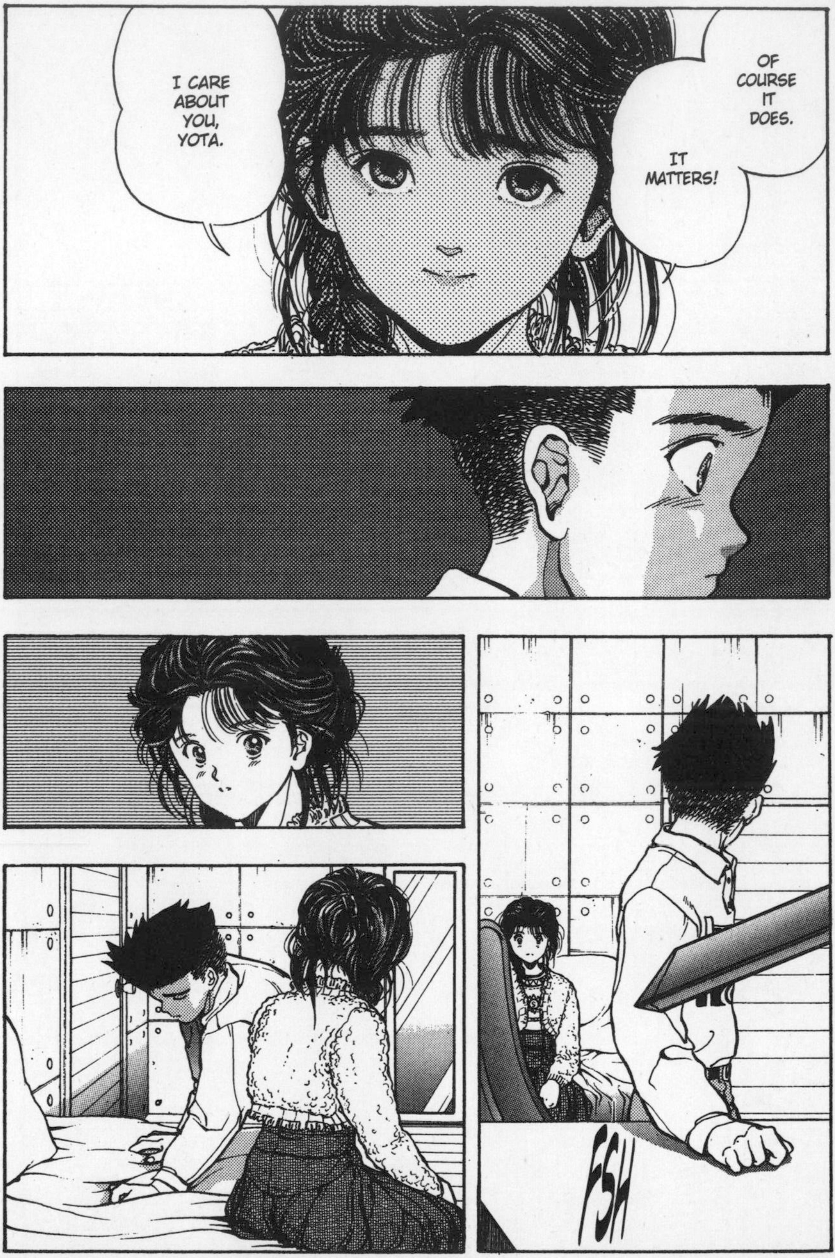
OF COURSE IT DOES.
IT MATTERS!
I CARE ABOUT YOU, YOTA.
FSH

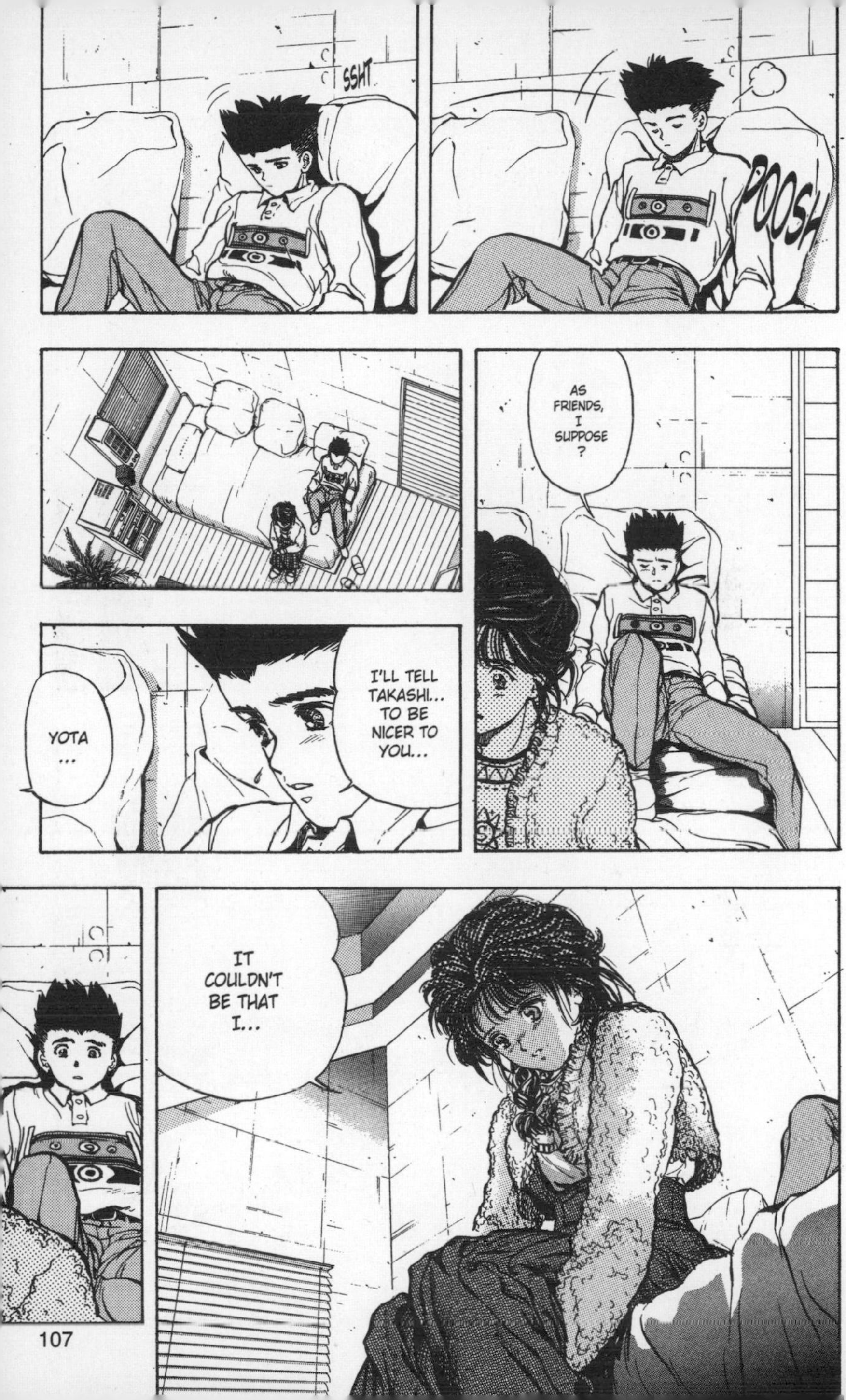
POOSH
SSHT
AS FRIENDS, I SUPPOSE?
I'LL TELL TAKASHI... TO BE NICER TO YOU...
YOTA...
IT COULDN'T BE THAT I...

CHAPTER FOURTEEN - I LIKE YOU

IT COULDN'T BE...

...THAT I...

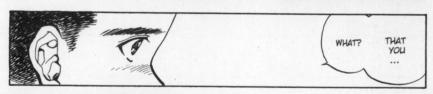

WHAT?

THAT YOU...

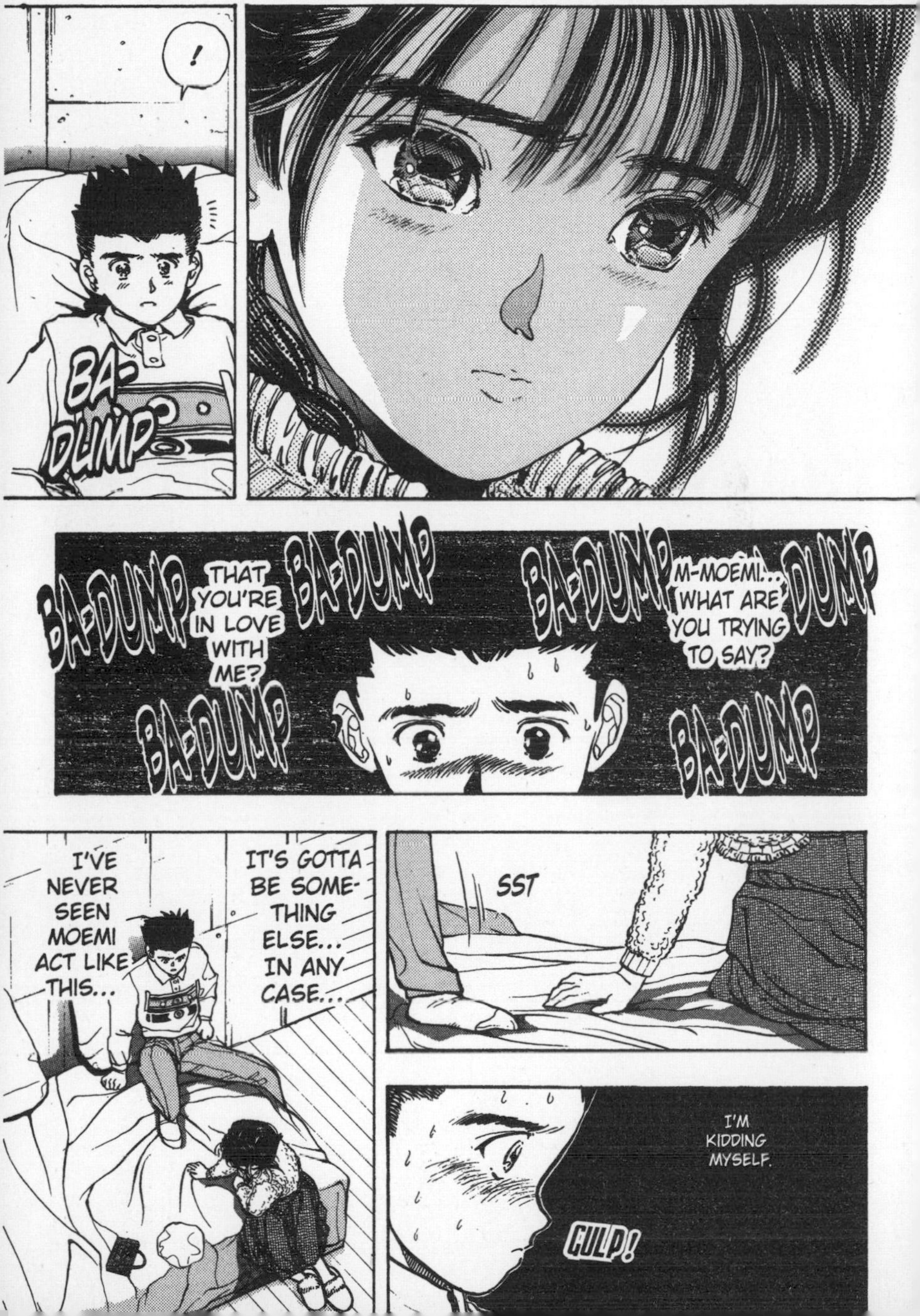
!
BA-DUMP
DUMP
BA-DUMP
M-MOEMI... WHAT ARE YOU TRYING TO SAY?
BA-DUMP
BA-DUMP
THAT YOU'RE IN LOVE WITH ME?
BA-DUMP
BA-DUMP
SST
I'M KIDDING MYSELF.
GULP!
IT'S GOTTA BE SOME-THING ELSE... IN ANY CASE...
I'VE NEVER SEEN MOEMI ACT LIKE THIS...

▲ ❚❚ ►► ► *CHAPTER FOURTEEN*
I Like You

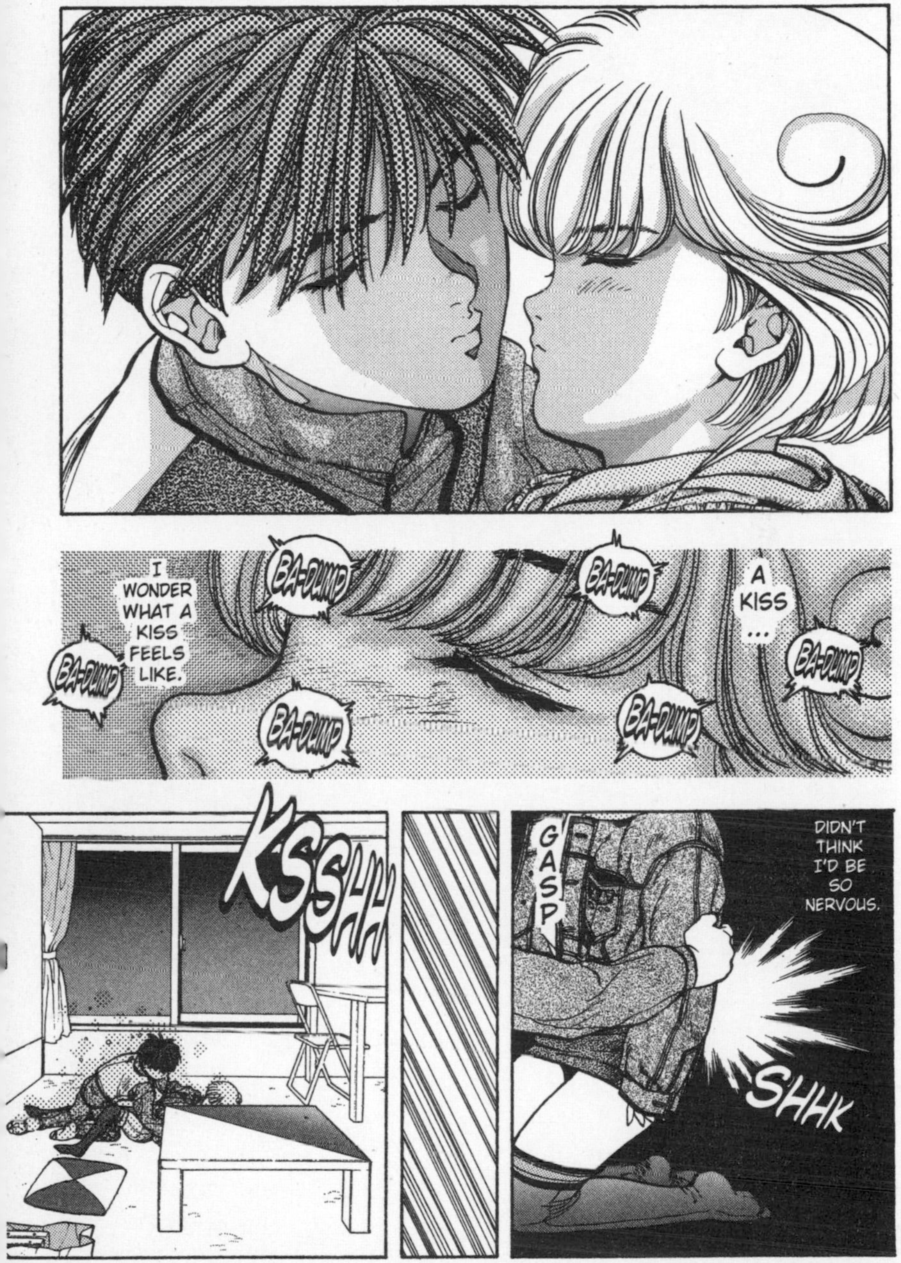
A KISS ...
BA-DUMP
BA-DUMP
BA-DUMP
BA-DUMP
BA-DUMP
I WONDER WHAT A KISS FEELS LIKE.
BA-DUMP
DIDN'T THINK I'D BE SO NERVOUS.
GASP
SHHK
KSSHH

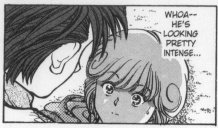

WHOA-- HE'S LOOKING PRETTY INTENSE...
HERE IT COMES! HERE IT COMES!
BUT... SHOULD I KISS HIM?
KRRL
ONLY PEOPLE IN LOVE KISS, RIGHT?
DOES HE REALLY LOVE ME?
HE MIGHT JUST BE LONELY... THAT'S NOT...
THAT'S *NOT* ENOUGH!

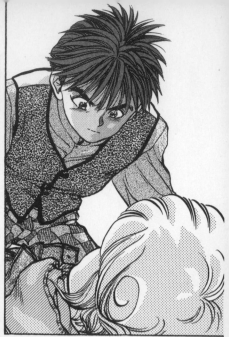

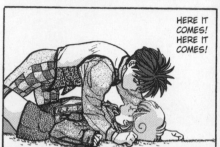

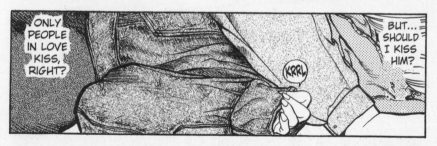

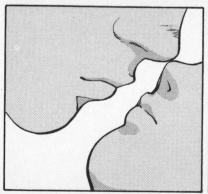

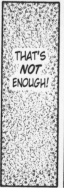

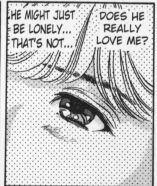

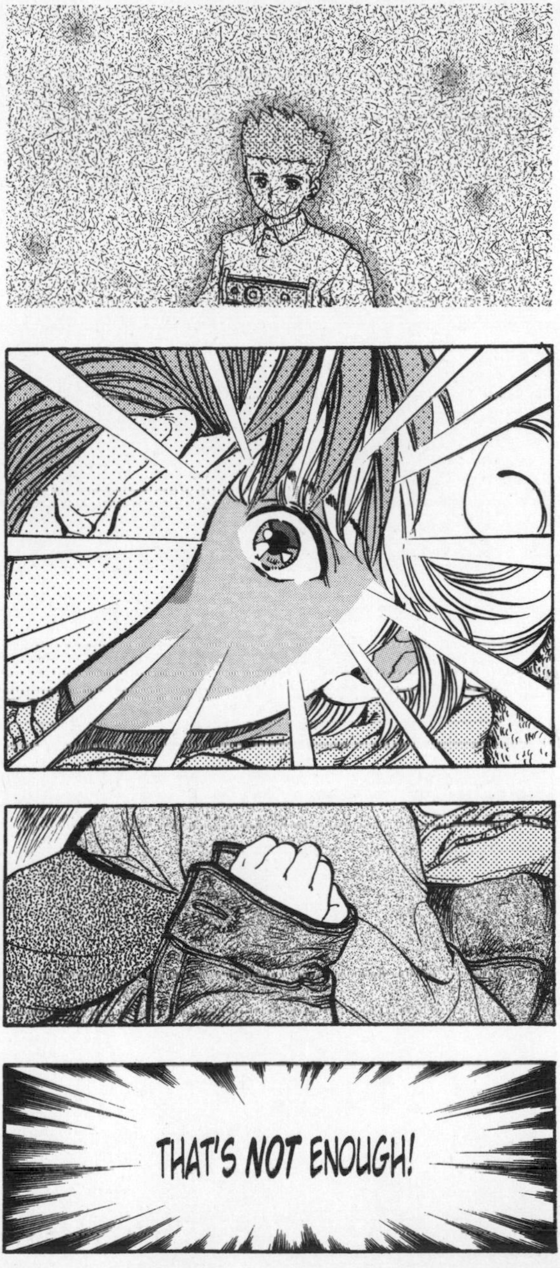
THAT'S NOT ENOUGH!
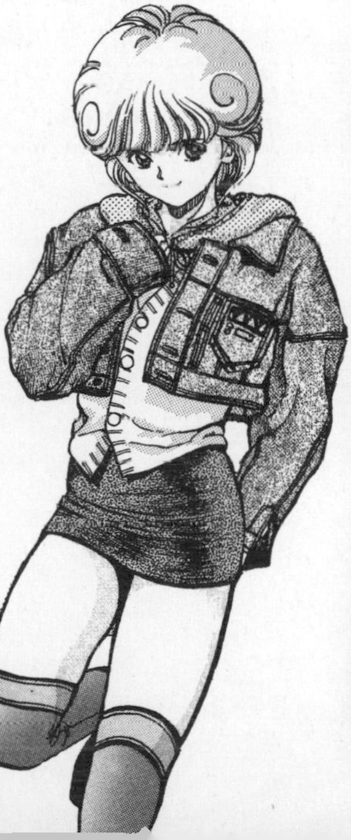

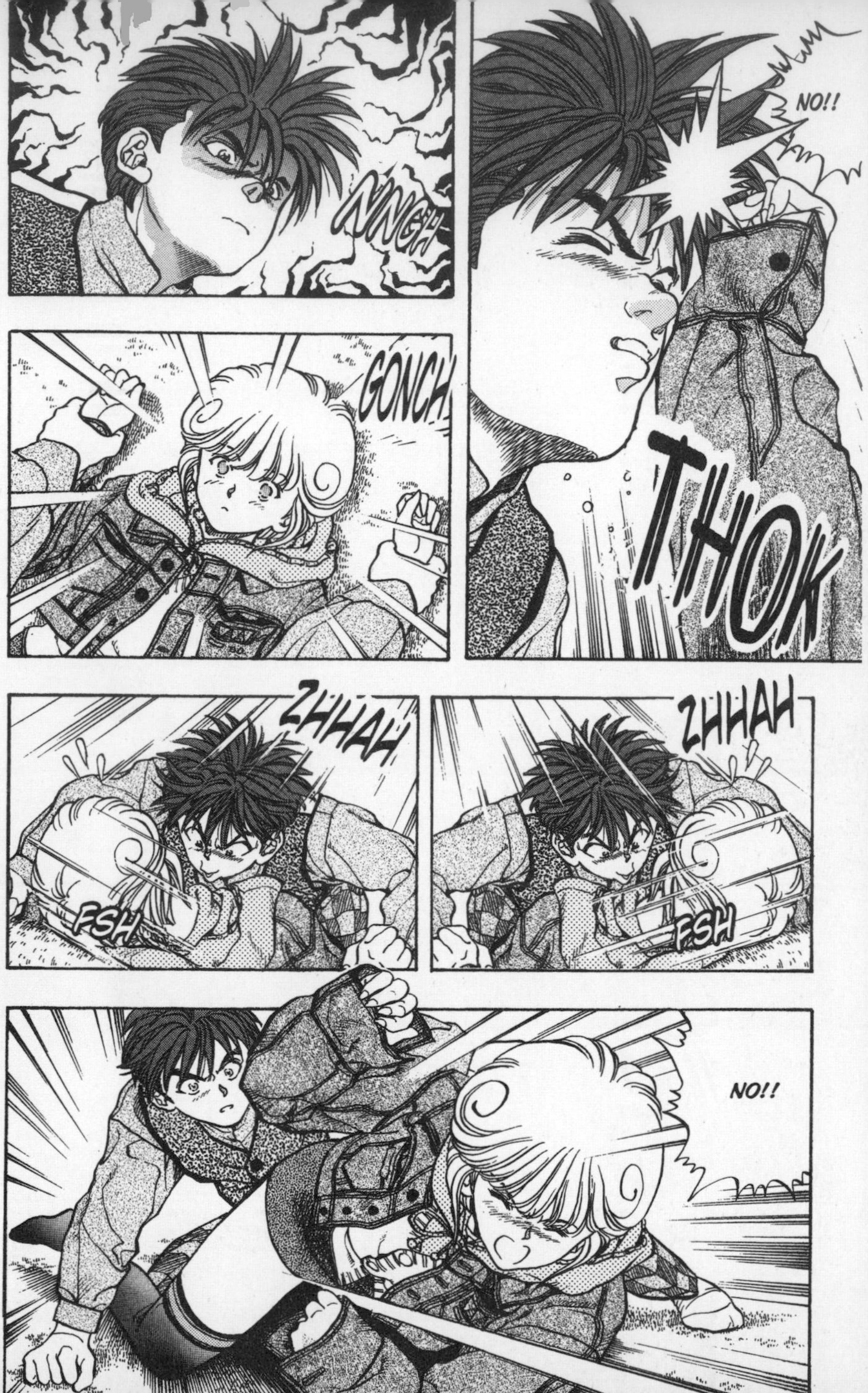
NO!!
THOK
NNGH
GONCH
ZHHAH
FSH
ZHHAH
FSH
NO!!

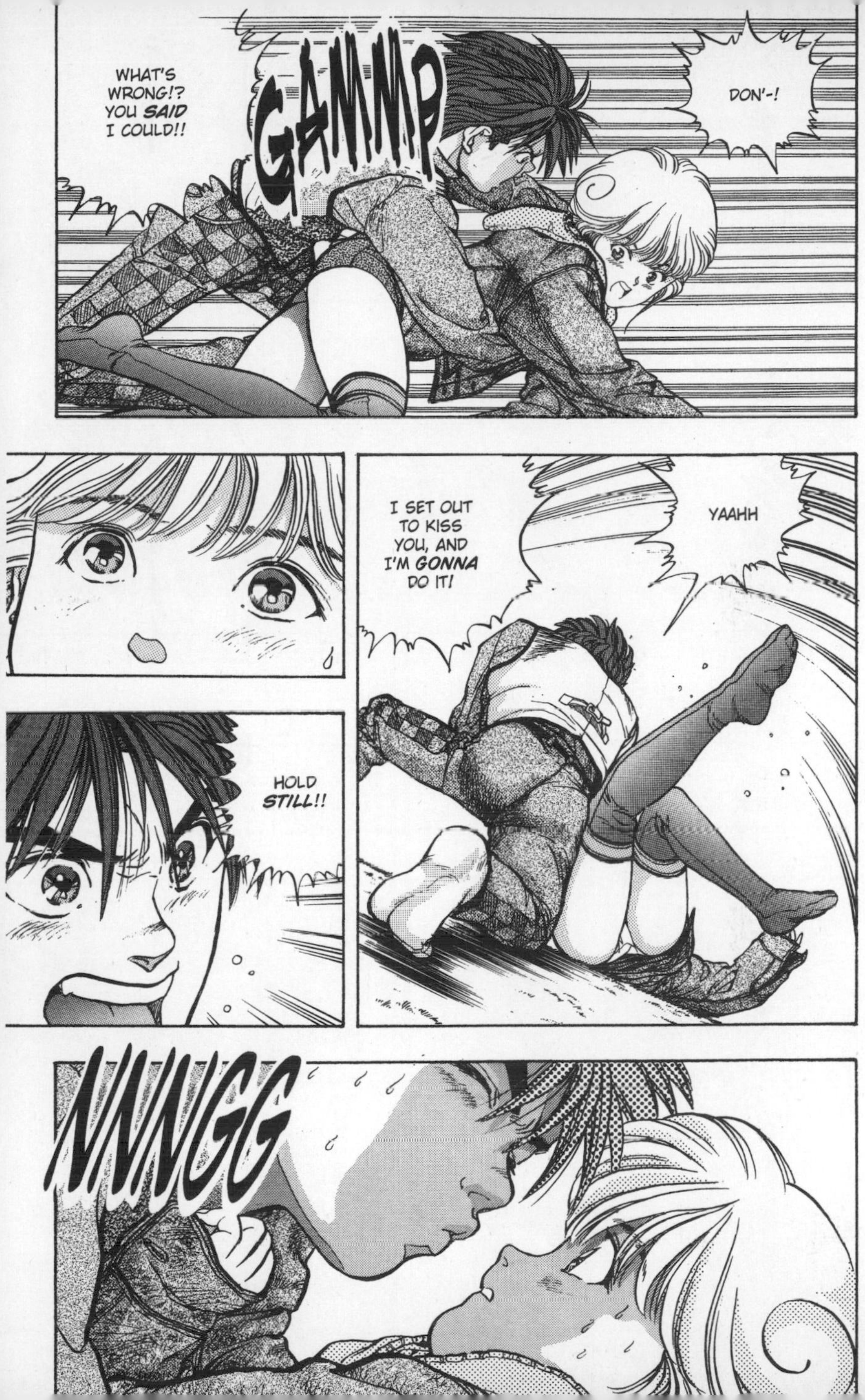
DON'-!
GAMMP
WHAT'S WRONG!? YOU *SAID* I COULD!!
YAAHH
I SET OUT TO KISS YOU, AND I'M *GONNA* DO IT!
HOLD *STILL*!!
NNNGG

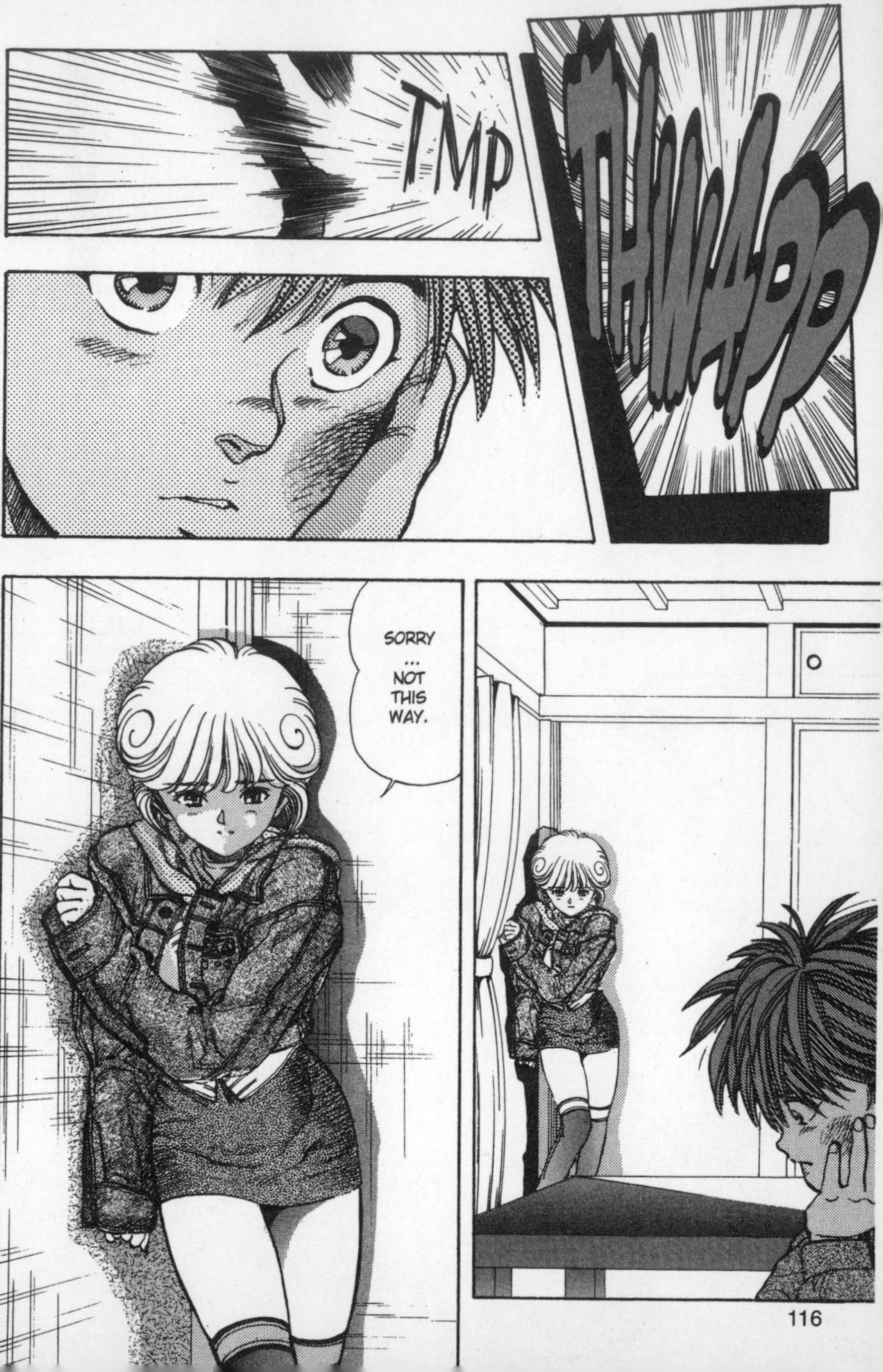
THWAPP
TMP
SORRY ... NOT THIS WAY.

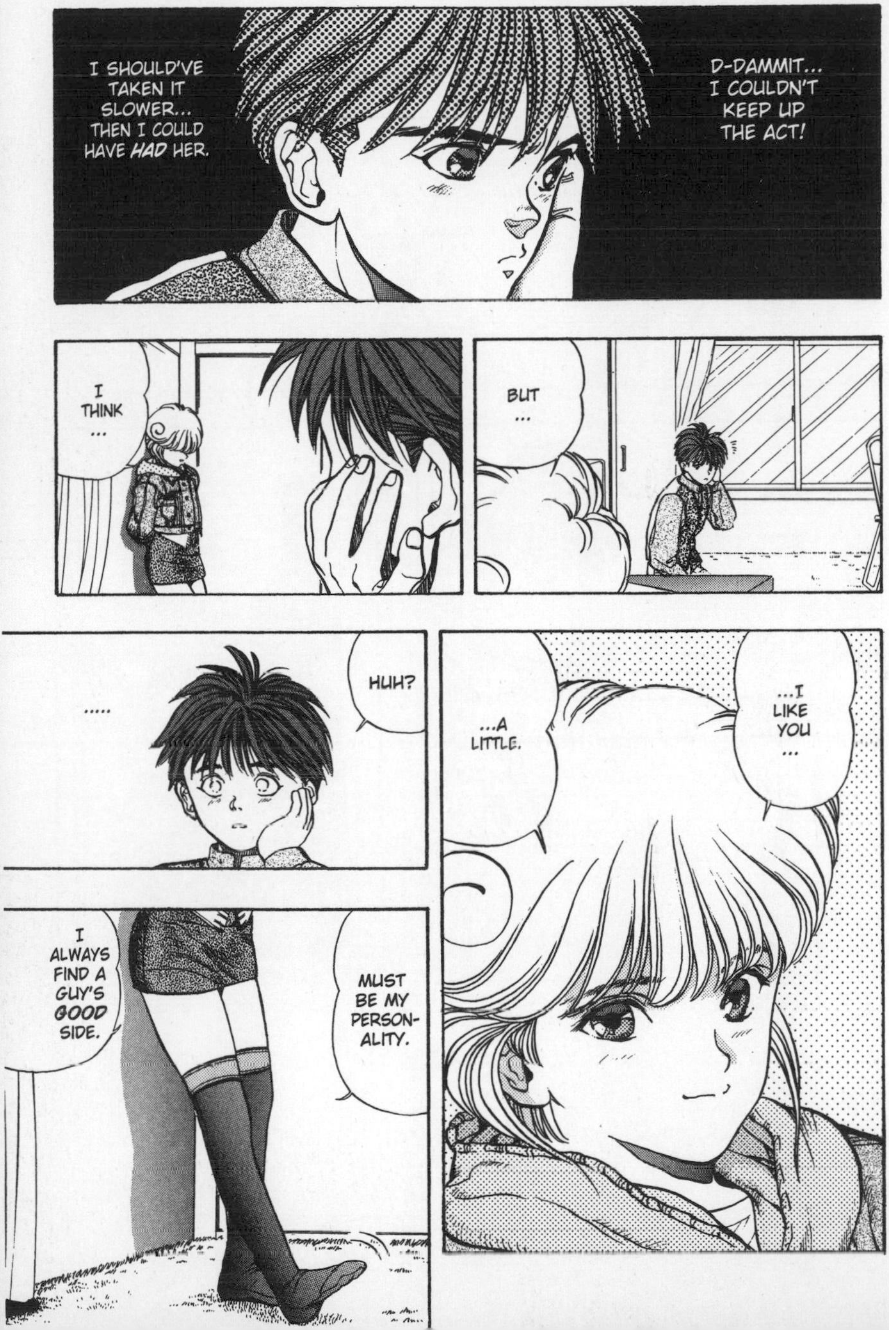
D-DAMMIT... I COULDN'T KEEP UP THE ACT!
I SHOULD'VE TAKEN IT SLOWER... THEN I COULD HAVE *HAD* HER.
BUT ...
I THINK ...
...I LIKE YOU ...
...A LITTLE.
HUH?
.....
MUST BE MY PERSON-ALITY.
I ALWAYS FIND A GUY'S **GOOD** SIDE.

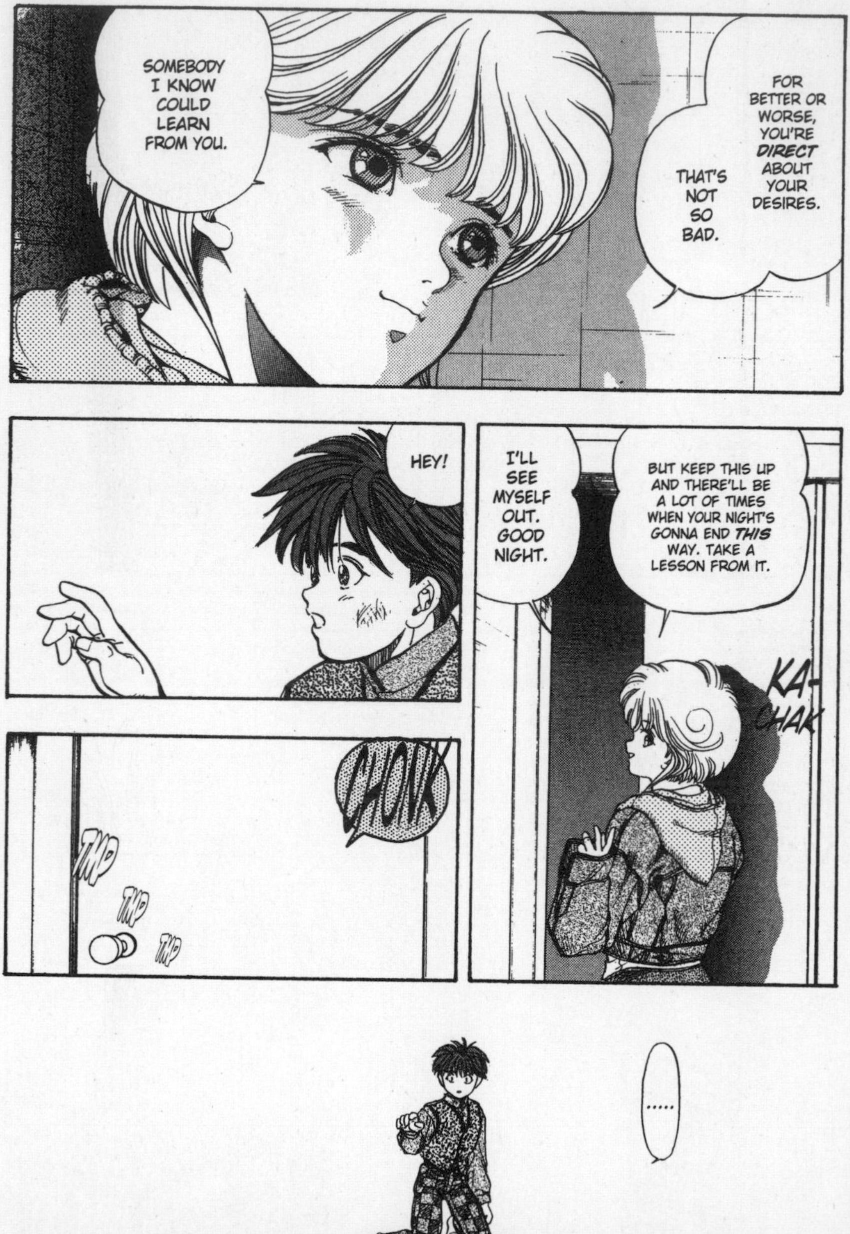
FOR BETTER OR WORSE, YOU'RE **DIRECT** ABOUT YOUR DESIRES.
THAT'S NOT SO BAD.
SOMEBODY I KNOW COULD LEARN FROM YOU.
BUT KEEP THIS UP AND THERE'LL BE A LOT OF TIMES WHEN YOUR NIGHT'S GONNA END ***THIS*** WAY. TAKE A LESSON FROM IT.
I'LL SEE MYSELF OUT. GOOD NIGHT.
KA-CHAK
HEY!
CHONK
TMP
TMP
TMP
.....

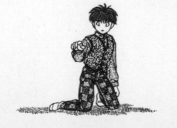

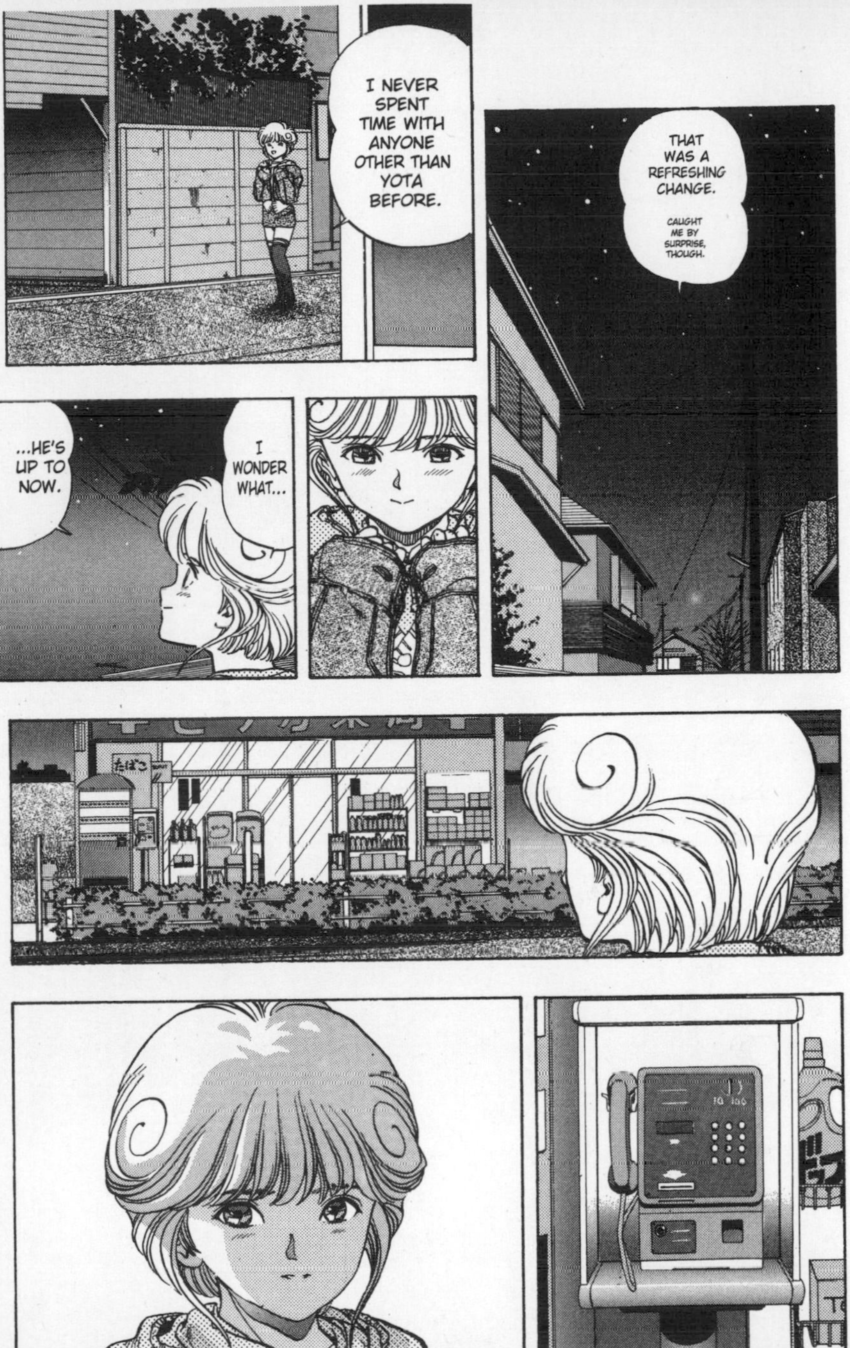
THAT WAS A REFRESHING CHANGE.
CAUGHT ME BY SURPRISE, THOUGH.
I NEVER SPENT TIME WITH ANYONE OTHER THAN YOTA BEFORE.
I WONDER WHAT...
...HE'S UP TO NOW.
たばこ

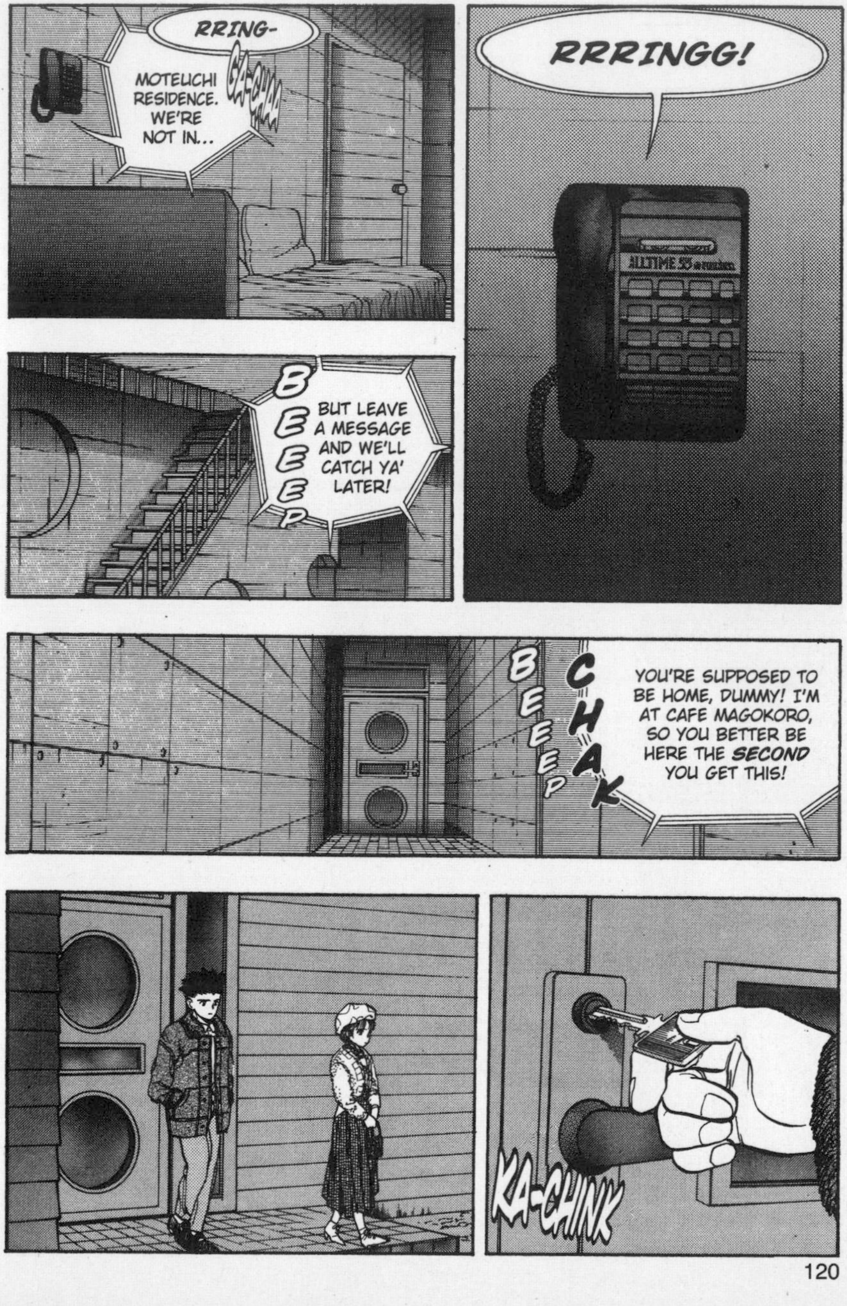
RRRINGG!
RRING-
MOTEUCHI RESIDENCE. WE'RE NOT IN...
BEEEEP
BUT LEAVE A MESSAGE AND WE'LL CATCH YA' LATER!
BEEEP
CHAK
YOU'RE SUPPOSED TO BE HOME, DUMMY! I'M AT CAFE MAGOKORO, SO YOU BETTER BE HERE THE ***SECOND*** YOU GET THIS!
KA-CHINK

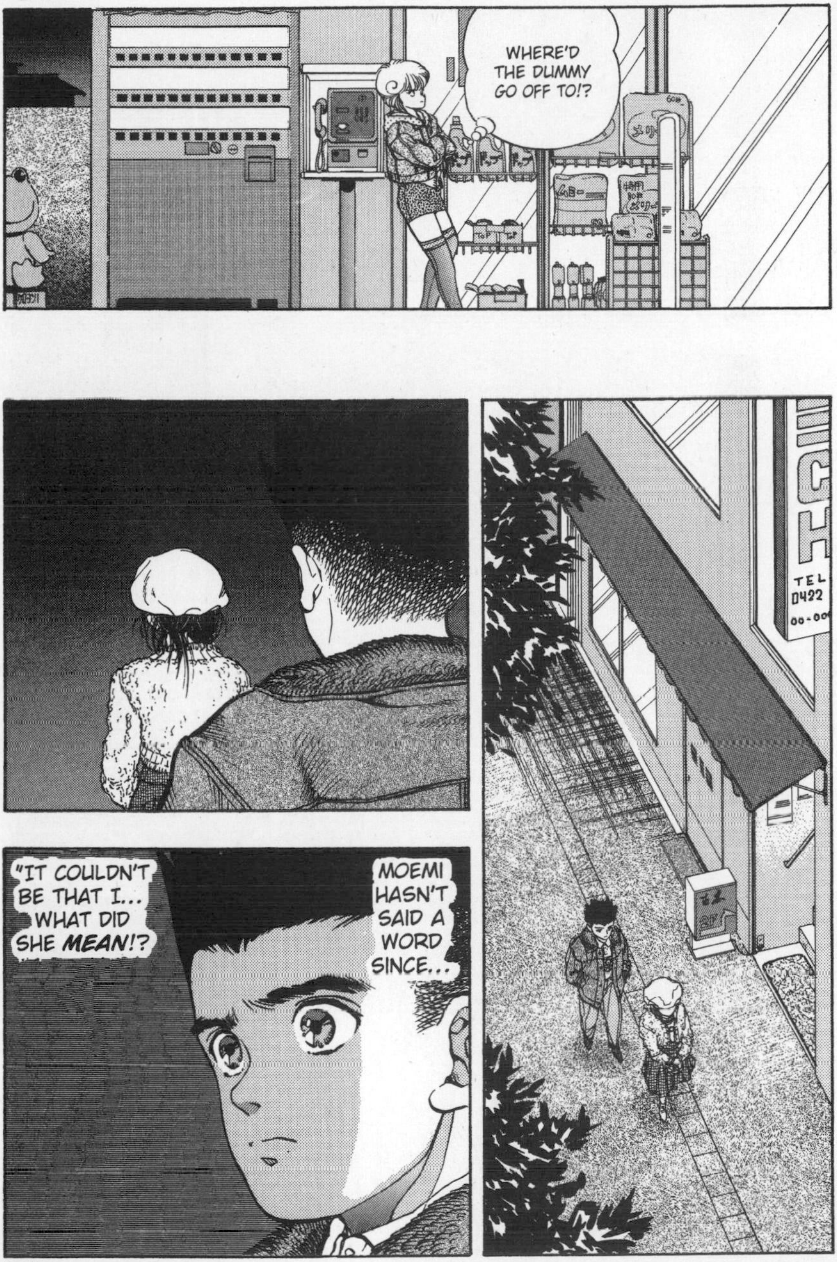
WHERE'D THE DUMMY GO OFF TO!?
TEL
0422
MOEMI HASN'T SAID A WORD SINCE...
"IT COULDN'T BE THAT I... WHAT DID SHE *MEAN*!?

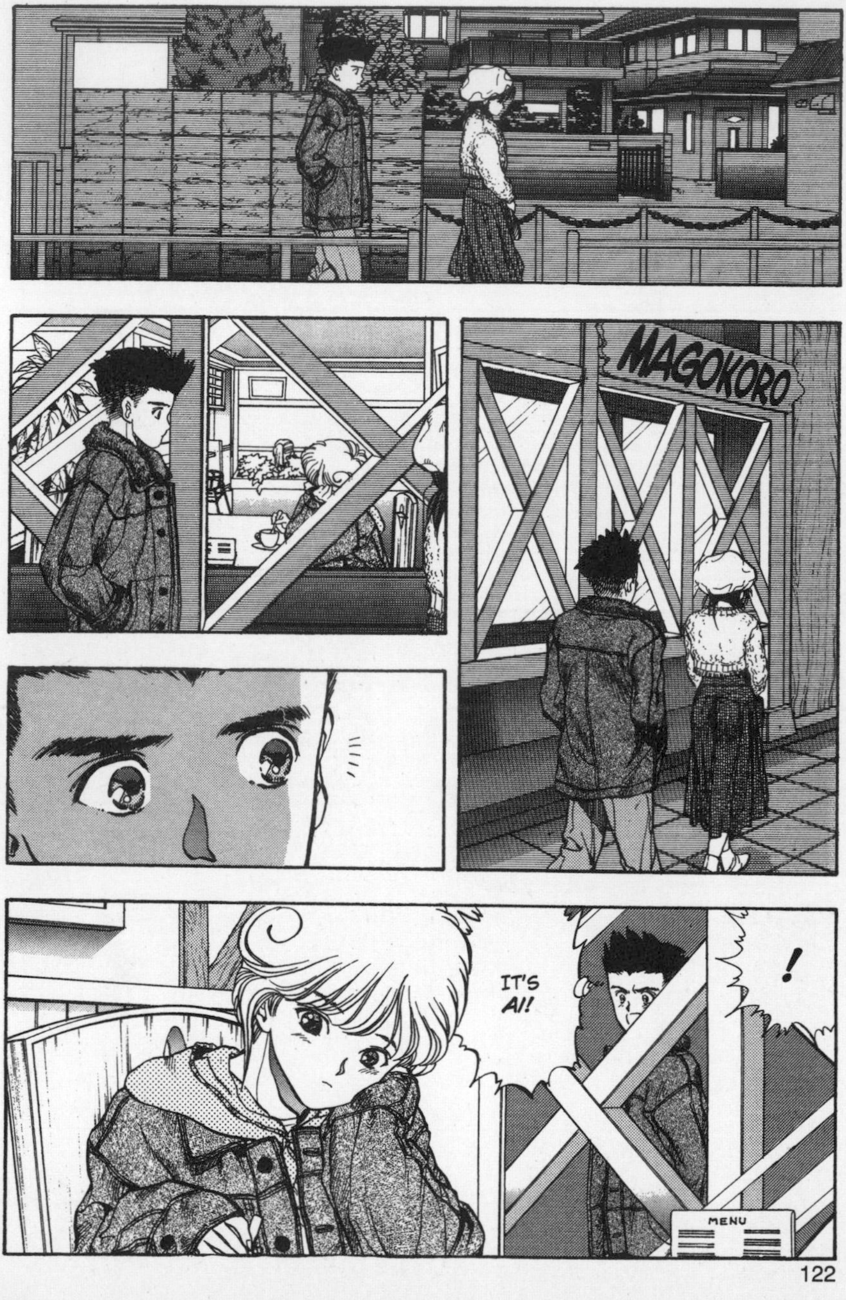
MAGOKORO
!
IT'S AI!
MENU

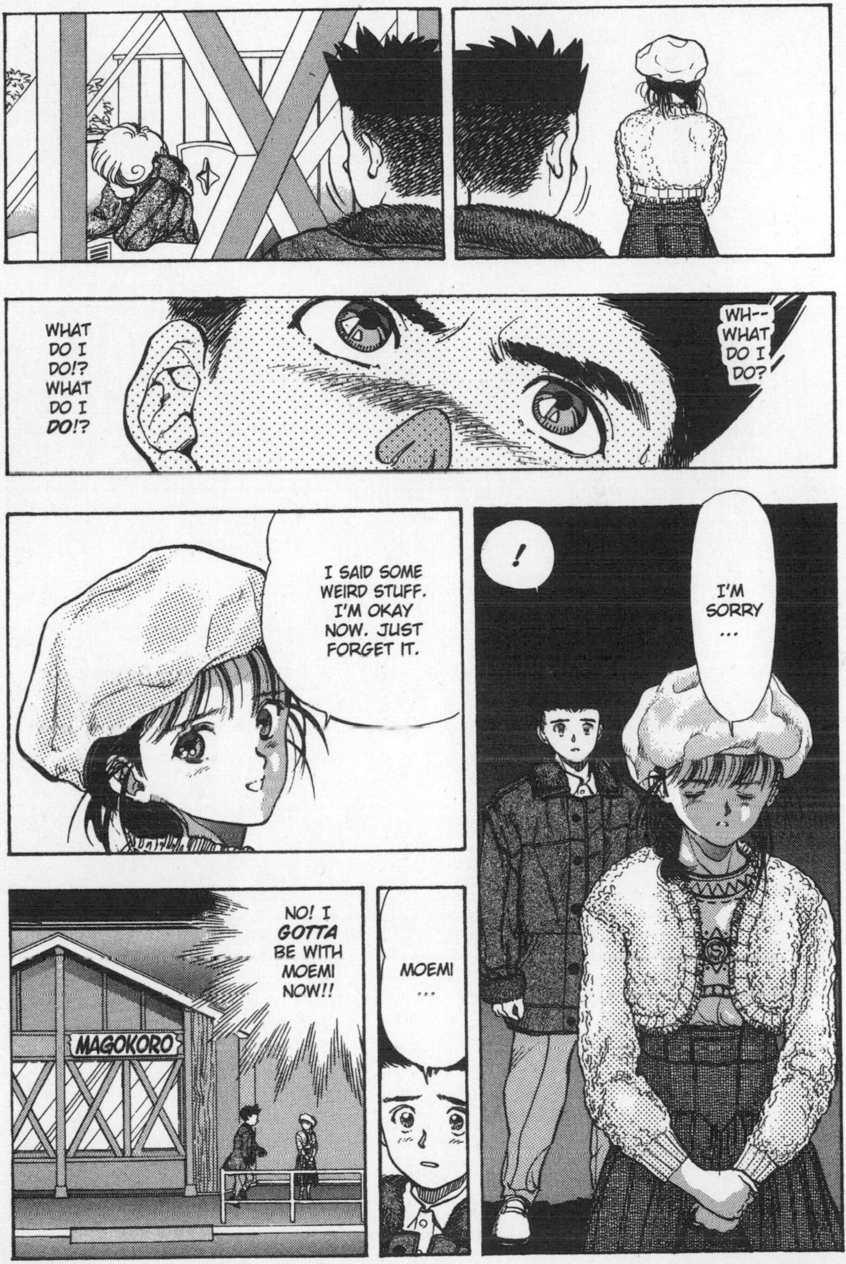
WH-- WHAT DO I DO?
WHAT DO I DO!? WHAT DO I DO!?
I'M SORRY ...
!
I SAID SOME WEIRD STUFF. I'M OKAY NOW. JUST FORGET IT.
MOEMI ...
NO! I GOTTA BE WITH MOEMI NOW!!
MAGOKORO

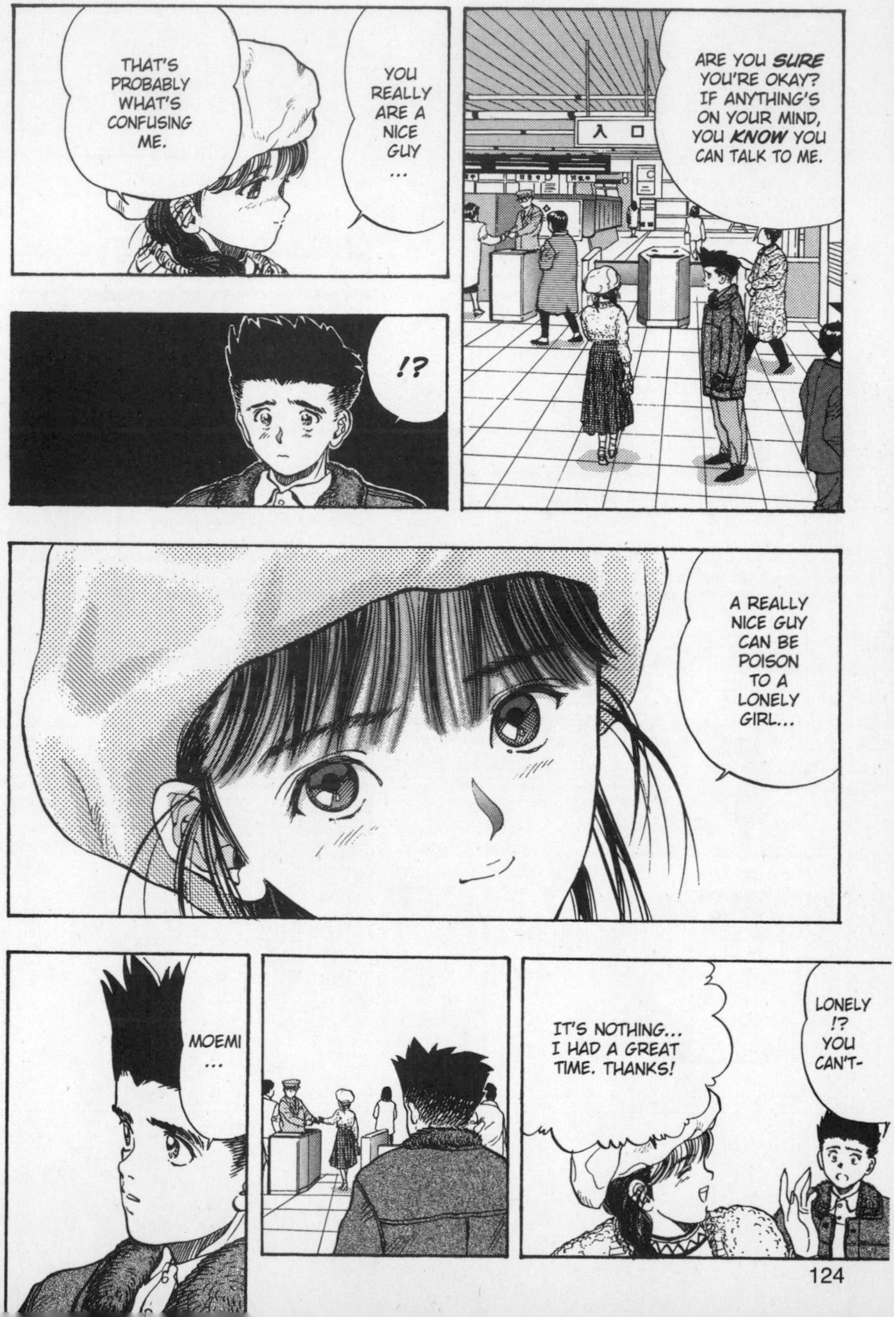
ARE YOU SURE YOU'RE OKAY? IF ANYTHING'S ON YOUR MIND, YOU KNOW YOU CAN TALK TO ME.
入口
YOU REALLY ARE A NICE GUY ...
THAT'S PROBABLY WHAT'S CONFUSING ME.
!?
A REALLY NICE GUY CAN BE POISON TO A LONELY GIRL...
LONELY !? YOU CAN'T-
IT'S NOTHING... I HAD A GREAT TIME. THANKS!
MOEMI ...

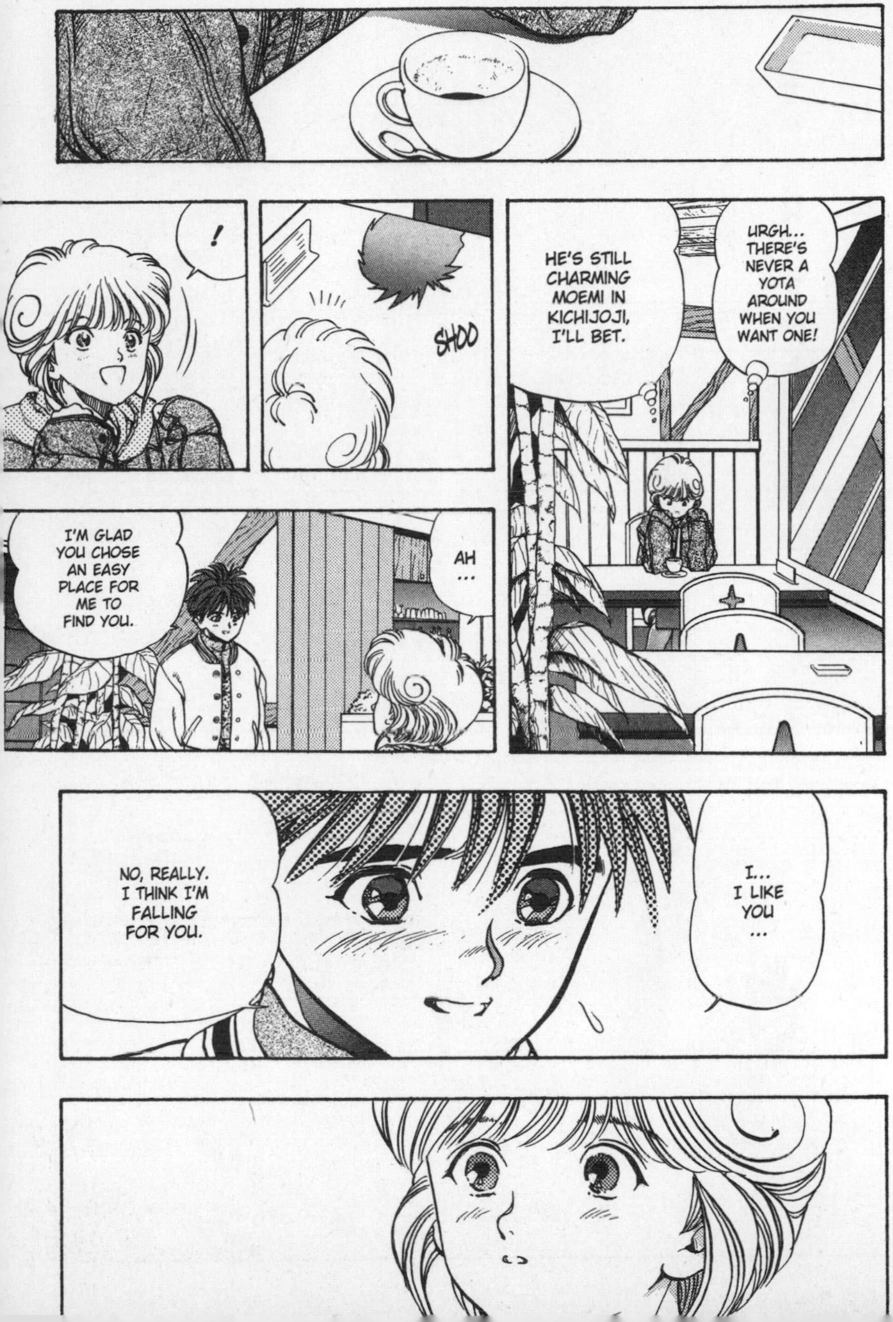
URGH... THERE'S NEVER A YOTA AROUND WHEN YOU WANT ONE!
HE'S STILL CHARMING MOEMI IN KICHIJOJI, I'LL BET.
SHOO
!
AH ...
I'M GLAD YOU CHOSE AN EASY PLACE FOR ME TO FIND YOU.
I... I LIKE YOU ...
NO, REALLY. I THINK I'M FALLING FOR YOU.

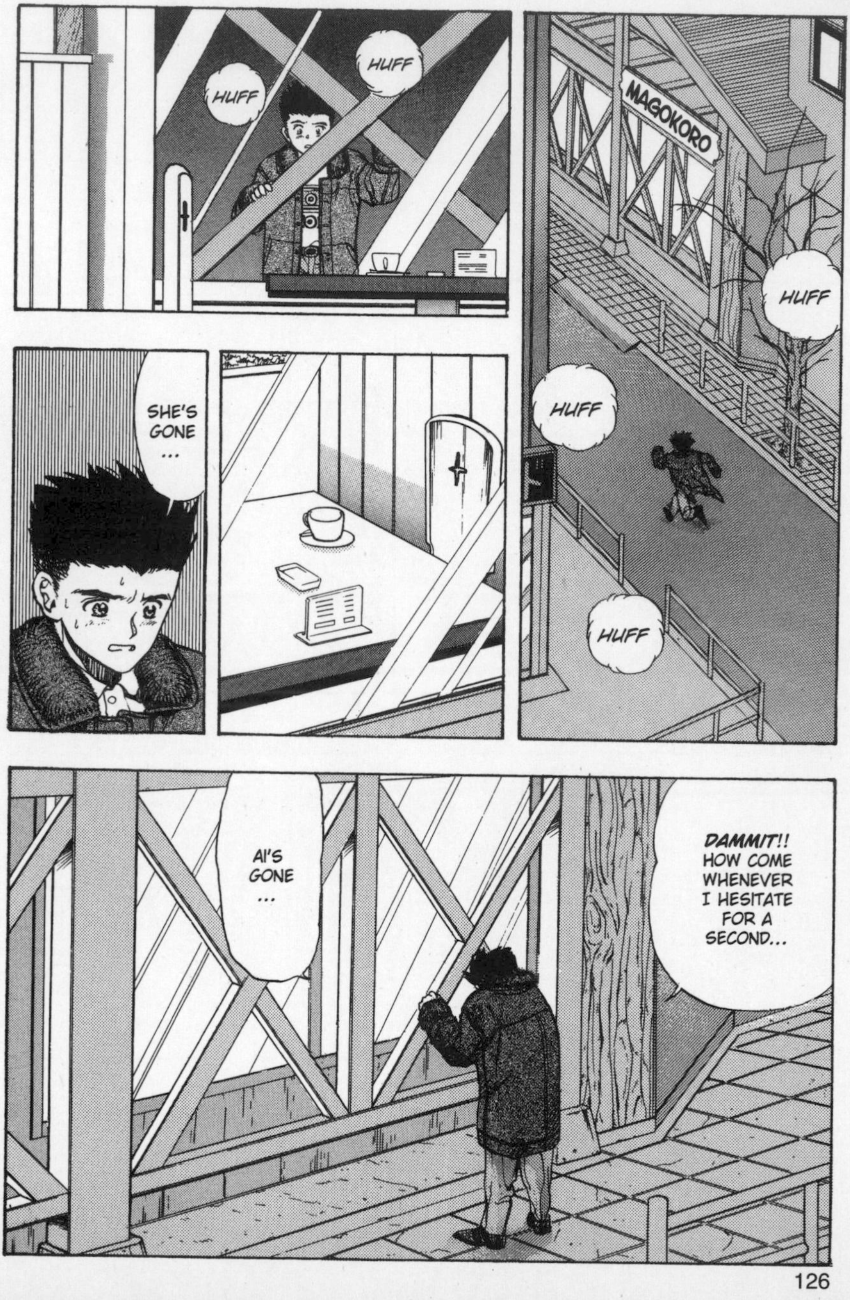
MAGOKORO
HUFF
HUFF
HUFF
HUFF
HUFF
SHE'S GONE ...
DAMMIT!! HOW COME WHENEVER I HESITATE FOR A SECOND...
AI'S GONE ...

⏏ ⏸ ⏩ ▶ *CHAPTER FIFTEEN*
Heartache

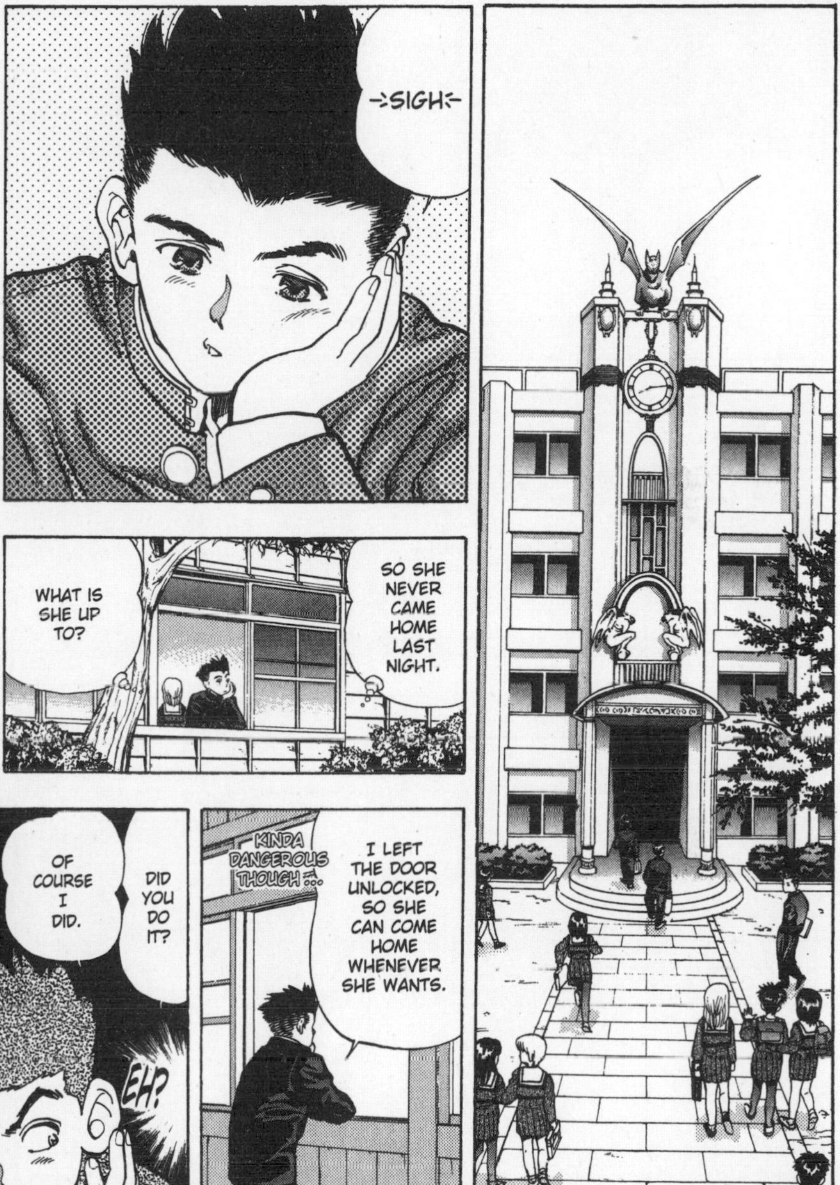
-SIGH-
SO SHE NEVER CAME HOME LAST NIGHT.
WHAT IS SHE UP TO?
I LEFT THE DOOR UNLOCKED, SO SHE CAN COME HOME WHENEVER SHE WANTS.
KINDA DANGEROUS THOUGH...
DID YOU DO IT?
OF COURSE I DID.
EH?

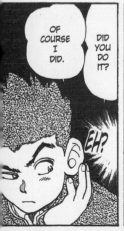

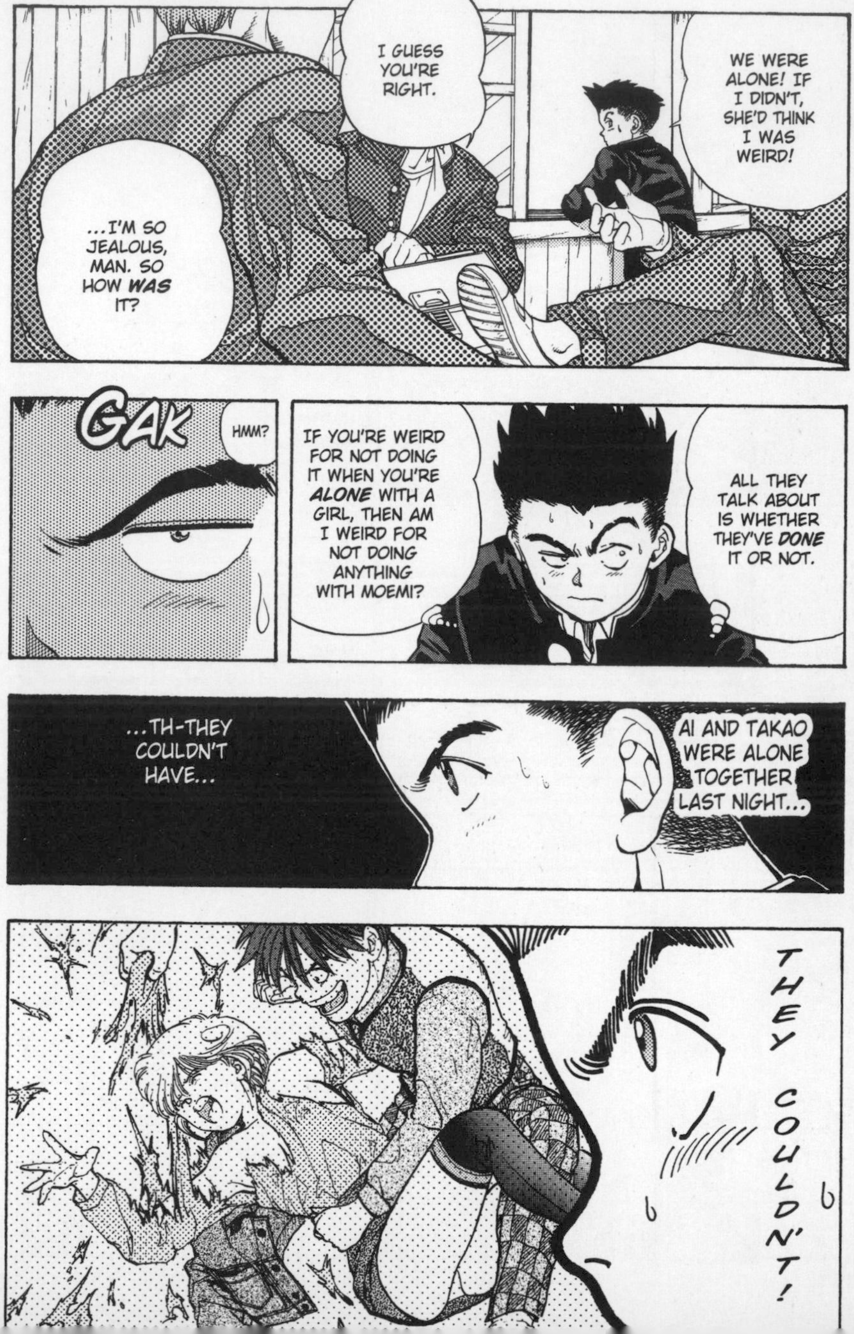
WE WERE ALONE! IF I DIDN'T, SHE'D THINK I WAS WEIRD!
I GUESS YOU'RE RIGHT.
...I'M SO JEALOUS, MAN. SO HOW WAS IT?
ALL THEY TALK ABOUT IS WHETHER THEY'VE DONE IT OR NOT.
IF YOU'RE WEIRD FOR NOT DOING IT WHEN YOU'RE ALONE WITH A GIRL, THEN AM I WEIRD FOR NOT DOING ANYTHING WITH MOEMI?
HMM?
GAK
AI AND TAKAO WERE ALONE TOGETHER LAST NIGHT...
...TH-THEY COULDN'T HAVE...
THEY COULDN'T!

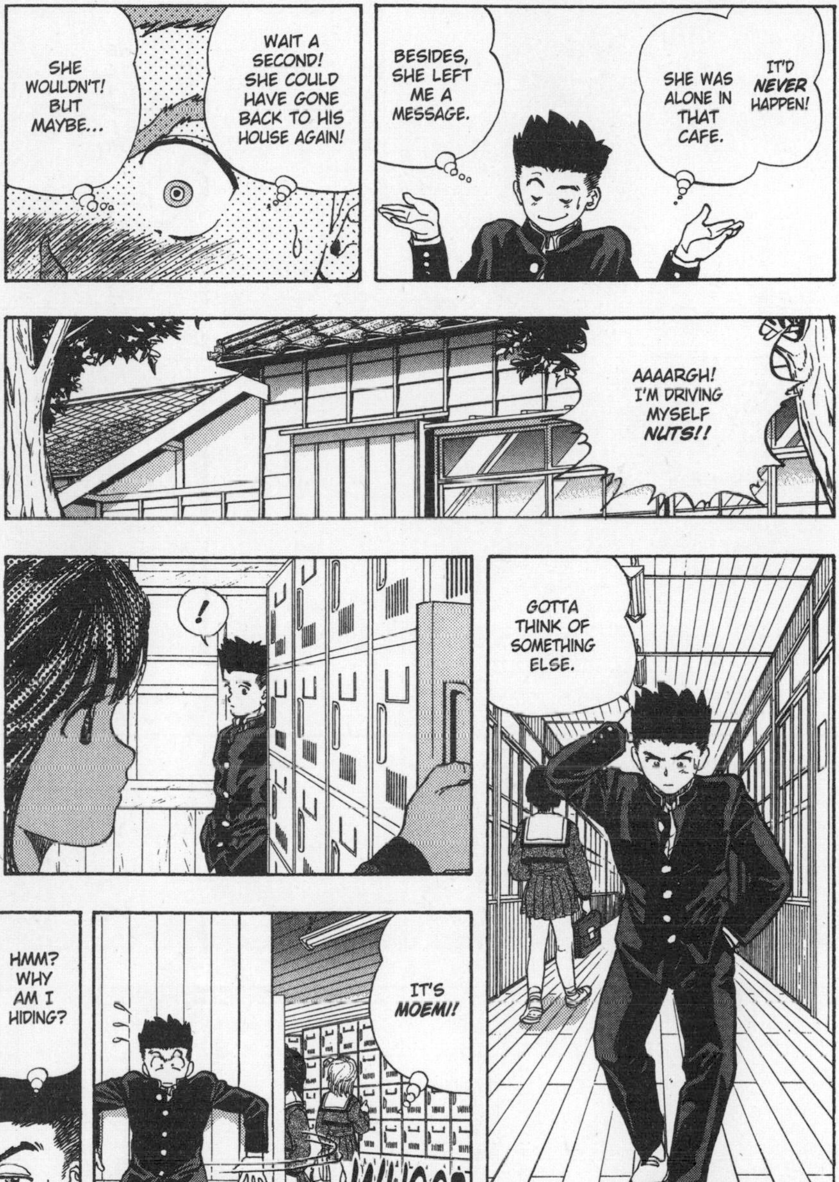
IT'D NEVER HAPPEN!
SHE WAS ALONE IN THAT CAFE.
BESIDES, SHE LEFT ME A MESSAGE.
WAIT A SECOND! SHE COULD HAVE GONE BACK TO HIS HOUSE AGAIN!
SHE WOULDN'T! BUT MAYBE...
AAAARGH! I'M DRIVING MYSELF NUTS!!
GOTTA THINK OF SOMETHING ELSE.
!
IT'S MOEMI!
WHOOP
HMM? WHY AM I HIDING?

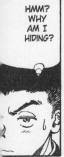

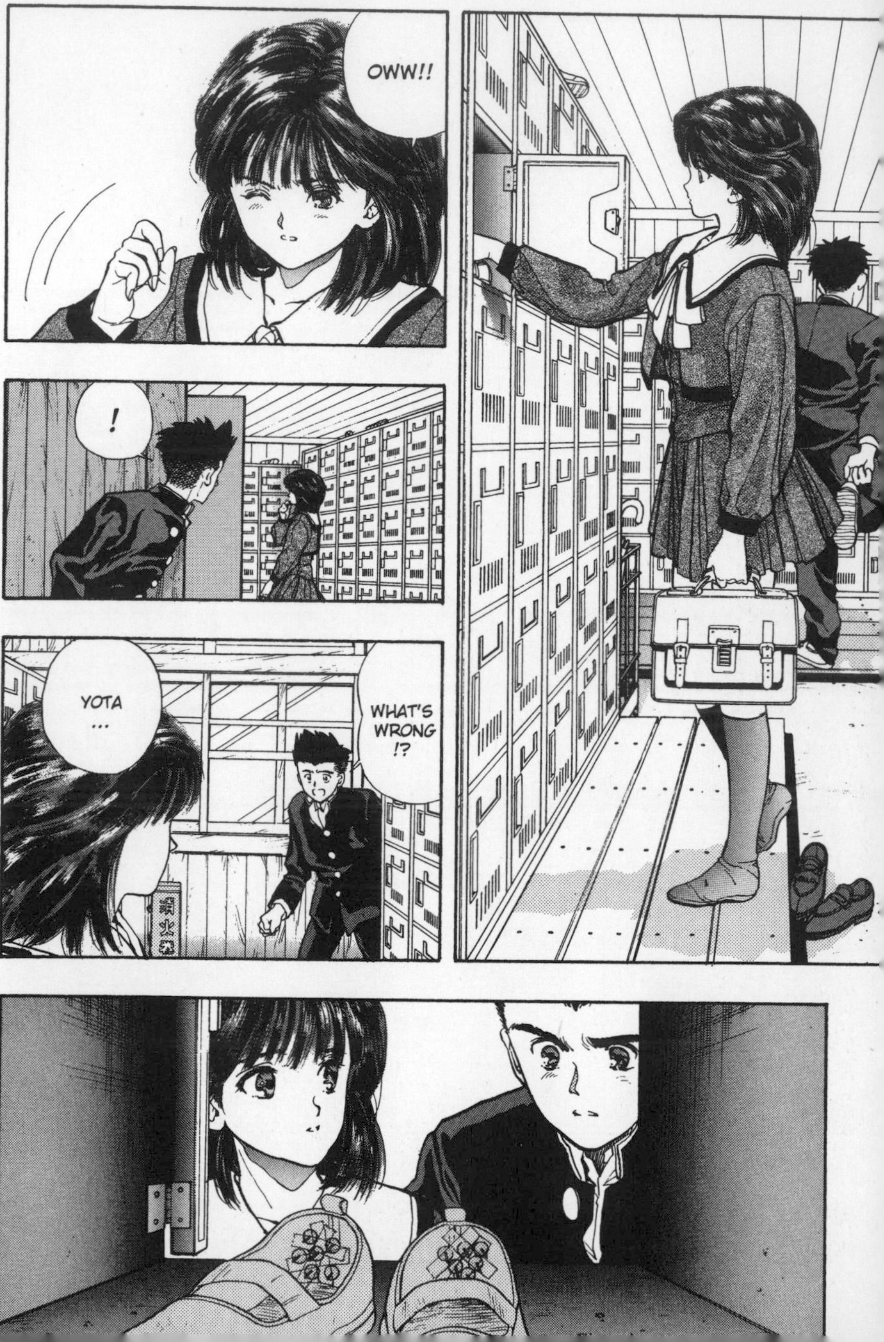
OWW!!
!
WHAT'S WRONG !?
YOTA ...

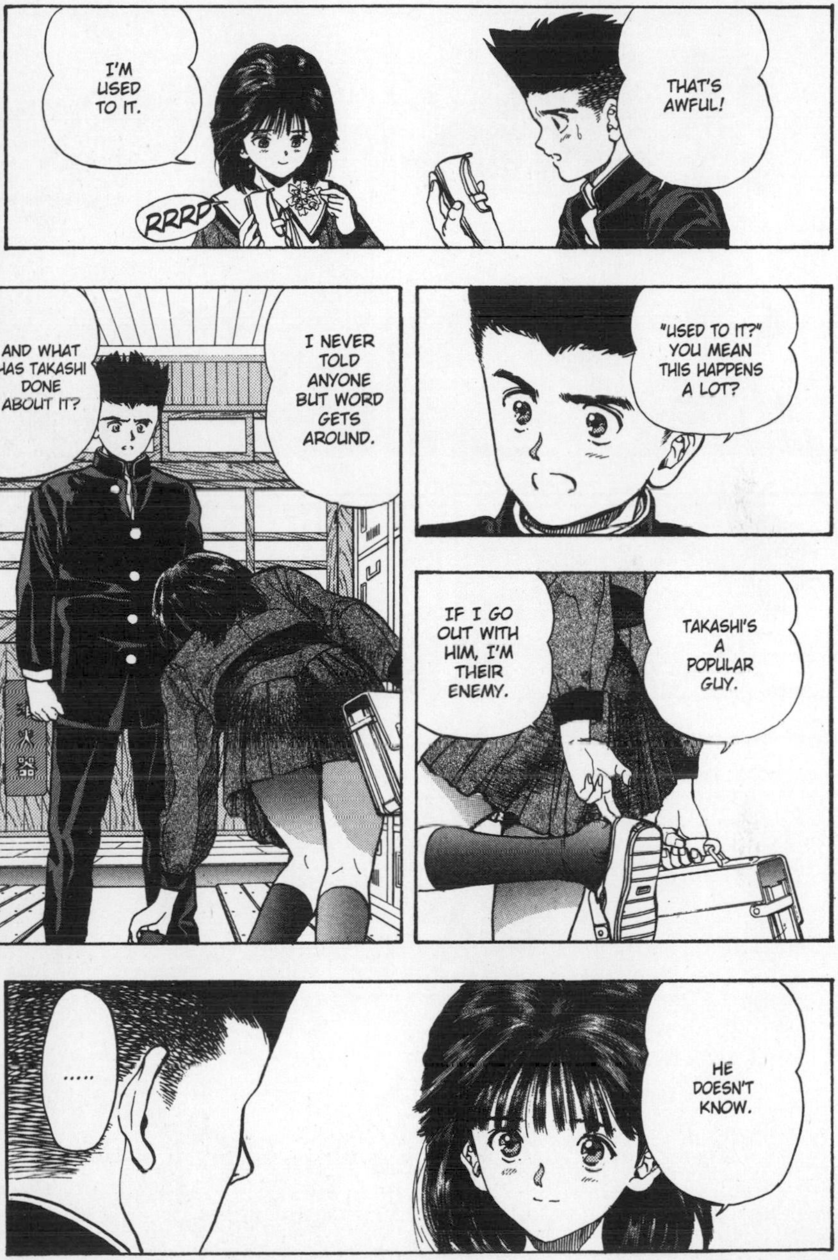
THAT'S AWFUL!
I'M USED TO IT.
RRRP
"USED TO IT?" YOU MEAN THIS HAPPENS A LOT?
TAKASHI'S A POPULAR GUY.
IF I GO OUT WITH HIM, I'M THEIR ENEMY.
I NEVER TOLD ANYONE BUT WORD GETS AROUND.
AND WHAT HAS TAKASHI DONE ABOUT IT?
HE DOESN'T KNOW.
.....

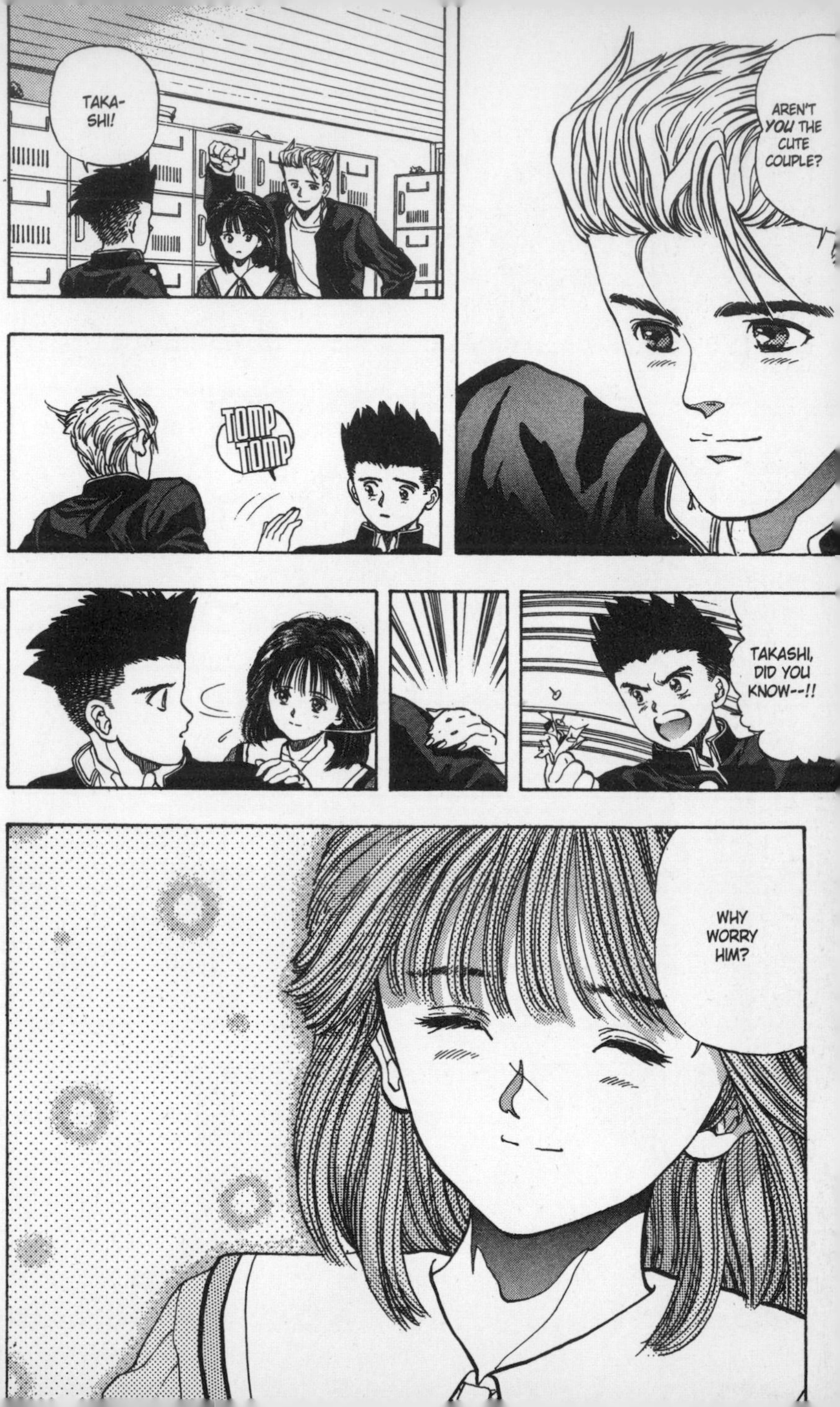
AREN'T YOU THE CUTE COUPLE?
TAKA-SHI!
TOMP TOMP
TAKASHI, DID YOU KNOW--!!
WHY WORRY HIM?

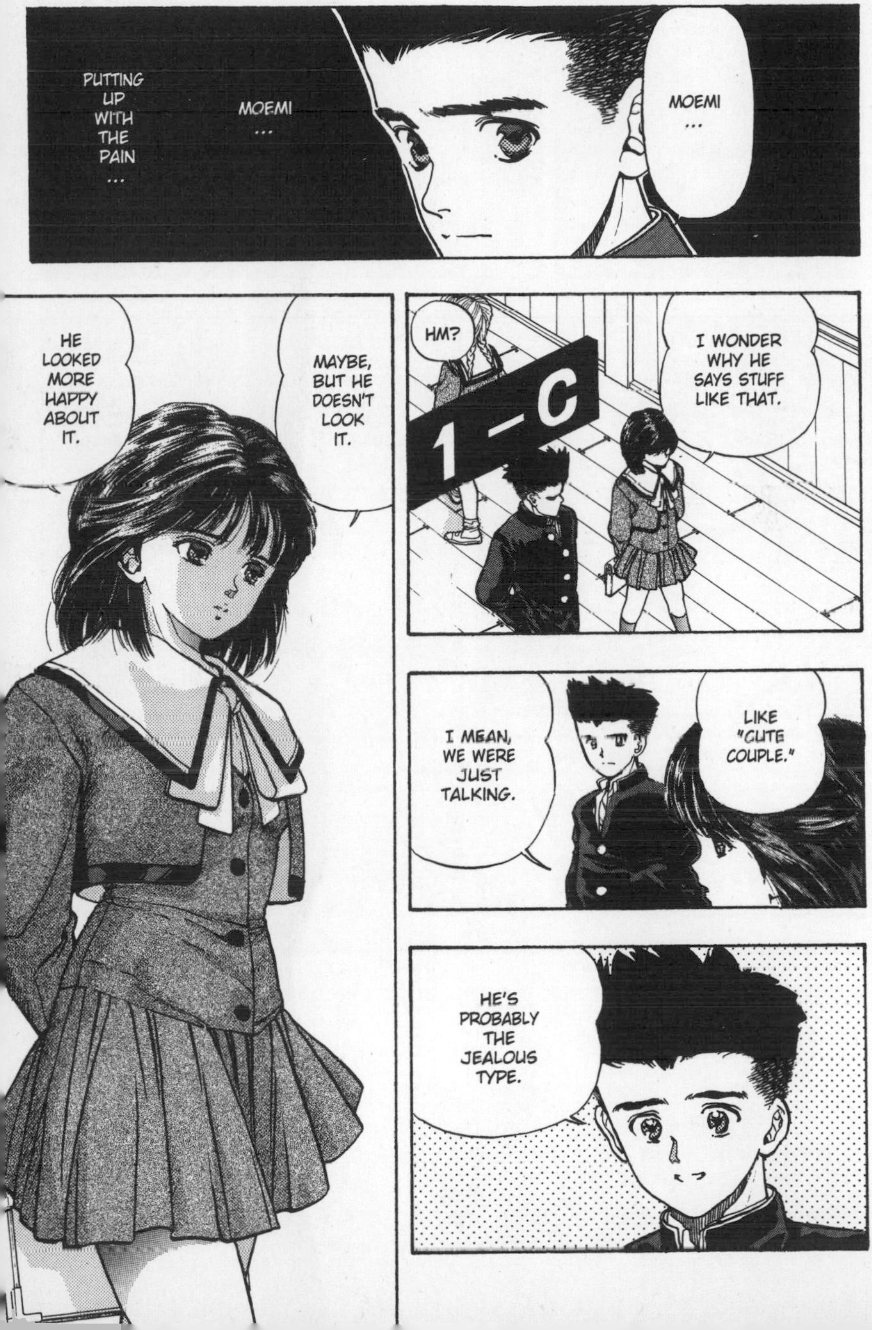
MOEMI ...
MOEMI ...
PUTTING UP WITH THE PAIN ...
I WONDER WHY HE SAYS STUFF LIKE THAT.
HM?
1-C
LIKE "CUTE COUPLE."
I MEAN, WE WERE JUST TALKING.
HE'S PROBABLY THE JEALOUS TYPE.
MAYBE, BUT HE DOESN'T LOOK IT.
HE LOOKED MORE HAPPY ABOUT IT.

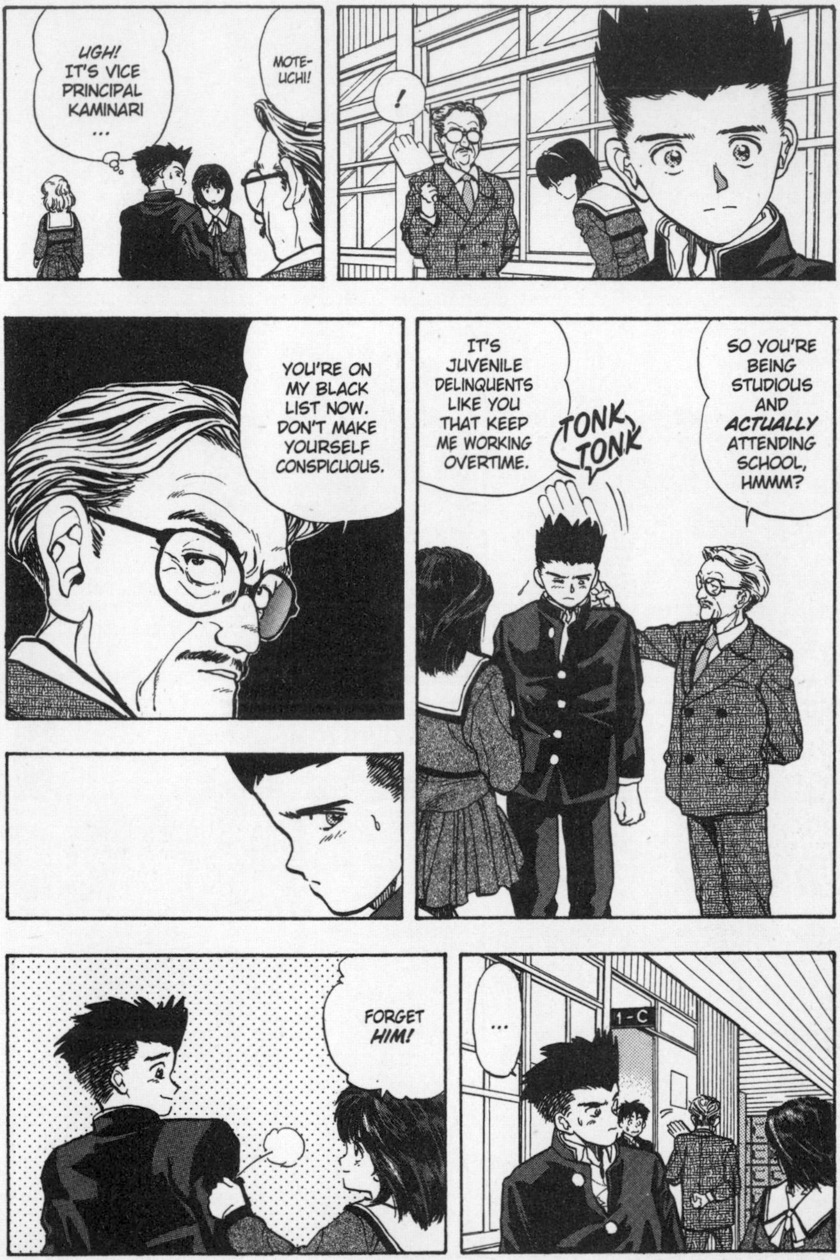
!
MOTE-UCHI!
UGH! IT'S VICE PRINCIPAL KAMINARI ...
SO YOU'RE BEING STUDIOUS AND ACTUALLY ATTENDING SCHOOL, HMMM?
TONK TONK
IT'S JUVENILE DELINQUENTS LIKE YOU THAT KEEP ME WORKING OVERTIME.
YOU'RE ON MY BLACK LIST NOW. DON'T MAKE YOURSELF CONSPICUOUS.
...
FORGET HIM!

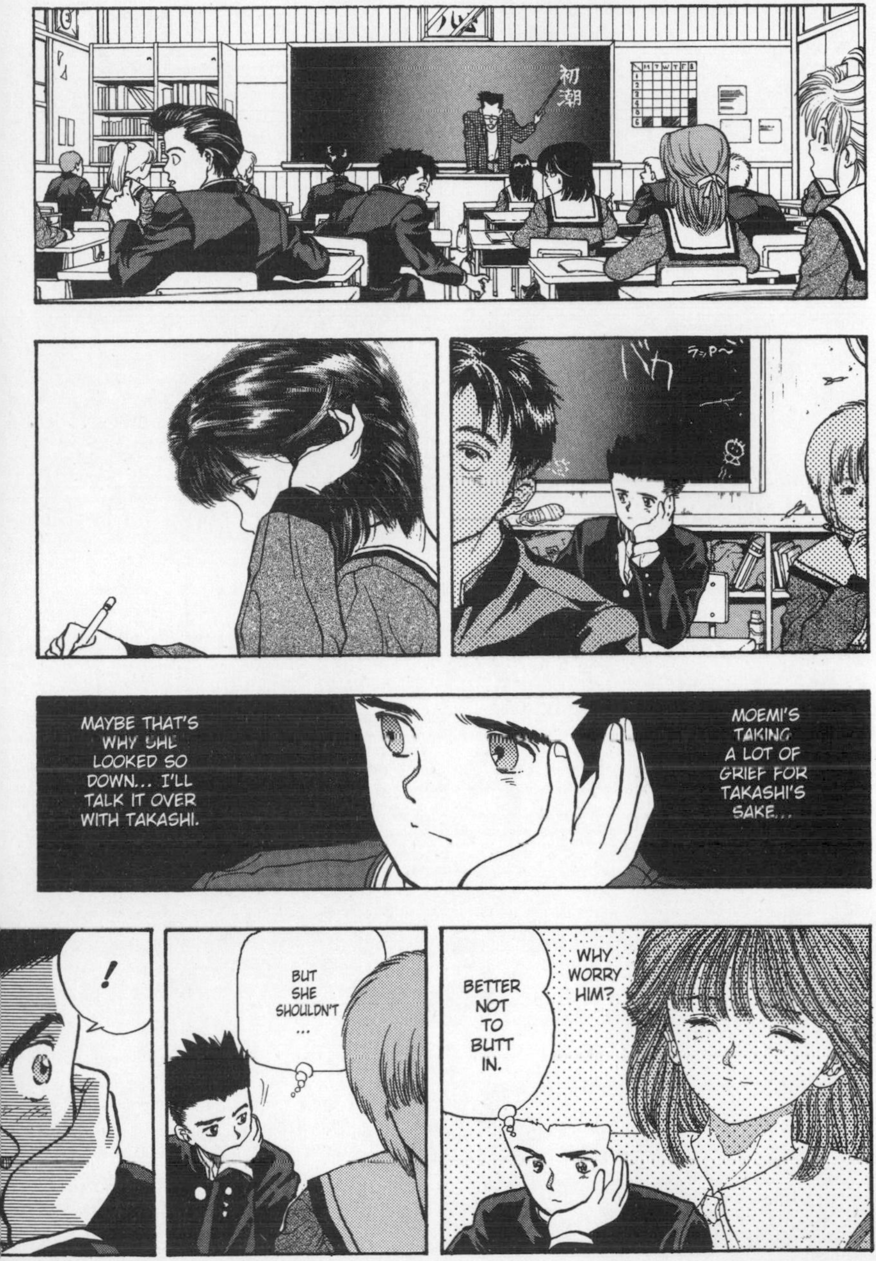
初潮
バカ
MOEMI'S TAKING A LOT OF GRIEF FOR TAKASHI'S SAKE...
MAYBE THAT'S WHY SHE LOOKED SO DOWN... I'LL TALK IT OVER WITH TAKASHI.
WHY WORRY HIM?
BETTER NOT TO BUTT IN.
BUT SHE SHOULDN'T ...
!

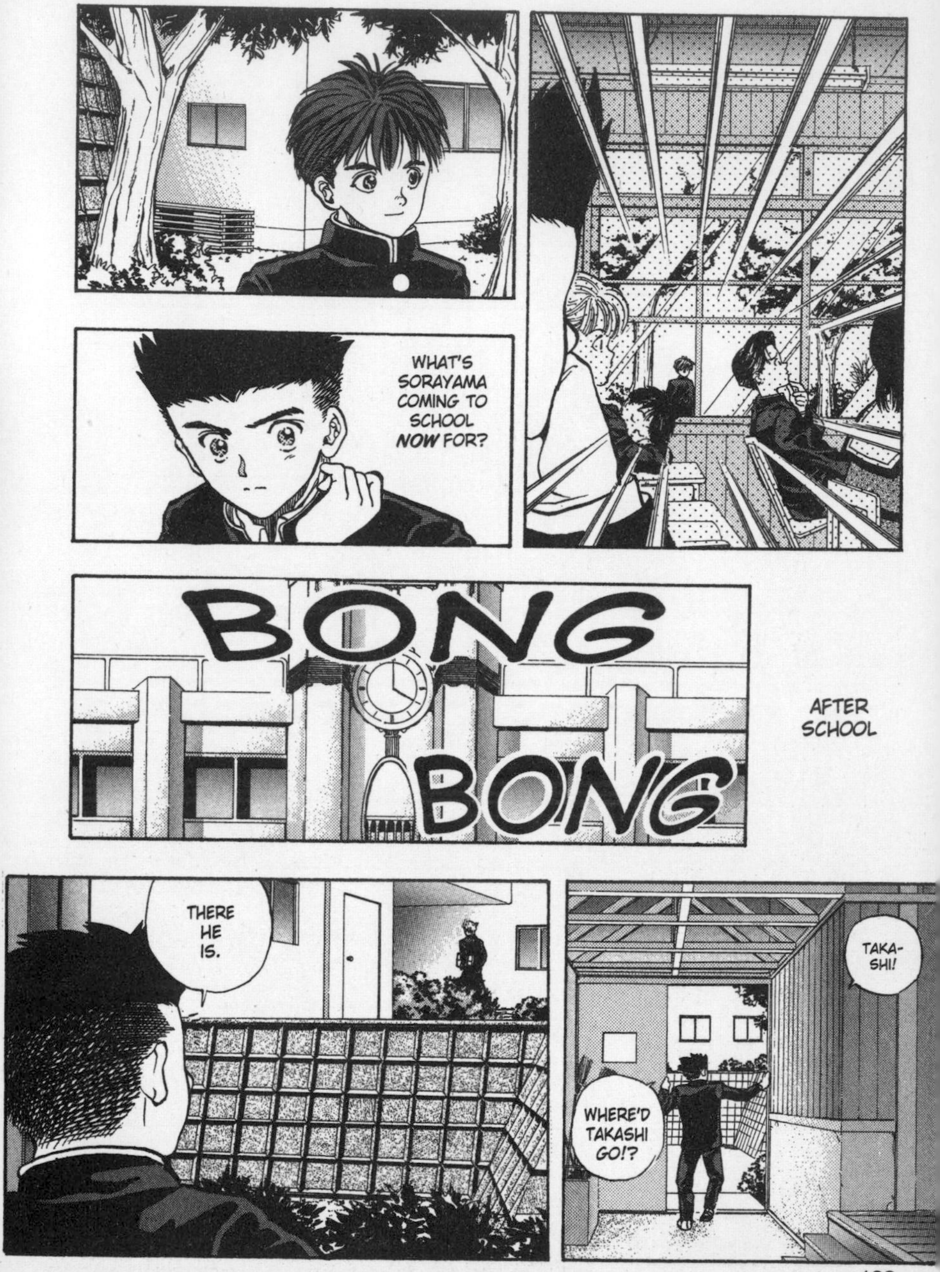
WHAT'S SORAYAMA COMING TO SCHOOL *NOW* FOR?
AFTER SCHOOL
BONG
BONG
TAKA-SHI!
WHERE'D TAKASHI GO!?
THERE HE IS.

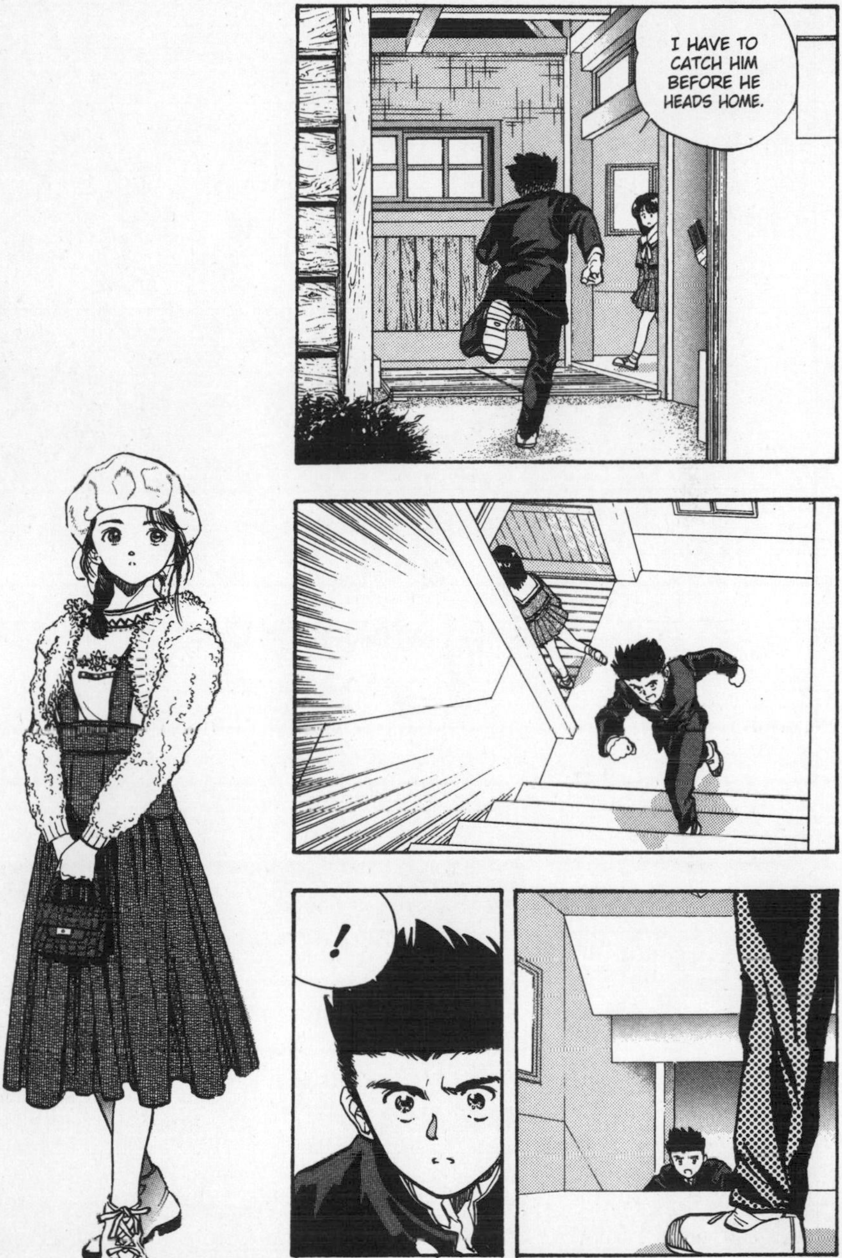
I HAVE TO CATCH HIM BEFORE HE HEADS HOME.
!

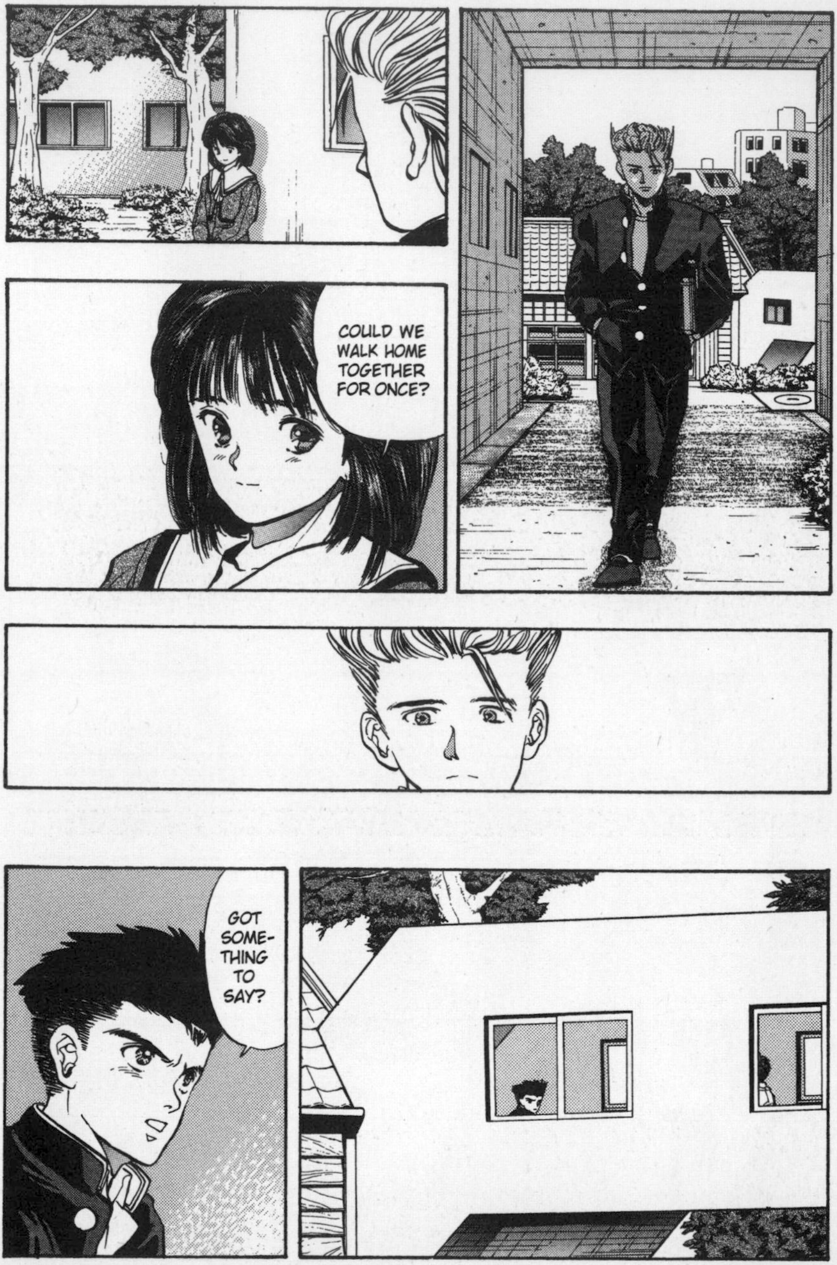
COULD WE WALK HOME TOGETHER FOR ONCE?
GOT SOME-THING TO SAY?

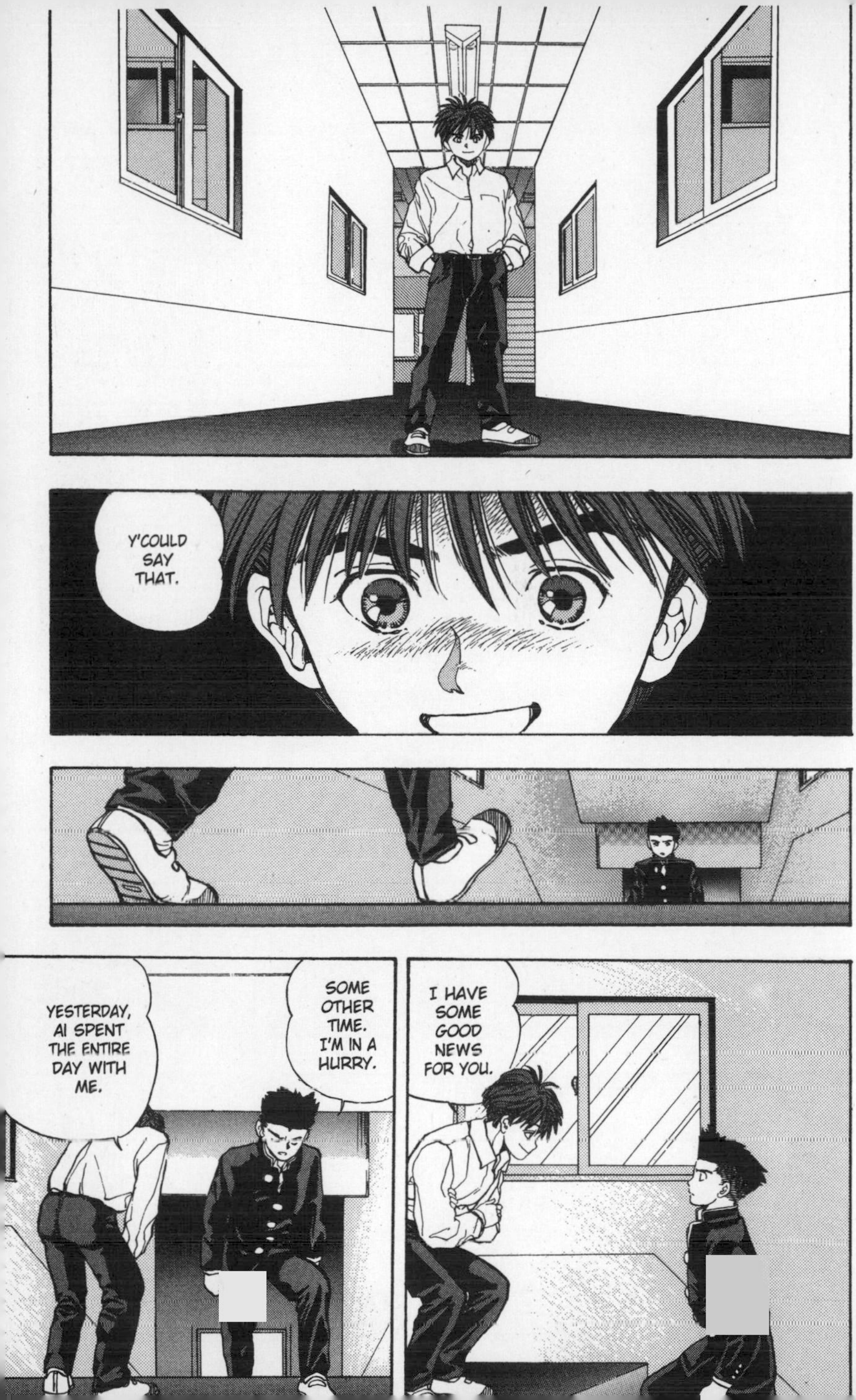
Y'COULD SAY THAT.
I HAVE SOME GOOD NEWS FOR YOU.
SOME OTHER TIME. I'M IN A HURRY.
YESTERDAY, AI SPENT THE ENTIRE DAY WITH ME.

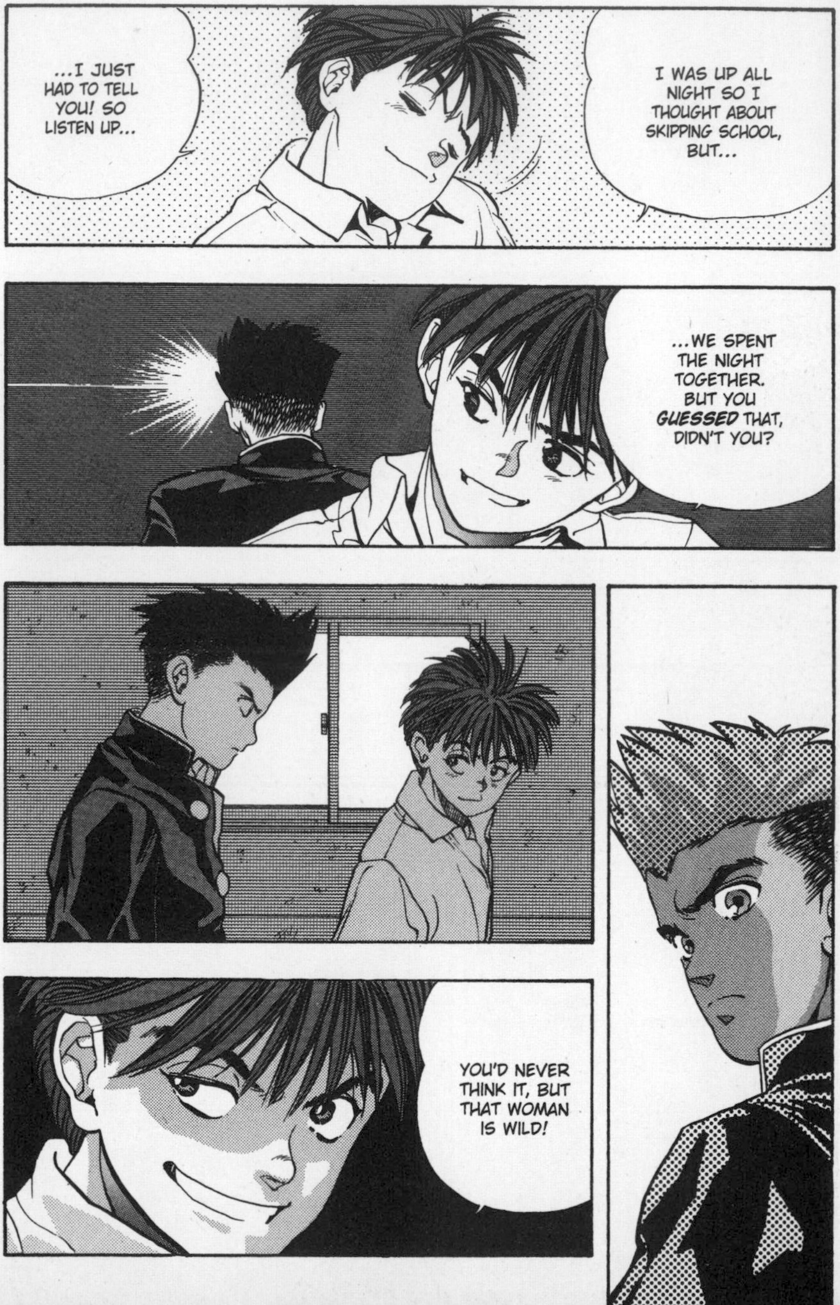
I WAS UP ALL NIGHT SO I THOUGHT ABOUT SKIPPING SCHOOL, BUT...
...I JUST HAD TO TELL YOU! SO LISTEN UP...
...WE SPENT THE NIGHT TOGETHER. BUT YOU *GUESSED* THAT, DIDN'T YOU?
YOU'D NEVER THINK IT, BUT THAT WOMAN IS WILD!

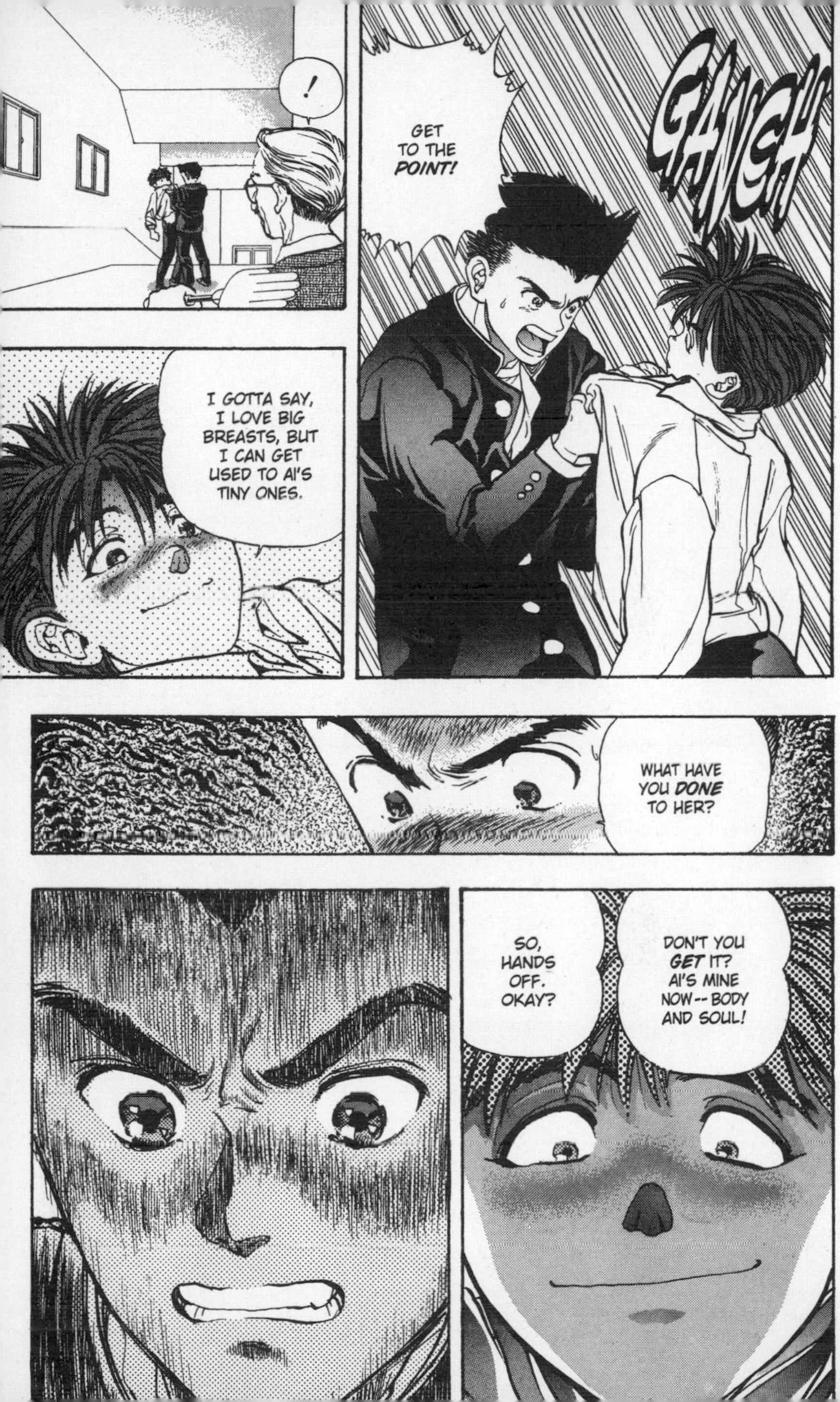
GANCH
GET TO THE POINT!
!
I GOTTA SAY, I LOVE BIG BREASTS, BUT I CAN GET USED TO AI'S TINY ONES.
WHAT HAVE YOU DONE TO HER?
DON'T YOU GET IT? AI'S MINE NOW--BODY AND SOUL!
SO, HANDS OFF. OKAY?

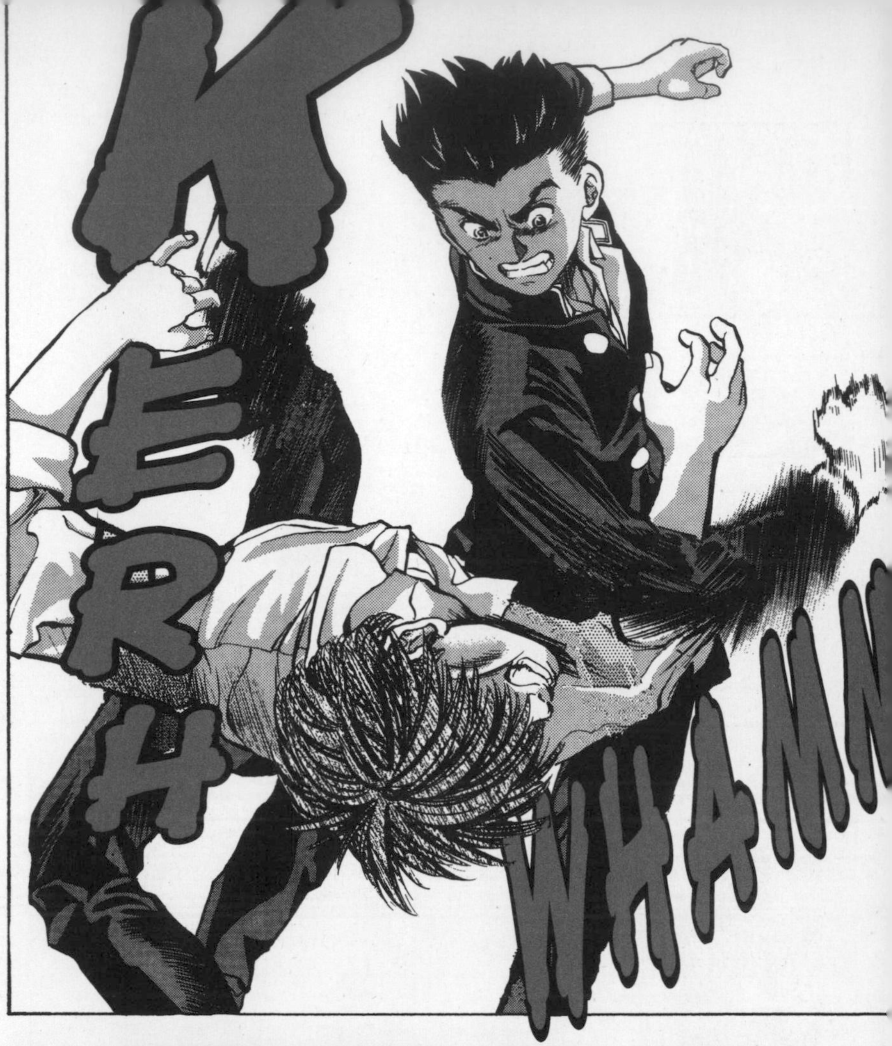
KERH
WHAMM

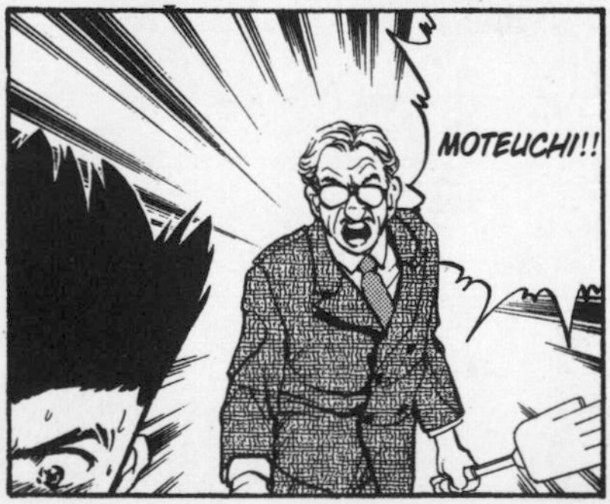
MOTEUCHI!!

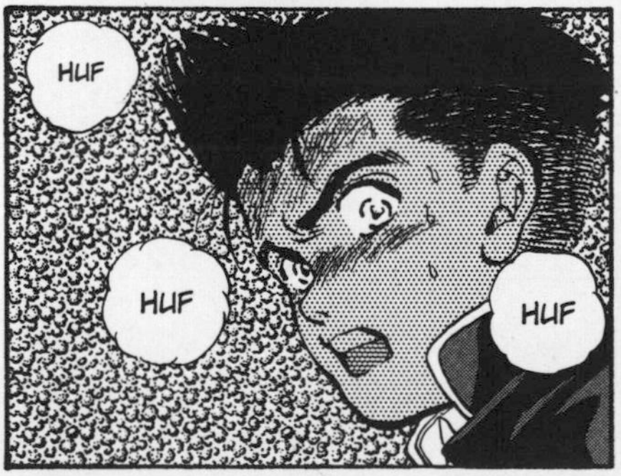
HUF
HUF
HUF

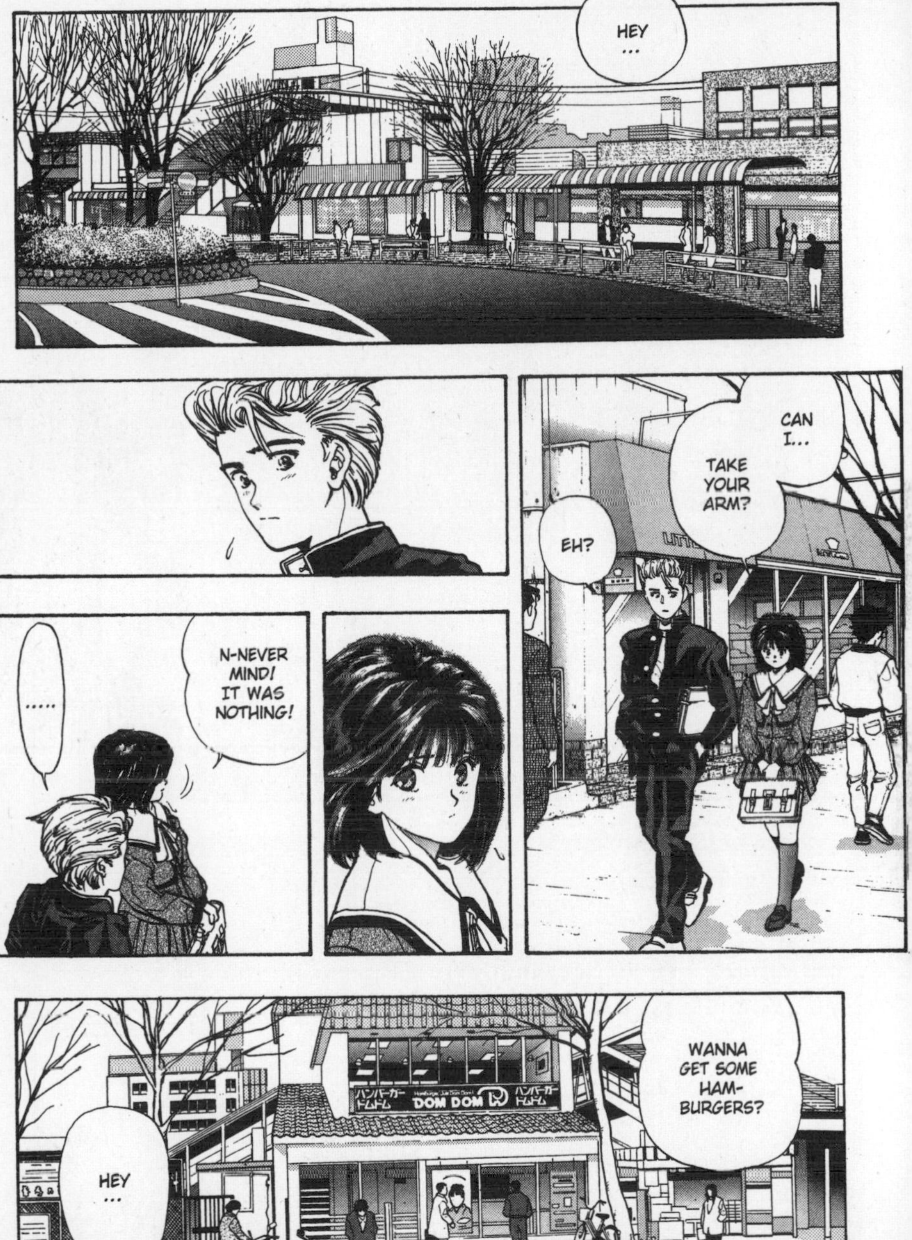
HEY ...
CAN I...
TAKE YOUR ARM?
EH?
N-NEVER MIND! IT WAS NOTHING!
......
WANNA GET SOME HAM-BURGERS?
ハンバーガー ドムドム
DOM DOM
ハンバーガー ドムドム
HEY ...

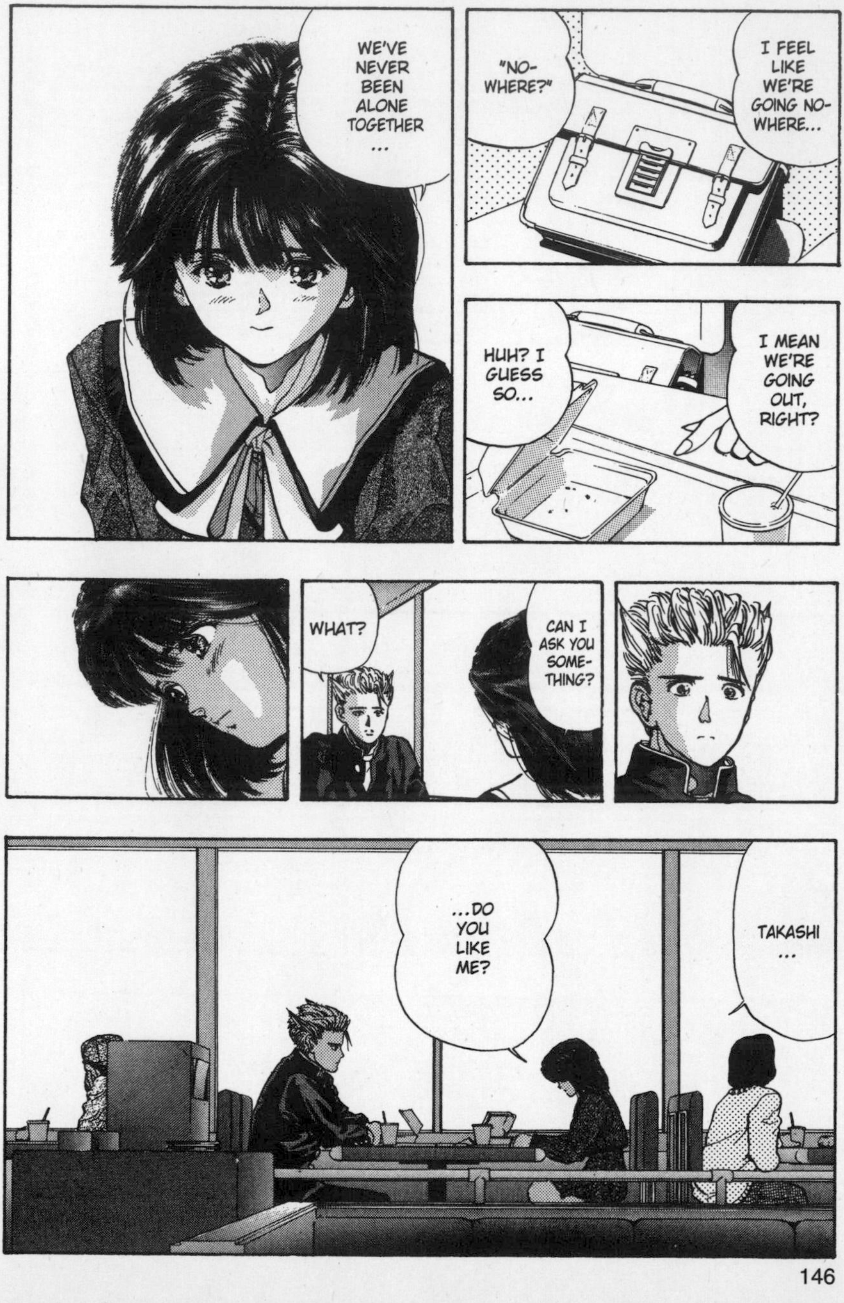
I FEEL LIKE WE'RE GOING NO-WHERE...
"NO-WHERE?"
I MEAN WE'RE GOING OUT, RIGHT?
HUH? I GUESS SO...
WE'VE NEVER BEEN ALONE TOGETHER ...
CAN I ASK YOU SOME-THING?
WHAT?
TAKASHI ...
...DO YOU LIKE ME?

■ ▲ ■ ❚❚ ■ ►► ■ ► *CHAPTER SIXTEEN*

Kindness

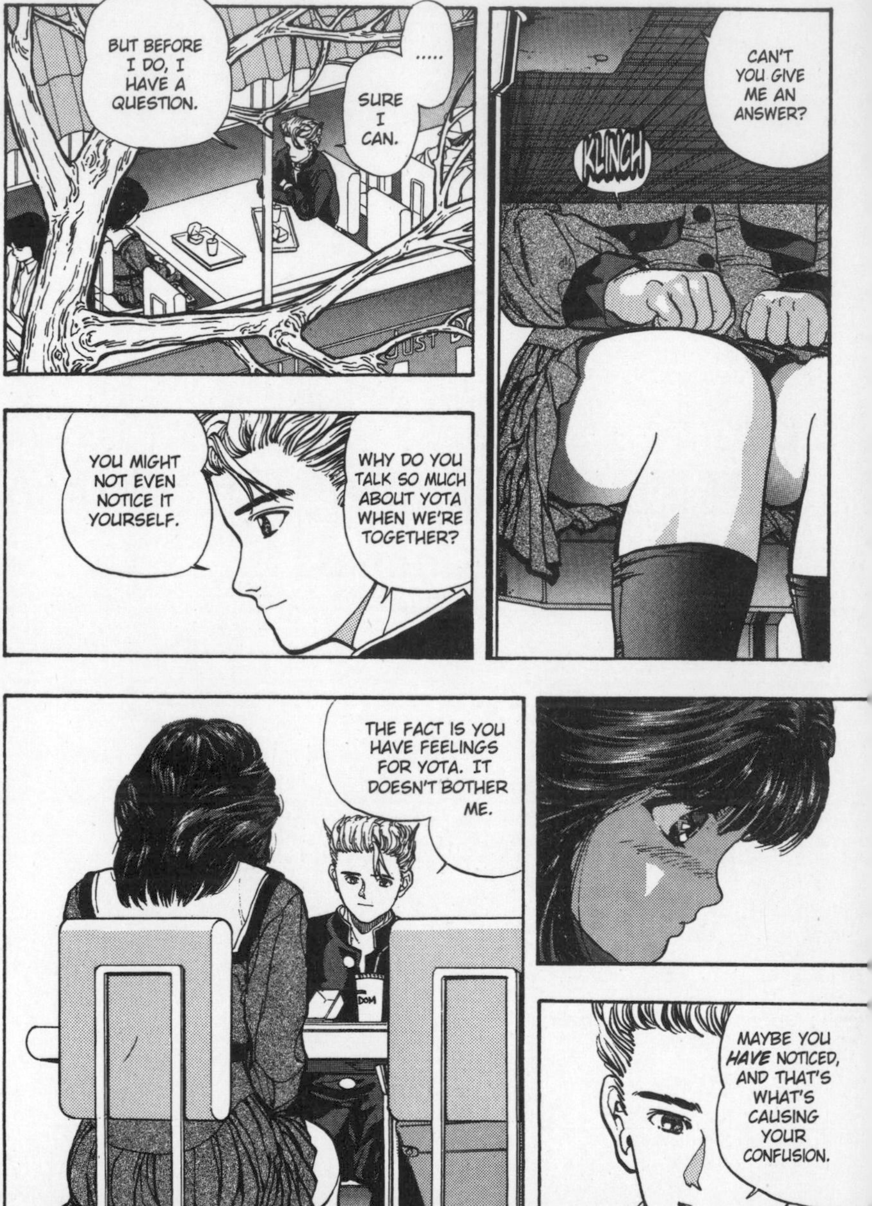
CAN'T YOU GIVE ME AN ANSWER?
KLINCH
.....
SURE I CAN.
BUT BEFORE I DO, I HAVE A QUESTION.
WHY DO YOU TALK SO MUCH ABOUT YOTA WHEN WE'RE TOGETHER?
YOU MIGHT NOT EVEN NOTICE IT YOURSELF.
MAYBE YOU *HAVE* NOTICED, AND THAT'S WHAT'S CAUSING YOUR CONFUSION.
THE FACT IS YOU HAVE FEELINGS FOR YOTA. IT DOESN'T BOTHER ME.

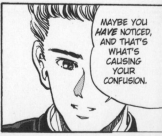

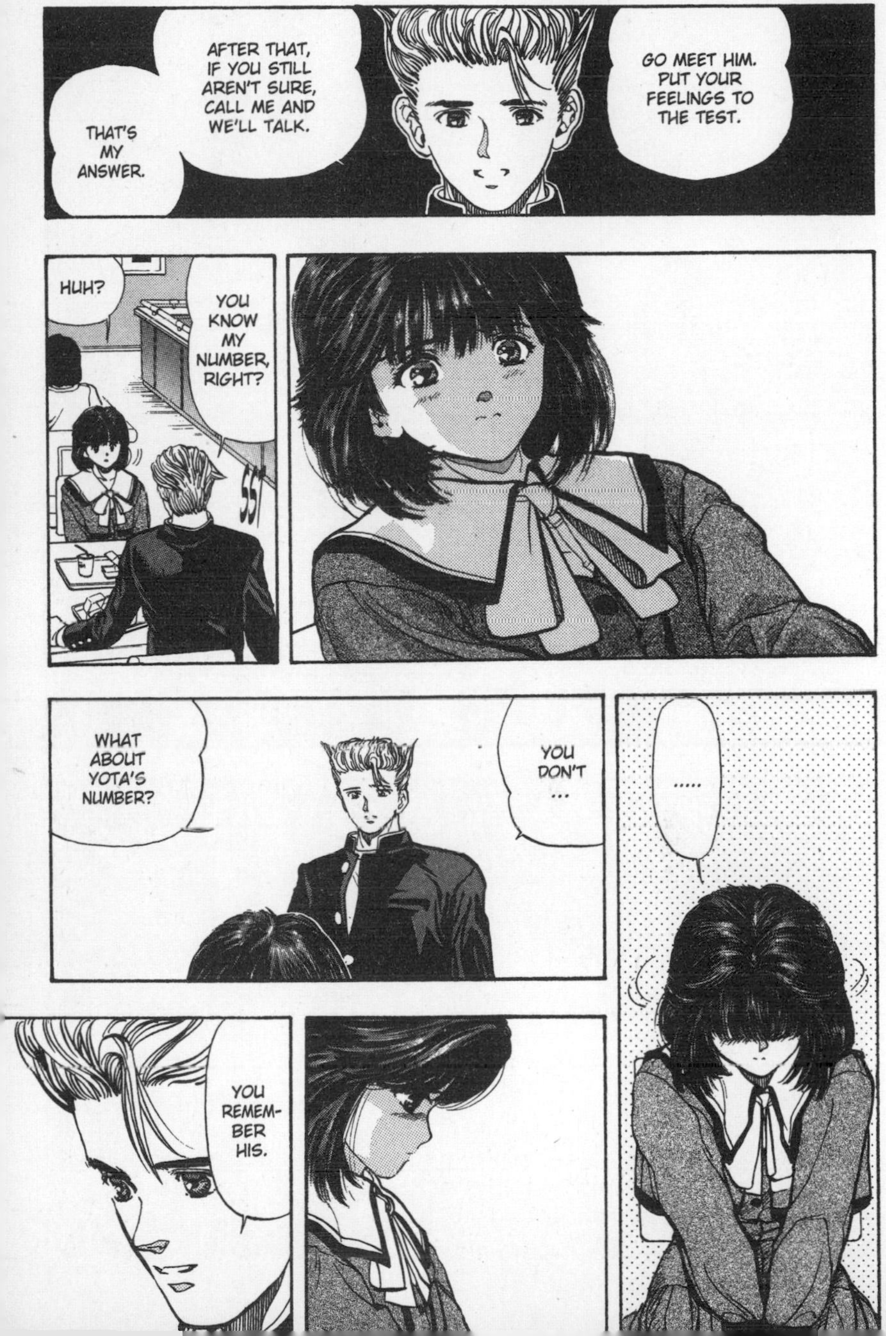
GO MEET HIM. PUT YOUR FEELINGS TO THE TEST.
AFTER THAT, IF YOU STILL AREN'T SURE, CALL ME AND WE'LL TALK.
THAT'S MY ANSWER.
YOU KNOW MY NUMBER, RIGHT?
HUH?
.....
YOU DON'T ...
WHAT ABOUT YOTA'S NUMBER?
YOU REMEMBER HIS.

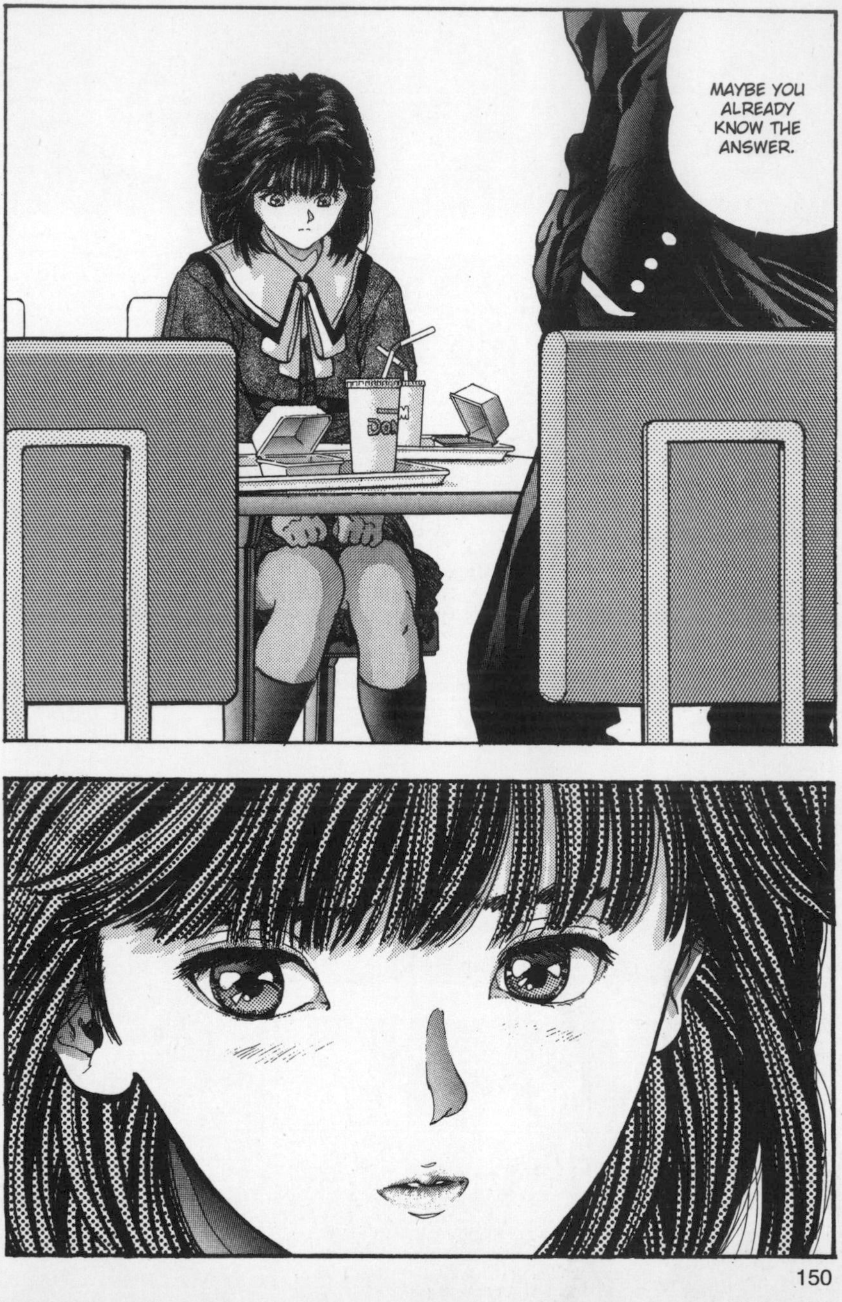
MAYBE YOU ALREADY KNOW THE ANSWER.
DON

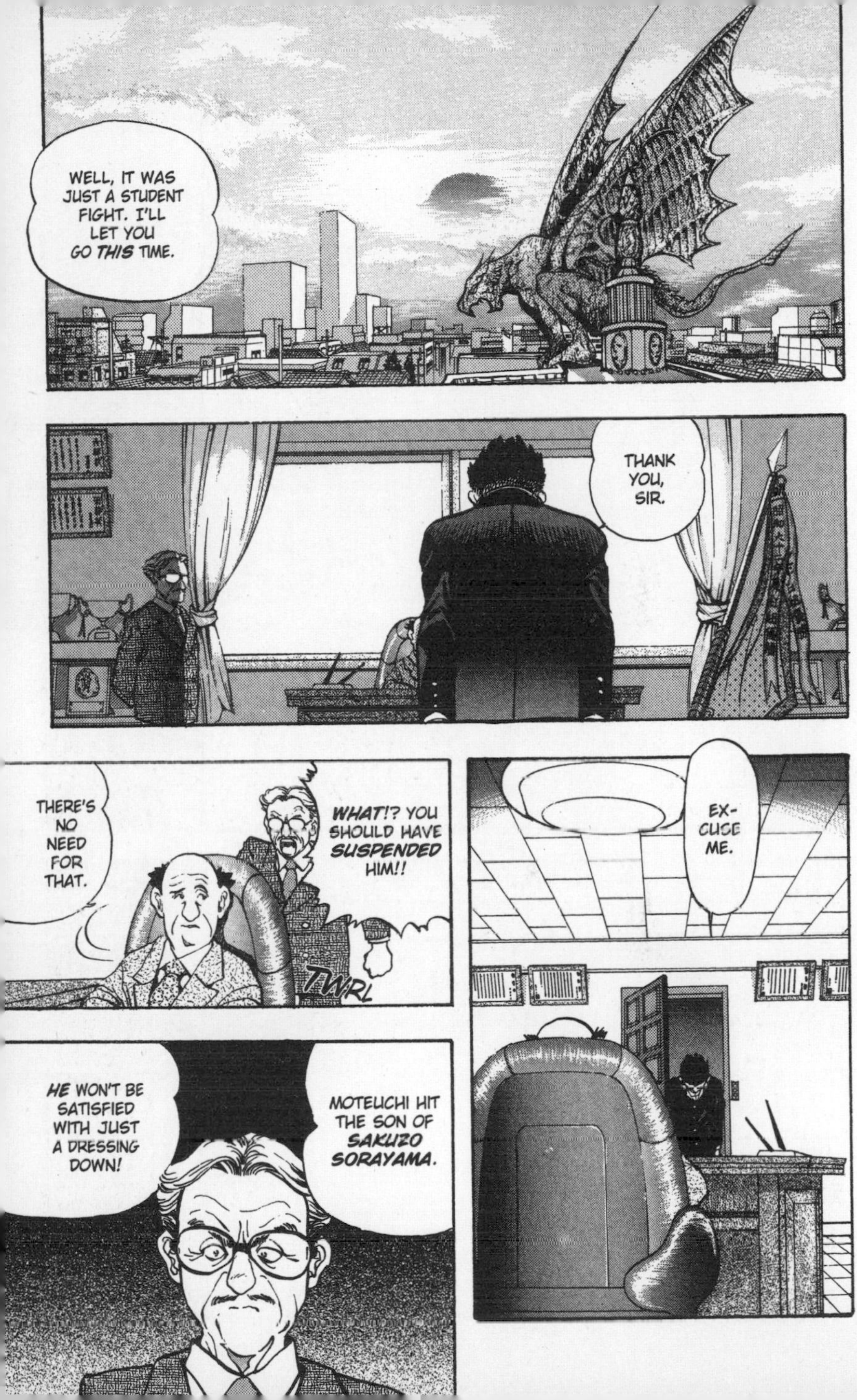

WELL, IT WAS JUST A STUDENT FIGHT. I'LL LET YOU GO THIS TIME.
THANK YOU, SIR.
EX-CUSE ME.
WHAT!? YOU SHOULD HAVE SUSPENDED HIM!!
THERE'S NO NEED FOR THAT.
TWIRL
MOTEUCHI HIT THE SON OF SAKUZO SORAYAMA.
HE WON'T BE SATISFIED WITH JUST A DRESSING DOWN!

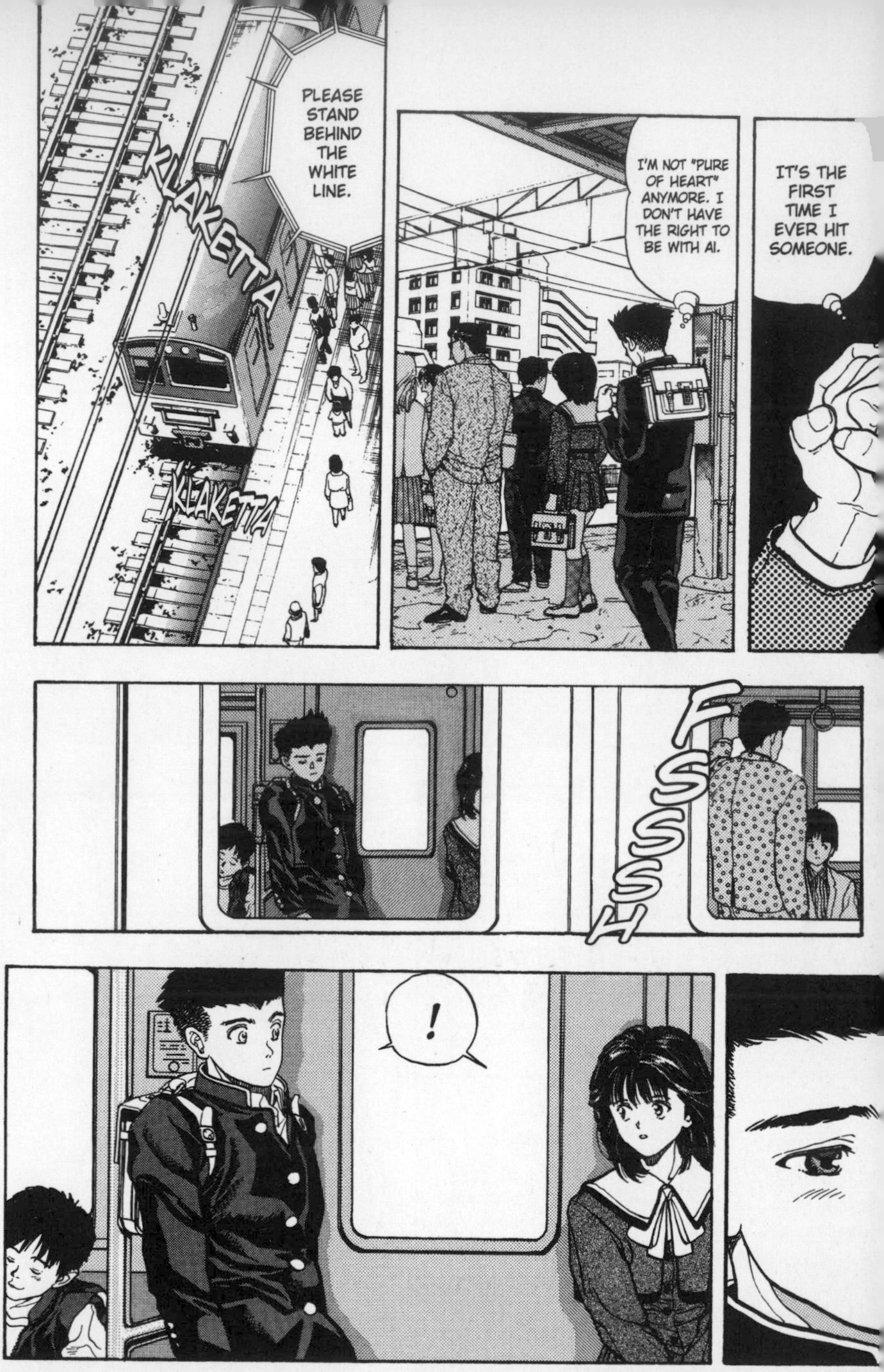
IT'S THE FIRST TIME I EVER HIT SOMEONE.
I'M NOT "PURE OF HEART" ANYMORE. I DON'T HAVE THE RIGHT TO BE WITH AI.
PLEASE STAND BEHIND THE WHITE LINE.
KLAKETTA
KLAKETTA
FSSSH
!

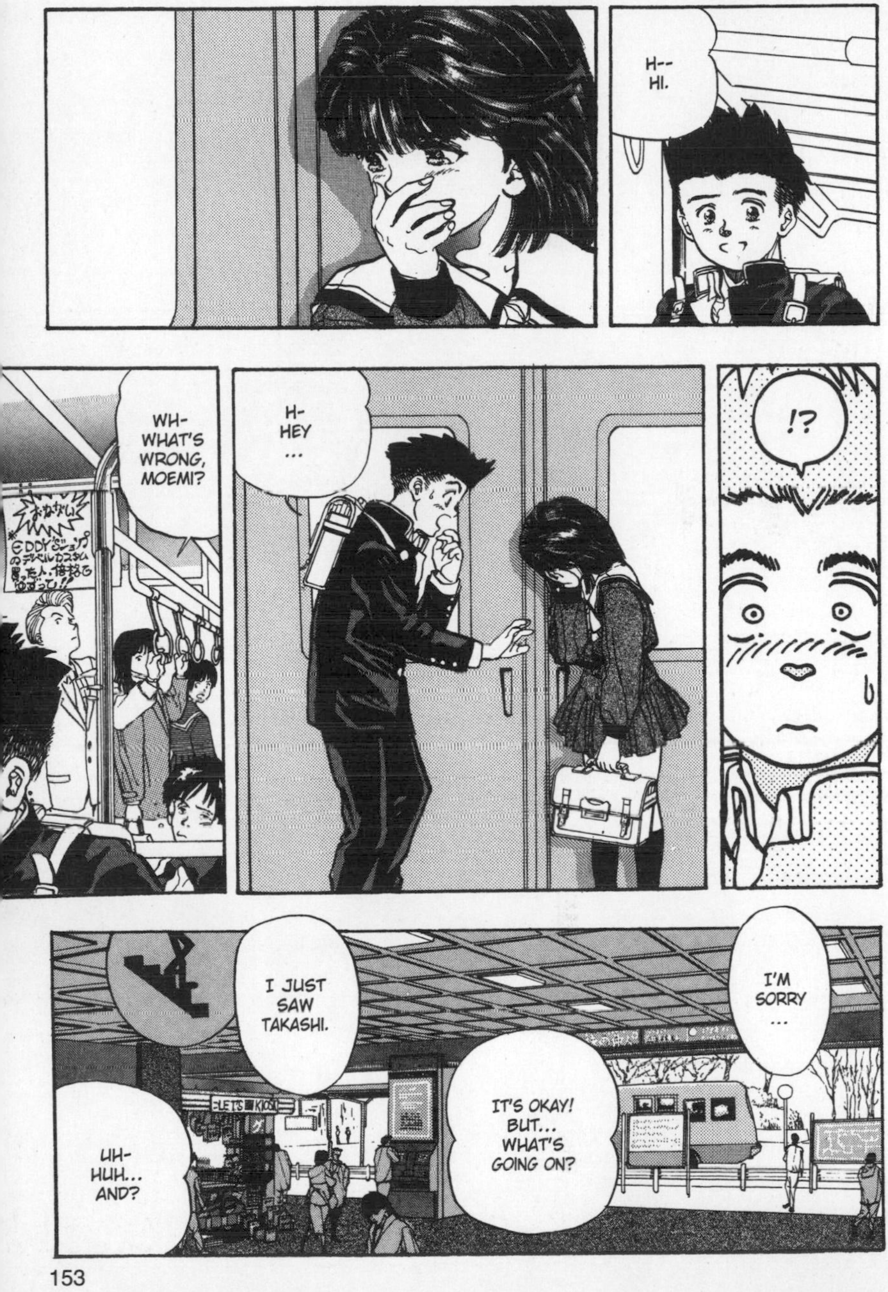
H-- HI.
!?
H- HEY ...
WH- WHAT'S WRONG, MOEMI?
I'M SORRY ...
IT'S OKAY! BUT... WHAT'S GOING ON?
I JUST SAW TAKASHI.
UH-HUH... AND?

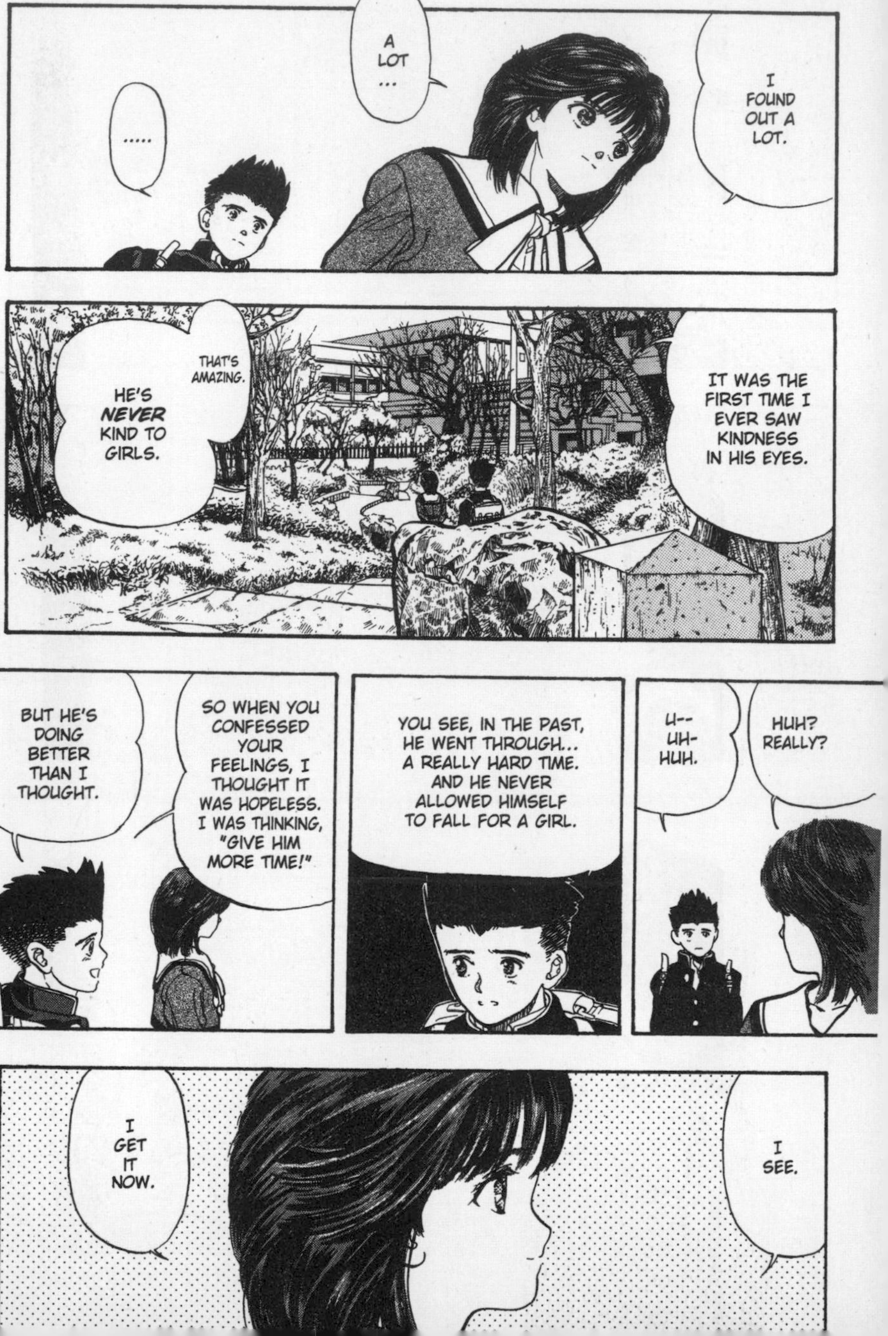
I FOUND OUT A LOT.
A LOT...
......
IT WAS THE FIRST TIME I EVER SAW KINDNESS IN HIS EYES.
THAT'S AMAZING.
HE'S *NEVER* KIND TO GIRLS.
HUH? REALLY?
U-- UH-HUH.
YOU SEE, IN THE PAST, HE WENT THROUGH... A REALLY HARD TIME. AND HE NEVER ALLOWED HIMSELF TO FALL FOR A GIRL.
SO WHEN YOU CONFESSED YOUR FEELINGS, I THOUGHT IT WAS HOPELESS. I WAS THINKING, "GIVE HIM MORE TIME!"
BUT HE'S DOING BETTER THAN I THOUGHT.
I SEE.
I GET IT NOW.

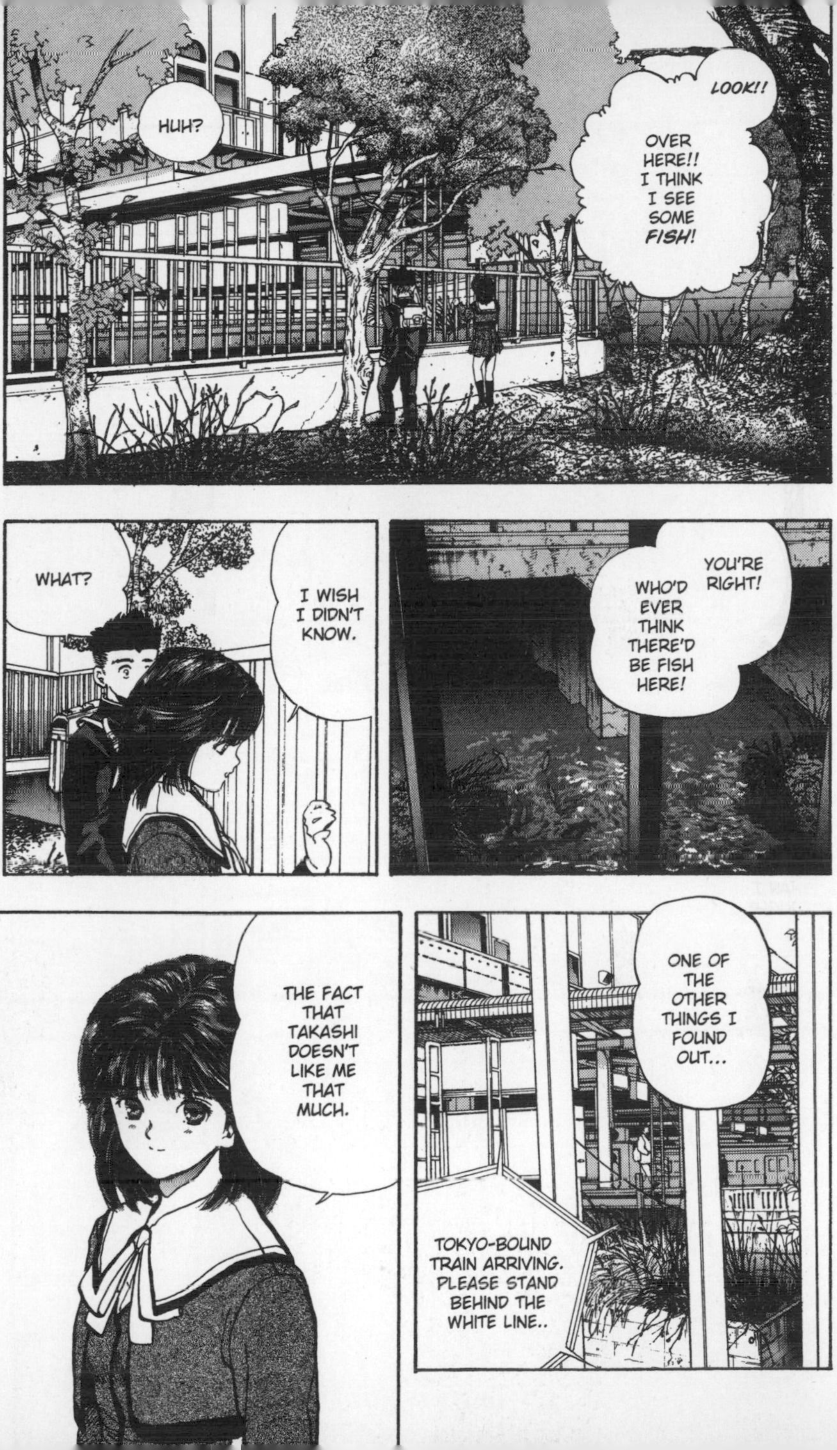
LOOK!!
OVER HERE!! I THINK I SEE SOME *FISH*!
HUH?
YOU'RE RIGHT!
WHO'D EVER THINK THERE'D BE FISH HERE!
I WISH I DIDN'T KNOW.
WHAT?
ONE OF THE OTHER THINGS I FOUND OUT...
TOKYO-BOUND TRAIN ARRIVING. PLEASE STAND BEHIND THE WHITE LINE..
THE FACT THAT TAKASHI DOESN'T LIKE ME THAT MUCH.

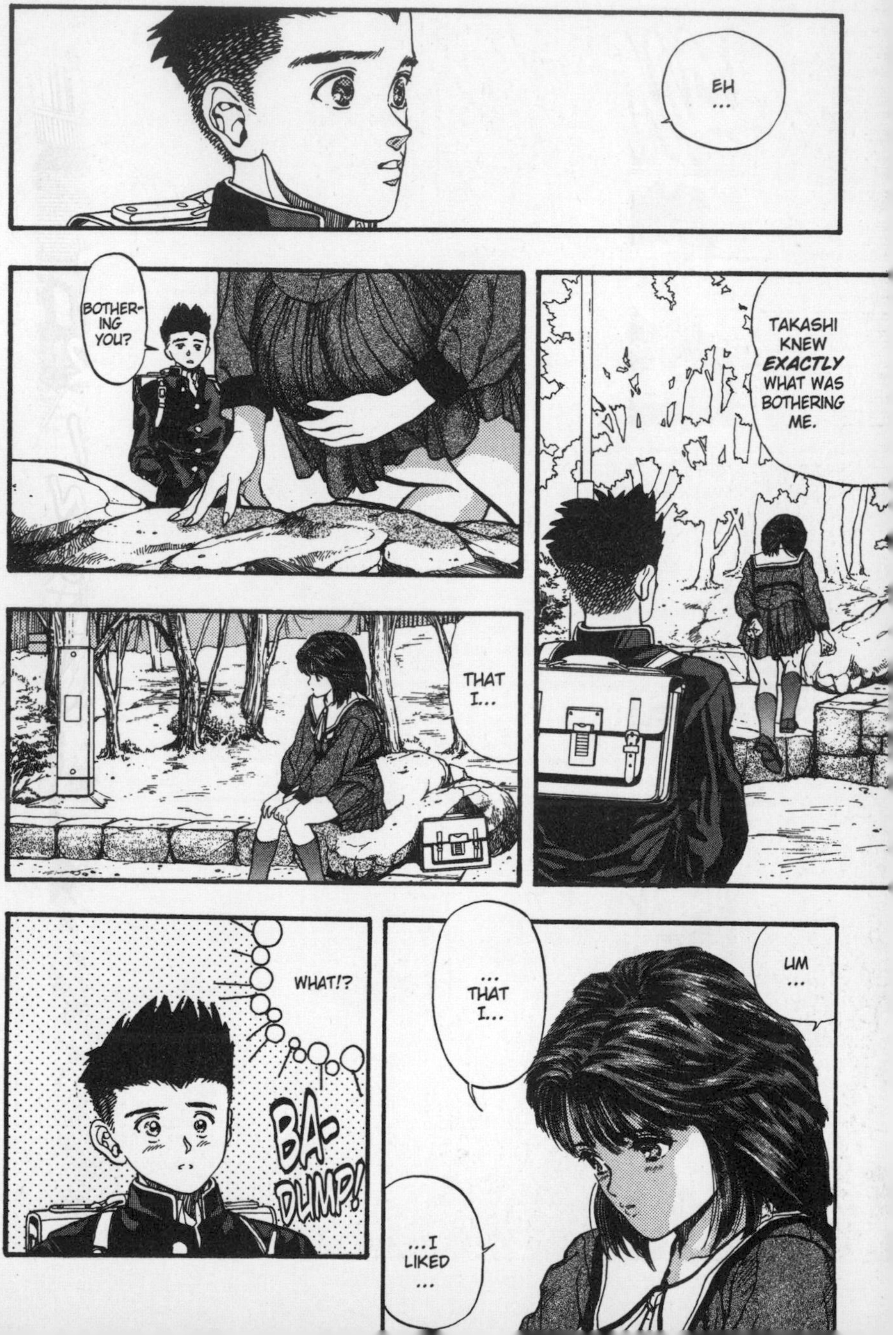
EH ...
TAKASHI KNEW *EXACTLY* WHAT WAS BOTHERING ME.
BOTHERING YOU?
THAT I...
UM ...
... THAT I...
...I LIKED ...
WHAT!?
BA-DUMP!

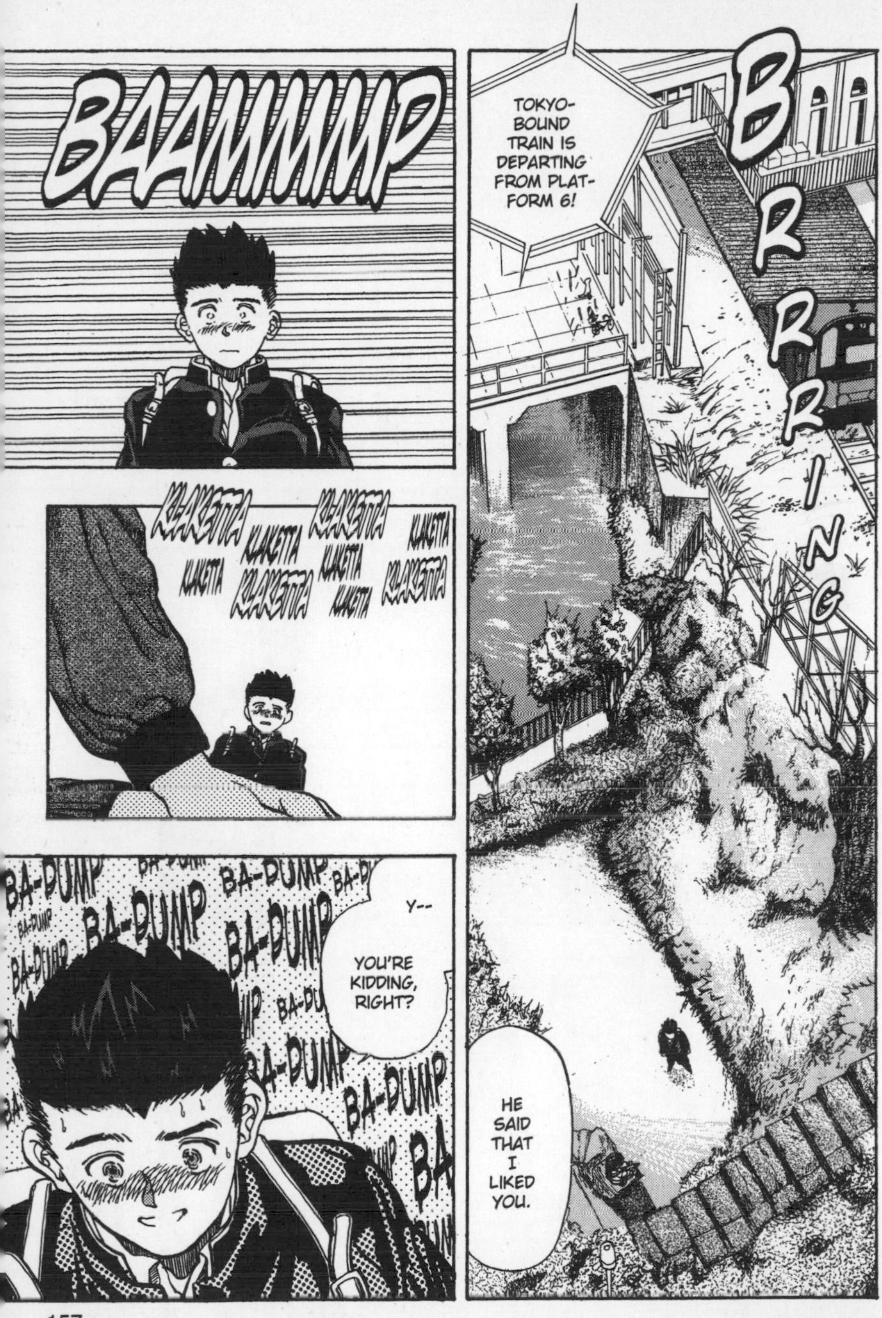
BRRRRING
TOKYO-BOUND TRAIN IS DEPARTING FROM PLATFORM 6!
HE SAID THAT I LIKED YOU.
BAAMMMMP
KLAKETTA KLAKETTA KLAKETTA KLAKETTA
KLAKETTA KLAKETTA KLAKETTA KLAKETTA
KLAKETTA KLAKETTA
BA-DUMP BA-DUMP BA-DUMP BA-DUMP
Y--
YOU'RE KIDDING, RIGHT?

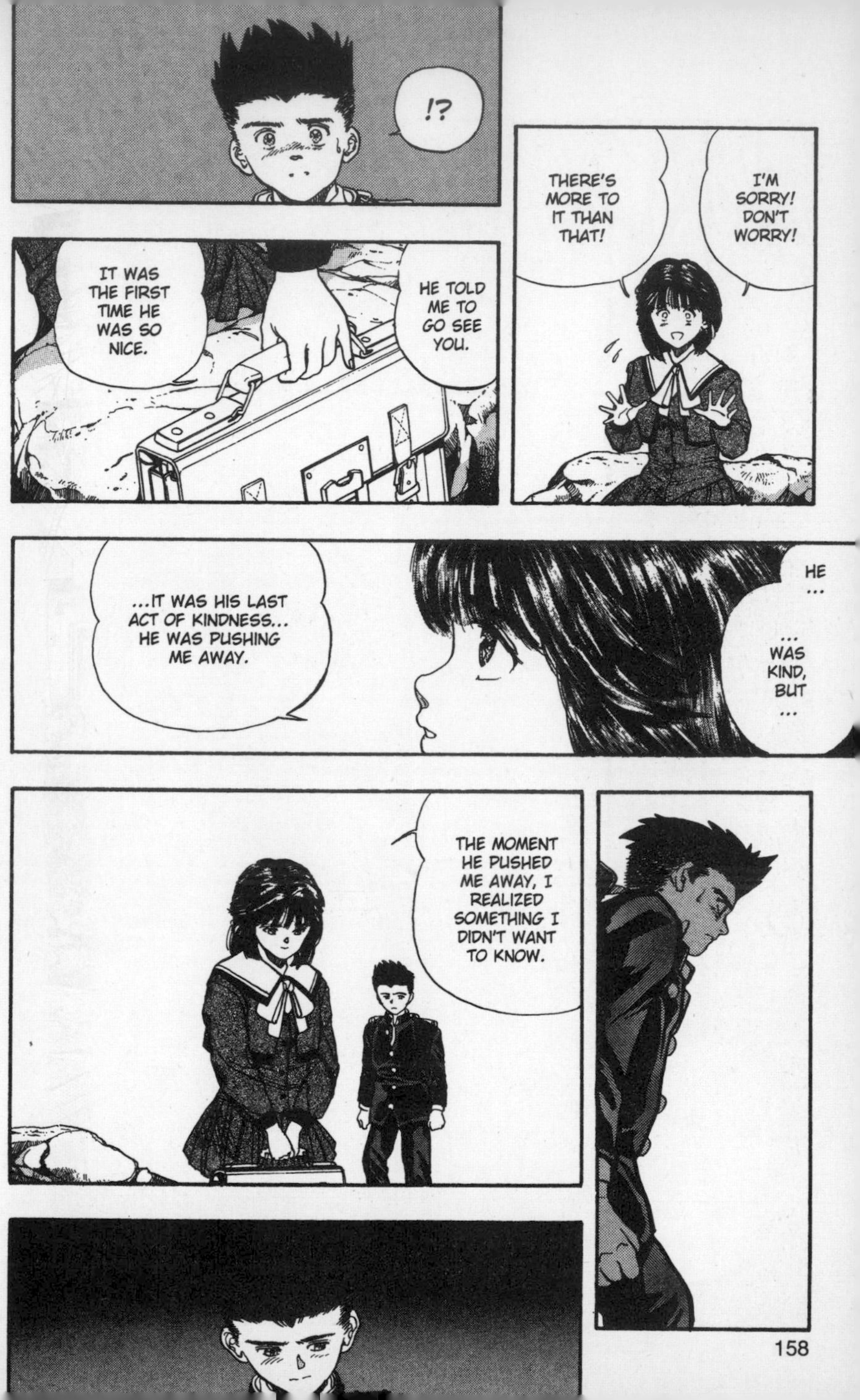
I'M SORRY! DON'T WORRY!
THERE'S MORE TO IT THAN THAT!
!?
HE TOLD ME TO GO SEE YOU.
IT WAS THE FIRST TIME HE WAS SO NICE.
HE ... ... WAS KIND, BUT ...
...IT WAS HIS LAST ACT OF KINDNESS... HE WAS PUSHING ME AWAY.
THE MOMENT HE PUSHED ME AWAY, I REALIZED SOMETHING I DIDN'T WANT TO KNOW.

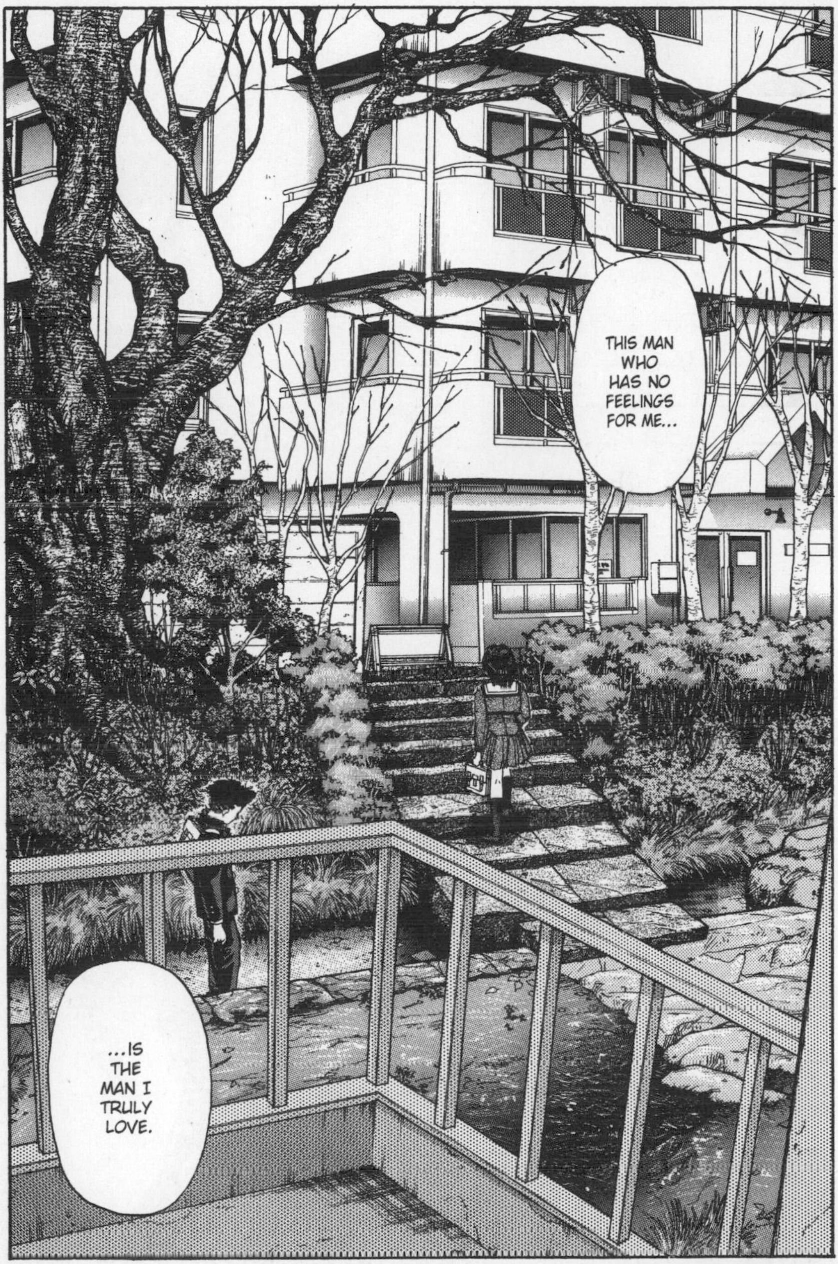
THIS MAN WHO HAS NO FEELINGS FOR ME...
...IS THE MAN I TRULY LOVE.

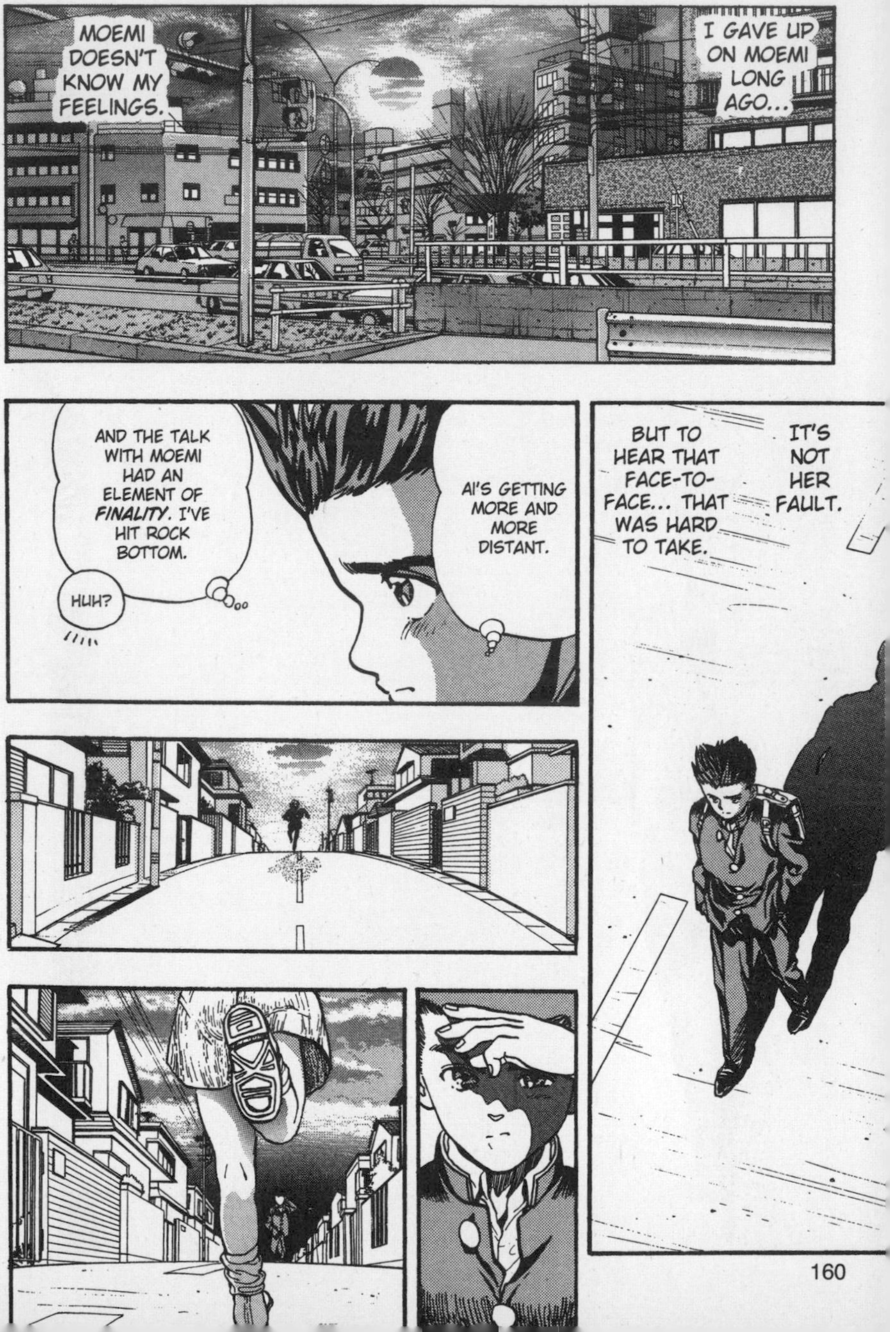
I GAVE UP ON MOEMI LONG AGO...
MOEMI DOESN'T KNOW MY FEELINGS.
IT'S NOT HER FAULT.
BUT TO HEAR THAT FACE-TO-FACE... THAT WAS HARD TO TAKE.
AI'S GETTING MORE AND MORE DISTANT.
AND THE TALK WITH MOEMI HAD AN ELEMENT OF *FINALITY*. I'VE HIT ROCK BOTTOM.
HUH?

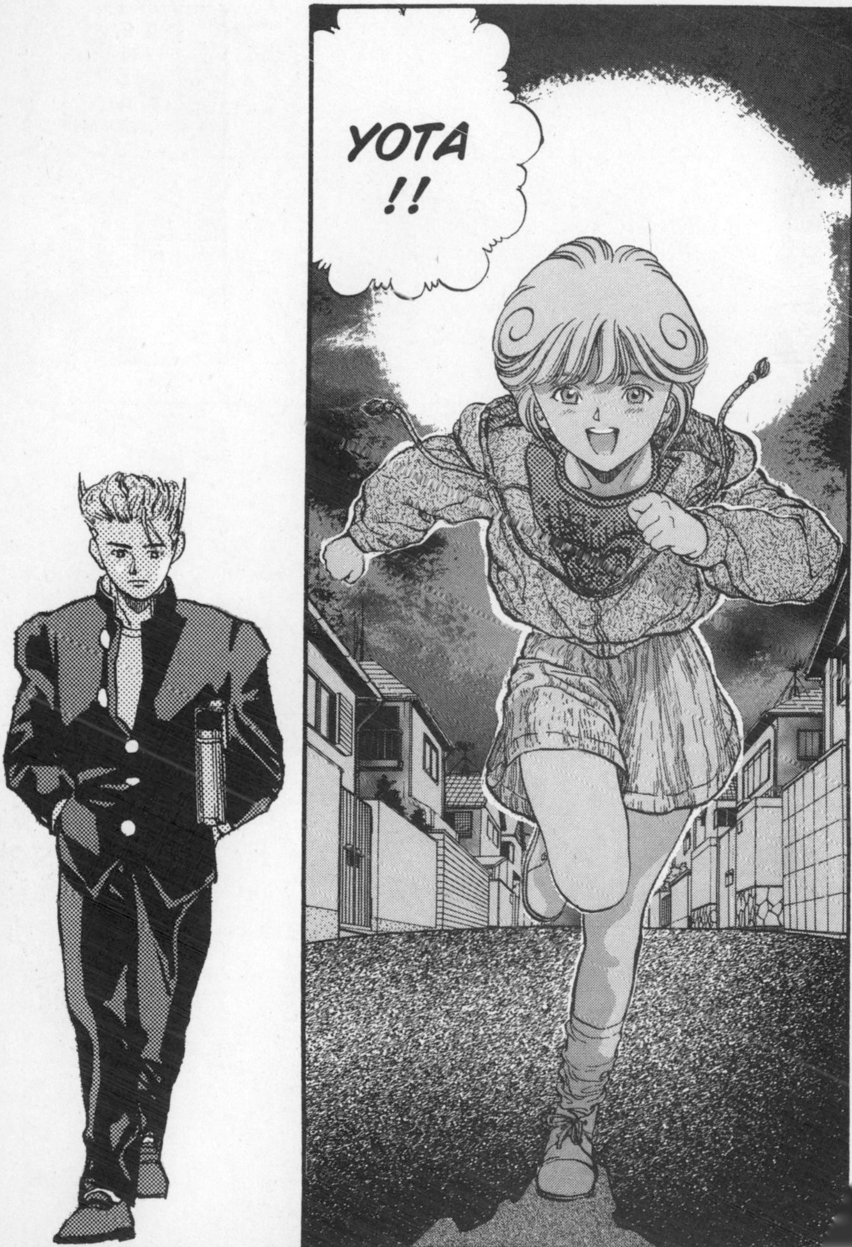
YOTA
!!

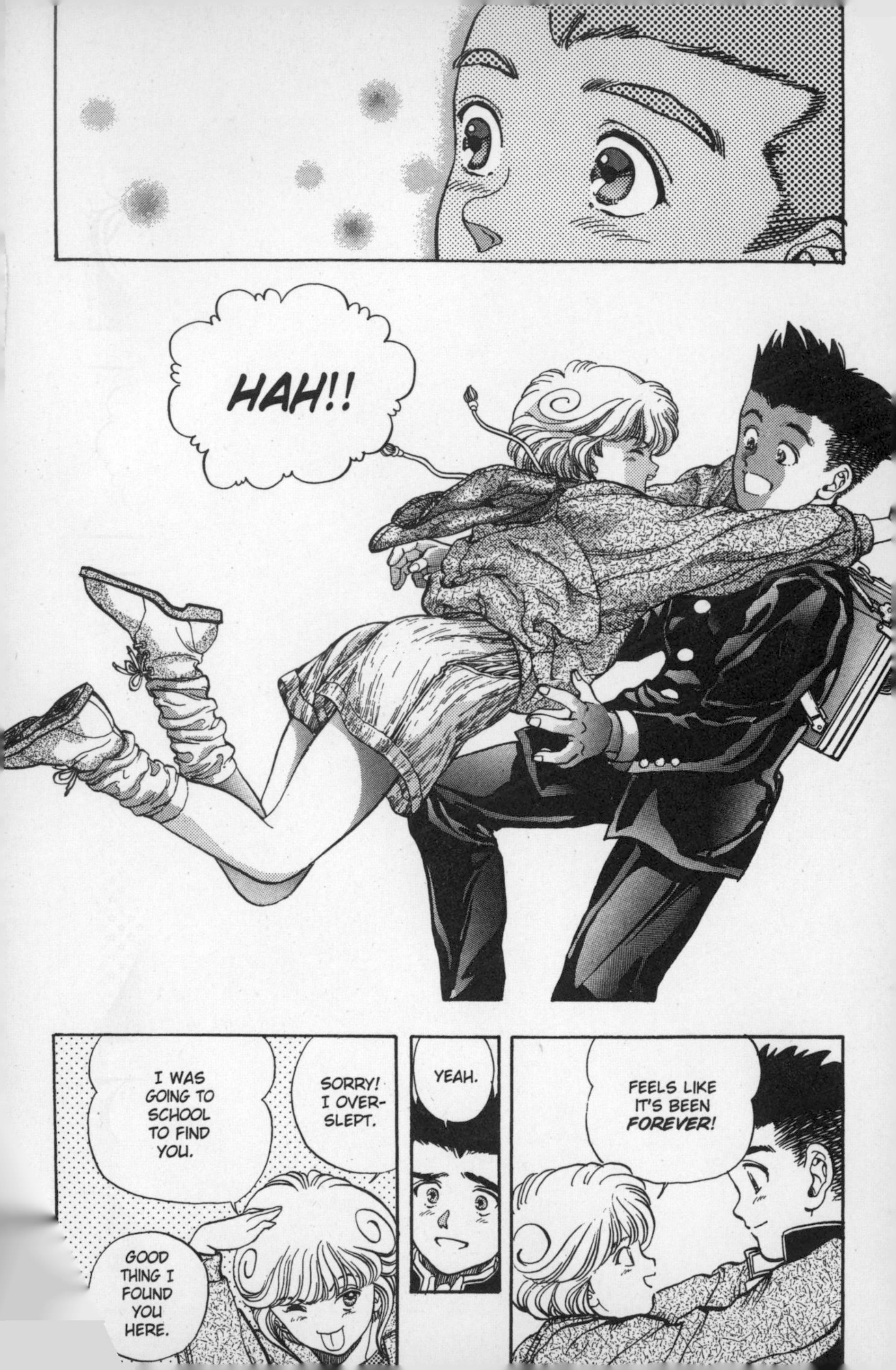
HAH!!
FEELS LIKE IT'S BEEN *FOREVER!*
YEAH.
SORRY! I OVER-SLEPT.
I WAS GOING TO SCHOOL TO FIND YOU.
GOOD THING I FOUND YOU HERE.

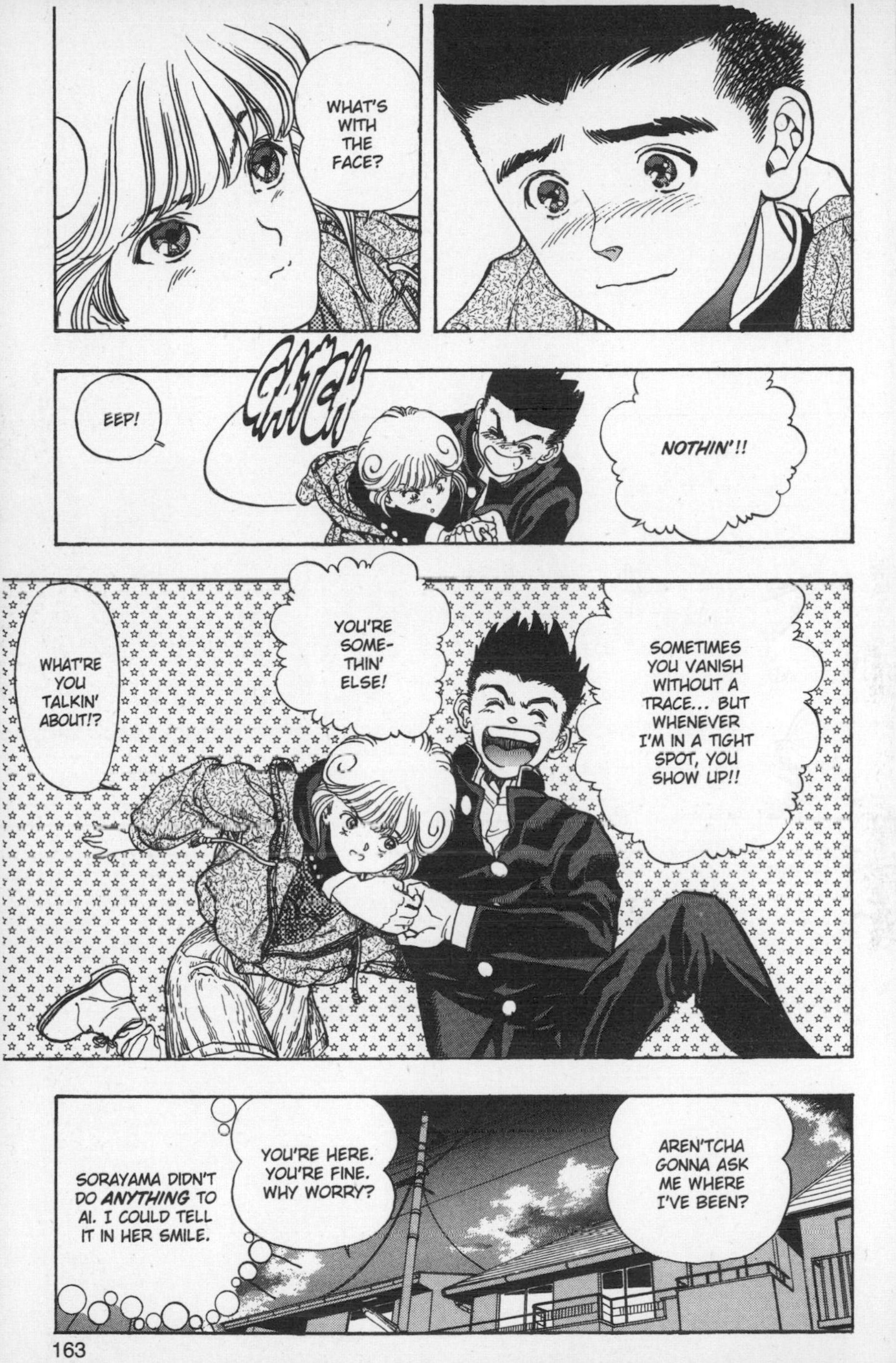
WHAT'S WITH THE FACE?
NOTHIN'!!
EEP!
SOMETIMES YOU VANISH WITHOUT A TRACE... BUT WHENEVER I'M IN A TIGHT SPOT, YOU SHOW UP!!
YOU'RE SOME-THIN' ELSE!
WHAT'RE YOU TALKIN' ABOUT!?
AREN'TCHA GONNA ASK ME WHERE I'VE BEEN?
YOU'RE HERE. YOU'RE FINE. WHY WORRY?
SORAYAMA DIDN'T DO *ANYTHING* TO AI. I COULD TELL IT IN HER SMILE.

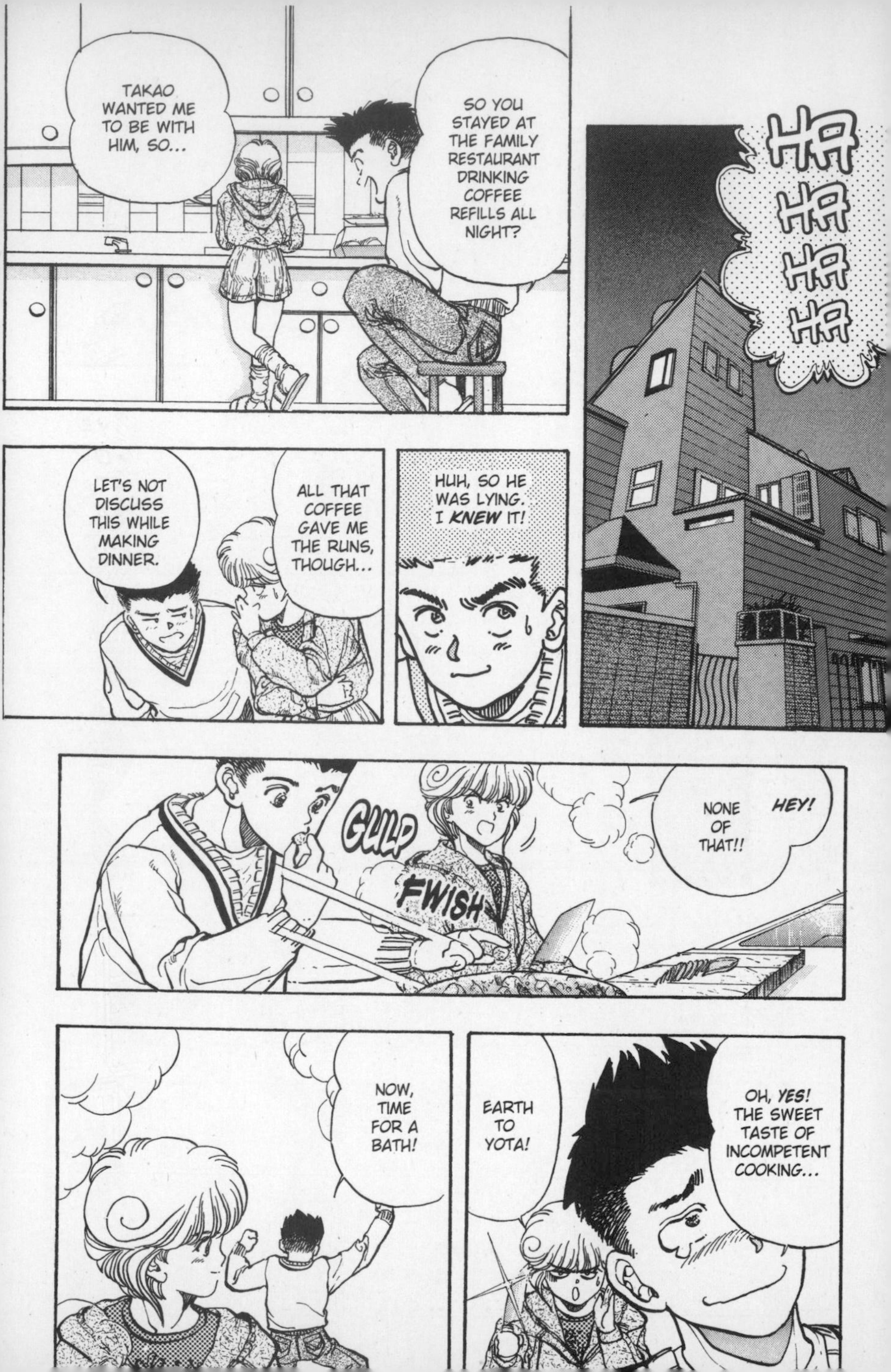
HA HA HA HA
SO YOU STAYED AT THE FAMILY RESTAURANT DRINKING COFFEE REFILLS ALL NIGHT?
TAKAO WANTED ME TO BE WITH HIM, SO...
HUH, SO HE WAS LYING. I *KNEW* IT!
ALL THAT COFFEE GAVE ME THE RUNS, THOUGH...
LET'S NOT DISCUSS THIS WHILE MAKING DINNER.
HEY!
NONE OF THAT!!
GULP
FWISH
OH, *YES!* THE SWEET TASTE OF INCOMPETENT COOKING...
EARTH TO YOTA!
NOW, TIME FOR A BATH!

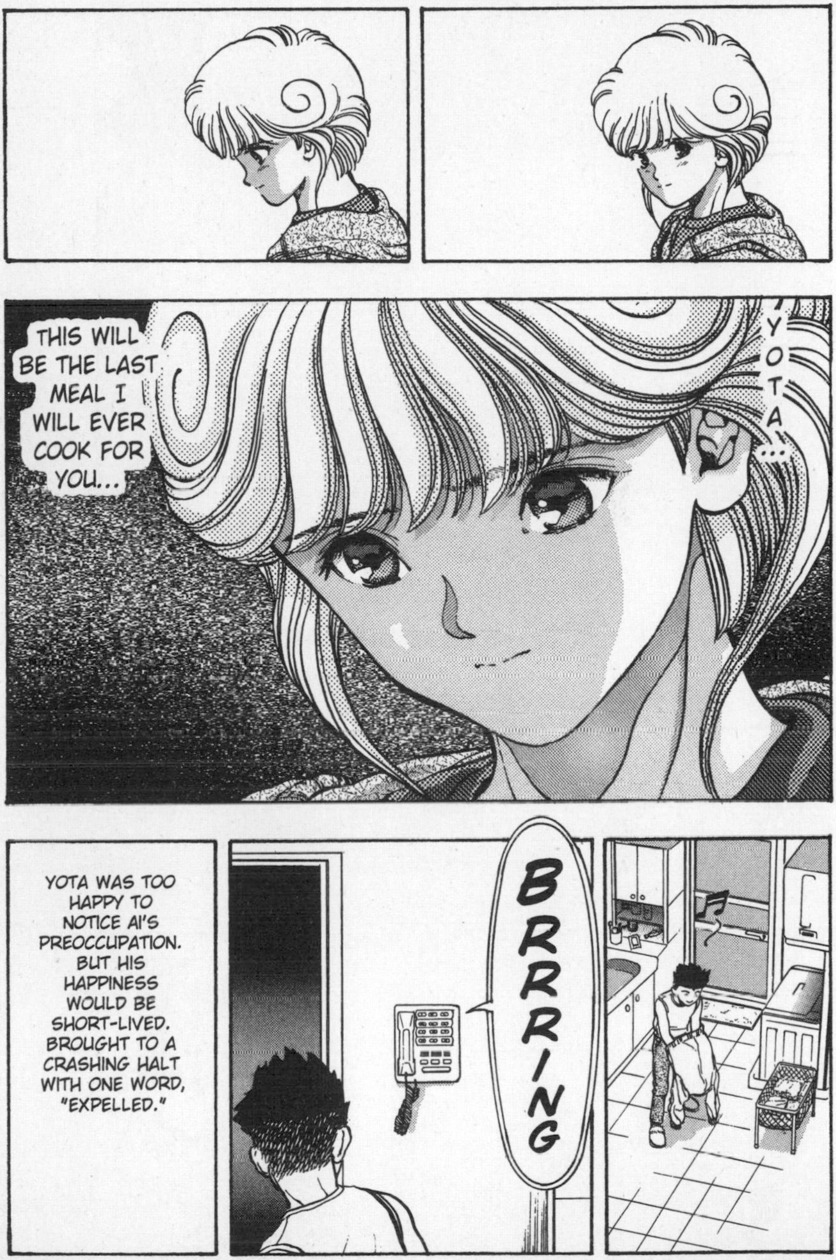
YOTA...
THIS WILL BE THE LAST MEAL I WILL EVER COOK FOR YOU...
BRRRING
YOTA WAS TOO HAPPY TO NOTICE AI'S PREOCCUPATION. BUT HIS HAPPINESS WOULD BE SHORT-LIVED. BROUGHT TO A CRASHING HALT WITH ONE WORD, "EXPELLED."

■ ⏏ ❚❚ ▶▶ ▶ *CHAPTER SEVENTEEN*

Melancholy Couple

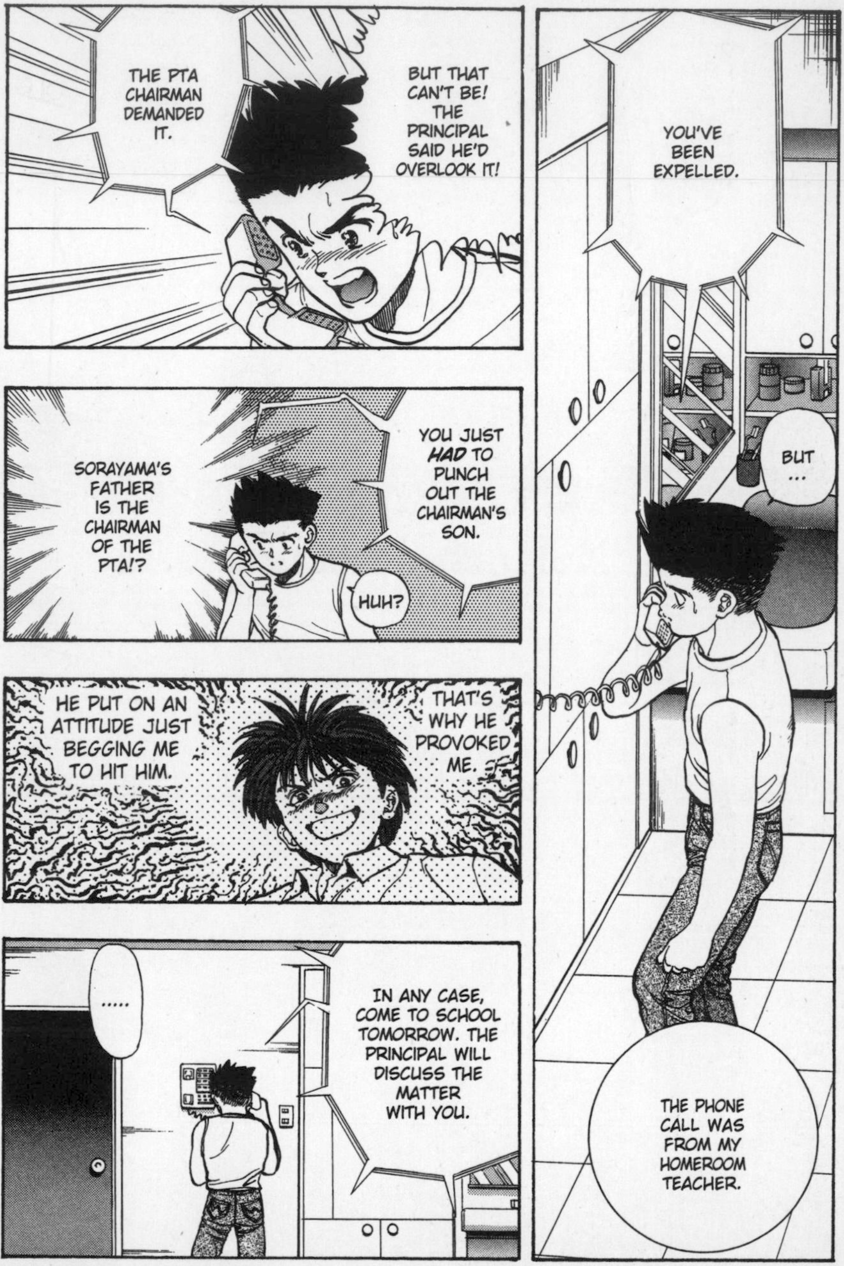

YOU'VE BEEN EXPELLED.
BUT ...
THE PHONE CALL WAS FROM MY HOMEROOM TEACHER.
BUT THAT CAN'T BE! THE PRINCIPAL SAID HE'D OVERLOOK IT!
THE PTA CHAIRMAN DEMANDED IT.
YOU JUST *HAD* TO PUNCH OUT THE CHAIRMAN'S SON.
HUH?
SORAYAMA'S FATHER IS THE CHAIRMAN OF THE PTA!?
THAT'S WHY HE PROVOKED ME.
HE PUT ON AN ATTITUDE JUST BEGGING ME TO HIT HIM.
IN ANY CASE, COME TO SCHOOL TOMORROW. THE PRINCIPAL WILL DISCUSS THE MATTER WITH YOU.
.....

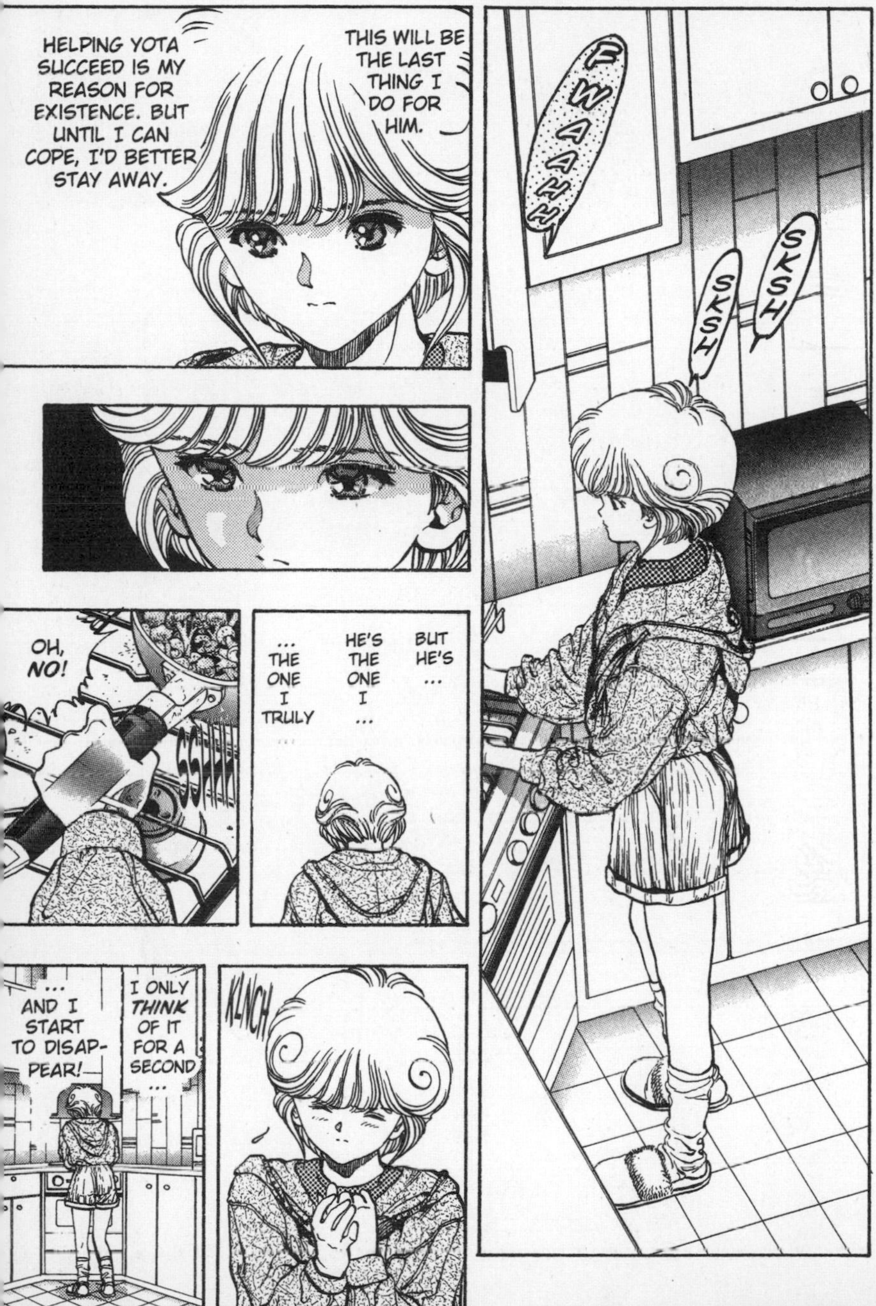
FWAAHH
SKSH
SKSH
THIS WILL BE THE LAST THING I DO FOR HIM.
HELPING YOTA SUCCEED IS MY REASON FOR EXISTENCE. BUT UNTIL I CAN COPE, I'D BETTER STAY AWAY.
BUT HE'S ...
HE'S THE ONE I ...
... THE ONE I TRULY ...
OH, *NO!*
KLINCH
I ONLY *THINK* OF IT FOR A SECOND ...
... AND I START TO DISAP-PEAR!

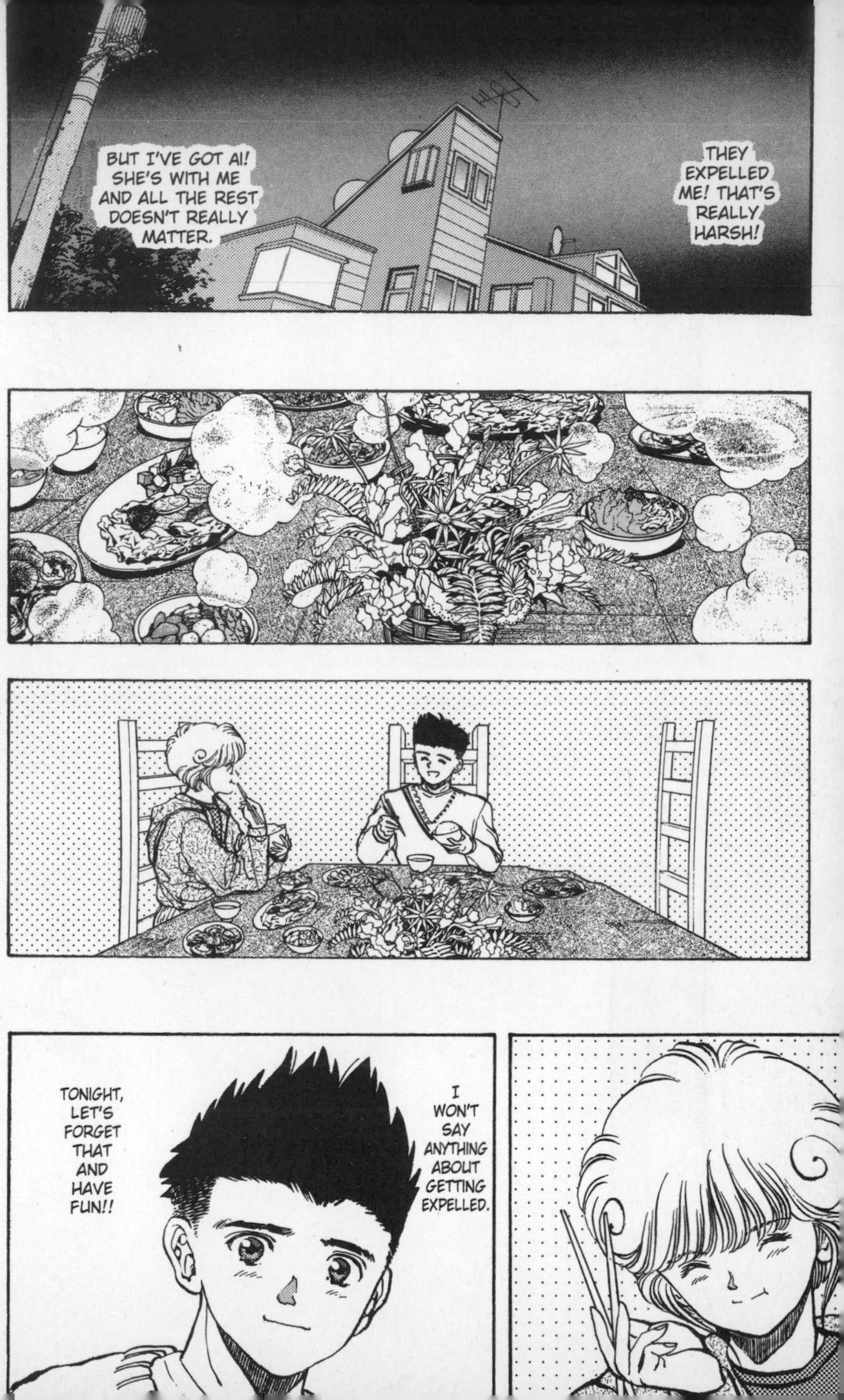
THEY EXPELLED ME! THAT'S REALLY HARSH!
BUT I'VE GOT AI! SHE'S WITH ME AND ALL THE REST DOESN'T REALLY MATTER.
I WON'T SAY ANYTHING ABOUT GETTING EXPELLED.
TONIGHT, LET'S FORGET THAT AND HAVE FUN!!

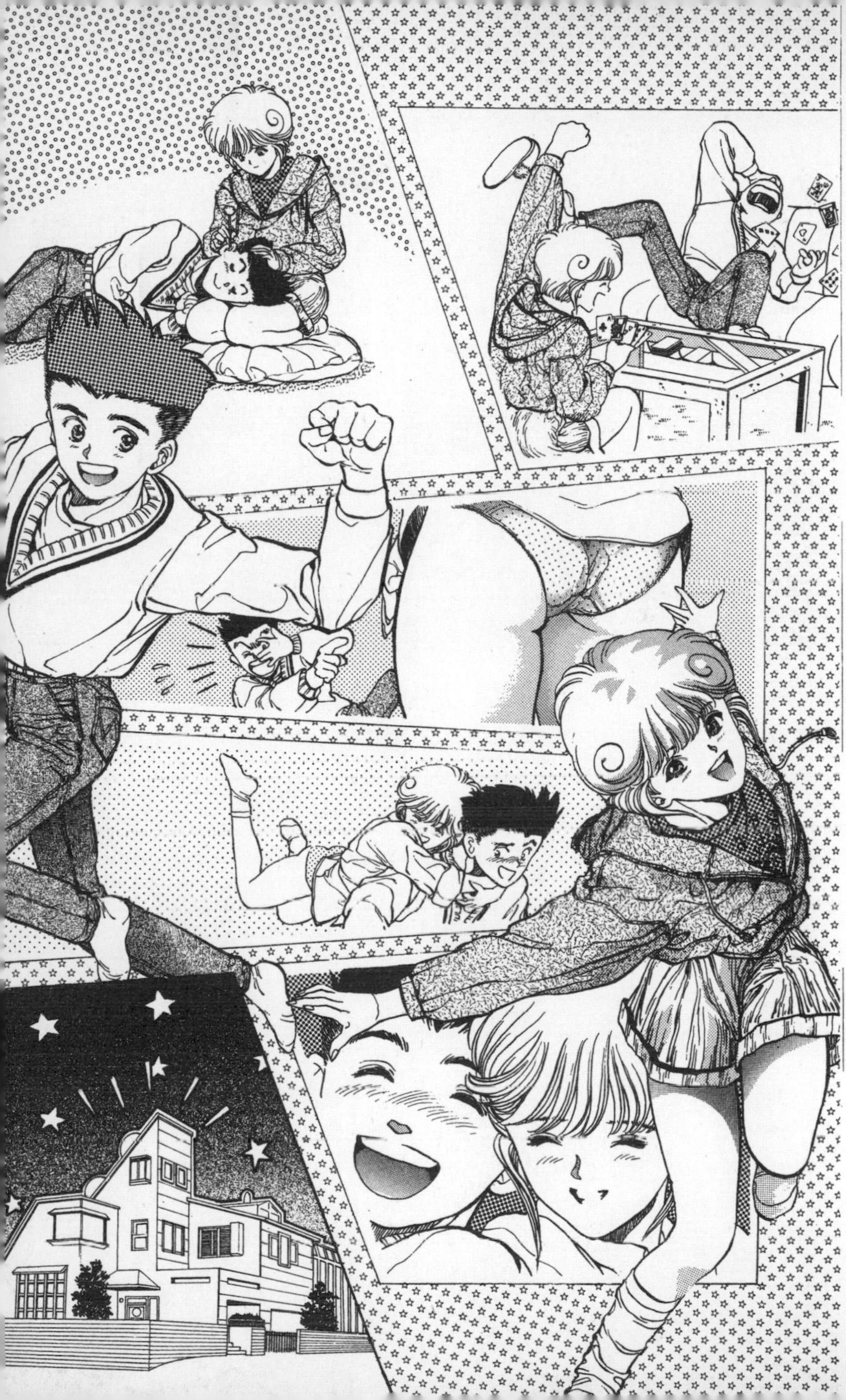

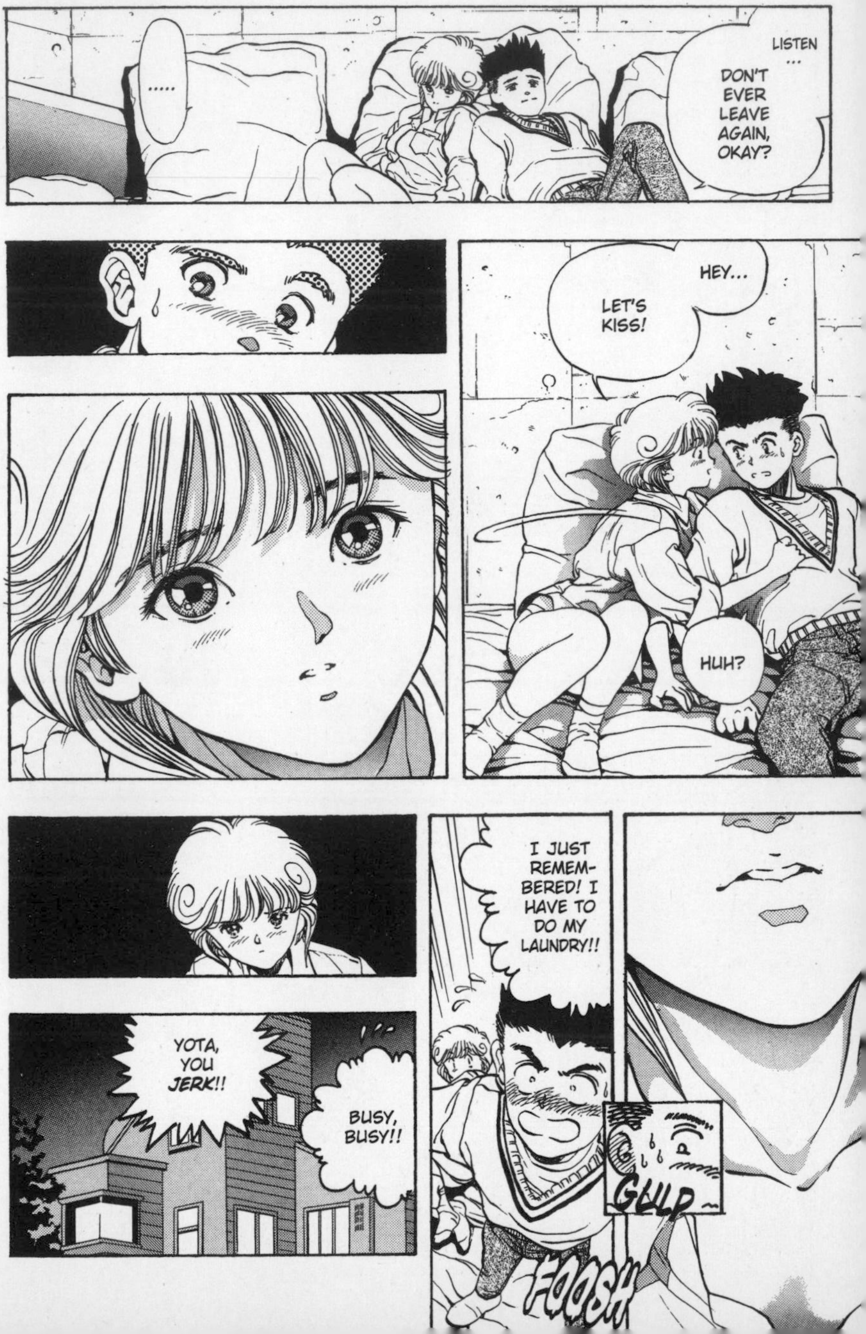
LISTEN ...
DON'T EVER LEAVE AGAIN, OKAY?
......
HEY...
LET'S KISS!
HUH?
I JUST REMEM-BERED! I HAVE TO DO MY LAUNDRY!!
GULP
FOOSH
YOTA, YOU JERK!!
BUSY, BUSY!!

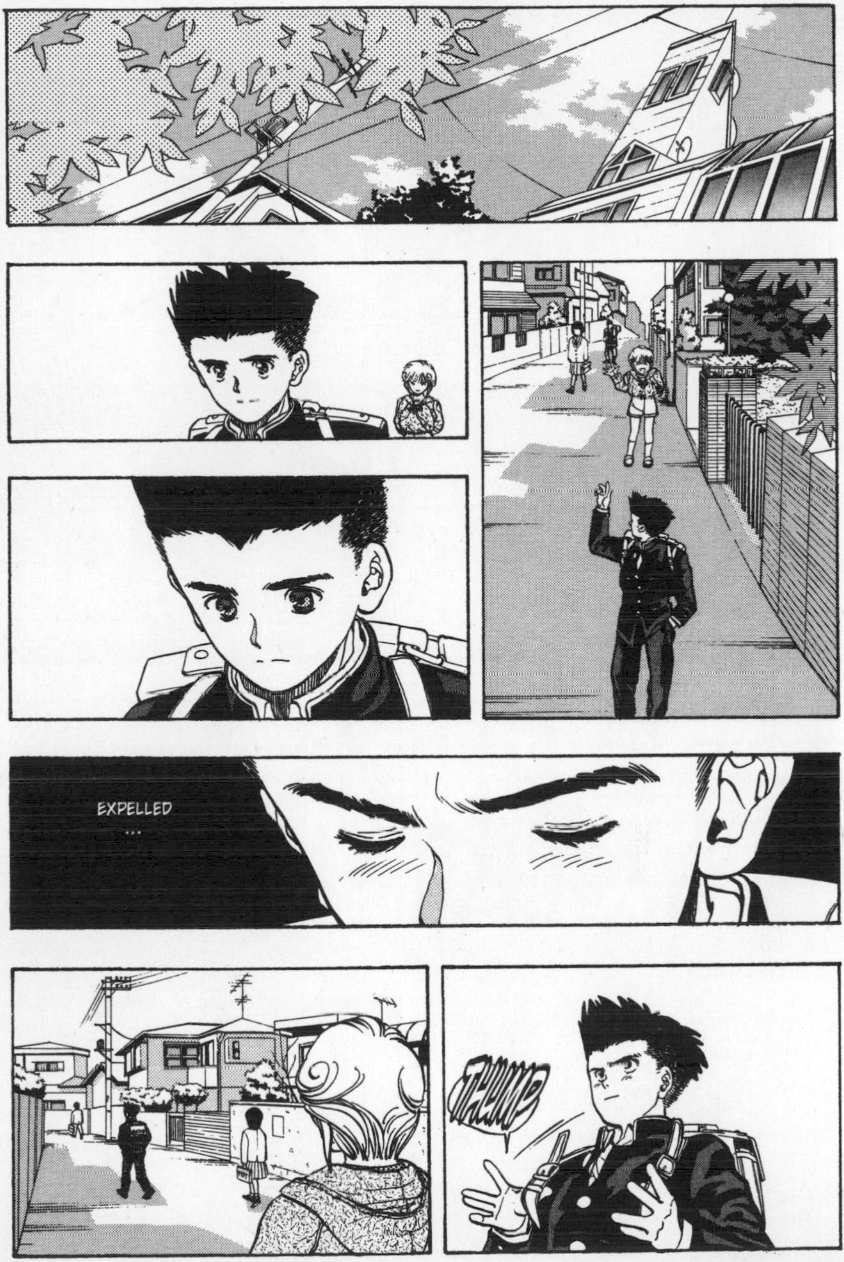
EXPELLED
...
THUMP

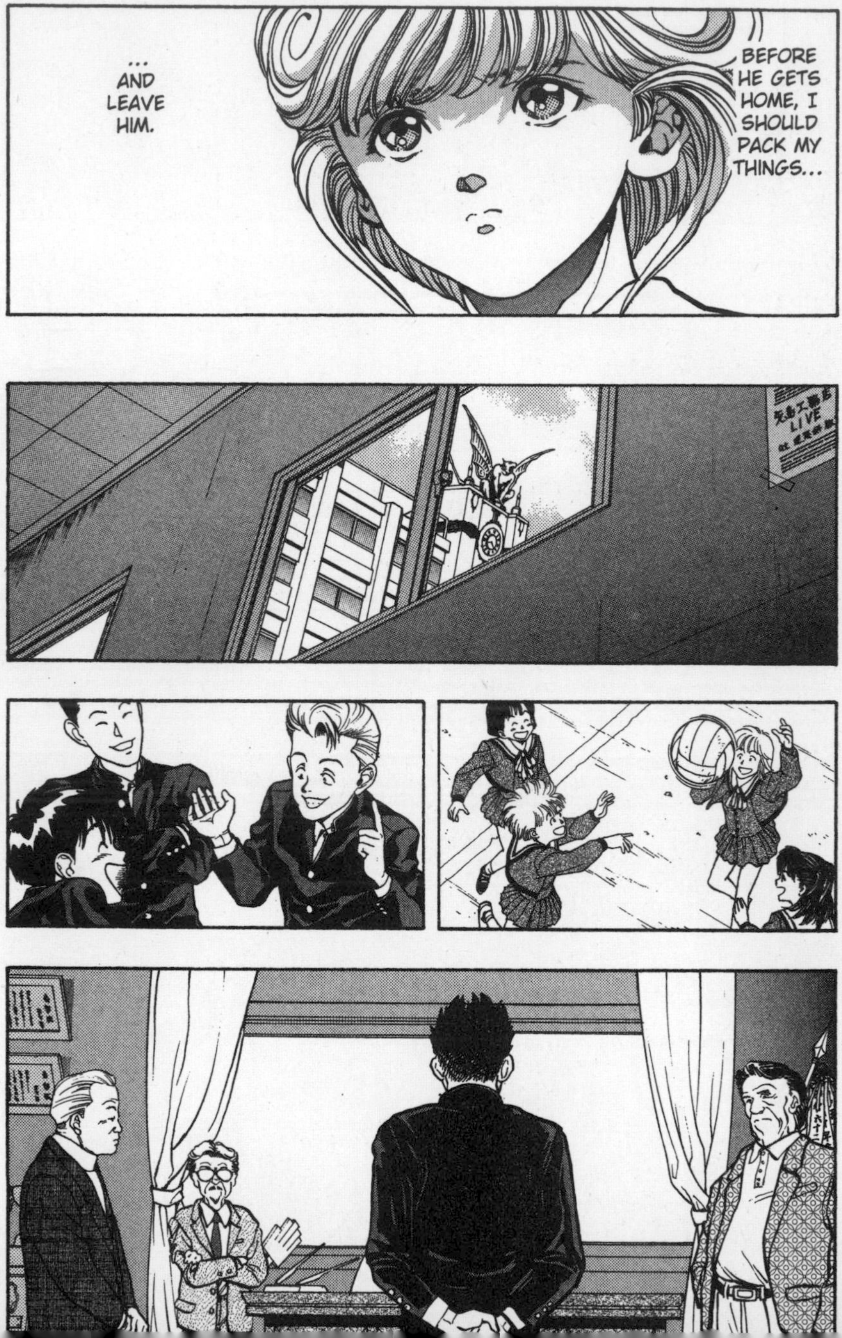
BEFORE HE GETS HOME, I SHOULD PACK MY THINGS...
... AND LEAVE HIM.
LIVE

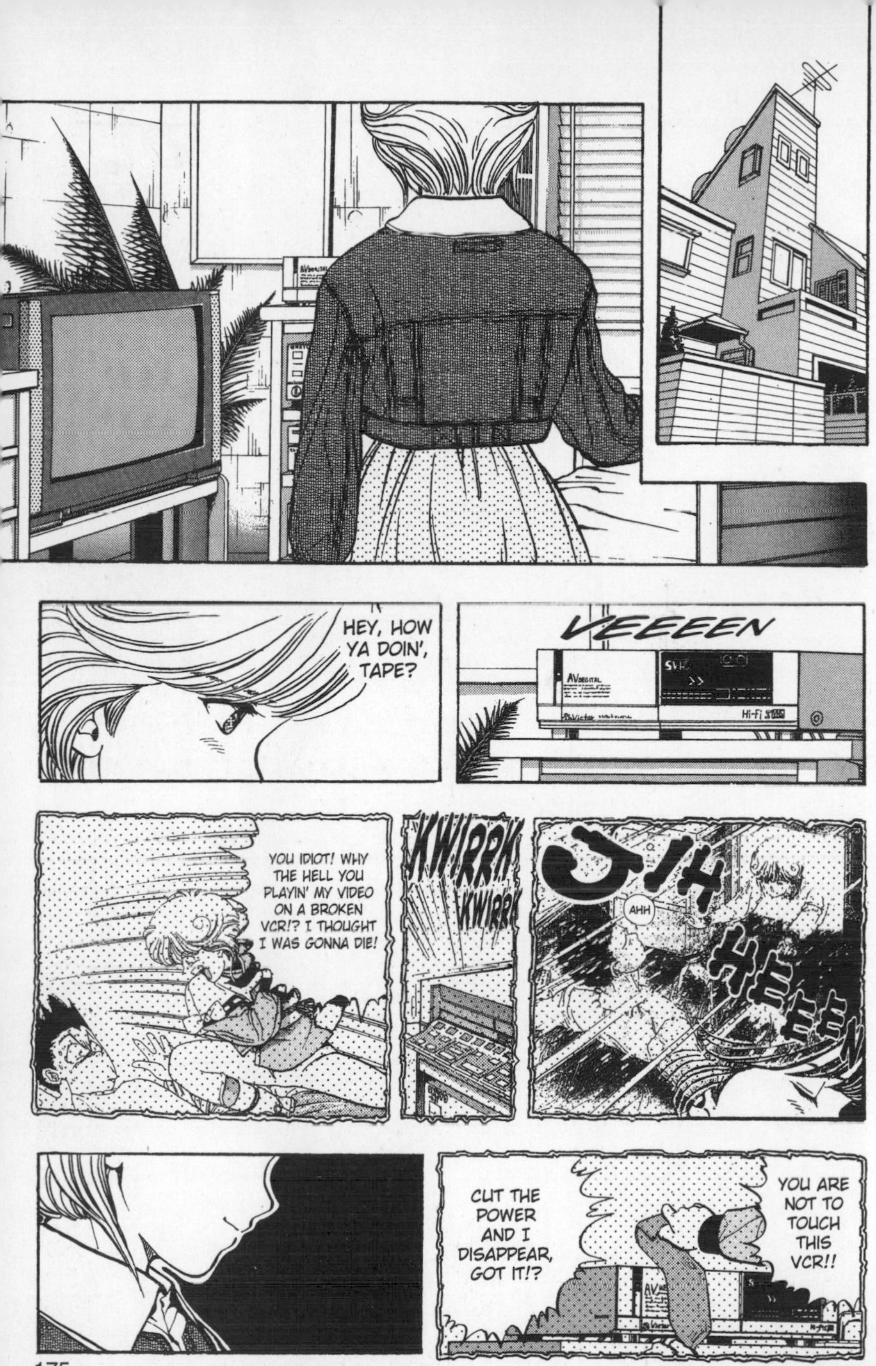
VEEEEN
HEY, HOW YA DOIN', TAPE?
AHH
KWIRRK
KWIRRK
YOU IDIOT! WHY THE HELL YOU PLAYIN' MY VIDEO ON A BROKEN VCR!? I THOUGHT I WAS GONNA DIE!
YOU ARE NOT TO TOUCH THIS VCR!!
CUT THE POWER AND I DISAPPEAR, GOT IT!?

THAT WAS A LOT OF FUN BACK THEN... ...WHEN I DIDN'T KNOW WHAT LOVE WAS. EVEN IF I WERE TO REWIND, THIS IS "I'M ROOTING FOR YOU"...

...I COULD NEVER GO BACK TO THE "I'LL CHEER YOU UP" DAYS.

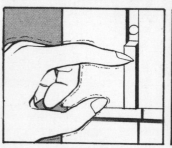

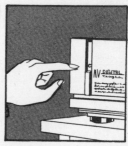

IT'S TOO PAINFUL! I SHOULD JUST CUT THE POWER.

YOU GUT- LESS ...

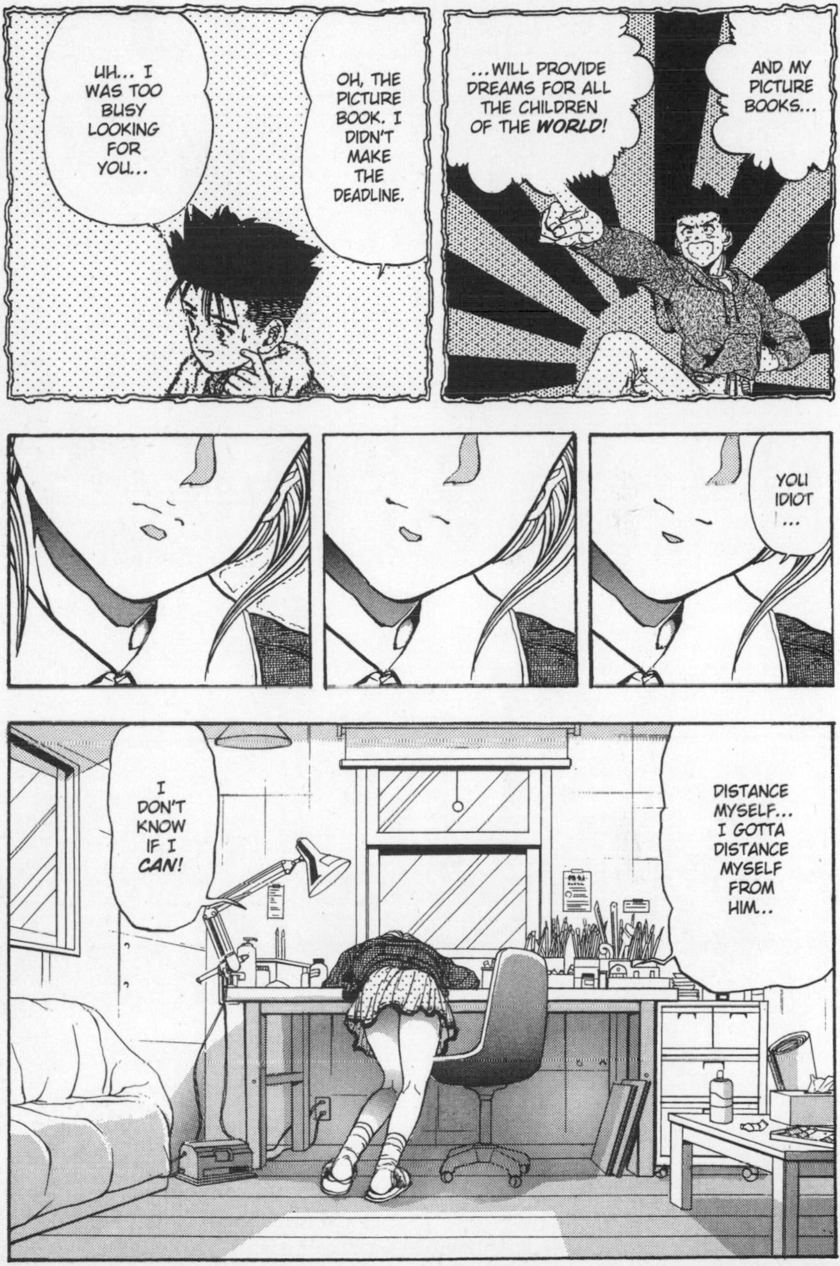
AND MY PICTURE BOOKS...
...WILL PROVIDE DREAMS FOR ALL THE CHILDREN OF THE *WORLD*!
OH, THE PICTURE BOOK. I DIDN'T MAKE THE DEADLINE.
UH... I WAS TOO BUSY LOOKING FOR YOU...
YOU IDIOT ...
DISTANCE MYSELF... I GOTTA DISTANCE MYSELF FROM HIM...
I DON'T KNOW IF I *CAN*!

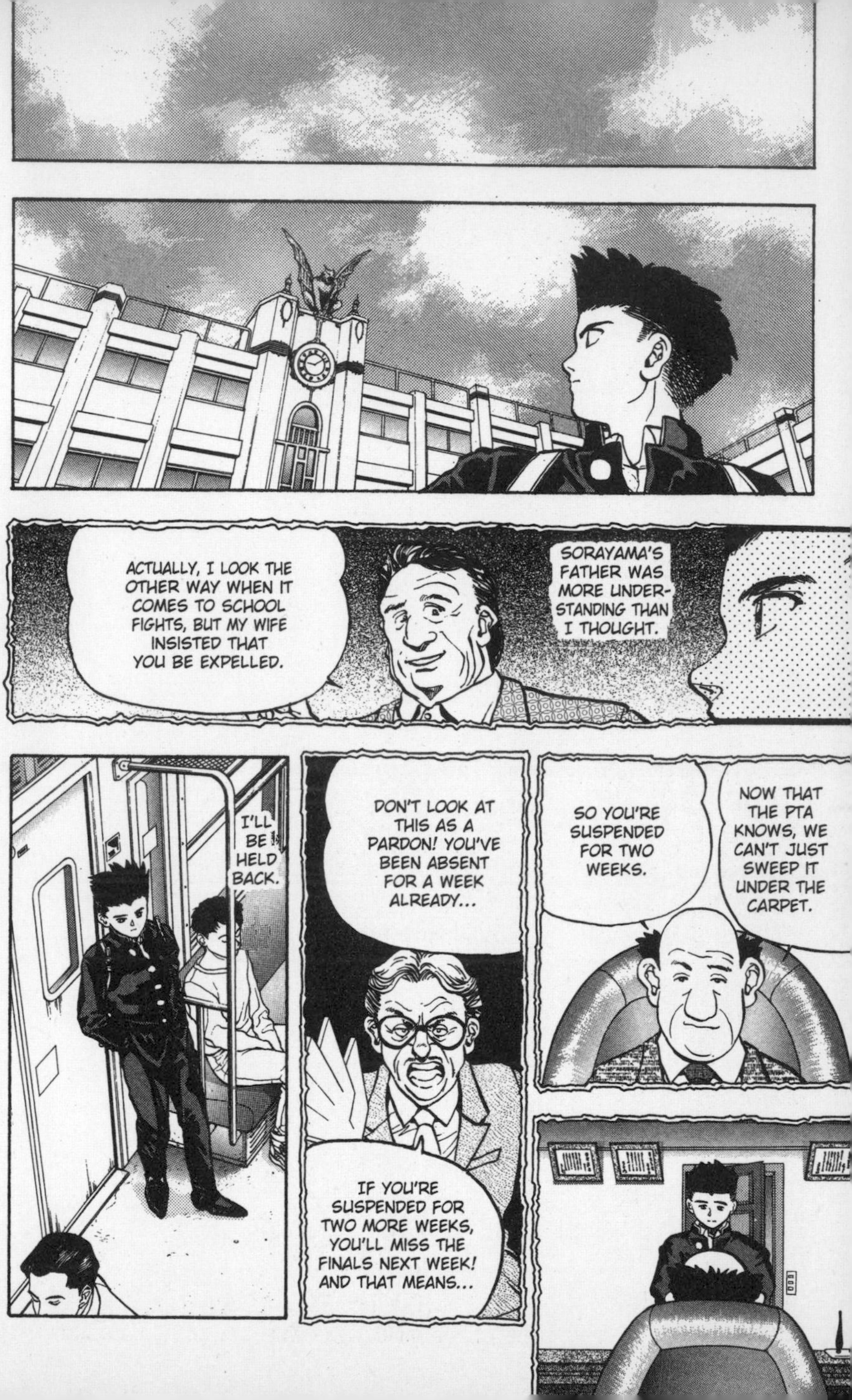
SORAYAMA'S FATHER WAS MORE UNDER-STANDING THAN I THOUGHT.
ACTUALLY, I LOOK THE OTHER WAY WHEN IT COMES TO SCHOOL FIGHTS, BUT MY WIFE INSISTED THAT YOU BE EXPELLED.
NOW THAT THE PTA KNOWS, WE CAN'T JUST SWEEP IT UNDER THE CARPET.
SO YOU'RE SUSPENDED FOR TWO WEEKS.
DON'T LOOK AT THIS AS A PARDON! YOU'VE BEEN ABSENT FOR A WEEK ALREADY...
IF YOU'RE SUSPENDED FOR TWO MORE WEEKS, YOU'LL MISS THE FINALS NEXT WEEK! AND THAT MEANS...
I'LL BE HELD BACK.

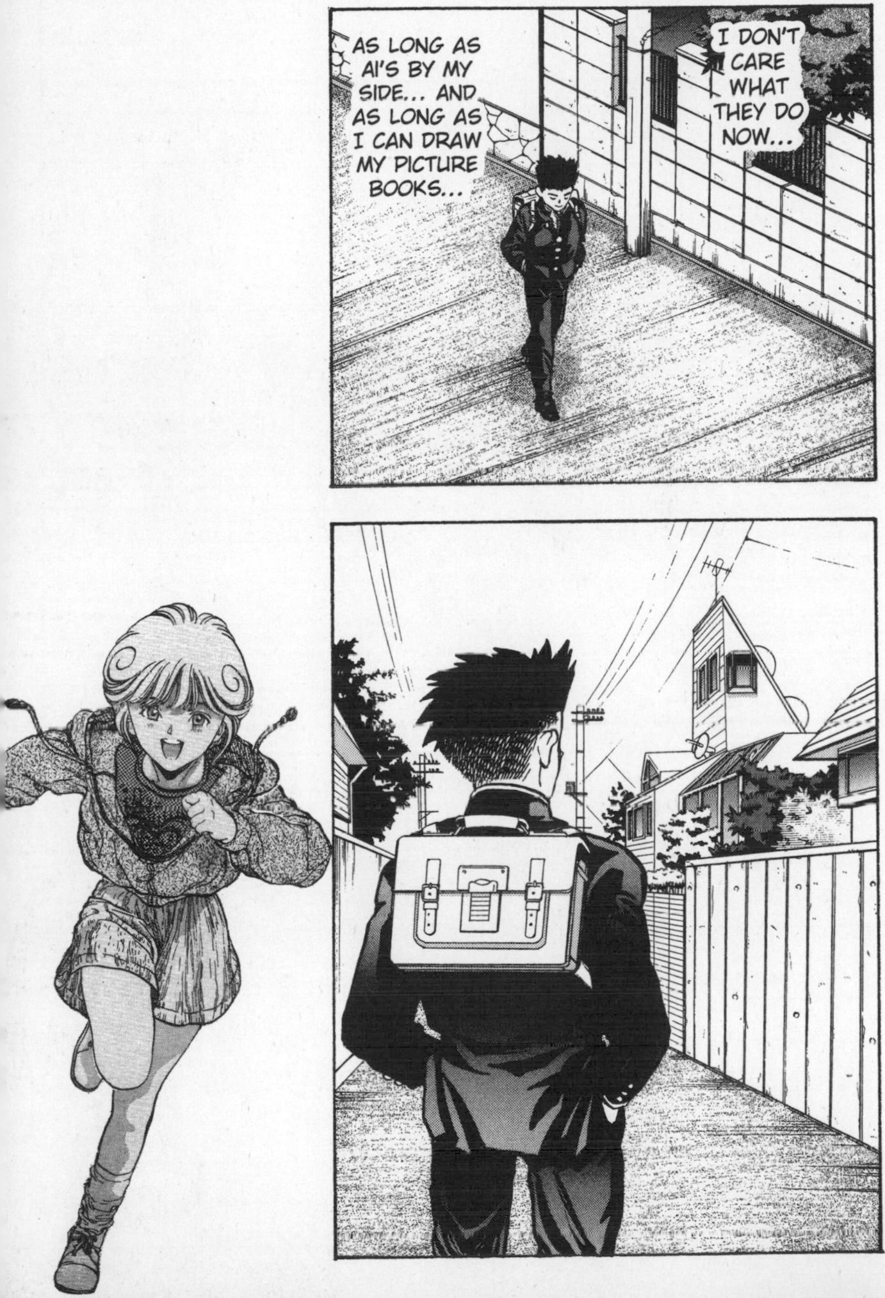
I DON'T CARE WHAT THEY DO NOW...
AS LONG AS AI'S BY MY SIDE... AND AS LONG AS I CAN DRAW MY PICTURE BOOKS...

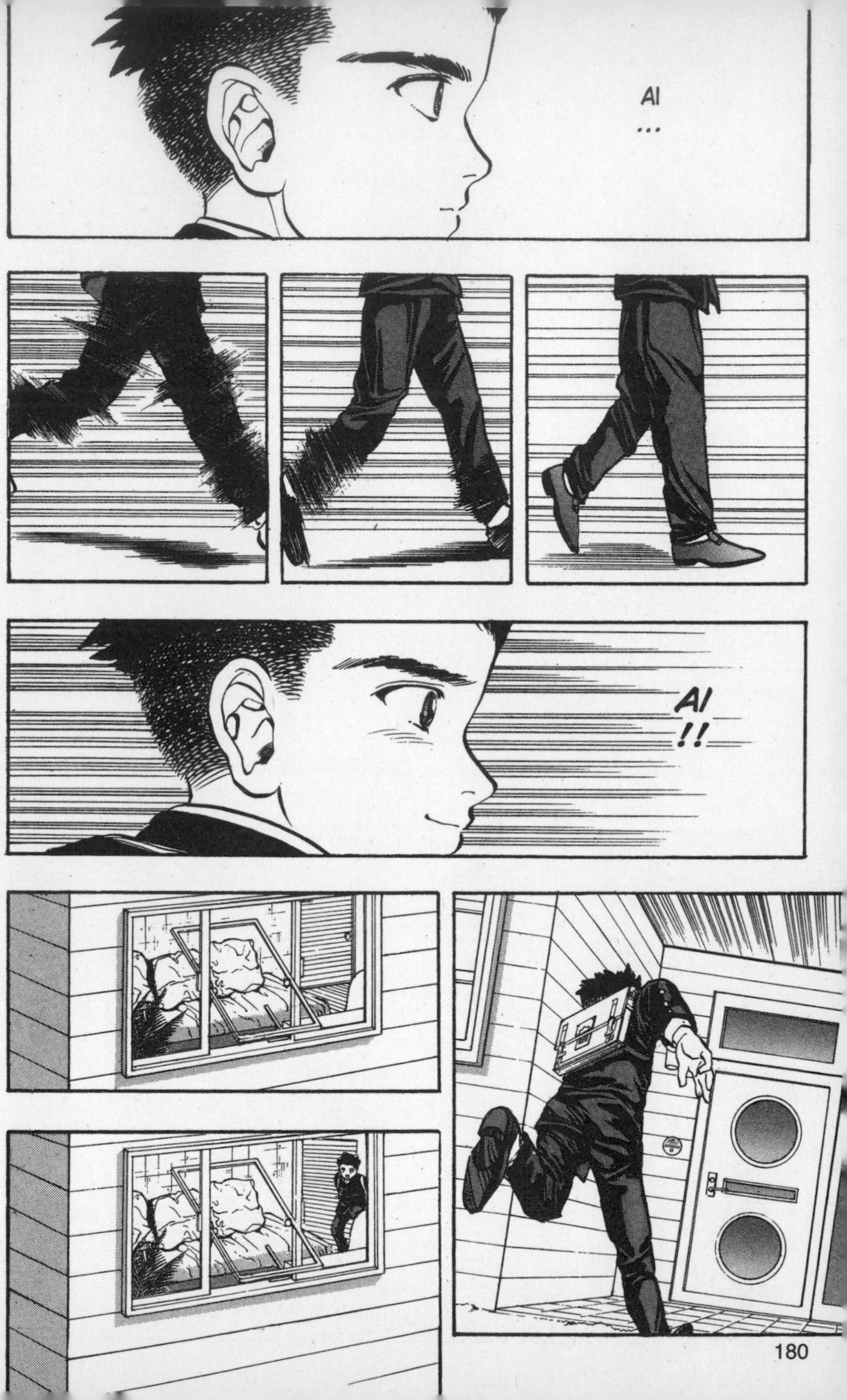
AI
...
AI
!!

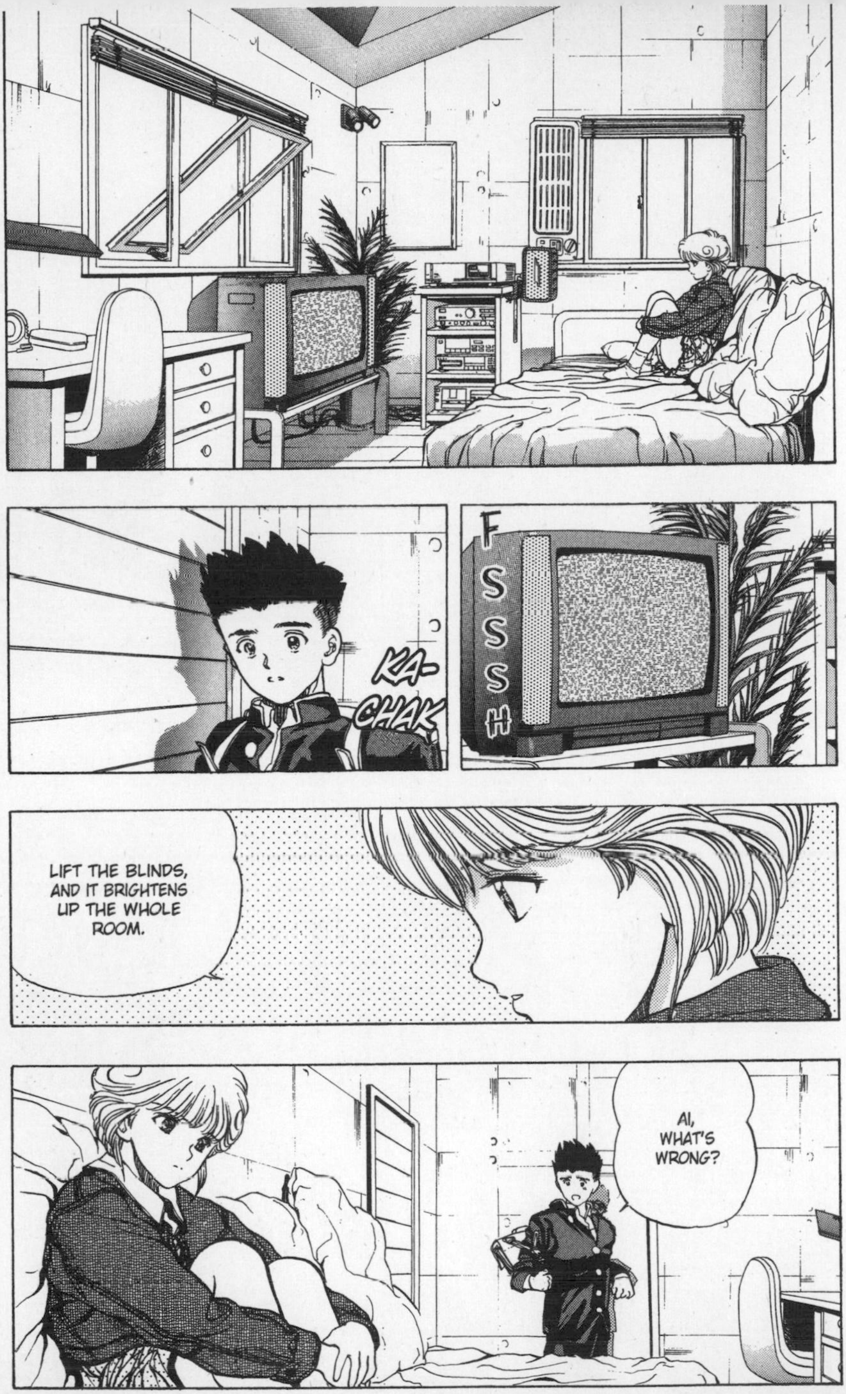
FSSSH
KA-CHAK
LIFT THE BLINDS, AND IT BRIGHTENS UP THE WHOLE ROOM.
AI, WHAT'S WRONG?

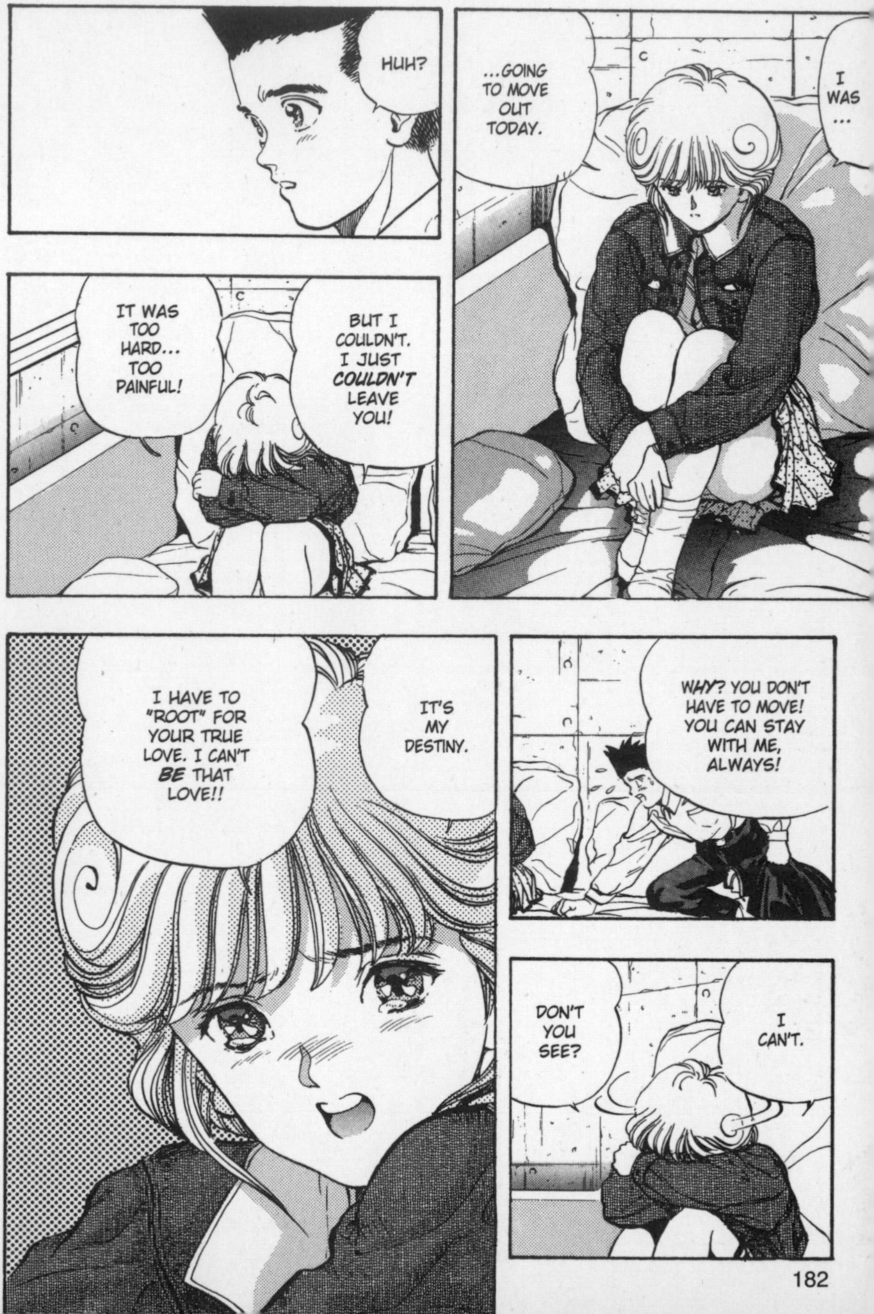
I WAS...
...GOING TO MOVE OUT TODAY.
HUH?
BUT I COULDN'T. I JUST COULDN'T LEAVE YOU!
IT WAS TOO HARD... TOO PAINFUL!
WHY? YOU DON'T HAVE TO MOVE! YOU CAN STAY WITH ME, ALWAYS!
I CAN'T.
DON'T YOU SEE?
IT'S MY DESTINY.
I HAVE TO "ROOT" FOR YOUR TRUE LOVE. I CAN'T BE THAT LOVE!!

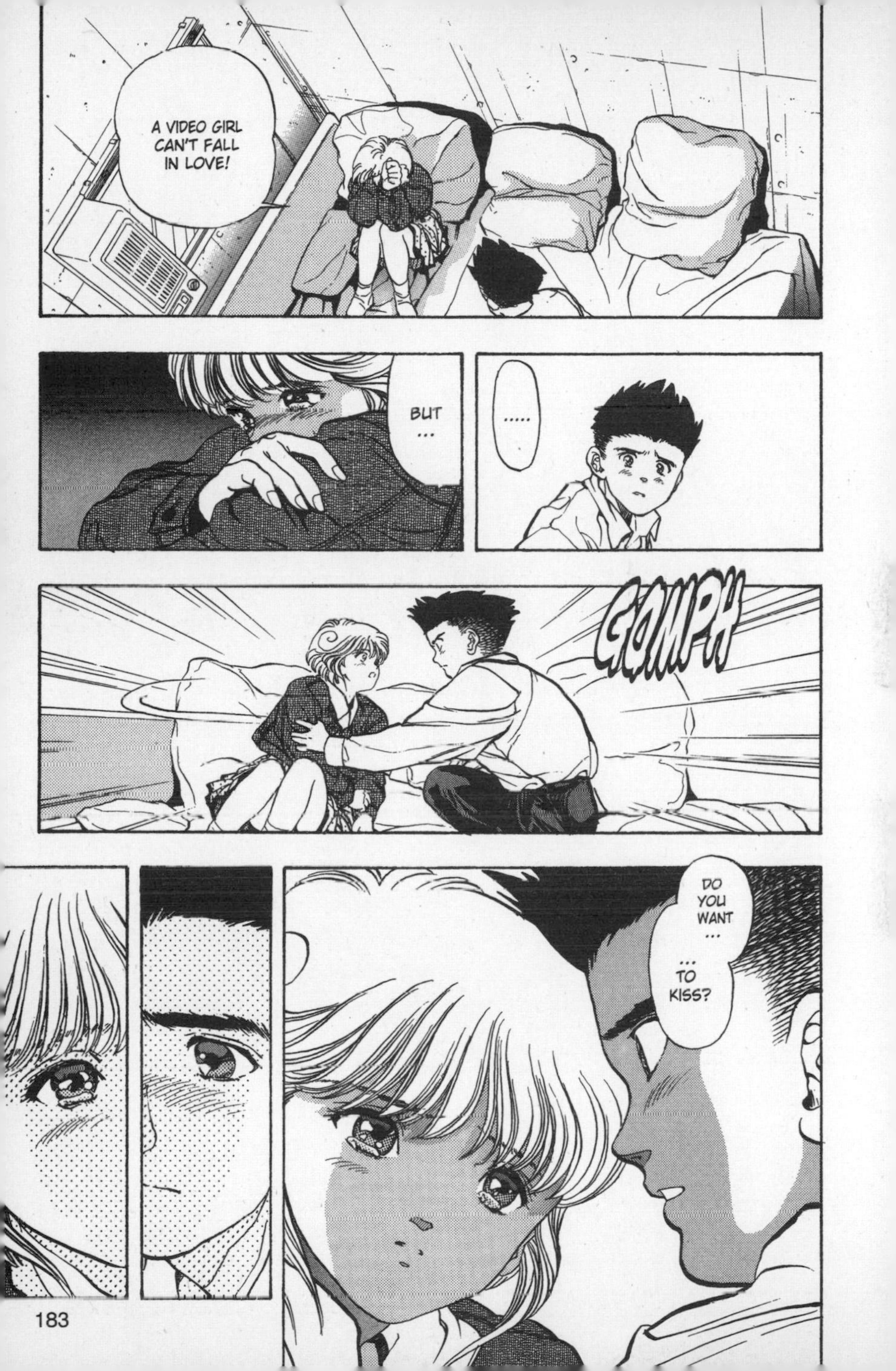
A VIDEO GIRL CAN'T FALL IN LOVE!
.....
BUT ...
GOMPH
DO YOU WANT ...
... TO KISS?

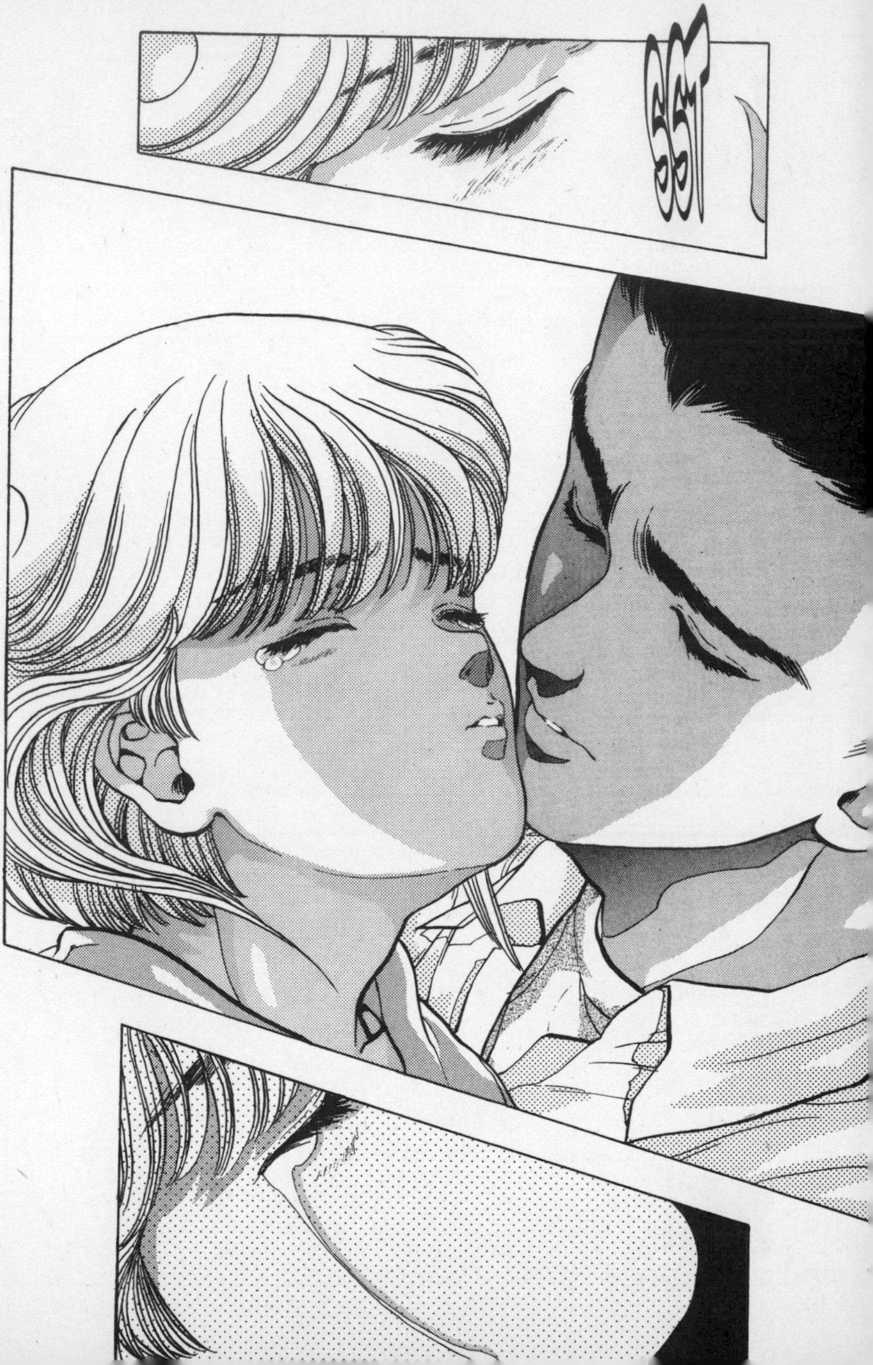
SST

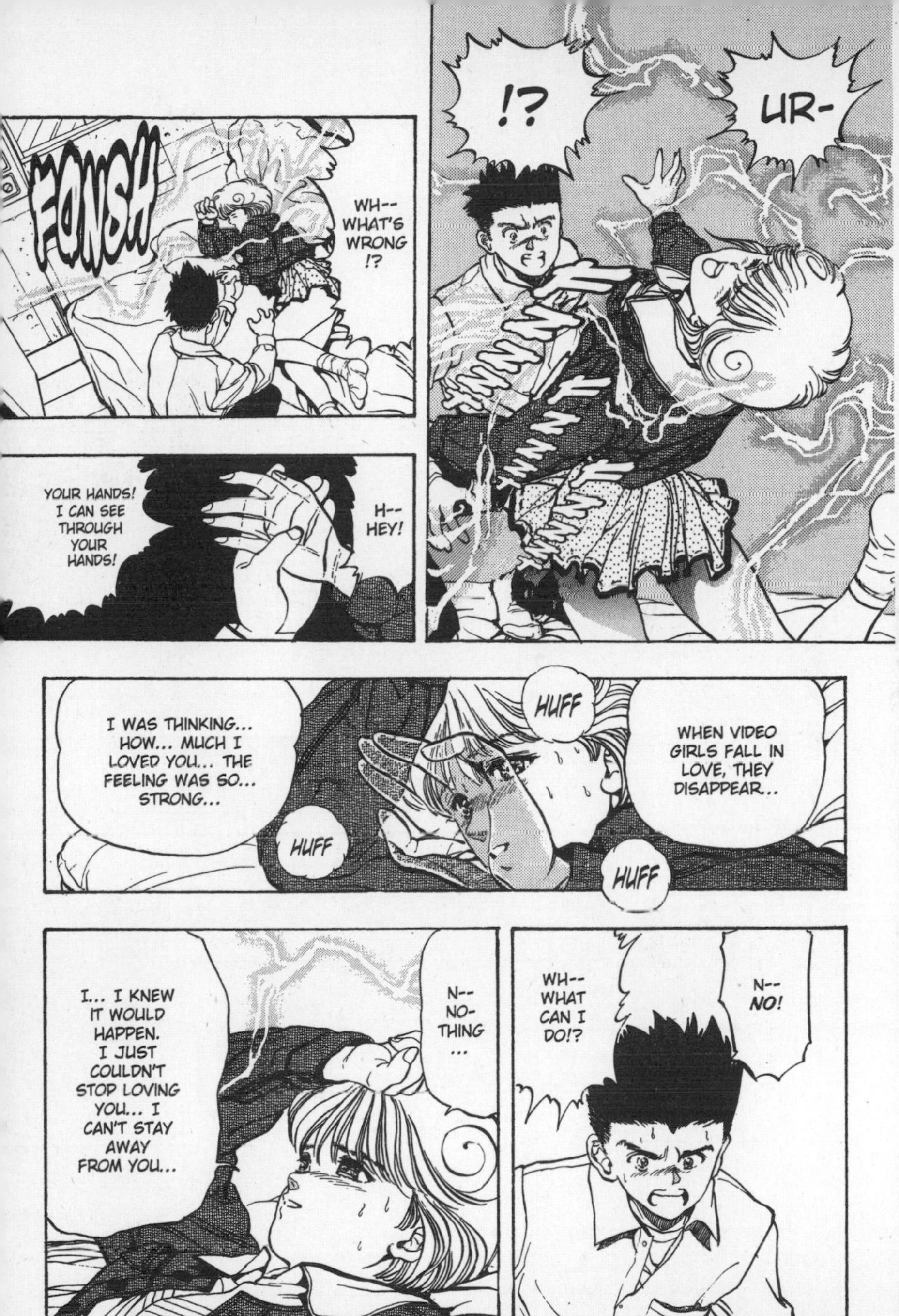
UR-
!?
WH-- WHAT'S WRONG !?
FONSH
H-- HEY!
YOUR HANDS! I CAN SEE THROUGH YOUR HANDS!
WHEN VIDEO GIRLS FALL IN LOVE, THEY DISAPPEAR...
HUFF
I WAS THINKING... HOW... MUCH I LOVED YOU... THE FEELING WAS SO... STRONG...
HUFF
HUFF
N-- NO!
WH-- WHAT CAN I DO!?
N-- NO- THING ...
I... I KNEW IT WOULD HAPPEN. I JUST COULDN'T STOP LOVING YOU... I CAN'T STAY AWAY FROM YOU...

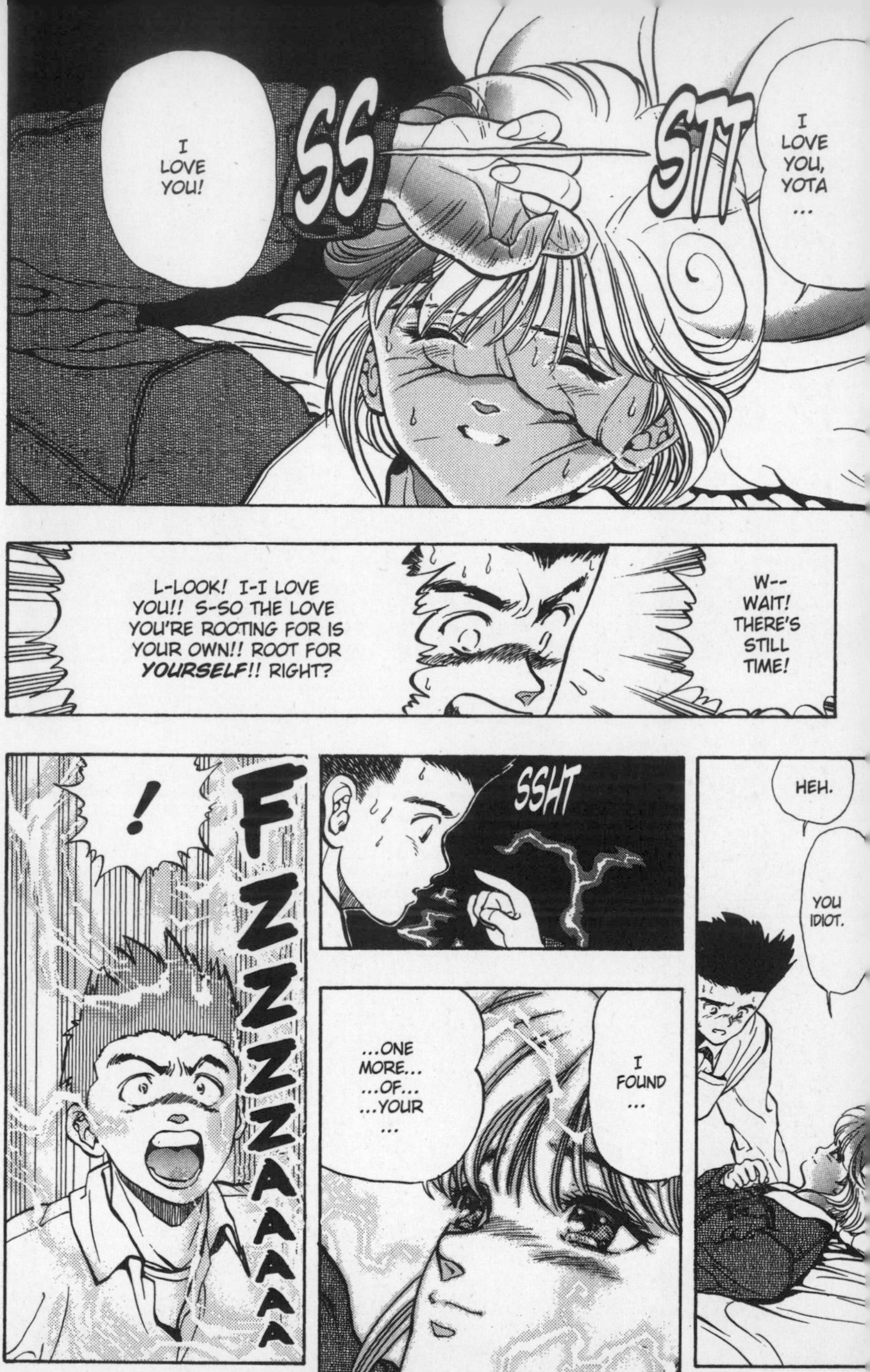
I LOVE YOU, YOTA ...
SS STT
I LOVE YOU!
W-- WAIT! THERE'S STILL TIME!
L-LOOK! I-I LOVE YOU!! S-SO THE LOVE YOU'RE ROOTING FOR IS YOUR OWN!! ROOT FOR **YOURSELF**!! RIGHT?
HEH.
YOU IDIOT.
SSHT
I FOUND ...
...ONE MORE... ...OF... ...YOUR ...
!
FZZZZAAAAA

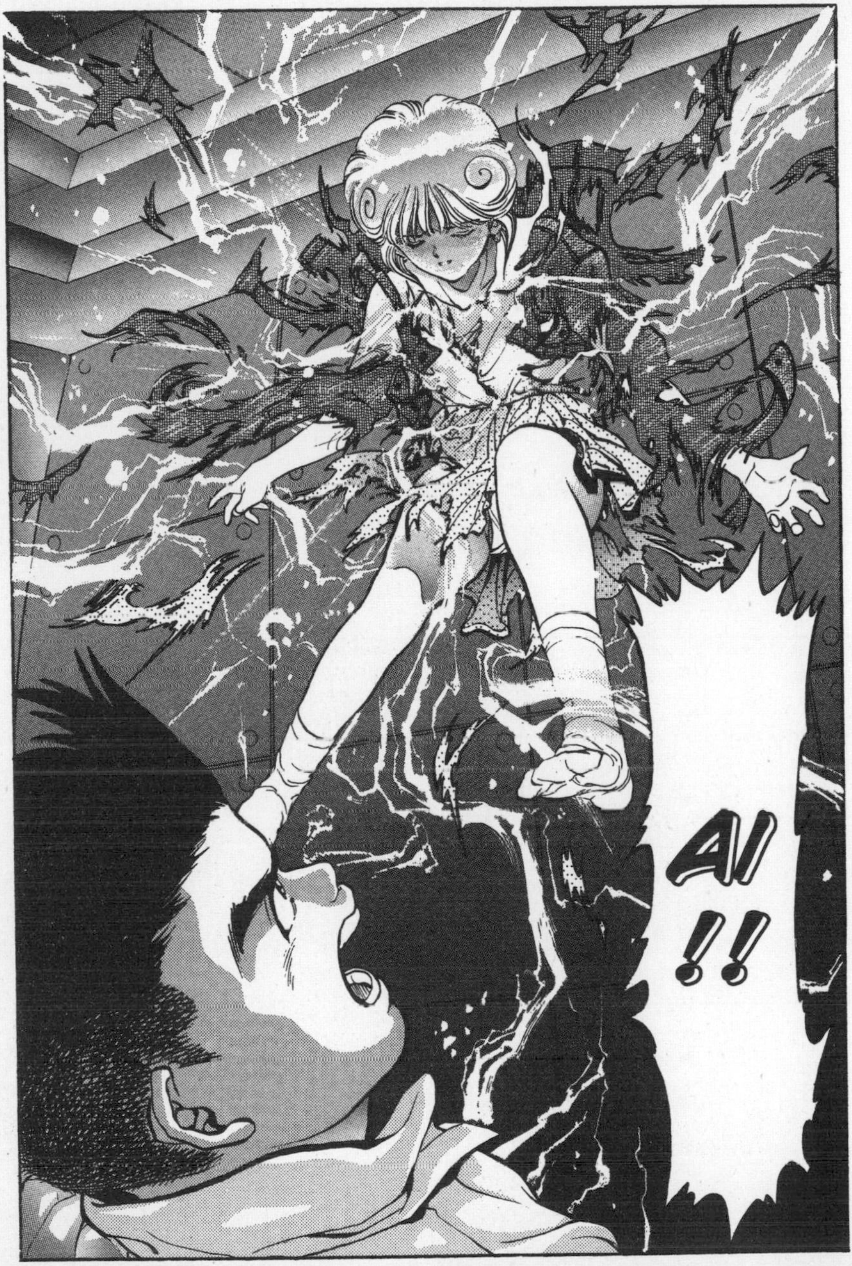
AI!!

To be continued in Volume 3: RECALL

Masakazu Katsura

When Masakazu Katsura was a high school student, he entered a story he had drawn into a manga contest in hopes of winning money to buy a stereo. He won the contest and was soon published in the immensely popular weekly manga anthology magazine *Shônen Jump*. Katsura was quickly propelled into manga-artist stardom and his subsequent comic series, *Wingman*, *Video Girl Ai*, *DNA2*, *Shadow Lady* and *I's*, are perennial fan favorites. Katsura lives in Tokyo, and possesses an extensive collection of Batman memorabilia (the occasional Batman reference pops up in the *Video Girl Ai* series).

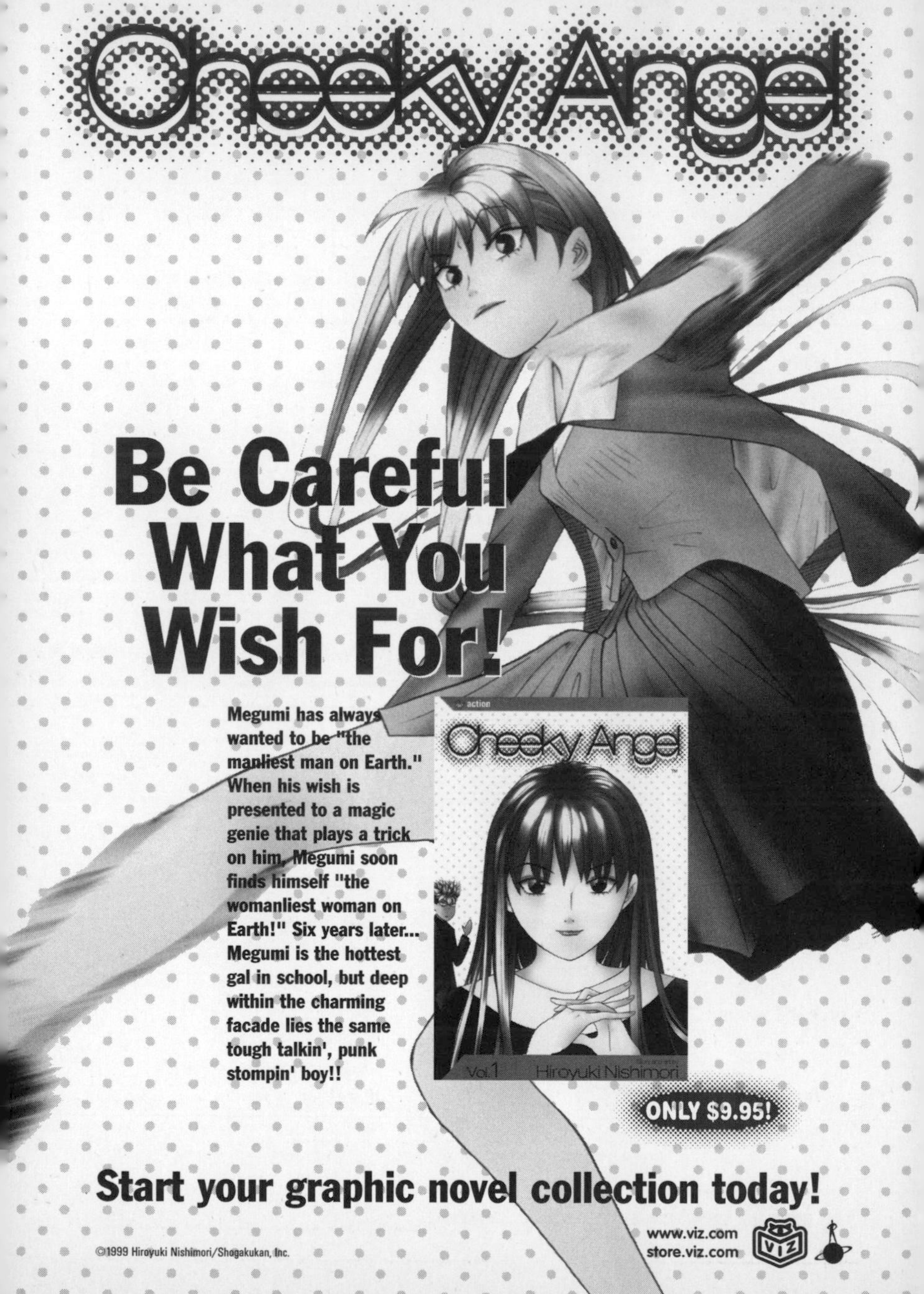
Cheeky Angel
Be Careful What You Wish For!
Megumi has always wanted to be "the manliest man on Earth." When his wish is presented to a magic genie that plays a trick on him, Megumi soon finds himself "the womanliest woman on Earth!" Six years later... Megumi is the hottest gal in school, but deep within the charming facade lies the same tough talkin', punk stompin' boy!!
action
Cheeky Angel
Vol. 1
Hiroyuki Nishimori
ONLY $9.95!
Start your graphic novel collection today!
www.viz.com
store.viz.com
VIZ
©1999 Hiroyuki Nishimori/Shogakukan, Inc.

COMPLETE OUR SURVEY AND LET US KNOW WHAT YOU THINK!

☐ Please do NOT send me information about VIZ products, news and events, special offers, or other information.

☐ Please do NOT send me information from VIZ's trusted business partners.

Name: _____

Address: _____

City: _____ **State:** _____ **Zip:** _____

E-mail: _____

☐ Male ☐ Female   Date of Birth (mm/dd/yyyy): ___ / ___ / _____ (Under 13? Parental consent required)

What race/ethnicity do you consider yourself? (please check one)

☐ Asian/Pacific Islander   ☐ Black/African American   ☐ Hispanic/Latino

☐ Native American/Alaskan Native ☐ White/Caucasian   ☐ Other: _____

What VIZ product did you purchase? (check all that apply and indicate title purchased)

☐ DVD/VHS _____

☐ Graphic Novel _____

☐ Magazines _____

☐ Merchandise _____

Reason for purchase: (check all that apply)

☐ Special offer   ☐ Favorite title   ☐ Gift

☐ Recommendation   ☐ Other _____

Where did you make your purchase? (please check one)

☐ Comic store   ☐ Bookstore   ☐ Mass/Grocery Store

☐ Newsstand   ☐ Video/Video Game Store ☐ Other: _____

☐ Online (site: _____)

What other VIZ properties have you purchased/own? _____

_____

How many anime and/or manga titles have you purchased in the last year? How many were VIZ titles? (please check one from each column)

ANIME	MANGA	VIZ
☐ None	☐ None	☐ None
☐ 1-4	☐ 1-4	☐ 1-4
☐ 5-10	☐ 5-10	☐ 5-10
☐ 11+	☐ 11+	☐ 11+

I find the pricing of VIZ products to be: (please check one)

☐ Cheap   ☐ Reasonable   ☐ Expensive

What genre of manga and anime would you like to see from VIZ? (please check two)

☐ Adventure   ☐ Comic Strip   ☐ Science Fiction   ☐ Fighting

☐ Horror   ☐ Romance   ☐ Fantasy   ☐ Sports

What do you think of VIZ's new look?

☐ Love It   ☐ It's OK   ☐ Hate It   ☐ Didn't Notice   ☐ No Opinion

Which do you prefer? (please check one)

☐ Reading right-to-left

☐ Reading left-to-right

Which do you prefer? (please check one)

☐ Sound effects in English

☐ Sound effects in Japanese with English captions

☐ Sound effects in Japanese only with a glossary at the back

THANK YOU! Please send the completed form to:

NJW Research
42 Catharine St.
Poughkeepsie, NY 12601

All information provided will be used for internal purposes only. We promise not to sell or otherwise divulge your information.